The Legacies of Liberalism

The Legacies of Liberalism

Path Dependence and Political Regimes in Central America

James Mahoney

The Johns Hopkins University Press
Baltimore and London

© 2001 The Johns Hopkins University Press
All rights reserved. Published 2001
Printed in the United States of America on acid-free paper
9 8 7 6 5 4 3 2 1

The Johns Hopkins University Press
2715 North Charles Street
Baltimore, Maryland 21218-4363
www.press.jhu.edu

Library of Congress Cataloging-in-Publication Data will be found at the end
of this book.

A catalog record for this book is available from the British Library.
ISBN 0-8018-6552-2

For Sharon

CONTENTS

Part IV: Legacies of the Liberal Reform Period

FIGURES, MAPS, AND TABLES

Figures

Maps

Tables

PREFACE

The notion of path dependence suggests that crucial actor choices may establish certain directions of change and foreclose others in a way that shapes long-term trajectories of development. This book develops this idea with the purpose of offering a new comparative-historical explanation of regime change in Central America. I argue that the liberal reform period in Central America in the nineteenth and early twentieth centuries was a critical juncture that profoundly influenced future political development in the region. During this period, the choices by liberal elites about how to pursue societal modernization led to the creation of differing state and agrarian structures, setting the various Central American countries on contrasting long-term paths of development. By the mid-twentieth century, I argue, liberals' decisions about modernization had culminated in the establishment of vastly different national political regimes, ranging from harsh military authoritarianism in Guatemala and El Salvador, to progressive democracy in Costa Rica, to traditional dictatorship in Honduras and Nicaragua.

This argument is developed through the application of a comparative-historical methodology. Comparative-historical analysis is designed to discover and test hypotheses by engaging theory with history; when successfully employed, it can both inspire new theoretical formulations and stimulate new interpretations of historical cases. By juxtaposing countries with one another, I use this method to anchor theoretical arguments about the workings of path-dependent development in Central America. For those scholars not particularly interested in Central America, my hope is that the application of this path-dependent approach will make the history worthwhile. I also use comparative history to ground arguments in fine-grained evidence about the unfolding of processes over time within each Central American country. For Central American specialists not particularly interested in the theory of path dependence, my hope is that these historical narratives will reveal the value of employing a systematic analytic and comparative framework.

The decision to pursue this comparative-historical study of liberalism and regime change in Central America has, for me, often felt like something approaching a personal critical juncture. Nevertheless, looking back, it is clear that this decision was deeply embedded in surrounding events. In the late 1980s, while still an undergraduate at the University of Minnesota, I cultivated an interest in Central American politics. Like many others, I was drawn to the region because of the extraordinary events that were taking place at the time, including the spread of revolutionary movements and the response of U.S.-backed counterinsurgency forces. My intellectual fascination with the Central American crisis led me to write a senior honors thesis on the causes of revolution in the region; my political sensibilities led me to become deeply opposed to U.S. foreign policy toward Central America.

The first ideas for this book were worked out while I was a graduate student at the University of California, Berkeley. At the time, Central America was declining in geopolitical importance, with the crises of the 1980s gradually giving way to peace settlements and new electoral regimes. Nevertheless, I remained interested in the region as I came to appreciate the scope and explanatory power of comparative-historical analysis. The Central American region seemed ideally suited for such analysis, given the striking political differences that existed alongside many important regional and contextual similarities. Moreover, when compared to prevailing explanations that put primary emphasis on short-term causes unique to each Central American country, the focus of comparative-historical analysis on juxtaposing cases and processes over time seemed to offer a much superior alternative. Comparative-historical analysis provided a means of making generalizations across cases while still remaining sensitive to the distinctive features of each country. My beliefs about the advantages of comparative-historical analysis were reinforced by the growing success of studies of this kind on other regions of the world, including works that analyzed critical juncture episodes in Europe and South America. I decided that these ideas could be brought together to frame a full-blown path-dependent explanation of Central American political development.

I had recognized for some time that scholars had largely "discovered" Central America in the 1980s, and that much of the social science literature about politics in the region focused primarily on these years. Thus, I felt that there was a real need for a study that attempted to explain the divergent trajectories of political development in the region *before* the crisis period. My sense of this empirical gap and my interest in exploring path-dependent development led me to hypothesize that key changes in nineteenth-century Central America might represent a critical juncture that could account for major political differences among the region's countries in the early and mid-twentieth century. In particular, I began to explore the possibility that the different ways in which countries experienced early state-building processes and the commercialization of agriculture—during a period known as the liberal reform—might account for the origins of different national regimes in the twentieth century.

Historians had already suggested that the liberal reform period was important for future development in the region. However, I was convinced that much work remained to be done. For one thing, I believed that the literature on the Central American liberal reform could benefit from the introduction of new theoretical ideas about the relationship of states to markets, domestic conditions to international processes, and human agents to social structure. While I saw much value in Marxist-inspired arguments about this period, I was skeptical of the way they mechanically reduced liberal politics to underlying economic structure. Likewise, I recognized that foreign intervention played an important role during the liberal reform period, but I doubted that such intervention could be understood solely in terms of economic factors. To test these theoretical hunches, I felt that new methodological approaches to comparison and causal analysis might provide more leverage than the narrative methods used in many histories of Central America.

From these experiences, the idea of carrying out this project took shape: I could develop a full-blown path-dependent approach to help make sense of Central American political development before the crisis period. And in my analysis of the liberal reform period, I could formulate new theoretical principles about the role of actor choices, states, and foreign intervention, while situating them within an explicitly employed comparative-historical methodology. Eventually, by way of many rounds of revision, I arrived at the argument about path dependence and regime change found in this book.

In pursuing this project, I have been fortunate to draw on the support of many colleagues and friends, whom I am pleased to acknowledge here. The original draft of this book took the form of a doctoral dissertation, and my most fundamental scholarly debts are to my advisors in political science and sociology. David Collier was a constant source of support during my years at graduate school. I decided to study at Berkeley in order to work with him, and it was one of the better decisions I have made. He shaped my intellectual development in profoundly positive ways. In very different but equally important ways, Ruth Berins Collier aided me during my years at Berkeley. She encouraged me to pursue a broadly conceived comparative-historical analysis, never once flinching when I decided to pursue a five-country comparative study that covered more than two centuries. Laura J. Enríquez was a big help in preparing for my research in Central America, and her extensive comments on chapters greatly improved the manuscript. Her support was uplifting at several points in the long process of writing. Peter Evans provided unfailing guidance throughout all phases of the process. His ability to help one see the big picture and offer advice on how to structure new theoretical arguments is truly remarkable. It is surpassed only by his genuine kindness and positive outlook. I thank all of these individuals for encouraging me to take on what proved to be a nearly impossible but ultimately highly rewarding project.

Much of the research for this book was conducted during a ten-month trip to Central America, which gave me a chance to visit libraries and archives throughout the region. Support for the trip came from the Institute of International Education in the form of a J. William Fulbright Scholarship. The staffs of the Archivo General de la Nación in San Salvador, the Archivo y Biblioteca Nacional de Honduras in Tegucigalpa, the Biblioteca Nacional in Managua, and the Archivo Nacional de Costa Rica in San José were particularly helpful. Several Central American scholars opened their office doors to me and offered useful comments and advice for my research. I especially single out Leticia Salomón, Ramón Oquelí, and Mario Posas. Special thanks also go to Oscar A. García and David and Lolita Symes, whose friendship and advice were invaluable.

Eric Selbin and Deborah Yashar provided important suggestions at various points, including when I was originally developing the project's ideas. Fellow students at Berkeley also offered helpful comments and support along the way. I owe thanks to Peter Houtzager, Timothy Kessler, Marcus Kurtz, Steven Levitsky, Matt Marostica, Carol Ann Medlin, Pierre Ostiguy, and Jeffrey Sluyter. Richard Snyder helped me in countless ways as friend and colleague, during and after graduate school. Major revisions were needed to convert earlier drafts into a publishable book. In this effort, I was assisted by the comments of Miguel Calderón Chelius, Erik Ching, Silvia E. Giorguli, José Itzigsohn, John Markoff, Paul Pierson, Sally Reover, Dietrich Rueschemeyer, Kenneth Shadlen, and Thomas E. Skidmore. I especially appreciate the help of Edgar Kiser,

David J. Meyer, and Gerardo L. Munck, who carried out the heroic task of commenting on every page of the manuscript. Ralph Lee Woodward Jr. suggested that I include the bibliography found at the back. Toward the end of the project, I was stimulated to make further changes by conversations with Kirk Bowman, Fabrice Lehoucq, and Jeffery M. Paige, three of the finest Central Americanists working today.

A number of senior colleagues at Brown University and elsewhere helped me arrive at the decision to publish the book with Johns Hopkins. These high-level consultants were Phil Brown, Miguel Centeno, Calvin Goldscheider, Frances K. Goldscheider, Lowell Gudmundson, Evelyne Huber, and Michael J. White. At the Johns Hopkins University Press, Henry Tom arranged for the publication of the book and offered helpful advice on the title and chapter organization. Nancy Trotic did a marvelous job copyediting the manuscript, and Barbara Lamb patiently oversaw the production of the book. Carrene W. Tracy skillfully prepared the maps on short notice.

Finally, I acknowledge the support of Sharon Kamra. She was my *compañera* in the field, and she allowed me to turn our living room into a personal office to complete the manuscript. Although Sharon still resists committing the names of my three patterns of liberal reform to memory, without her steady encouragement I could never have completed this analysis of radical, reformist, and aborted liberalism.

The Legacies of Liberalism

PART I

Introduction

CHAPTER I

Explaining Political Development in Central America

In nineteenth-century Central America, the rise of liberal elites to political power launched an historic episode of change known as the liberal reform period. During this time, national governments sought to increase the overall role of the state in promoting economic development, while simultaneously removing state-imposed constraints on private property and free trade. Furthermore, governments aimed to weaken the socioeconomic position of traditional corporate groups such as the Church. In each of the Central American countries, the reforms enacted by liberals to meet these ends had the effect of significantly advancing commercial agriculture, greatly increasing exports, and dramatically enhancing the role of the state within society and the economy.

Yet the specific manner in which liberals implemented reform agendas varied among countries. Under a pattern of "radical liberalism," which characterized Guatemala and El Salvador, liberals enacted policies that attacked communal landholding structures, encouraged rapid agrarian capitalist expansion, and offered no long-term protection to peasant communities and small producers. This pattern saw the creation of a highly polarized agrarian economy and a militarized state apparatus. By contrast, under "reformist liberalism" in Costa Rica, liberals promoted a less dramatic shift to commercial agriculture and actively worked to maintain small farms as the central agricultural unit over the long run. This pattern saw the development of an advanced but nonpolarized agrarian economy and a centralized but nonmilitarized state apparatus. Finally, under "aborted liberalism" in Honduras and Nicaragua, liberal efforts to promote development were not fully successful. In this pattern, foreign intervention undermined ongoing processes of liberal transformation, allowing many traditional state and agrarian structures to persist from the preliberal to the postliberal period.

These three patterns of liberal reform—radical liberalism, reformist liberalism, and aborted liberalism—help to explain subsequent political dynamics in the region, including the dominant political regime that characterized each country in the twentieth century. In all countries, the liberal reform brought on significant reactions from actors who were excluded or marginalized during the reform process. These contrasting reactions—ranging from major democratizing efforts to episodes of authoritarianism to anti-imperialist movements—can in part be explained as a consequence of the type of liberal reform period that occurred in a given country. Furthermore, the persistence of military-authoritarian regimes in Guatemala and El Salvador, a democratic regime in Costa Rica, and traditional dictatorships in Honduras and Nicaragua over many decades in the twentieth century can be explained in part as legacies of the three patterns of radical, reformist, and aborted liberalism. Thus, the liberal reform period helps account for major contrasts among these countries in the character of national political regimes.

The study of the liberal reform period and its legacies affords an opportunity to assess the theoretical frameworks most commonly employed to explain Central American development and political change. This work adopts a "path-dependent" approach that stresses the importance of actor choices during critical junctures for structural development and for long-run trajectories of change. This path-dependent approach contrasts with alternative perspectives that emphasize short-term causes or more gradual processes of change. In addition, the specific causal argument developed in this study contrasts with previous explanations of Central American political development, including those that explain regime outcomes in terms of agrarian structure, U.S. intervention, and historical periods such as colonialism and the depression of the 1930s.

A Path-Dependent Approach

Social scientists commonly describe their explanations as "path-dependent," but the term is often used without careful elaboration.[1] To serve as a useful concept, path dependence must mean something more than the notion that "history matters" or that "past events influence future events."[2] Likewise, path dependence cannot simply be used as a blanket label to describe all explanations that employ a long time horizon or that examine temporally sequenced variables. Such broad definitions of path dependence fail to distinguish this mode of analysis from standard social

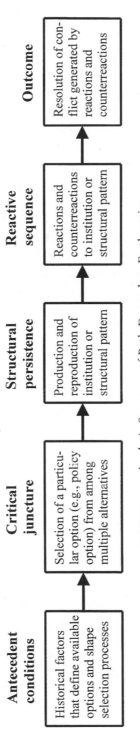

FIGURE 1.1   Analytic Structure of Path-Dependent Explanation

Antecedent conditions

Historical factors that define available options and shape selection processes

Critical juncture

Selection of a particular option (e.g., policy option) from among multiple alternatives

Structural persistence

Production and reproduction of institution or structural pattern

Reactive sequence

Reactions and counterreactions to institution or structural pattern

Outcome

Resolution of conflict generated by reactions and counterreactions science explanations and reduce path dependence to a vague catch-all phrase for characterizing historical analyses.

In this study, path dependence refers to a specific type of explanation that unfolds through a series of logically sequential stages (see fig. 1.1). With this formulation, antecedent historical conditions define a range of options available to actors during a key choice point. This key actor choice point, or what can be called a "critical juncture," is characterized by the selection of a particular option (e.g., a specific policy, coalition, or government) from among two or more alternatives. The selection made during a critical juncture is consequential because it leads to the creation of institutional or structural patterns that endure over time. In turn, institutional and structural persistence triggers a reactive sequence in which actors respond to prevailing arrangements through a series of predictable responses and counterresponses. These reactions then channel development up to the point of a final outcome, which represents a resolution to the conflicts marking reactive sequences.

Several major comparative-historical analyses of regime change analyze path-dependent causal patterns, including the work of Barrington Moore, Gregory M. Luebbert, and Ruth Berins Collier and David Collier.[3] These analysts show how differences among countries in selection processes during critical junctures lead to the formation of contrasting structural patterns, and how these differing structural patterns in turn trigger reactions and counterreactions that culminate in the establishment of distinct types of national regimes. For example, Collier and Collier's *Shaping the Political Arena* illustrates how different policies toward labor movements adopted by eight Latin American governments led to the formation of new institutions governing state-labor relations. These new institutional arrangements in turn triggered a series of reactions and counterreactions that culminated in the creation of differing party-system regimes. Likewise, Moore's *Social Origins of Dictatorship and Democracy* and Luebbert's *Liberalism, Fascism, or Social Democracy* explore how the coalitional allies selected by key actors (e.g., the decision of the bourgeoisie to ally with landed elites or the decision of liberals to ally with labor) represent critical junctures that established new structures and institutions, which in turn triggered a sequence of political reactions that led to the emergence of enduring national political regimes.

Critical Junctures and Antecedent Conditions

Critical junctures are choice points when a particular option is adopted from among two or more alternatives.[4] These junctures are "critical" because once an option is selected, it becomes progressively more difficult to return to the initial point when multiple alternatives were still available. Popular examples of such choice points are found in the economic history literature on competing technologies, which has examined the selection processes that enabled inefficient technologies such as the QWERTY keyboard to prevail over more efficient rivals.[5] These examples are interesting because they show how small events and random processes can shape developments during critical junctures, leading to the adoption of options that could not have been predicted by theory. They demonstrate that the explanation of path-dependent outcomes may require a careful analysis of the historical events that condition distant selection processes.

The options available during critical junctures, as well as the choices ultimately made by actors, are typically rooted in prior events and processes. The degree to which these antecedent conditions determine actor choices during critical junctures can vary, ranging from choices characterized by a high degree of individual discretion to choices that are more deeply embedded in earlier occurrences.[6] In many cases, critical junctures are moments of relative structural indeterminism when willful actors shape outcomes in a more voluntaristic fashion than normal circumstances permit. Regardless of the degree to which actor choices during critical junctures can be considered truly random events, these choices demonstrate the power of agency by revealing how long-term development patterns can hinge on distant actor decisions of the past.

Not all choice points represent critical junctures. Critical junctures are specifically those choice points that put countries (or other units) onto paths of development that track certain outcomes—as opposed to others—and that cannot be easily broken or reversed. Before a critical juncture, a broad range of outcomes is possible; after a critical juncture, enduring institutions and structures are created, and the range of possible outcomes is narrowed considerably. An assessment of the narrowing of possible future outcomes by critical junctures must be developed in relation to prevailing theory. To assert that a given choice closes off future outcomes, one must show how this choice activates key variables that favor certain outcomes over others. Although the choice itself may have been caused by prior events, it is the variables activated by the choice, not the antecedent conditions that led to the choice, that predict final outcomes.

A focus on critical junctures enables historical researchers to avoid the problem of infinite explanatory regress into the past.[7] This problem arises when analysts lack criteria for establishing a meaningful beginning point of analysis and keep reaching back in time for ultimate causes that underlie subsequent events and outcomes. Critical junctures provide a basis for cutting into the seamless flow of history and overcoming this problem: the analyst focuses attention on those key choice points in history when (from the perspective of theory) the range of possible outcomes is substantially narrowed.[8] Hence, in a path-dependent framework, the centerpiece of analysis is a critical juncture period, because after this period major alternative development trajectories are increasingly closed off.

Structural and Institutional Persistence

A defining feature of path dependence is the idea that it is difficult for actors to reverse the effects of choices made during critical junctures; critical junctures lock countries into particular paths of development. As Margaret Levi suggests, "Path dependence has to mean, if it is to mean anything, that once a country or region has started down a track, the costs of reversal are very high. There will be other choice points, but the entrenchments of certain institutional arrangements obstruct an easy reversal of the initial choice."[9] Choices during critical junctures make path reversal difficult because they lead to the formation of institutions or structures that tend toward persistence and that cannot be easily transformed.

   Institutions and structures can endure over time in one of two basic ways. First, some institutional or structural patterns are reproduced through what Arthur Stinchcombe calls "constant causes."[10] In this case, a specific set of causal factors first produces a given outcome and then works in an analogous way over time to reproduce the outcome. With constant causes, then, a common set of factors is responsible for both the production and reproduction of an institution. By contrast, other institutions and structures persist over time in the absence of the processes responsible for their original development.[11] In this case, an initial set of causal factors first produces the institution—what Stinchcombe calls "historical causes"—and a subsequent set of processes reproduces the institution without the recurrence of the original causes. Path-dependent analyses emphasize specifically historical causes, not constant causes, when explaining institutional and structural formation and persistence; path-dependent structures and institutions endure in the absence of the processes that initially led to their establishment.

   Explaining the persistence of institutions and structures created by historical causes requires one to identify specific mechanisms of reproduction. In the social sciences, analysts working from different theoretical traditions have identified a wide array of such mechanisms. For example, researchers associated with the new institutionalism literature in economics have shown how rational utilitarian actors are prone to reproduce organizations and technologies due to the benefits of learning effects, coordination effects, and adaptive expectations, as well as the costs imposed by irretrievable investments.[12] Earlier functionalist explanations likewise argued that institutional reproduction may occur because institutions serve some function (e.g., integration, adaptation, survival) for larger systems within which they are embedded.[13] In this sense, both rational utilitarian and functional explanations trace institutional reproduction back to the beneficial consequences of the institution for either actors or overall systems.

Other analysts emphasize that institutions and structures distribute costs and benefits unevenly, and individuals in different power positions will typically have conflicting interests vis-à-vis institutional continuity. These scholars argue that institutions and structures can persist even when most individuals prefer to change them, provided that a powerful elite that benefits from existing arrangements has sufficient strength to resist their transformation.[14] Institutional transformation in these situations may be contingent on the ability of subordinate actors to force change on a resistant elite. Still other researchers emphasize how institutional and structural reproduction may be grounded in actors' subjective orientations and beliefs about what is appropriate or morally correct.[15] These kinds of explanations point out that institutional persistence may occur because actors view institutions as legitimate and voluntarily opt for their reproduction out of a belief that it is the right thing to do. Here institutions are assumed to persist until actors develop new subjective codes concerning appropriateness.

In short, several plausible theoretical perspectives for understanding structural and institutional persistence can be used in conjunction with path-dependent explanation. Although these different perspectives might be viewed as rival explanations for the persistence of any given structural or institutional pattern, they do not necessarily represent mutually exclusive explanations. For example, an institution could be reproduced both because it is highly functional for an overall system and because it is legitimate in the eyes of societal members. In this sense, evidence in support of one mechanism does not preclude the possibility that other mechanisms are also at work.

Reactive Sequences and Final Outcomes

With many path-dependent patterns, the endurance of institutions and structures over time triggers a chain of causally linked events that, once itself in motion, unfolds independently of the institutional or structural factors that initially produced it. This sequence of events, while ultimately linked to a critical juncture period, can culminate in an outcome that is far removed from the original critical juncture. These chains of reactions and counterreactions can be called "reactive sequences," and such sequences can be thought of as defining the "aftermath" of a critical juncture period.[16]

Reactive sequences are chains of temporally ordered and causally connected events. These sequences are marked by what Andrew Abbott calls an "inherent logic of events," whereby one event triggers another through predictable reaction-counterreaction dynamics.[17] Actor resistance to prevailing institutions or structures is often the initial force that launches a reactive sequence. Counterreactions to this actor resistance may then drive subsequent events in the sequence. Reactive sequences are therefore often marked by properties of backlash and counterresponse as actors challenge or support structural and institutional patterns established during critical juncture periods. Even if such resistance does not actually transform these institutions and structures, it can set in motion an autonomous process that encompasses events that lead to a final outcome of interest.

The mechanisms driving reactive sequences differ substantially from those that characterize processes of structural and institutional reproduction. Whereas mechanisms of institutional and structural reproduction are marked by self-reinforcing and positive-feedback processes, reactive sequences are characterized by transformative and backlash processes in which there is movement toward reversing previous patterns. The processes that trigger actor resistance to a prevailing institution will vary depending on the particular mechanism responsible for the reproduction of the institution. For instance, institutions that persist only by virtue of the support of a small elite are inherently susceptible to mass challenges from groups that do not benefit from the prevailing arrangements. Here reactive sequences may be launched when subordinate groups mobilize against established institutions. By contrast, institutions that persist because their endurance is in the rational interests of broad populations are less vulnerable to mass pressure from below, but may face competitive pressures when new and superior institutional arrangements are developed. In this case, a reactive sequence will be launched as actors question whether their interests are still best served by the institutional status quo. Thus, knowledge about the mechanisms that sustain an institution can be helpful in understanding the reactive pressures likely to emerge in response to institutional persistence.

In a path-dependent pattern, the conflicts of a reactive sequence eventually give way to more stable final outcomes, which can be considered the "heritage" of a critical juncture period. Final outcomes typically entail the formation of new institutional or structural patterns, such as national regimes, party systems, types of industrial economies, national value systems, class structures, or electoral realignments. Understanding the persistence of these institutional or structural outcomes again requires an analysis of the specific mechanisms that underpin self-reinforcing processes. Even when such mechanisms are identified, the analyst must keep in mind that new periods of discontinuity will inevitably dislodge and replace final outcomes. Such periods of discontinuity signal the end of the legacy of a given critical juncture and perhaps the beginning of a new critical juncture.

In sum, a path-dependent approach emphasizes how actor choices create institutions and structures, which in turn shape subsequent actor behaviors, which in turn lead to the development of new institutional and structural patterns. Such a mutually constitutive approach to actors and institutions resonates well with many recent calls in the study of national political regime change for frameworks that go beyond voluntaristic and structural approaches.[18] Unlike voluntaristic analyses of regime change, a path-dependent approach avoids an excessive emphasis on contingency, crafting, and choice by highlighting the crucial role of structures and institutions in channeling long-term development. At the same time, by emphasizing the role of actor choice in creating institutions and structures, this approach avoids the tendency of some structuralist accounts to read human agency out of the analysis. Although a path-dependent approach is not the only integrative "solution" to the agent-structure problem, it represents one concrete research strategy that can be readily applied in empirical analysis.

THE HISTORICAL ARGUMENT

This study hypothesizes that the nineteenth-century liberal reform period was a critical juncture in Central American history. During this period, the Central American countries witnessed their first major expansion of commercial agriculture and their incorporation into the international market through coffee and/or banana export production. The exact dates of this period differ for each country, though they roughly correspond to 1870–1920—with the important exceptions of Costa Rica, which launched a reform episode much earlier, and Nicaragua, which experienced a notably brief liberal reform period (see table 1.1). This epoch of state-building and agrarian capitalist development is typically called the liberal reform period because the political leaders who exercised control over government embraced a Central American variant of liberalism as an ideology.

The liberal reform period grew out of an intra-elite conflict between liberals and conservatives whose origins pre-date Central American independence in 1821. This conflict initially reflected different class bases within the colonial elite, but by the mid-nineteenth century both political factions drew membership from the same wealthy classes of landlords and well-to-do merchants. With increased world demand for potential Central American exports in the mid-nineteenth century, conservatives gradually gave up an earlier commitment to common land systems and concurred with liberals on the necessity of land privatization and export agriculture. However, the two factions disagreed about the pace and scope of economic change: conservatives advocated a more gradual and less thoroughgoing transition to commercial agriculture than liberals. Hence, not until liberals actually wrested power from conservatives did

TABLE 1.1 Chronological Overview

Cases	Liberal Reform	Full-Blown Liberalism	Aftermath of Liberalism	Regime Heritage
Guatemala	1871–1926	1873–85 (Barrios)	1926–54	1954–86
El Salvador	1871–1927	1876–83 (Zaldívar)	1927–48	1948–79
Costa Rica	1821–1914	1838–42 (Carrillo) 1870–82 (Guardia)	1914–49	1949–present
Honduras	1873–1919	1876–83 (Soto)	1919–32	1932–82
Nicaragua	1893–1909	1893–1909 (Zelaya)	1909–36	1936–79

an explosion of commercial agriculture and primary product exportation occur.

One or two presidents were especially influential in each country during the liberal reform years, leading periods of "full-blown liberalism" and enacting policy legislation that defined the overall direction of change for the entire era. These key liberal presidents are Justo Rufino Barrios (1873–85) in Guatemala, Rafael Zaldívar (1876–83) in El Salvador, Braulio Carrillo (1838–42) and Tomás Guardia (1870–82) in Costa Rica, Marco Aurelio Soto (1876–83) in Honduras, and José Santos Zelaya (1893–1909) in Nicaragua. In this study, the choices made by these liberal presidents concerning state-building and agricultural modernization are argued to have critically shaped future development.

Liberals faced a basic choice between a *radical* policy option and a *reform* policy option. These options reflected differences in the pace and scope of agrarian modernization and in how the state was used to promote commercial agriculture. With a radical policy option, which characterized Guatemala, El Salvador, and Nicaragua, liberals pursued rapid and highly encompassing land privatization policies that marginalized peasants, either by coercively seizing their land or by using the market to squeeze them onto estates that could not provide them long-term security. By contrast, with a reform policy option, which characterized Costa Rica and Honduras, liberals pursued land privatization in a gradual fashion and took steps to ensure that peasants and small producers would have access to land over the long run. Thus, radical and reform policy options were differentiated by the pace and scope of land privatization and by the implications of privatization policies for small producers.

The decision of liberals to implement either a radical or a reform policy option was rooted in antecedent conditions (see fig. 1.2). Liberals pursued a radical policy option in those countries (Guatemala, El Salvador, and Nicaragua) that were characterized by more developed agrarian economies and state structures at the beginning of the liberal reform period. By contrast, countries marked by lower levels of development (Costa Rica and Honduras) at the beginning of the reform period saw the enactment of a reform policy option. Nevertheless, preexisting socioeconomic structures did not make the adoption of a particular policy choice inevitable. Liberals' choices were most immediately influenced by political considerations, especially threats from conservative rivals and other groups that sought to win state power. In Guatemala, El Salvador, and Nicaragua, liberals faced significant political challenges and were consequently led to build powerful militaries that made it structurally possible to pursue radical policy options. By contrast, liberals in Costa Rica and Honduras faced fewer political challenges and never constructed the military and bureaucratic infrastructure necessary for the effective implementation of radical policy options.

When key liberal presidents implemented either a radical or a reform policy option, major structural transformations were set in motion. In Guatemala and El Salvador, the pursuit of radical policy options led to the establishment of relatively centralized and highly militarized state apparatuses along with polarized agrarian class structures in which landless and land-poor peasants were faced with a politically powerful agrarian-commercial elite. This overall constellation of structural patterns can be referred to as "radical liberalism." In Costa Rica, the implementation of a reform policy option brought about a substantial modernization of the state and the agrarian economy, including the emergence of a politically powerful coffee elite class, but it did not lead to intense class polarization in the agrarian sector or substantial militarization in the state. This overall set of structural transformations can be called "reformist liberalism." Finally, in Honduras and Nicaragua, policy options were not successfully implemented. In these countries, major episodes of U.S. intervention acted as an intervening variable that stunted domestic structural changes during the liberal reform period. These countries thus followed a pattern of "aborted liberalism."

Different patterns of liberalism were consequential to long-term development because they triggered reactive sequences. In the three countries where liberalism was not aborted by foreign intervention—Guatemala, El Salvador, and Costa Rica—disadvantaged actors responded to the structural patterns established during the liberal reform period by leading democratizing episodes in which major political and socioeconomic issues were brought to the forefront of national politics. In the cases of radical liberalism—Guatemala and El Salvador—these democratizing episodes ultimately failed when military and economic elites initiated powerful counterresponses against democratic reformers, which led to the establishment of harsh military-authoritarian regimes. By contrast, in the case of reformist liberalism in Costa Rica, important factions of the elite actively mobilized democratizing movements to generate electoral support in the course of ongoing political struggles. The inclusion of previously excluded groups in the political system increased the stakes of political competition among the elite and eventually convinced most factions that full democracy was the type of national regime most compatible with their interests. Finally, in the two countries that followed the

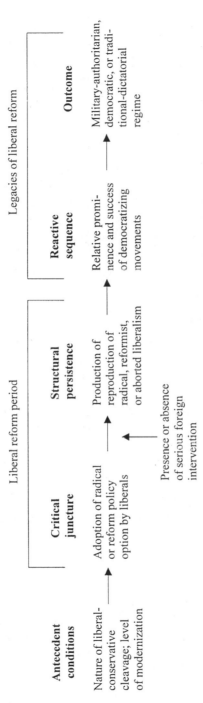

FIGURE 1.2 Path-Dependent Explanation of Political Development in Central America

pattern of aborted liberalism—Honduras and Nicaragua—the limited structural transformation of the reform period provided no basis for the emergence of powerful democratizing movements. In these cases, the political reactions of the aftermath period were directed at U.S. actors who had established semicolonial authority during the reform period. Once the U.S. presence was removed, backward traditional dictatorships similar to those that had prevailed in the nineteenth century emerged at the level of national politics.

The contrasting political outcomes of military authoritarianism in Guatemala and El Salvador, democracy in Costa Rica, and traditional dictatorship in Honduras and Nicaragua constitute the regime heritage of the liberal reform period. Given the many other similarities shared by these countries—a common colonial experience, cultural orientation, geographic location, and position in the global capitalist economy—this contrast in regime outcomes is nothing short of remarkable. Indeed, over several decades in the twentieth century, the Central American region featured Latin America's most violent political systems (Guatemala and El Salvador), its most stable and least militaristic political system (Costa Rica), and its archetypal banana republic (Honduras) and personalistic dictatorship (Nicaragua). Hence, this study offers an explanation for why the countries of Central America were characterized by some of the most different political systems in the world during the twentieth century.

These contrasting regimes did not, of course, mark the end of political development in the region. In the 1980s and 1990s, the Central American countries experienced substantial political convergence through the creation of electoral and democratic regimes. Although this recent period has seen an erosion of the nineteenth-century liberal heritage analyzed here, this study nonetheless argues that an understanding of the earlier liberal reform period offers a powerful lens through which to assess contemporary changes.

RIVAL EXPLANATIONS

Many thoughtful analysts have attempted to unravel the puzzle of political differences among the Central American countries. These scholars have developed several plausible arguments that highlight diverse explanatory factors ranging from class structures in the agrarian sector to external actors such as U.S. corporations. In addition, analysts have emphasized the importance of historical periods as different as the colonial era and the depression period in the 1930s to explain political divergence in the region. Previous explanations have much to contribute to an understanding of Central American development, and it would be a serious error to simply dismiss them as invalid. Nevertheless, I shall argue that, taken on their own terms, prevailing theories provide an incomplete or inadequate basis for explaining the region's political outcomes.

Before turning to these specific alternative explanations, two basic points about the explanatory approach of this study should be made. First, in adopting a path-dependent approach, this study rejects commonplace arguments that emphasize solely or primarily short-term causes that immediately precede regime outcomes. For example, military authoritarianism in Guatemala is commonly explained in terms of events surrounding the fall of Jacobo Arbenz in the early 1950s; the origins of Costa Rican democracy are often linked to an elite pact following the 1948 civil war; and the rise of traditional dictatorship in Nicaragua is sometimes understood in terms of the skillful political maneuvering of Anastasio Somoza in the early and mid-1930s.[19] While these short-term processes will figure into the analysis below, they will be situated in relationship to more fundamental historical causes associated with the liberal reform period.

Second, the explanation of this study is developed at a middle level of generality in which both similarities and differences among cases are highlighted. By contrast, "the historiography shows two tendencies . . . it either stresses trends common to all of Central America using broad brush strokes that obscure the individuality of each case or concentrates on specific countries without making any substantial effort to refer to what was happening in others."[20] The basic limitation of arguments that highlight idiosyncratic causal factors is that they fail to develop meaningful generalizations of the type that interest social scientists. In the field of Central American studies, however, the opposite problem—overgeneralization—is equally common. Specifically, many scholars have characterized the entire region in terms of patterns that are really appropriate for only one or two cases. The Guatemalan case, in particular, has been repeatedly treated as a model for all of Central America, leading scholars to skip over or discuss only briefly certain cases that do not fit well, especially Honduras.[21] In order to deal with Costa Rica, which does not fit the Guatemala model but is seen as too important to be ignored, some analysts have developed a dichotomous characterization in which one pattern supposedly characterizes Central America's four northern states and Costa Rica is the region's exception.[22] By contrast, this study rejects efforts to interpret the entire region in light of only one or two particularly salient cases, offering instead an argument located between the extremes of whole-region generalization and country-specific particularism.

Agrarian Class Structure and the State

Perhaps the most persuasive explanations of Central American political development are historically grounded and comparative analyses that emphasize differences among countries in the nature of agrarian class structure. R. Lee Woodward's famous distinction between coffee republics and banana republics pointed to the value of such an approach, even though a limited focus on commodity differences has proved unable to explain twentieth-century regime outcomes.[23] More recent efforts at elaborating the agrarian roots of modern politics in Central America have been undertaken by talented scholars such as James Dunkerley, Lowell Gudmundson, Jeffery Paige, and Robert G. Williams.[24] These analysts have demonstrated that countries in which polarized class structures were created in the coffee sector during the nineteenth century, such as Guatemala and El Salvador, were far more likely to develop authoritarian political systems than countries in which more harmonious class structures were formed, such as Costa Rica. In my view, these studies have convincingly shown that a focus on class relations rooted in control over productive property and the processing and marketing of agrarian products is an indispensable theoretical tool for understanding Central American development. Hence, in this study, I shall draw freely on the ideas elaborated by these scholars as I develop a comparative-historical analysis of the liberal reform period and its legacies.

Yet it is also the case that this study emphasizes states as actors and as organizational structures to a much greater degree than most works that focus on agrarian class relations.[25] Studies centered on agrarian relations have tended to overlook the role of states, either because they assume the countries of Central America were essentially "stateless" in the nineteenth century[26] or, more commonly, because they assume that state structures and behavior are outgrowths of agrarian elite interests and the overall organization of coffee production.[27] As a result, agrarian-centered analyses have presented little information concerning state activities and organization at the time when key agrarian structural patterns were established.

Such omissions have led to misleading portraits of Central American history in which class structural changes are assumed to have driven state structural changes in a unidirectional fashion. In fact, during the liberal reform period, the organization of economic production was to a considerable degree an outcome, not a cause, of the organization and policies of states. Most basically, liberal states were indispensable to the development of export agriculture in the region. Their role included not only the minimal regulatory and policing duties of a "nightwatchman" state, but also actively stimulating production through a range of promotional activities: signaling government support for the production of key agrarian products, providing information on agricultural techniques in government bulletins, encouraging foreign investment and the immigration of foreign capitalists, making cheap land available for export crop production, offering loans for the purchase of agricultural inputs, and distributing free coffee seedlings to producers. Liberal states were also active in efforts to secure a workforce for export crop producers— which sometimes involved "extra-economic," coercive means, such as vagrancy laws that kept peasants on plantations. Moreover, the growth of the agrarian economy was tied to state efforts to promote railways, roads, ports, and improved communication and financial facilities. Hence, rather than posit class relations in the agricultural sector as the ultimate driving force behind agrarian development, this study shows how states were key determinants of agrarian structural transformation.

Furthermore, this study rejects the idea that liberal state activity was simply an expression of oligarchic interests or a response to the needs of an incipient agrarian capitalist mode of production. Rather, liberal states were typically headed by personalistic dictators who were capable of making decisions without negotiation or consultation with classes and groups from civil society. Liberal rulers and their cohort of close allies dictated the terms of state policies, often with little direct input from major societal actors, and sometimes in accordance with their own personal whims. To be sure, dominant-class interests were one important consideration that liberal presidents had to keep in mind, especially given that some of Central America's liberal dictators were linked to members of the agrarian elite through social networks or by direct membership in this class.[28] Nevertheless, liberal dictators were fundamentally state-building political actors interested in maintaining and expanding their own personal power. When faced with the choice of protecting their political interests or supporting local agrarian elites, liberals could and did make decisions that directly contradicted the socioeconomic interests of dominant-class actors.

New state structures were forged during the liberal reform period, and when these structures are treated as independent variables, they can help explain political outcomes that agrarian class structure variables alone cannot. Throughout Latin America, unequal power relations in the countryside have closed off democracy as an historical possibility only when combined with and closely linked to extensively militarized state structures. Had Guatemala and El Salvador not witnessed extensive militarization by the 1920s, it is quite possible that, even with the polarized class structures that developed there, they would have followed the democratic path of countries such as Chile, where coercive agrarian structures did not prevent the early establishment of democracy. Furthermore, state structures are important to this analysis because differences in state formation can help explain variations among countries that experienced the same type of liberal reform. For instance, to understand why Guatemala underwent a major social and democratic reform period in the late 1940s and early 1950s whereas El Salvador broke down into military authoritarianism without such a reform, differences in the degree to which the military was autonomous from the ruling government provide answers that agrarian class structures alone cannot.

Finally, state structures are essential to understanding and explaining the persistence of major twentieth-century regime outcomes. Continuity in the organization of state institutions, especially the military, was often more important to twentieth-century regime endurance than continuity in the organization of agrarian production. For example, even before a democratic regime was established in Costa Rica, land concentration became an increasing problem as the subdivision of family plots left significant numbers of rural producers with smaller and smaller estates. Nevertheless, the state remained demilitarized and generally committed to promoting social development for poorer citizens. This persistence in state organization and orientation underpinned a high level of democratic stability despite the fact that land concentration had become a real problem for Costa Rica in the mid- and late twentieth century.

U.S. Intervention and Domestic Politics

In contrast to analysts who focus on agrarian structure, other scholars of Central America emphasize U.S. intervention and external dependence when explaining political development in the region. These scholars argue that outside entities such as the U.S. State Department, the Central Intelligence Agency, and multinational corporations have profoundly shaped development trajectories through indirect political pressures or more direct interventionist operations. In this study, I build on these accounts by suggesting that U.S. intervention during the liberal reform period had enormous implications for national development in Central America. However, I maintain that the dependency theory foundation of these arguments needs to be reworked to incorporate the autonomous role of domestic political processes in the analysis of intervention.

From the perspective of this study, dependency theory is on its strongest footing when offering regionwide generalizations about the occurrence of the liberal reform period in the nineteenth century. This period did indeed correspond with a massive demand by industrialized nations for primary goods from less developed countries. Most important, the market for coffee exploded in the nineteenth century as the Industrial Revolution spread across northern Europe and the California gold rush opened up the western frontier in the United States.[29] With the technological improvements of this era, especially the advent of the steam engine, it became profitable for the Central American region to enter export trade through coffee production. Furthermore, the development of refrigerated ships and improvements in maritime navigation enabled another sought-after Central American product—the highly perishable banana crop—to be profitably exported to markets in advanced nations.[30] I thus follow the dependency theory tradition in arguing that technological improvements and changes in the international economy were necessary facilitating conditions for the liberal reform period.

Yet it is now widely accepted that variants of dependency theory that focus too narrowly on external processes provide a poor guide to understanding many important facets of development.[31] One obvious reason is that an external-dependency perspective overlooks the role of domestic structures and processes and consequently cannot differentiate the development trajectories of countries—such as those of Central America—that are similarly situated in the global capitalist economy. To their credit, however, analysts of Central America have been sensitive to intraregional variations, and they employ more sophisticated dependency theory perspectives that clearly link external conditions with internal ones.[32] Nevertheless, these analyses remain centered on *economic* factors, stopping short of considerations about the role of linkages between *domestic politics* and international contexts in shaping Central American development.

The failure to emphasize domestic politics has left many Central American specialists unable to distinguish processes of foreign intervention that undermine an ongoing political project from those that do not. While most Central American countries experienced serious foreign intrusion during the liberal reform period, including the establishment of major banana enclave sectors in Guatemala, Costa Rica, and Honduras, such intervention did not necessarily spell the demise of a given liberal reform policy option. Rather, in all cases except Honduras and Nicaragua, state actors were able to carry out policy options to their logical conclusion in spite of the foreign presence. Even in the cases of Honduras and Nicaragua, where U.S. intervention did abort liberal reform projects, dependency theory ill prepares us to understand the long-run consequences of this intervention. Dependency theorists nearly always assume that because intervention is morally objectionable, it necessarily has negative implications for political development. Yet if we take seriously the domestic political project pursued by Central American actors, it becomes clear that such conclusions are not always warranted. For example, U.S. intervention in Nicaragua aborted a radical policy option that, had it been left unchecked, might well have led to a much harsher form of military authoritarianism. By contrast, U.S. intervention in Honduras did have the anticipated negative effects, undermining a reform policy option that could have laid the foundation for a future democracy.

Furthermore, the economistic focus of dependency theory has directed attention away from important differences between political and economic forms of foreign intervention. Just as the Central American countries are embedded in both an international states system and a world capitalist economy, foreign intrusion in the region has included political forms of domination as well as economic forms of imperialism.[33] Many comparative-historical analysts of Central America have not given sufficient weight to forms of intervention in which advanced nations use their *military* power to establish *political* control over foreign states and territories. While this type of political intervention may be accompanied by economic domination, it is analytically separate from, and not necessarily reducible to, economic imperialism.

Such a distinction is crucial to grasping the relationship between policy options and U.S. intervention during the liberal reform period. The more modest transformative initiative entailed in a *reform* policy option, as was pursued in Costa Rica and Honduras, was particularly vulnerable to failure due to *economically* based intervention. The comparative gradualness associated with this policy option opened up opportunities for foreign capitalists to establish enclave sectors that developed more rapidly than domestically controlled sectors of the economy. By contrast, the rapid, encompassing changes embodied in a *radical* policy option, as was pursued in Guatemala, El Salvador, and Nicaragua, made these countries more vulnerable to *political* forms of foreign intervention. The comparatively dramatic initiatives of this policy option promoted a process of development in which there was less space and time for foreign capital to assert a dominant influence over the economy. The abortion of this transformative process required covert and overt foreign military intervention that replaced ruling government authorities with proxy leaders sympathetic to the political agenda of the United States.

In either pattern, however, the likelihood that foreign intervention would actually occur was influenced by domestic political struggles among actors seeking control over the state. These struggles conditioned possibilities for foreign intervention by providing opportunities for foreign actors to work through local political factions to achieve their economic or political goals. In certain cases, local factions actually encouraged foreign intervention in order to bolster their efforts to gain or maintain state power in the course of a political struggle. This reality points to the limitations of explanations that assume Central American countries are simply passive recipients of foreign intervention. Even without such active domestic encouragement, however, unstable political situations made it easier for foreign actors to establish direct or indirect control over the state. When domestic actors exercised only a tenuous hold over the state, foreigners could readily develop ideological justifications for intervention and could more easily seize control of key political and economic sectors. State structural cohesion is thus inversely related to the likelihood of foreign intervention, and in Central America it was precisely the noncohesive states of Honduras and Nicaragua that fell victim to foreign intervention during the liberal reform period.

In sum, transnational processes have greatly affected Central American political development, including during the liberal reform period, but to understand these processes it is necessary to move beyond even the most sophisticated variants of dependency theory. In this study, I adopt an approach to transnational relations that emphasizes the link between domestic political initiatives and foreign intervention. I suggest that domestic political events in Central American countries—independent of the domestic or global economy—were crucial to the onset of U.S. intervention. In addition, I argue that a theoretical emphasis on domestic politics can help differentiate periods of intervention in Central America that critically affected long-term trajectories of change from periods of intervention that did not fundamentally redirect paths of national development.

Alternative Critical Juncture Explanations

Scholars have suggested that other episodes of change besides the liberal reform period were of tremendous importance to political development in Central America. Three periods in particular—the colonial period, the depression period beginning in 1929, and the democratic and social reform period that followed World War II in the 1940s and 1950s—stand out as salient examples. Each of these periods has been treated by analysts as a founding epoch in more or less the sense of "critical juncture" as employed here. Hence, one must ask why specifically the liberal reform period should be regarded as the crucial turning point in Central American political development.

A first alternative suggests that the different ways in which the individual provinces of Central America experienced colonialism can help explain differences in post-independence trajectories.[34] No historically minded scholar would seriously question the assertion that differences during the colonial period had an important impact on future development in Central America. Yet the importance of colonial differences for long-term *political* development has often been exaggerated. For example, while many scholars have argued that the roots of Costa Rican democracy are found in individualistic settlement patterns formed during the colonial period, in fact Costa Rican villages were more nucleated than those in Honduras (as we shall see below). Likewise, while Guatemala is sometimes contrasted with the rest of Central America because of its extensive economic development during colonialism, El Salvador was in many ways the region's most vibrant economy during the colonial period; and outright stagnation was not present in any of the colonies, including Costa Rica.

In truth, differences among countries during the colonial period often do not correspond to stereotypes that have developed over the years. According to David Scott Palmer's index of Spanish colonial penetration for Latin America—which focuses on a variety of factors such as colonial bureaucratization, economic production, Church revenues, and population density—colonialism was most pronounced in Guatemala and then gradually declined to the south such that colonial institutions were most limited in Costa Rica.[35] Yet differences between any two neighboring countries were quite small. Based on the level of colonial penetration, one would not expect El Salvador and Honduras, and Nicaragua and Costa Rica, to have emerged with profound differences in political outcomes. Indeed, based on colonial differences alone, perhaps only the polar cases of Guatemala and Costa Rica could be expected to have developed sharply contrasting political systems. The picture for the region as a whole is one in which various colonial differences—political and social cleavages, modes of land tenure and state organization, and extent of indigenous population—were small enough to have left future regime options largely undefined.

In contrast to scholars of colonialism, analysts who point to a second potential critical juncture—the Great Depression—assert that the crucial turning point in Central America occurred after the liberal reform period. For example, Enrique A. Baloyra-Herp argues that the Great Depression led to major and broadly similar regime changes throughout Central America.[36] According to Baloyra, a political system of "reactionary despotism" was set up after the Depression and characterized the region until at least the late twentieth century (with the exception of Costa Rica). This political system was marked by a governmental coalition of oligarchic merchants and planters, large financiers and bankers, and military officers—actors who together ruled in a repressive and highly exclusionary manner. The establishment of reactionary despotism is viewed as an important shift away from an earlier pattern of "oligarchic domination."[37] Specifically, Baloyra argues that the Depression triggered pressures from below for land and labor reforms and forced the traditional oligarchy to call upon other elite economic actors and the military "to restore order through repression."[38] The outcome was a new government partnership and the political weakening of the traditional oligarchy.

The argument of this study, by contrast, suggests that the Great Depression was not a critical turning point. I basically follow Woodward in contending that the Depression did not lead to a fundamental regime change in the region.[39] The dictatorships established in the 1930s share the main features of the liberal political systems present in the late nineteenth and early twentieth centuries. Not until the mid-twentieth century and the advent of full-blown military-authoritarian regimes in Guatemala and El Salvador and a democracy in Costa Rica was the old pattern broken (in Honduras and Nicaragua the pattern managed to persist past the mid-twentieth century). In addition, Baloyra's argument that pressures from below associated with the Depression forced the hand of elites is not correct. In Guatemala and El Salvador, middle-sector pressures from below preceded the Great Depression (they took place in the mid- to late 1920s) and were ultimately ineffectual. In Costa Rica, no major lower-class pressures accompanied the Depression. In Nicaragua, the only significant lower-class movement was the Sandino revolt of 1927–33, which began well before the Depression and was directed at the U.S. occupation. In Honduras, the most important pressures from below occurred in the banana enclave and were also not directed at the national elite. Hence, my disagreement with Baloyra about whether the Great Depression was a critical juncture centers largely on basic empirical differences.

Finally, we turn to the 1940s and 1950s as a candidate for a critical juncture in Central American history. In her excellent book *Demanding Democracy,* Deborah J. Yashar explicitly develops a critical juncture argument that seeks to explain two of the major regime outcomes explored in this study: military authoritarianism in Guatemala and democracy in Costa Rica. Yashar looks at the liberal reform period and argues that differences in the construction of state-society relations during this time conditioned future regime outcomes by helping to produce contrasting reform contexts during the 1940s and 1950s. However, she argues that the state-society differences of the liberal reform period were associated with broadly *similar* nondemocratic political regimes in Guatemala and Costa Rica. By contrast, during the democratic and social reform period of the 1940s and 1950s, key differences in the strategy, goals, and social class composition of reform coalitions and countercoalitions led directly to the formation of a military-authoritarian regime in Guatemala and a democracy in Costa Rica. Without the events of the 1940s and 1950s, Yashar argues, Guatemala and Costa Rica could have still followed a similar regime trajectory. Hence, she reasons that the 1940s–1950s period is a better candidate for a critical juncture than the liberal reform period.

From the perspective of the five-country comparison employed in this study, however, the 1940s–1950s period appears less useful for explaining regime outcomes. Specifically, the three Central American countries not analyzed by Yashar (El Salvador, Honduras, and Nicaragua) highlight the importance of the liberal reform period as opposed to the social reform period of the 1940s and 1950s. In El Salvador, the 1940s saw the emergence of a reform movement, but it was moderate in its goals and strategies, and it in fact paralleled the Costa Rican reform movement of the 1940s and 1950s as much as the Guatemalan reform movement of the same era. Thus, based on evidence from the post–World War II reform period, one would expect El Salvador to have developed a regime heritage more similar to that of Costa Rica than Guatemala. Given that El Salvador's military-authoritarian regime did not resemble Costa Rica's democracy, the 1940s–1950s reform period emerges as a weak explanatory factor. There are additional empirical problems when Honduras and Nicaragua are considered. The traditional dictatorships of Honduras and Nicaragua were consolidated *before* the 1940s and 1950s. In these cases, reform movements of the mid-twentieth century had no impact on basic regime properties. Any explanation of these cases must look to variables antecedent to the 1940s and 1950s.

Yashar's analysis was not focused on the five-country comparison, and it might be argued that from the perspective of only Guatemala and Costa Rica, the 1940s–1950s period was indeed a critical juncture, whereas from the perspective of Central America as a whole the liberal reform period was a critical juncture. However, to sustain this argument, it would be necessary to establish reasons why the limited comparison of only Guatemala and Costa Rica is more appropriate than the broader, five-country comparison. In the absence of such reasons, one must conclude that the liberal reform period—not the 1940s–1950s period—was the key turning point in Central American political development.

The Analysis to Come

The analysis that follows shall put the path-dependent approach and theoretical principles outlined in this chapter to work in understanding Central American development. Two basic kinds of comparison will inform the discussion. First, some of the comparisons presented below will involve juxtaposing aspects of different cases with one another. These cross-case comparisons will be used to assess hypotheses through what have been called "nominal" and "ordinal" strategies of causal analysis.[40] Second, other comparisons will focus on within-case features to supplement the cross-case analysis. These within-case comparisons will show how particular features of specific cases conform to what would be expected if cross-case hypotheses are true.[41]

Evidence for the arguments below is drawn significantly from "secondary" sources—that is, published books and articles by historians and analysts of the region. This study does not rely on new documents previously undiscovered by historians. However, I have examined some of the primary source material that informs leading studies of particular countries, and I use this knowledge as a foundation for questioning the evidentiary basis from which the traditional historiography derives conclusions. Nevertheless, even with this probing of documents, the novelty of the argument offered in this book must grow out of the systematic use of comparison and theory to develop new lines of argumentation from existing sources.

The next chapter, which completes Part I, presents an overview of the major concepts that inform this analysis of liberalism and its legacy in Central America. Subsequent chapters are grouped into three parts based on their chronological relationship to the liberal reform period. Part II examines the time before the liberal reform period, including the development of a liberal-conservative cleavage and the conservative episode of the mid-nineteenth century. The liberal reform period itself is the focus of Part III, with separate chapters on radical, reformist, and aborted liberalism. In Part IV, the legacy of liberalism is traced from initial reactions following the liberal reform period to the consolidation of military-authoritarian, democratic, and traditional-dictatorial regimes. Finally, in the Conclusion, I consider the overall argument in relation to path-dependent explanations of political change in other regions and historical contexts.

CHAPTER 2

The Liberal Reform Period and Its Legacies: A Conceptual Framework

The emergence of liberalism as a movement for reform in the nineteenth and early twentieth centuries decisively shaped the course of modern world history. In Europe, the birthplace of liberal thought, liberal reformers played a leading role in the transition from absolutist to constitutional forms of government. From Paris and London to Stockholm and Zurich, liberals spearheaded reforms that led to the fall of monarchs and the institutionalization of popular sovereignty, marking what Reinhard Bendix has called the transition "from royal authority to popular mandate."[1] European liberal reformers were also instrumental in shaping new roles for the state in the promotion of capitalism and the protection of private property. And liberals were responsible for helping to define new social positions for aristocratic elites, peasants, working classes, and religious authorities.[2]

The influence of liberalism has hardly been confined to the European continent, however. The ideals embraced by European liberals have diffused throughout the world system, sometimes mixing with local belief systems to form new ideological models. In certain cases, such as the United States, liberal ideals were directly incorporated into national political culture.[3] Yet even when liberal ideas have not been central features of national culture, liberalism has profoundly shaped the basic institutions of nearly all societies, including societies ruled by governments that are expressly antiliberal. This influence can be seen in the nearly universal tendency of governments to legitimate themselves by drawing on core elements of liberal ideology, including the notions of popular sovereignty, individual liberty and freedom, private property, and secular state au-

29

thority. Liberalism is thus a worldwide cultural institution, a basic feature of contemporary "world society."[4]

Despite Central America's status as a small, peripheral area of the world system, there are good reasons to hypothesize that nineteenth-century liberalism played a major role in the region's development. For one thing, like Europe, this region saw the development of explicitly liberal movements. In Central America, liberalism became organizationally grounded in political movements consciously seeking to enact its ideological principles. Furthermore, during a relatively well defined period in each Central American country, these liberal movements seized political power and initiated major reform efforts. In all five countries, liberals carried out reforms that led to the creation of more advanced agrarian economies characterized by commercial agriculture and significant primary product exportation. In this sense it is meaningful to speak of a "liberal reform period" in Central America, as in Europe.

CENTRAL AMERICAN LIBERALISM

During the nineteenth century, a political cleavage between liberal and conservative political factions was present to a greater or lesser degree in the five Central American countries. This division emerged in the late colonial period, as liberal European ideas spread into the region through the enactment of the Spanish Bourbon reforms and the promulgation of the Cádiz Constitution in 1812. At this time, Central American conservative factions tended to be composed of elite actors who had benefited from the existence of colonial institutions, and who sought to keep the basic political, cultural, and socioeconomic structures of the colonial period intact. Accordingly, they advocated monarchical or authoritarian regimes, local autonomy for landlords, preservation of traditional landlord-peasant relations, special privileges for the Catholic Church, and extensive state regulation of the market. Early-nineteenth-century liberals, by contrast, found their strongest political base within the urban middle class, important elements of which were socially and politically marginalized under colonialism. Influenced by liberal political doctrines of the time, liberal leaders called for constitutional rule, free trade and markets, a separation of church and state, an expanded state role in the promotion of development, and incorporation into the international market through agro-exports.

Following the breakup of the Federation of Central America (1823–

38), the region was generally dominated by political elites organized into conservative factions. During this period of conservative rule, the social class differences between liberals and conservatives gradually eroded as both factions came to draw membership from wealthy landowners and merchants. In addition, in the mid-nineteenth century, conservatives gradually came to accept liberal beliefs concerning the advantages of development through agro-exportation, and some Central American countries underwent incipient processes of state-building and experienced modest commercial development. However, under conservative rule, national-level legislation still tended to promote agrarian structures— such as communal and *ejidal* lands—that were antithetical to the liberal commitment to private property. Likewise, conservatives failed to fully use the state to promote agrarian capitalism. Hence, before the liberal reform, capitalist agriculture and agro-exportation were relatively limited throughout the region, and national states played only a small role in stimulating agrarian development.

By the late nineteenth century, conservative rule had come to an end in all five countries. Liberal leaders took power and greatly extended the initial modernization policies embraced by conservatives, while undermining the lingering policy orientations of their colonial predecessors. With varying degrees of success, liberals spearheaded reforms that led to the creation of more modern state apparatuses, the expansion of export agriculture, and the incorporation of national economies into the world market. This period saw ambitious attempts by government leaders to use the state as an active promoter of agrarian capitalism through infrastructural development, financial incentives, and the imposition of order in the countryside. In most cases, the liberal reform period also witnessed the rise of a new agrarian export elite and in some cases the emergence of a vast class of marginal peasants. Thus, the liberal reform was a foundational period in the sense that all Central American countries definitively broke free of colonial legacies and achieved a basic transformation of state roles and socioeconomic relations.

Defining the Liberal Reform Period

The liberal reform period is defined here as an historical epoch in each Central American country during which (1) reformist leaders who embraced "liberalism" as an ideology exercised power over the state; and (2) these leaders successfully implemented reforms that led to a dramatic expansion of commercial agriculture and the incorporation of national economies into the international market. This definition highlights both a specific type of political leadership and the transformations actually produced by these leaders.

The leaders of the liberal reform were often members of Liberal political parties, but this was not true across all cases; the trait that was common to all was a commitment to a particular belief system known as liberalism. Liberalism has roots going back to the seventeenth century, finding expression in the thought of major social theorists such as Adam Smith, John Locke, and John Stuart Mill. Since then, its meaning has been variously—even contradictorily—understood across different regional and historical contexts. I focus on the form of liberalism that was present in mid- to late-nineteenth-century Central America—an ideology that is distinct from both classical liberalism in Western Europe and the liberal ideology dominant in Central America of the late eighteenth and early nineteenth centuries. I define this ideology in terms of three features: political positivism, economic individualism, and social anticorporatism.[5]

In the eighteenth and nineteenth centuries, various European ideologies made their way into Central America, but it was ultimately the philosophical positivism of Auguste Comte that formed the political cornerstone of liberalism in the region.[6] Comtean positivism rejected the Enlightenment doctrine of natural human rights, instead viewing the individual as a component of a hierarchically ordered society. Mid-nineteenth-century liberals were attracted to Comte's idea that social hierarchy and elitism were not only a natural state of affairs, but a necessary condition for the effective operation of society. Whereas pre-independence liberals in Central America had generally followed classical liberals in Western Europe by calling for more democratic forms of government and a broad series of individual rights and freedoms for male citizens, later in the nineteenth century liberals advocated "enlightened" republican dictatorships that systematically excluded those large populations of individuals whose race or level of wealth prohibited them from membership in the liberal definition of a citizen. Furthermore, Comte's emphasis on empiricism, scientific rationality, and the inherent value of progress strongly influenced Central American liberals. Indeed, his motto "order and progress" became a rallying cry for liberals. This expression reflected their belief that while modernization was a benign and progressive process, a means to move from "barbarism" to "civilization," the achievement of progress required strong governments willing to assert their dominance in the face of societal anarchy.[7]

Mid-nineteenth-century Central American liberals generally followed their West European counterparts in believing that Adam Smith's doctrine of economic individualism offered a valid model for achieving development. Liberals accepted the proposition that if individuals could be left to their own initiatives—that is, free from state restrictions that stood in the way of their "natural" economic interests—then individual creativity, a division of labor, and free exchange would bring about socioeconomic modernization. In the context of Central America, this translated into a major concern with promoting land privatization and free trade. Since classical liberalism is often associated with "limited government," it is important to note that Central American liberals (like liberals in Western Europe)[8] were in fact simultaneously opposed to and in favor of greater state involvement in the economy. On the one hand, liberals were against the use of the state to support monopolistic practices, communal forms of agriculture, and most tariffs that obstructed free trade. On the other hand, they sought to actively use the state to promote economic development; a major goal was to invest in the creation of a material and legal infrastructure to facilitate agrarian capitalist development. Liberals were often obsessed with the development of railroads, highways, ports, and communication facilities, all of which they associated with Western "civilization" and "progress." Similarly, they sought to establish legal codes that would benefit commerce and agrarian production. In addition to offering direct incentives such as tax breaks and land grants to agrarian producers, this involved the creation of laws regulating plantation labor, vagrancy, and civil codes of conduct. Thus, liberals believed that it was necessary to guide the invisible hand that Adam Smith envisaged would bring about the wealth of nations.

Finally, liberalism in Central America was based on opposition to traditional "corporate" entities within society. Liberals sought to replace or reorganize the Church, guilds, Indian communities, and other corporate groups by imposing new forms of social organization. For example, the liberal agenda called for the replacement of the traditional "moral economy" that often existed between hacienda owners and peasants—in which personal responsibility and obligation linked landed elites and peasants—with relations based on impersonal legal standards.[9] Above all, the liberal anticorporatist drive was aimed at the Catholic Church. Tax-exempt and inactive ecclesiastical properties were viewed by liberals as inhibiting agrarian capitalist expansion and blocking public capital accumulation, and the Church's tight grip on banking and financial activities was seen as a drag on the economy. Liberals favored a broad secularization of all public institutions, especially educational facilities. Ending Church control of education was seen as a crucial step toward the "privatization" of religious matters vis-à-vis matters of reason and science. More generally, liberals sought to weaken the Church's position as the premier source of ideological and moral guidance within society— particularly when political disputes were at issue—since such guidance was, again, viewed as an obstacle to progress.

Besides the presence of reformers who embraced the political, economic, and social components of liberalism, the transformations in the state and economy actually produced by these reformers represent the second broad defining feature of the liberal reform period. In all five countries, this period saw a major expansion of commercial agriculture and the incorporation of local economies into the international market as primary product producers. Except in Honduras, these transformations occurred as a result of the spread of coffee production, which commercialized agriculture and led to huge increases in exportation.[10] To varying degrees across cases, an initial experimentation with export-led growth policies (especially at the municipal level) had stimulated coffee production and exportation in the decade or so prior to the reform period. With the liberal reform, however, national governments implemented policies that sought to dramatically reorganize land structures and actively use the state to facilitate coffee production. As a consequence, coffee production for exportation exploded and came to dominate these economies.

This definition of the liberal reform period differs somewhat from the criteria conventionally used to identify the liberal period in Central American history. Scholars often view this period as corresponding with a set of years when liberal governments tended to be present in much of Central America, most commonly the years from 1870 to 1930.[11] By contrast, the definition here allows for the possibility of distinct beginning and ending points for the reform period in different countries. An alternative definition occasionally found in the literature identifies the liberal reform period more narrowly with the specific reforms of a particular liberal administration.[12] It is indeed the case that one or two distinct phases occurred in each of the Central American countries during which a single leader carried out a particularly ambitious reform program, defining the overall direction of the liberal reform period for many years to come. However, rather than date the entire liberal reform period with these administrations, I choose to treat them as phases of "full-blown liberalism" within a larger reform process. My reasoning is that the reforms initiated during full-blown liberalism often took decades to be carried out to their logical conclusion and should not be analytically separated from this larger transformation process.

Types of Liberal Reform

The liberal reform period occurred in different ways across the five Central American countries, and this study offers an account of the causes and consequences of these differences. Key variations concern the degree to which, and the ways in which, class and state structures were transformed in individual countries. Based on such variations in state and class transformation, I identify three types of liberal reform: radical liberalism, reformist liberalism, and aborted liberalism (see table 2.1).

In all of these countries, the liberal reform period saw a major expansion of commercial agriculture and the incorporation of local economies into the international market as primary product producers. A central component of these transformations was the shift from common lands to privately owned lands. The common land system in preliberal Central America was complex, and it varied from one country to another.

TABLE 2.1   Types of Liberal Reform

	Radical Liberalism (Guatemala & El Salvador)	Reformist Liberalism (Costa Rica)	Aborted Liberalism (Honduras & Nicaragua)
Massive expansion of commercial agriculture	Yes	Yes	Yes
Incorporation into international market	Yes	Yes	Yes
Emergence of agrarian bourgeoisie with significant political power	Yes	Yes	No
Emergence of centralized state apparatus	Yes	Yes	No
Emergence of polarized rural class structures	Yes	No	No
Emergence of powerful military-coercive apparatus	Yes	No	No
	Scope of transformation		
	← Greatest		Least →

Nevertheless, three basic types of land tenure were present in most countries. First, some lands were controlled by municipalities and rented to villagers in relatively well defined plots (referred to as *ejidal, censo,* or *legua* lands). Second, there were lands occupied by indigenous groups who enjoyed communal ownership rights based on colonial precedent and custom (known as *común,* or communal, lands). Third, some lands were officially declared unoccupied, though they were legally owned by the national government (referred to as *baldíos,* or public, lands). In all five countries, a substantial portion of the total land area was held in one of these forms prior to the liberal reform period. During the reform period, this common land system was partially or completely replaced with private landed property in conjunction with the transition to commercial agriculture and agro-exportation.

In Guatemala, El Salvador, and Costa Rica, the liberal reform period saw the rise of a politically powerful "agrarian bourgeoisie"—a class of individuals who derived wealth from estate ownership and the production of agro-export products, and from the financing, processing, and/or export of these products.[13] Because the Central American political systems were generally closed authoritarian regimes during the liberal reform, the political power of this class was not usually exercised in an electoral arena. Instead, political power was rooted in control and influence over state institutions—including the presidency, agricultural agencies, and the military—and in the ability of the agrarian bourgeoisie to shape public policy by virtue of its substantial economic power. The historical evidence presented below demonstrates that this class actor was able to exercise substantial political influence in the cases of Guatemala, El Salvador, and Costa Rica. In Honduras and Nicaragua, by contrast, the agrarian bourgeoisie was a much weaker actor and, at the end of the reform period, had little influence within semisovereign states.

Prior to the liberal reform period, Central America was characterized by weak national states that lacked significant bureaucratization, professional armies, and substantial power within society. Politics during this time tended to be dominated by local authorities, and major political decisions were often made at the level of municipal governments. In three cases—Guatemala, El Salvador, and Costa Rica—the liberal reform period saw a dramatic transformation of the state. Compared to those of earlier periods, the new states that emerged were much larger, more centralized, and more bureaucratic. Moreover, they wielded significantly greater influence within society. Local authorities and local governmental institutions, which had previously been the major locus of decision-making power, were superseded by national-level agencies. The new states were more capable of penetrating regional departments, regulating social relations, and fostering economic growth, thus more directly impinging on the lives of small agrarian producers and large landowners alike. By contrast, in Honduras and Nicaragua, foreign actors had assumed significant control over national politics by the conclusion of the reform period, stunting the development of centralized states.

Finally, in Guatemala and El Salvador, the liberal reform period also saw the establishment of highly polarized rural class structures and an extensive role for the military and other coercive institutions within the state and society. In judging whether class relations became highly polarized, I focus on the degree of land concentration and the situations of peasant and plantation workers at the conclusion of the reform period. The Guatemalan and Salvadoran cases—in which liberal leaders attacked communal land systems and promoted a rapid shift to commercial agriculture—exhibit a noticeably higher degree of land concentration, along with agrarian class relations in which large-scale lower-class revolts against landlords and state agents were distinct possibilities. The dimension of the establishment of a powerful military-coercive apparatus is reflected in the size of the army and other state-sponsored coercive bodies and in their prominence within the state and society by the conclusion of the liberal reform. Comparisons among the countries reveal that Guatemala and El Salvador were characterized by significantly larger and more socially prominent military-coercive institutions than the other cases.

The structural patterns that define these three types of liberalism—as summarized in table 2.1—persisted beyond the liberal reform period. Such persistence was not rooted in any functional logic in which agrarian or state structures were maintained because they coordinated and synchronized overall social systems. Nor were structural patterns reproduced through legitimation mechanisms in which the majority consented to existing arrangements because their subjective needs were met by the status quo. Rather, in quite straightforward ways, power mechanisms underpinned the reproduction of radical, reformist, and aborted liberalism. In Guatemala and El Salvador, the blatantly coercive nature of the agrarian economy and the state makes it easy to see the role of elite domination in sustaining structural persistence. Likewise, in Honduras and Nicaragua, the presence of U.S. imperialists working through local political and economic allies during and after the liberal reform period points toward a profoundly coercive process of structural reproduction. Even in Costa Rica, where one might be tempted to emphasize legitimation mechanisms because substantial modernization occurred without the development of polarized class structures, power dynamics were crucial to the maintenance of liberal structures. Most important, the liberal state in Costa Rica was an exclusionary and illegitimate apparatus that was maintained by political and economic elites without popular consensual support.

Given the crucial role of elite actors in sustaining radical, reformist, and aborted liberalism, it makes sense to inquire about the logic guiding their behavior. Here utilitarian notions of rational cost-benefit decision making prove useful. Despite a highly advantageous position in society, Central American elites faced real predicaments in reproducing liberal structures. In Guatemala and El Salvador, the elite was susceptible to class-based revolts from below and dependent on a partially autonomous militarized state to maintain political influence. Elite actors may have preferred some way out of radical liberalism through incremental reforms that gradually reduced societal polarization without fundamentally altering the class structure of society, but they feared that any effort to rearrange the agrarian economy would play into the hands of non-elite actors by triggering large-scale revolts and unraveling the entire radical liberal agrarian-state complex. Hence, Guatemalan and Salvadoran elites were led to defend structural arrangements that were not optimal for their interests. In Honduras and Nicaragua, privileged actors were faced with the choice of working with U.S. political advisors and capitalists, which many considered to be semicolonial occupiers, or losing their position of authority in the aftermath of the liberal reform period. Local elites in Honduras and Nicaragua sold themselves out to foreign occupying forces and multinational corporations not because it was a particularly tasteful option, but because it was the best option available in a context where national sovereignty had been lost. Finally, in Costa Rica, elite actors were faced with difficult choices about how to resolve intraclass conflicts without threatening their monopoly of governmental power. Their solution was to abolish authoritarian liberal political structures, but they did so only after a civil war had been fought that taught them that democracy was indeed the most reliable means of protecting their interests.

By the mid-twentieth century, the Central American elite had invented certain myths to provide ideological justification for the liberal systems from which they benefited. Thus, in countries such as El Salvador and Nicaragua, the elite developed stories of "liberty and progress" to describe their histories, and in Costa Rica the elite created a "rural democracy" discourse to characterize the nation.[14] These myths eventually became part of the national culture, and they developed a certain autonomy such that elite actors accepted them as a description of reality without realizing their instrumental aspects. Nevertheless, these ideologies were originally formulated as tools to justify and disguise fundamentally self-interested behavior. At the conclusion of the liberal reform period, the Central American elite could hardly have believed that the narratives they propagated were something more than an ideological rationale for maintaining the power mechanisms from which they benefited.

CAUSES OF RADICAL, REFORMIST, AND ABORTED LIBERALISM

To explain the development of radical, reformist, and aborted liberalism, this study emphasizes the contingent choices pursued by key Central American presidents at the height of the liberal reform period. To explain in turn the origins of these choices themselves, the study focuses centrally on the political dilemmas that faced liberals and the types of state structures they developed to solve governance problems.

Liberal Leaders and Policy Options

Once in power, liberals had to make a choice between two basic strategies for achieving societal modernization: a reform policy option and a radical policy option. These policy options represented overall packages of related agrarian reforms, entailing a range of specific land and labor provisions designed to stimulate agricultural modernization. As table 2.2 illustrates, radical and reform policy options can be defined along three dimensions: scope of privatization, size of estate promoted, and level of state coercion. Scope of privatization refers to the extent to which common lands were targeted for privatization by liberals. In Central America, this ranged from the one extreme of El Salvador and Nicaragua, where all common lands were subject to privatization, to the other extreme of Honduras, where agricultural commercialization was pursued with comparatively limited changes to previous landholding structures. In the middle on this dimension were Guatemala and Costa Rica, where

TABLE 2.2   Agricultural Policy Options

	Scope of Land Privatization[a]	Size of Estate Promoted[a]	Level of State Coercion[a]	Type of Policy Option[b]
Guatemala	Partial (2)	Large estates (3)	High (3)	Radical (8)
El Salvador	Full (3)	Large and small estates (2)	Moderate (2)	Radical (7)
Nicaragua	Full (3)	Large and small estates (2)	High (3)	Radical (8)
Honduras	Limited (1)	Large and small estates (2)	Low (1)	Reform (4)
Costa Rica	Partial (2)	Small estates (1)	Low (1)	Reform (4)

[a]1 = least, 3 = most.
[b]Sum of scores.

liberals privatized substantial amounts of land but also deliberately retained significant tracts of common land for much or all of the liberal reform period. The second dimension concerns the size of the commercial landholding estate promoted by liberals. The cases range from explicit efforts to privilege large plantations at the expense of small farms (Guatemala), to the promotion of both large and small estates (El Salvador, Nicaragua, and Honduras), to direct efforts to favor family-based agriculture (Costa Rica). Finally, level of state coercion refers to the degree to which public and quasi-public security organizations were used in the implementation and enforcement of land and labor legislation. The Central American cases range from the feudal-like promotion of coercive labor (Guatemala and Nicaragua), to the use of some coercion in a basically free labor system (El Salvador), to the near absence of public coercion in labor promotion during the reform period (Honduras and Costa Rica).

The initial design and implementation of policy options are identified with the one or two liberal presidents in each country who headed the phase of full-blown liberalism. Once enacted by these leaders, policy options had the effect of defining an overall trajectory of state and class transformation throughout the liberal reform period. Subsequent liberal administrations pushed forward the implementation of these policy options and were unable or unwilling to significantly break with their transformative logic. This policy continuity existed because the enactment of policy options by major liberal reformers stabilized reform inclinations among liberal leaders and created a kind of bureaucratic path dependence in which liberals could not "easily switch to expand into other fields of action."[15]

Which policy option was selected is a powerful explanatory variable for understanding the type of liberal reform period that characterized a particular country (see fig. 2.1). When successfully implemented, a radical policy option gave rise to radical liberalism, as in Guatemala and El Salvador. Likewise, the successful implementation of a reform option led to reformist liberalism, as was the case for Costa Rica. In contrast, when a particular policy option was not successfully implemented, as in Honduras and Nicaragua, the outcome was aborted liberalism.

Policy options in Honduras and Nicaragua were not successfully implemented because episodes of U.S. intervention occurred shortly after their initiation, stunting the domestic structural changes sought by liberal leaders. Liberals initially adopted opposing policy options (i.e., a reform option in Honduras and a radical option in Nicaragua), but once intervention occurred, these two countries followed a similar pattern of aborted liberalism. Despite different initial choices, then, an exogenous shock in the form of U.S. intervention brought the two cases together.

Antecedent Conditions

In Central America, similar ideologies and state-building interests guided liberals in their efforts to modernize agriculture and augment central state power. However, because ideology and state-building interests were *common* to all liberal leaders, they cannot explain the *variation* in policy options pursued by liberals. To explain this variation, it is necessary to examine the contrasting antecedent conditions that characterized the preliberal Central American countries.

The level of national socioeconomic modernization varied before the liberal reform period in a pattern that corresponds with the policy option eventually selected by liberal leaders. Specifically, at the initiation of the reform period, the three countries where radical policy options were adopted—Guatemala, El Salvador, and Nicaragua—had somewhat more advanced commercial economies and somewhat more developed state apparatuses than Honduras and Nicaragua, the two countries where liberals followed a reform policy option. This contrast in level of modernization affected policy choices by providing liberals with different kinds of economic and bureaucratic resources for transforming agriculture. Yet the importance of preliberal modernization should not be exaggerated.

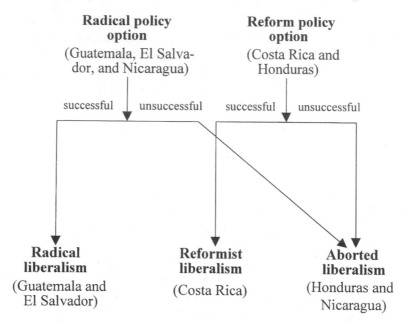

FIGURE 2.1   Policy Options and Types of Liberal Reform

At this early stage of development, the socioeconomic differences between most countries were rather small, and in no case did antecedent conditions prohibit the adoption of either a radical or a reform policy option. Liberals in Guatemala could have pursued a reform policy option, just as liberals in Costa Rica could have promoted a radical policy option. One cannot simply read the adoption of a particular policy option from knowledge of antecedent socioeconomic conditions.

In this study, I emphasize the historical contingency of liberals' choices by showing how their decisions were influenced most fundamentally by immediate political situations. Above all else, liberal leaders were concerned with political challenges to their authority, and these challenges figured as crucial considerations in their calculations about how to promote state development and agrarian modernization. In nineteenth-century Central America, political challenges took the form of armed movements led by rival domestic elites and neighboring Central American presidents. Across the region, the degree of threat faced by liberal presidents varied depending on evolving regional alliance patterns and political dynamics within and between liberal and conservative factions. These differing levels of political threat led liberals to construct particular kinds of state apparatuses that were more or less congruent with a specific policy option. When opposition movements posed major threats, as they did in Guatemala, El Salvador, and Nicaragua, liberals were inclined to pursue political preservation through building up the military and establishing tight state control over society. In turn, the construction of larger and more powerful states was highly conducive to radical policy options. By contrast, where liberals were less threatened by a political opposition, as in Honduras and Costa Rica, military development and state monitoring of social groups were pursued far less zealously. In the absence of a severe political threat, liberals found a reform policy option a useful means of maintaining political stability and avoiding the kind of societal upheaval that a radical option might have brought forth.

LEGACIES OF RADICAL, REFORMIST, AND ABORTED LIBERALISM

The legacies left by different types of liberalism encompass both a series of reactions and counterreactions set in motion by the liberal reform period and the emergence and consolidation of enduring national political regimes. What I call the "aftermath" period corresponds specifically with the political struggle that followed the liberal reform period. What I call the "heritage" period corresponds with the establishment of contrasting regime outcomes.

The Aftermath of Liberalism

Different types of liberal reform periods set in motion contrasting political reactions and counterreactions that ultimately culminated in the formation of distinct political regimes. As table 2.3 suggests, a key distinction is whether or not major "democratizing episodes" emerged in the aftermath of the liberal reform. These democratizing episodes were periods when elite state actors and popular-sector movements brought the issue of democracy to the forefront of national politics by actively pursuing goals such as incorporation of the lower class into the political arena, expanded electoral contestation, increased democratic freedoms and civil liberties, and enhanced socioeconomic equality.

Major democratizing episodes occurred in Guatemala, El Salvador, and Costa Rica during the aftermath period, but not in Honduras and Nicaragua. This difference was rooted in the kinds of state structures that

TABLE 2.3   Aftermath of the Liberal Reform

	Radical Liberalism (Guatemala & El Salvador)	Reformist Liberalism (Costa Rica)	Aborted Liberalism (Honduras & Nicaragua)
Major democratizing episodes	Yes	Yes	No
Successful	No	Yes	—
Regime heritage	Military authoritarianism	Liberal democracy	Traditional dictatorship

were established during the liberal reform. In Guatemala, El Salvador, and Costa Rica, relatively centralized state apparatuses that effectively held a monopoly on organized force were present at the end of the reform period. These state apparatuses facilitated democratizing episodes by putting an end to a prior pattern in which regionally based military rebellions kept national politics in a state of constant instability.[16] In Honduras and Nicaragua, by contrast, regional warfare persisted beyond the liberal reform period, postponing consolidation of the state and delaying any real movement toward democracy until the mid-twentieth century. Furthermore, the creation of centralized states in Guatemala, El Salvador, and Costa Rica provided politicians with the necessary machinery for implementing democratizing reforms. Only with the aid of state bureaucracies capable of launching, directing, and enforcing governmental policies could progressive national political leaders actually initiate, rather than simply advocate, democratization processes. In Honduras and Nicaragua, progressive politicians may have been interested in democratization, but they lacked the requisite apparatus to effectively pursue their goals at the national level. Indeed, even for mass actors, the possibility of democratic mobilization was shaped by structural relationships of state and class during the liberal reform period. In Guatemala, El Salvador, and Costa Rica, the coffee oligarchy's political leverage in the national state represented an obvious impediment to political influence for mass actors, which helped promote large-scale democratic demands from below. By contrast, in Honduras and Nicaragua, popular-sector groups might well have sought democratization, but the target against which they might direct their democratic aspirations was not transparent: centralized states did not exist, and no clearly visible elitist class dominated national politics. Hence, popular-sector protest in these two countries often focused on local conditions, serving more to fuel re-gionally based conflict than to force democratization onto the national political agenda.

Democratizing episodes broke the hold of the coffee elite over the state in Guatemala, El Salvador, and Costa Rica alike, but only in Costa Rica did they actually bring about the establishment of a democratic regime.[17] In part, this was because in Costa Rica, incorporation of the popular sector into the political system could take place without posing immediate threats to the country's commercially based coffee elite. Of equal importance, the marginal position of the armed forces within the Costa Rican state and society mitigated the potential for a harsh military response to democratizing movements. Matters were quite different in Guatemala and El Salvador, where incorporation of the lower rural class into national politics might well have led to a revolutionary transforma-tion of the agrarian economy, directly threatening the economic well-being of dominant-class actors. Furthermore, in Guatemala and El Sal-vador, state actors could employ powerful military-coercive institutions to put down lower-class movements seeking political inclusion. Indeed, the armed forces were themselves threatened by movements that sought to transform agrarian relations, and thus they had their own organiza-tional interest in defeating democratizing movements even without di-rection from civilian elites or government officials.

In Honduras and Nicaragua, where no significant democratizing movements appeared in the aftermath of the reform period, major polit-ical opposition did emerge, but it was often directed at U.S. actors, not the domestic state or dominant classes. The absence of democratizing movements in these two countries meant that traditional political au-thoritarianism persisted well into the mid-twentieth century in forms not much different from those of the nineteenth century.

The Heritage of Liberalism

In all five countries, the polarization of the aftermath period eventually gave way to the formation of relatively stable national regimes. These regimes represent the heritage of the liberal reform period. In the cases of radical liberalism (Guatemala and El Salvador), political order was established in the form of military-authoritarian regimes; in the pattern of reformist liberalism (which characterized Costa Rica), a progressive democracy was the regime heritage; and in the cases of aborted liberal-ism (Honduras and Nicaragua), it was traditional dictatorship.

The concept of "national political regime" refers both to the organization of the center of political power (e.g., the structure of governmental roles and processes) and to formal and informal relations between government and society (e.g., mechanisms of representation and patterns of repression). As Robert Fishman puts it, "A regime determines who has access to political power, and how those who are in power deal with those who are not."[18] Regime is therefore a relational concept referring to a set of institutions; regimes are not actors. Regime is typically distinguished from the concepts of "government" and "state."[19] Government refers to the head of state and the surrounding political leadership, including top presidential aides and congressional legislators. In contrast, state refers to the bureaucratic, military, and legal institutions of the public sector and the incumbents of those institutions.

In the context of mid-twentieth-century Central America, it is useful to operationalize the concept of regime along two dimensions: the nature of the ruling governmental elite (i.e., organization of the center of political power) and the primary means through which this governmental elite generated support and/or compliance from societal groups (i.e., government-society relations). Based on these two dimensions, it is possible to offer a stylized characterization of the regime outcomes explored in this study (see table 2.4).

The ruling elite varied significantly across the countries. From 1954 to 1986 in Guatemala and from 1948 to 1979 in El Salvador, key state agencies and governmental decision-making roles were dominated by the military as an institution. Institutional military rule contrasts with personalistic rule by an individual military officer or general, as often occurred during the liberal reform period. Things could hardly have been more different in Costa Rica, where government was led by freely elected

TABLE 2.4   Types of Regime Heritage

	Military Authoritarianism (Guatemala & El Salvador)	Democracy (Costa Rica)	Traditional Dictatorship (Honduras & Nicaragua)
Nature of ruling governmental elite	Military as institution	Elected politicians	Personal dictator
Primary means of generating support/compliance	Coercion	Electoral mobilization	Patronage

politicians beginning in 1949 and continuing to the present. While elected politicians controlled key legislative offices and sometimes the presidency in the Central American countries before the 1980s, only in Costa Rica did freely elected leaders actually have the effective power to govern. Finally, in Honduras from 1932 to 1982 and in Nicaragua from 1934 to 1979, government was controlled by personal dictators who ruled in a fashion similar to that of the presidential leaders of the liberal reform period. While mid-twentieth-century dictators in Honduras and Nicaragua sometimes competed for power with incumbents of the state—including military officers—these dictators exercised a level of individual authority and arbitrary influence far surpassing that of leaders of the other Central American republics.

The means through which governmental elites interacted with societal groups also varied greatly. In Guatemala and El Salvador, military leaders sustained their rule to an important degree through repression against urban and rural popular sectors. Although elections were sometimes held, they were always strictly controlled, occurring in a context in which basic civil liberties and freedoms were denied and in which coercion was often a major feature of the electoral process. By contrast, in Costa Rica, where democratic elections were held, politicians used electoral mobilization as the primary means for generating support from societal groups. Like all formally democratic political systems, Costa Rican democracy occasionally featured the use of coercion against antigovernmental groups (e.g., the Communist Party), and patronage was used by politicians to generate political support. However, the dominant characteristic of relations between the governmental elite and societal groups was the use of electoral mobilization to win votes in free electoral processes. Finally, in Honduras and Nicaragua, personal dictators relied extensively on patronage and clientalistic practices for the co-optation of societal groups. Here again, one can point to the occasional use of elections and certain episodes of severe repression against key opposition actors. However, the exchange of goods and services for political loyalty was the dominant means through which dictators sustained themselves.

In the 1980s and 1990s, the heritage of the liberal reform period was partially eclipsed as the so-called third wave of democracy swept electoral and democratic regimes to power across the region.[20] Although the new regimes of Central America represent an erosion of the legacies analyzed in this book, an understanding of liberalism and its legacies nonetheless provides insight into contemporary regional politics. For in contemporary Central America, the challenges facing countries have been shaped by the nature of the antecedent authoritarian regimes. This is obviously true in Guatemala and El Salvador, where the legacies of military authoritarianism have been slow to disappear. But it also applies in important ways to Honduras and Nicaragua as well, where past experiences with traditional dictatorship have affected the nature of party competition. By understanding the kinds of regimes that dominated Central America before the 1980s and 1990s, therefore, we can gain insight into current political dynamics in the region.

A Note on the Historiography of the Liberal Reform Period

Before we turn to the task of developing the overall argument, it must be pointed out that any analysis of the liberal reform period in Central America is bound to stir at least some controversy among historians, for the historiography of Central America is currently divided over the importance of this period. Traditional histories often asserted or implied that the transformations of the liberal reform were so consequential that the period could be treated as a social revolutionary break. In reaction to such conclusions, many recent histories have been dedicated to scaling back earlier interpretations of the liberal reform period.[21] These analyses point out that the liberal reform did not represent a period of complete discontinuity, that liberal processes of transformation were already beginning to take place during earlier periods, and that the distinction between liberals and conservatives was often not well grounded in social class or ideological differences. Furthermore, revisionist analyses show that in certain cases, such as Guatemala, the traditional historiography has grossly overstated the extent of changes actually accomplished by liberal reformers.

The argument of this study draws heavily on evidence developed in revisionist works of Central American history—by scholars such as Patricia Alvarenga, Julie A. Charlip, Erik Ching, Aviva Chomsky, Elizabeth Dore, Darío A. Euraque, Jeffrey L. Gould, Lowell Gudmundson, Aldo A. Lauria-Santiago, Héctor Lindo-Fuentes, David McCreery, Iván Molina Jiménez, and Mario Samper—but reaches conclusions about the liberal reform period that in some respects correspond with the traditional historiography. This study does not endorse the traditional argument that the liberal reform period was a social revolutionary break in Central American history. Nor does it see late-nineteenth-century liberals and conservatives as distinct class factions representing diametrically opposed ideologies. However, based on a systematic comparative analysis of the historiography, including especially recent historical works, the study shows that major political divergencies among the Central American countries can be explained by what we currently know about the liberal reform period.

This study can therefore be seen as making an effort at integrating the traditional and revisionist strands of the historiography. Such an effort will please neither those older historians who refuse to part with the idea that the liberal reform was a true social revolution nor recent researchers unwilling to acknowledge that the liberal reform period involved something more than a continuation of an earlier period. Fortunately, as the chapters that follow will establish, these extreme positions are embraced by very few historians. Indeed, a synthesis of the Central American historiography is possible because most historians present arguments and evidence that point to important—but not revolutionary—changes accomplished during the liberal reform period. When these findings are brought together into a systematic comparative framework, it becomes possible to see the specific ways in which the liberal reform period represented a critical juncture throughout the region.

PART II

Antecedent Conditions

CHAPTER 3

Liberals and Conservatives before the Reform Period

Liberals and conservatives developed when local actors responded in varying ways to the introduction of Enlightenment thought into the Kingdom of Guatemala, beginning in the late eighteenth century. By the time of Central American independence in 1821, when the question of a postcolonial order loomed large, loosely defined liberal and conservative political factions had formed. Early-nineteenth-century liberals were generally represented by those notables and professional men who called for the creation of republican forms of government, the promotion of private property and free markets, and the removal of matters of religion from the public sphere. By contrast, early-nineteenth-century conservatives were represented by those privileged merchants and landed elites who sought the preservation of key colonial institutions, including quasi-monarchical forms of governance, restrictions on private property and free trade, and special privileges for the Church.

Although liberal leaders in Central America could never appeal to a significant base of middle-class individuals as their European counterparts did, there were certain parallels between liberalism in the two regions during the early nineteenth century. In both Europe and Central America, liberal movements formed in opposition to conservative elites as Enlightenment ideals spread across the globe in the aftermath of the French Revolution and the Napoleonic invasions. Liberals in both regions advocated an expansion of political freedoms, economic individualism, and social anticorporatism. Yet liberalism clearly fared differently in the two regions. In Europe, the success of liberals was mixed: in some countries they won comprehensive victories and established democratic regimes, in others they won partial victories, and in a few countries they failed altogether and succumbed to authoritarian leaders.[1] In early-nineteenth-century Central America, the fate of liberal movements largely followed only this last pattern—that of outright defeat and a turn toward authoritarianism. By the mid-nineteenth century, Central American liberals had converged politically with conservatives and ceased to seriously advocate individual rights for all citizens, especially peasant and indigenous groups.

The understanding of this earlier episode of failed liberalism provides essential background for the analysis of the liberal reform period that would take place in each of the Central American countries later in the nineteenth century. This discussion also illustrates that, from the perspective of Western Europe, liberalism was a failure in Central America. The liberals who eventually led successful reform periods in Central America were socially and politically distinct both from European liberals and from their early-nineteenth-century predecessors in Central America. By recognizing this distinction, it is possible to understand why the most radical pattern of liberalism in Central America had the effect of promoting extremely authoritarian political systems, an outcome that could only be seen as contradictory from the perspective of Western Europe.

The early-nineteenth-century liberal failure in Central America occurred alongside the dismal performance and eventual breakdown of the Federation of Central America—a single, sovereign territorial unit headed by liberal leadership that encompassed the five Central American countries following independence. Under the Federation, liberal reform efforts were repeatedly thwarted by conservative and anti-union resistance, and liberals increasingly turned to coercion to hold the union together. Ultimately, however, the inability of liberals to come to terms with peasants dealt the final crushing blow to the Federation. Conservatives exploited a wave of massive peasant revolts against liberal leadership and reestablished control over most of the Central American region. Liberals would reemerge in the decades following the Federation debacle and lead more-successful reform periods in the individual countries, but they would do so working from an authoritarian standpoint that was contrary to the original political goals of many early-nineteenth-century liberals.

THE ORIGINS OF LIBERAL AND CONSERVATIVE POLITICAL FACTIONS

The liberal-conservative cleavage first emerged at a time when Central America was united as a single Spanish colony known as the Kingdom of Guatemala.[2] This Kingdom encompassed as constituent provinces the five territories that more or less make up the contemporary countries of Central America, plus the region of Chiapas, now a state of Mexico. Under colonial rule, the province of Guatemala was the bureaucratic capital of the Kingdom, and it was here that the liberal-conservative cleavage first developed.

Bourbon Liberalism

The replacement of the Habsburg monarchy with Bourbon rule in Spain during the eighteenth century introduced Enlightenment thought and liberal practices into the Kingdom of Guatemala.[3] To defend their American possessions in the face of challenges from European rivals, Bourbon monarchs aimed to stimulate economic growth in the colonies through a series of liberalizing reforms, including efforts to increase trade between Spain and the colonies through tax reforms and the removal of local monopolies, and attempts to enhance government power by modernizing central bureaucracies and weakening ecclesiastical forces.[4] However, by the time these reforms were introduced under Charles III (1759–88), the economy of the Kingdom was dominated by an entrenched monopoly of wealthy Guatemalan merchants who oversaw the trade of indigo, Central America's only important export to the Spanish mainland.[5] Through their control over commerce and their connections with the trading port of Cádiz in Spain, these merchants were the main source of loans and cash and the principal buyers and distributors of goods in the Kingdom.[6] While Guatemalan merchants supported some liberalizing reforms, such as the abolition of price-fixing, they "were part of the monopolistic trading structure established by Spain at the beginning of the colonial era . . . [and] they were Spanish mercantilists in their fundamental outlook."[7] Captain generals appointed by the Bourbon crown to enact liberalizing reforms were thus confronted with well-established merchants who had vested interests in seeing the continuation of many traditional colonial practices.

In addition to Guatemalan merchants, Spanish Bourbon reformers faced an aristocratic landowning elite that had risen to substantial wealth and power under the previous Habsburg monarchy. These aristocrats dominated the *ayuntamiento* (municipal government) of Guatemala— the center of local political power within the Kingdom that was semiautonomous from Spanish authority exercised through the captain general. Although Guatemala's aristocrats were "closely allied to the interests of the indigo producers . . . [and thus] to some degree hostile to the merchants,"[8] they firmly supported the Church and existing government institutions. Because these institutions were threatened by the reform, the aristocratic political elite also represented a source of opposition for the Bourbons. Indeed, since the vast majority of the colonial population—the subsistence-farming peasantry—was virtually ignored by the Bourbons,[9] the only politically relevant group with which the reformers could make an alliance was small and medium-sized indigo planters concentrated in El Salvador who were outside of the aristocracy and openly hostile to the merchants. In 1782 these planters were organized by Bourbon colonialists as the Indigo Growers Society, a group that "constituted one of the clearest manifestations of the diffusion of liberal ideas in the Kingdom of Guatemala."[10]

Outside of some Salvadoran indigo planters, then, the Kingdom of Guatemala was an unlikely setting for liberal changes, at least under strict colonial guidance, and the Bourbon reform had little immediate impact. Guatemalan merchants organized in opposition to the Indigo Growers Society through a powerful guild association of their own, the Real Consulado de Guatemala, which was formed in 1794.[11] And aristocrats of the *ayuntamiento* offered little assistance to Bourbon reformers beyond encouraging more open trade.

The Emergence of Political Factions

No reformist colonial monarchy—Bourbon or otherwise—could have much hope of success in fashioning a liberal political movement in Central America so long as dominant political and economic groups were content with existing (Habsburg) colonial arrangements. Eventually, however, a liberal movement did develop, stimulated by events occurring outside of the Kingdom: France's invasion of Spain and the collapse of the Bourbon monarchy in 1808, along with the nearly simultaneous decline of indigo in the world market. The weakening of Spanish power and the downturn in indigo brought increased resentment toward colonial rule.[12] As Spanish officials looked to the colonies for expanded revenues and imposed greater taxes, many well-to-do Central Americans came to favor independence from a declining Spain. At the same time, the economic depression heightened resentment toward Guatemala City in the other provinces. By the early nineteenth century, regional sentiments were flourishing, and there was a major division in the Kingdom between Guatemala and the outside provinces.[13]

Political liberalism was introduced into Central America with the promulgation of the famous Cádiz Constitution in 1812, which was drawn up by the first modern parliament of Spain. The framers of the constitution reinforced the earlier Bourbon concern with economic liberalization and expanded the liberal agenda to the political sphere by advocating individual rights and liberties and elections for new political bodies.[14] According to historian Mario Rodríguez, the new Spanish parliament "coined the political term 'liberal' for the world" and laid out a political program that would influence Central American liberals for the remainder of the century.[15]

Within Guatemala, the core of fervent liberals emerged among urban professionals of the upper middle classes.[16] Individuals from this group were politically marginal, in that they had little influence within the colonial government. Furthermore, they were socially marginal, in that most were the illegitimate ladino offspring of liaisons between aristocrats and Indians. Not surprisingly, Enlightenment notions of political and social equality articulated in the 1812 constitution appealed to this group. More surprising were the aristocratic political elites of Guatemala, best represented by the Marqués de Aycinena and his "family," who also tactically supported the Cádiz government and its liberal policies. The majority of these political elites remained fundamentally conservative in their outlook, but a general disdain for the failing colonial system and the fact that the Cádiz changes implied greater political autonomy from Spain led them to stand behind the constitutional reforms. In a strange tactical alliance, these aristocratic individuals united with urban middle sectors, thereby bringing Guatemala's "best families" and its "social outcasts" into a pro-Cádiz coalition that held together until independence.[17]

On the other side, Guatemalan merchants represented through the Consulado were opposed to the reforms suggested by the Cádiz Constitution and formed the conservative opposition to the liberals. Until 1818, the conservative merchants of the Consulado largely had their way in shaping politics in the Kingdom because Captain General José de Bustamante Guerra detested the Cádiz experiment and suppressed Cádiz supporters. During Bustamante's tenure (1811–18), Guatemalan merchants controlled the advisory councils of the Kingdom and prevented the implementation of the liberal changes called for by the 1812 constitution.[18]

The removal of Bustamante in 1818 and the calling of elections for seats in the *ayuntamiento* and a new provincial deputation set the stage for the emergence of the first political parties in Guatemala.[19] The Aycinena family and members of the traditional aristocracy maintained their tactical alliance with urban liberals. This party was led by Pedro Molina in the newspaper press. Merchants found an ally in certain artisans who were opposed to free trade, and these groups together developed their own newspaper, edited by José Cecilio del Valle. Molina labeled the merchant group the *bacos* (drunks), while his party was in turn called the *fiebres* (hotheads) or *cacos* (thieves). Free trade emerged as the first major issue that divided these parties, and elections left the more liberal *cacos* with a slight advantage. However, the question of independence soon forced a broader set of issues into Guatemalan politics.

Political Divisions over Independence

Unlike in the rest of Spanish America, independence in Central America was not accompanied by violent revolts and bloody wars. Rather, Mexico's successful liberation simply left it up to the municipal council of Guatemala City to decide for itself if the Kingdom should follow suit. In general, the liberal *cacos* strongly favored an independent status, while the conservative *bacos* remained loyal to Spain. The threat of an invasion from Mexico to "liberate" Central America tipped the balance in favor of independence, as many *bacos* reluctantly came to support the break with Spain. In September 1821 Guatemala formally declared independence; the municipalities outside of Guatemala City eventually confirmed the decision.

Although independence changed very little in terms of the formal structure of governance (the Spanish bureaucracy remained intact, and the *ayuntamiento* continued to function as the center of political power), political dynamics and alliances were substantially affected. The merchants who had long been a bastion of conservatism began to decline. In part this decline can be traced to the fall of indigo at the turn of the century, but more important was the fact that with independence Cádiz ceased to be the main trading port for Central America, and merchants lost their monopoly over trade within the Kingdom.[20] One might expect that liberalism would therefore have thrived within Guatemala City, but in fact quite the opposite happened. With independence achieved, Guatemalan aristocrats had little use for an alliance with urban liberals. Having tactically supported the Cádiz experiment in order to gain increased political autonomy, many members of this group now moved swiftly in a conservative direction. Through the control they reestablished over most key offices, Guatemalan aristocrats became the leading conservative force in independent Central America.[21]

In the years following independence, the original political parties that had been pejoratively labeled the *cacos* and *bacos* gradually declined, but political divisions between conservative and liberal factions remained. These factions divided over the question of absolute independence or annexation to Mexico. Within Guatemala City, liberals—still with a base in the upper middle classes—favored complete independence, while the Aycinena family and the aristocratic power bloc championed annexation.[22] Underlying the question of Mexican annexation was a basic ideological cleavage. Conservatives advocated annexation because it accorded with their desire to maintain familiar colonial institutions such as quasi-monarchical rule, traditional patron-peasant relationships in the countryside, special privileges for the Church, and substantial public regulation of the economy. By contrast, liberals were dedicated to Enlightenment ideals and advocated independence precisely because they believed it would enable Central America to overcome the colonial legacy. This early-nineteenth-century liberal-conservative cleavage is well described by Ralph Lee Woodward Jr.:

> Conservatives felt more secure with monarchism while the successful republican example of the United States and the more open political and judicial form of the United States, France, and Great Britain enchanted the liberals. . . . The liberals sought to disestablish and remove the church from political and economic power, while the conservatives cherished it as a defender of their privileges and a vital link to control of and support from the masses. It was, in fact, the conservatives' privileged and monopolistic control of the economy that the liberals sought to destroy, and elimination of the fueros [judicial privileges] of the conservatives—ecclesiastical, commercial, university, and so on—were targets of the liberals.[23]

In the provinces outside of Guatemala, hostility toward Guatemala tended to condition political alliances and shape responses to the question of annexation to Mexico. Within each province, rival towns representing liberal or conservative causes fought battles with one another and formed alliances for or against Guatemala City as they sought to gain increased local political power.[24] Woodward has argued that a basic liberal-conservative cleavage characterized each of the provinces, in which "conservatives represented the wealthy, established families of the late colonial period, whereas liberals represented more especially the upper-middle sector, professional classes and illegitimate offspring of the elite families."[25] However, the ideological differences between liberals and conservatives were probably less meaningful outside of Guatemala. In the outside provinces, the middle classes simply represented a much smaller portion of society, and consequently any political mobilization most likely had to take place within the landed elite itself.[26]

Drawing on the support of Captain General Gabino Gaínza, conservatives initially had their way in most provinces, and annexation to Mexico was proclaimed in January 1822. This experiment proved short-lived.[27] As Héctor Pérez Brignoli notes, "Problems inherent in a power center too far removed were added to difficulties in reconciling manifold local interests. . . . Soon . . . the Mexicans were viewed as crude invaders."[28] Once the Mexican government's promises of financial resources failed to materialize, troops were necessary to ensure the compliance of the Central American provinces, especially in El Salvador, where major revolts against Mexico were launched.[29] The annexation experiment ended in 1823 with the abdication of Mexican emperor Agustín de Iturbide and the rise to power of liberals in Mexico, which again raised the question of the future of the Central American region. In July 1823, a congress was convened in Guatemala City and "proclaimed the 'United Provinces of Central America' to be a nation, 'sovereign, free, and independent of old Spain, of Mexico, and of all other powers whether of the Old or the New World.'"[30]

Central America thus emerged independent as a single republic marked by deep political and regional divisions. During the Federation years that followed, liberals would have their first real opportunity to enact changes in Central American society. However, their failure would set the stage for the breakup of the region into five independent countries and, with the exception of Costa Rica, delayed the liberal reform period until well into the nineteenth century.

THE INITIAL RISE AND FALL OF LIBERALS

One of the most celebrated episodes in Central American history is the period during which liberals attempted to forge a single, modern Central American nation known as the Federation of Central America. Caught up in the Enlightenment thought of the day and stimulated by the example of the United States, the rhetoric of idealist liberal reformers called for a democratic social revolution that would sweep away the old colonial order and propel Central America into the ranks of the world's advanced nations. Yet as it turned out, not only did liberals fall far short of their goals, but the Federation experiment worked to preserve colonial values and institutions in the region and transformed liberalism into an authoritarian political ideology.

To explain the initial rise and fall of liberals, it is useful to consider the conditions favoring liberal dominance in a broader comparative context. Comparisons with Europe are especially enlightening, not only because the original liberal democratic revolutions took place there, but also because the varied experience of European liberals serves to isolate the key factors that would prevent liberal success in early-nineteenth-century Central America.

Liberal Dominance in Comparative Perspective

In Western Europe, liberal political movements found their primary base of support among urban middle classes.[31] Although emerging in a much less economically advanced context, liberal middle-sector groups in early-nineteenth-century Central America shared certain social characteristics with the middle-class liberals of Europe. Like their European counterparts, Central American liberal supporters (especially in Guatemala) included significant numbers of professionals, bureaucrats, and university-educated men. In addition, Central American liberals were drawn to liberal ideology because they were politically marginal within reigning monarchical government structures and economically disadvantaged by highly regulated, predominantly agrarian economies. Finally, early-nineteenth-century liberal reformers in Central America and Europe shared a similar ideology centered on the elements of political freedom, economic individualism, and opposition to an established church.

European liberals met with varied success in their attempts to establish new political orders, ranging from comprehensive victories (e.g., in Switzerland) to outright defeats (e.g., in Germany). Andrew Gould's recent comparative work argues persuasively that approaches rooted in economic factors—for example, explanations that stress level of industrialization or the timing and character of economic development—are by themselves inadequate to account for the different fortunes of European liberals.[32] While not completely rejecting the relevance of economic factors, Gould suggests that additional political conditions shaped liberal dominance in Europe, particularly the ability of liberals to form movements capable of defeating conservative enemies and unifying key social groups behind liberal projects. In part, the capacity of liberals to form powerful movements was simply a product of the strength and cohesion of urban middle classes. Equally important, however, was the ability of liberals to attract support from rural social groups. As Gould writes: "If urban liberals won allies in the countryside, then liberals could build political parties and stable regimes. If, however, urban liberals did not find allies in the countryside, then liberals could not move beyond urban cliques and could not build stable regimes."[33] Gould's comparative-historical analysis shows that in cases where liberals failed to win significant rural support, such as Germany, not only were they unable to establish stable regimes in the early and mid-nineteenth century, but they moved ideologically in an authoritarian direction by the late nineteenth century.

Specialists on Central America have identified numerous factors to explain the failure of the liberal-led Federation: a lack of resources and the poor financial basis of the Federation,[34] the presence of regionalism among the five states,[35] contradictions inherent in the constitutional system,[36] and the absence of effective leadership.[37] However, each of these factors was conditioned by and intertwined with ongoing factional conflict between liberals and conservatives. Drawing on lessons from Europe, the crucial factors behind the fall of liberals during the Federation can be recast in terms of the political failure of liberals to form movements capable of defeating conservatives.[38] Both the strength of the core of liberal supporters—urban middle sectors—and their relationship with rural groups are relevant, and both varied within and outside of Guatemala.

In the peripheral states, outside of Guatemala, urban middle sectors were always a small and politically weak group, often little more than a fragment of the urban classes that led liberal movements in Europe.[39] This weakness was in part due to the extremely low level of economic development that characterized the peripheral states of Central America (with the partial exception of El Salvador) and in part due to the high concentration of social activity in Guatemala. Liberal movements outside of Guatemala could and did draw support from rural classes. Some large landowners and rural middle-sector groups identified with the liberal faction, including many indigo producers of various sizes in El Salvador. Yet liberals made few efforts to forge alliances with the diverse lower rural classes that made up the traditional peasantry in early-nineteenth-century Central America. Because educated middle classes constituted only a small portion of the population, liberals were forced to make decisions about how to treat those small rural producers and villagers who did not fit the liberal understanding of "citizen" because they were illiterate or destitute or racially inferior. In the end, the liberal reaction was to largely ignore this vast peasant population, removing them from consideration as worthy allies to be mobilized under the banner of liberalism.

Conditions were more auspicious for the formation of a powerful liberal movement in Guatemala, if only because urban middle classes composed a larger portion of the population. Here a true base of urban liberals could be found. The difficulties of Guatemalan liberals centered more squarely on the peasant problem and their inability to come to terms with this social class. Though liberals did have the political strength to mollify conservatives, their reform program ultimately isolated lower rural classes and triggered a major peasant insurrection that brought down the Federation.

In sum, one can best understand the failure of liberals under the Federation of Central America in terms of the cleavage between liberals and conservatives and the relationship between liberals and the peasantry. In the peripheral areas, outside of Guatemala, liberals generally lacked a core of supporters sufficient to defeat conservatives on their own. In Guatemala, the failure of politically dominant liberals to forge alliances with the peasantry undermined their reform efforts. The end result was similar to certain European cases: an early failure of liberalism and the movement of liberals in an authoritarian direction.

The Federation of Central America, 1823–1838

Right from the start, the union of the Central American provinces—which came to be known as the Federation of Central America after 1825—was hampered by intra-elite divisions between liberals and conservatives. With conservatives discredited by their association with the Mexican government during the brief annexation period, the composition of the Constituent Assembly that was set to write a constitution for the new nation was decidedly liberal. As conservatives returned from Mexico, however, a civil war nearly broke out and was avoided only by the inclusion of more-moderate elements in the Assembly.[40] The constitution finally promulgated in November 1824 was an unstable compromise between radical liberals and moderate factions, but it nonetheless reflected the dominance of liberalism at the time. Influenced by both the 1812 Cádiz Constitution and the U.S. Constitution of 1789, the document established a "popular, representative, federal" republic of five states and immediately put into effect several liberal measures, such as popular elections, free trade, and restrictions on special privileges for clergy.[41]

Despite this progressive constitution, the extent to which liberal reform policies were actually implemented under the Federation of Central America was limited. The Federation's first elected president, Manuel José Arce (1825–28), came to power seemingly representing liberal interests, but he quickly alienated his original backers and formed an alliance with conservatives.[42] As a result of Arce's political about-face, a disjuncture developed in which the individual state governments attempted to pursue liberal programs while the federal government in Guatemala sought to weaken the power of state authorities and check their reform efforts. This federal-state tension came to a head when Arce, drawing on the financial backing of conservatives and the moral authority of the Church, used federal troops to remove liberal state governments throughout the region and return conservatives to power. Liberals responded in turn by launching rebellions, throwing the region into a destructive civil war lasting from 1826 until 1829.[43] Although the financial problems of the Federation ran deep and stemmed from many sources,[44] the peaceful period from 1823 to 1826 was accompanied by modest economic growth, and stagnation did not set in until after the outbreak of civil war between liberals and conservatives.[45] Even after liberals regained control over the Federation, ongoing wars fueled a continuous state of economic crisis that severely constrained their ability to successfully carry out a reform program.

Under the leadership of the famous Honduran general Francisco Morazán, liberals won decisive victories against conservatives and reestablished formal control over the Federation in April 1829. Ironically in light of Morazán's later reputation as a democratic idealist, however, his rule revealed that liberals were quite willing to sacrifice political liberty to maintain and further political control. Immediately after regaining power, liberals in the federal congress passed laws justifying the use of exceptionally repressive measures to deal with opponents of the state. Significant numbers of conservative officials, military officers who had served in the federal army during the 1826–29 period, and wealthy conservative families were exiled, jailed, or issued death sentences.[46] Conservatives who remained often saw their property confiscated or were called upon by the government for forced loans. Morazán also approved measures that dealt quite harshly with conservative clergymen and peasants loyal to the Church.[47]

In conjunction with his consolidation of power, Morazán overturned conservative legislation put into place the previous three years and encouraged state governments to use all means necessary to pursue a broad range of socioeconomic reform legislation. Yet little in the line of liberal transformation was actually accomplished in most states. The reason is that even though "Morazán used the full powers of his office—and more—to achieve order and stability in the republic,"[48] he ultimately failed to contain conservative-led uprisings and movements in favor of greater state autonomy within the Federation. Repeated rebellions throughout the republic and calls for an end to the union forced Morazán to engage in continuous warfare merely to hold the union together, and most state governments failed to get significant liberal reforms off the ground in this conflictive and chaotic climate. In El Salvador, for example, liberal legislation initiated in the early 1830s was undermined by uprisings from below among indigenous communities who simply rejected the legitimacy of Federation authorities.[49] Within the republic as a whole, liberal reforms "were only effectively implemented in Guatemala under the government of Mariano Gálvez (1831–1838), and gradually in Costa Rica since the rise of Braulio Carrillo (1835)."[50] The exception of Costa Rica will be treated in the next chapter. For now we need to focus on Guatemala, because it was here "that the stage was set for the Liberal-Conservative conflict that would end both with the destruction of Liberalism and the collapse of the Central American Republic."[51]

In Guatemala, the implementation of a broad series of liberal reforms initially met with little elite opposition, due both to the weak political position of conservatives following Morazán's repressive policies and to Guatemalan governor Gálvez's ability to mollify remaining conservative groups. The liberal reform package was quite encompassing, including land grants, privatization policies, public works projects to build roads and ports, the implementation of the Livingston Codes, anticlerical reforms, the secularization of education, and the promotion of foreign colonization. However, these reforms were ultimately undermined by a peasant-led uprising that began in 1837 and destroyed liberalism within two years. "Unlike earlier civil wars," Woodward explains, "this one . . . erupted among the peasants of the eastern mountains, the region in Guatemala known as *la montaña*. It was not another quarrel between Liberals and Conservatives for control of the government, but rather a popular rebellion engendered by a growing list of grievances against the Gálvez government and triggered by a catastrophic epidemic of cholera."[52] Although some historians have emphasized the influence of conservative leaders and Church agitators on the peasantry in explaining the revolt,[53] the careful scholarship of Hazel Marylyn Bennett Ingersoll and Woodward points to the central role of peasant grievances caused by Gálvez's liberal reform program.[54]

The revolt against the liberal government was led by Rafael Carrera, an illiterate man of peasant origin who would dominate Guatemalan politics until his death in 1865.[55] Once the Carrera revolt was under way, Gálvez sought an alliance with conservatives to quell the insurrection. This action led Federation president Morazán to remove Gálvez in favor of more radical leadership, but, more important, it enabled conservatives to reemerge on the political scene. As events unfolded in the late 1830s, conservatives and Carrera's movement increasingly found common ground in their opposition to liberalism and formed a working alliance. Supported by popular revolts, conservatives were able to regain control over the Guatemalan government in the summer of 1838. As a result, "conservatives restored much of the institutional structure of the colonial period. The new legislation installed in Guatemala on May 29, 1839, dismantled the remains of the Gálvez program."[56] Morazán attempted to turn back the tide, but his forces were simply no match for the peasant army, which grew to huge proportions (estimates run as high as twelve thousand members). The war dragged on until March 1840, when Carrera's peasant troops stormed the Guatemalan capital and routed the liberal forces.

Meanwhile, during the course of the Carrera revolt, the Federation had finally disintegrated into sovereign countries. With Guatemala in a chaotic state and conservative forces regaining strength throughout the region, the federal congress declared the states to be sovereign bodies in July 1838. Morazán attempted to salvage the union, but again his efforts proved ineffective. To a significant extent, the declaration of state sovereignty merely formalized a situation that had already taken shape.

In the years following Morazán's defeat, Carrera would consolidate both his personal rule and conservatism in Guatemala. Although Carrera was hardly a representative member of the Guatemalan conservative elite, he gradually came to identify with their wealthy lifestyle and political philosophy, and conservatives came to recognize that they had to work with the caudillo to recoup losses from the Federation period and ensure that their political doctrines predominated.[57] Outside of Guatemala, Carrera worked to defeat liberal resistance and to support conservative forces. With the exception of Costa Rica, significant liberal legislation had not been successfully implemented in these neighboring countries during the Federation, easing the task of restoring conservative power. By the early 1840s, in all countries except Costa Rica, liberal legislation had been wiped from the books and conservative rule had been reestablished.

From the perspective of only Central America, the failure of liberals during the Federation years seems overdetermined: numerous idiosyncratic factors could be drawn on to account for this outcome. Yet when viewed in light of the failure of liberals in Western Europe, the story becomes less complex. Early-nineteenth-century liberals failed because they lacked a strong core of middle-class supporters, especially outside Guatemala, and because they were unwilling to make alliances with important rural groups, especially the peasantry within Guatemala. Taken together, these factors allow us to make sense of the initial rise and fall of liberals in Central America.

As a consequence of the failure of the Federation, the liberal reform period was delayed in Central America and would not occur as a single regional phenomenon. Rather, with the region divided into separate sovereign units, the liberal reform would necessarily take place at a different pace and a different rhythm in each of the five countries. Moreover, the Federation's failure ensured that the political elites who headed up later reform efforts would adopt a kind of liberalism quite distinct from that of the idealistic reformers who had emerged in colonial Central America and originally embraced the Federation experiment.

The Evolution of Liberals and Conservatives

Especially in Guatemala, urban middle classes attracted to both the political and socioeconomic aspects of Enlightenment thought made up the core of liberal supporters in the late eighteenth and early nineteenth centuries. However, as the nineteenth century progressed under generally conservative leadership in Central America, the class composition and ideological orientation of liberals changed in significant ways. To be sure, "first-generation" liberals concerned with developing a Central American union and promoting political liberties did not simply vanish. Yet they became but one faction of a new generation of liberals that emerged in the middle of the nineteenth century. To round out our analysis of liberals and conservatives before the liberal reform period, it is necessary to explore the distinct ideological beliefs and social class background of this new generation of liberals.

The core *political* aspects of Enlightenment thought embraced by middle sectors in Guatemala ceased to be central ideological tenets of most liberal movements in the aftermath of the Federation. We have seen how, even during the Federation, liberals turned in an authoritarian direction to meet the exigencies of stabilizing their hold on power. As the nineteenth century progressed, doctrines of political democracy and political individualism declined in the face of liberal efforts to reestablish control over what they increasingly viewed as a hostile and uncivilized society. Auguste Comte's philosophical positivism, explicitly fashioned as a critique of political Enlightenment thought, became the new political orientation of most Central American liberals. This shift in ideology can be seen in, for example, liberals' attitudes toward the peasantry. During the Federation, liberals made at least some legislative efforts to extend political rights to indigenous and peasant groups. By contrast, "for many second-generation Liberals, the attempt to legislate equality for the Indians had been a simple error, not to be repeated again."[58] Furthermore, although liberals would always be identified with the cause of Central American union, the salience of this goal gradually declined over time. By the late nineteenth century, the union cause often served as little more than a means for power-seeking reform leaders to justify aggression against their neighbors.

As conservatives evolved politically during the nineteenth century, increasingly detaching themselves from a commitment to monarchical forms of government and downgrading their haughty rhetoric about the special place of nobility within society, the differences in political ideology between liberals and conservatives declined. Most basically, liberals and conservatives converged on an elitist vision of society that was deeply imbued with classism and racism, and neither faction seriously advocated a democratic system in which broad populations would be entitled to equal rights and protection under the law. Nevertheless, as part of their continuing enchantment with Western society, liberals maintained a rhetoric of egalitarianism and were far more oriented toward introducing modern political institutions. Thus, they were concerned with creating republican governments based on modern constitutions, extending the suffrage to a broader spectrum of society, and carrying out nominal elections to legitimate their rule.

Important ideological differences between liberals and conservatives continued to exist in the social and economic spheres. Socially, the two factions were deeply divided throughout the nineteenth century over the status of corporate entities, such as guild associations and especially the Church. These entities were major targets for elimination by liberals; they were major bases of power for conservatives. Economically, conservatives were influenced by liberal doctrines that stressed the benefits of agrarian capitalism. However, the two factions disagreed about the pace and means through which commercial agriculture should be pursued.

Conservatives advocated a gradual shift, in which the state would protect traditional social arrangements and, to a large extent, existing land tenure relations. Liberals, by contrast, sought to use the state as a cornerstone of development and were interested in dismantling existing land tenure relations.

The other major transformation of liberalism concerned the individuals who made up the core of liberal supporters. During the mid-nineteenth century, the class composition of this faction became similar to that of conservatives. Liberals increasingly drew membership from landed elites and wealthy merchants, the original social bases of support for conservatives. As noted above, this trend was always partially true outside of Guatemala, but by the mid- to late nineteenth century it often applied to liberals within Guatemala. The evidence suggests that liberals throughout the region may have been represented more by newly established wealthy families, especially those who experimented with large-scale commercial agriculture, while conservatives were more likely to come from "old money" dating back to the colonial days. However, there are many exceptions to this generalization,[59] and little documented evidence actually points to significant class or socioeconomic conditions underlying the liberal-conservative cleavage in most countries during the mid-nineteenth century.[60]

For some individuals, identification with a particular faction was a highly calculated move, representing little more than a vehicle for enhancing personal power. The occasional tendency of individuals to switch political sides underscores this point.[61] Furthermore, the party labels "Liberal" and "Conservative" did not always correspond with underlying ideology (e.g., early-nineteenth-century liberals in Costa Rica were affiliated with the Conservative Party in the region). Nevertheless, especially outside of Honduras, it is a mistake to treat liberals and conservatives as nothing more than self-seeking individuals lacking any genuine ideological and political conviction. The differences between liberal and conservative ideologies were often of passionate importance to elites in the mid-nineteenth century. This is true even though the ideologies were hardly meaningful to the peasant groups who were mobilized under liberal or conservative flags and who fought battles defending the partisan beliefs.

Enduring patterns of political alignment characterized certain townships in the region, which stabilized political affiliation over time for many families and individuals. In Central America, as in much of Latin America, conservatives tended to draw their membership from areas near former colonial centers, while liberals tended to draw support from areas peripheral to the colonial system.[62] Some analysts have viewed one township in each Central American country as corresponding to a liberal stronghold and another as a conservative stronghold, such that the following liberal-conservative cleavages prevailed across the region: Quezaltenango versus Guatemala City in Guatemala; San Salvador versus San Miguel in El Salvador; Tegucigalpa versus Comayagua in Honduras; León versus Granada in Nicaragua; and San José versus Cartago in Costa Rica. Yet actual alliance patterns were more complex than this image suggests. In Guatemala, first-generation liberals continued to exist within Guatemala City throughout the mid-nineteenth century, despite the fact that the town was a conservative stronghold. Most of El Salvador was a stronghold for liberals, and the township of San Salvador was probably the most liberal area in the entire region. Liberalism was so strong among the elite that it often prevailed even in San Miguel, despite its traditional identification as conservative. In Nicaragua, the liberal-conservative conflict between León and Granada was legendary, but the most important second-generation liberals actually emerged in the Sierras de Managua and were often removed from the liberals of León. In Honduras, the liberal-conservative cleavage was extremely weak, though the liberals that did exist were often centered in Tegucigalpa and opposed to the old politicians of Comayagua. Finally, in Costa Rica, the San José–Cartago division was the axis of a liberal-conservative cleavage, but liberalism prevailed so strongly that conservatives were defeated in all but name before the mid-nineteenth century.

Conclusion

Two final observations concerning the altered class basis and ideological shift of liberals during the nineteenth century may be noted. First, while comparisons with West European liberals are meaningful when applied to the first generation of liberals in Central America, this frame of comparison is inappropriate for second-generation liberals. From the perspective of Europe, liberalism in Central America failed with the demise of the Federation. The remainder of this analysis will therefore consider liberalism only within the context of Central America, and arguments put forth about the liberal reform period are intended to apply specifically to this context. Second, because the class actors who led the Federation of Central America were sometimes urban middle sectors following mainstream Enlightenment doctrines, one might be tempted to see the Federation experiment as a failed bourgeois revolution. Yet it is worth underscoring again that the middle classes throughout Central America were extremely limited in size, and any bourgeois revolution would necessarily have had to rely on political support from the vast rural masses— a population that first-generation liberals were unwilling to include in their political project. In the end, the failure of the Federation ensured that no such bourgeois revolution would be forthcoming in the future of the region either. By the time liberals regained control of governments, they had incorporated authoritarian landlords into their movement, shedding any prior claims to bourgeois roots, and were poised only to lead revolutions that would play into the hands of state-building personal dictators.

When we recognize the distinctly authoritarian aspects of Central American liberalism, the conservative interlude between the Federation and the liberal reform period ceases to appear as a sustained holding period when national governments only stood as obstacles to progressive liberal transformation. Although there were real ideological differences between liberals and conservatives, the latter group was simply not the reactionary aristocrats portrayed by later liberal historians. As we shall see, conservatives carried out some reforms that were consistent with the modernizing goals of liberals, and the changes enacted during their rule are important for understanding the eventual shape that the liberal reform would take across different countries.

CHAPTER 4

Routes to Liberal Political Dominance

By the late nineteenth century, liberals had returned to power and launched reform periods in all five countries of Central America. Yet the domestic and international conditions prevailing at the beginning of the reform period varied across the region, with important consequences for the type of liberal reform period that would characterize each country. Specifically, the decision of liberals to pursue either a radical or a reform policy option was conditioned by the kinds of state, class, and agrarian structures existing at the initiation of the reform period. Furthermore, the likelihood of whether a given policy option would be successfully implemented or would fall prey to foreign intervention was shaped by the world-historical and international environments facing liberals. Thus, to explain the historical origins of reformist liberalism in Costa Rica, radical liberalism in Guatemala and El Salvador, and aborted liberalism in Honduras and Nicaragua, it is necessary to explore the different routes through which liberals established dominance in the region.

This chapter employs two broad classification schemes to locate the political and socioeconomic evolution of each Central American country before the liberal reform period. First, based on the timing and process of liberals' rise to power, the five countries are grouped into three patterns that correspond to the type of liberal reform period they would ultimately experience (see table 4.1). In this classification, Costa Rica is characterized as a unique case in which liberals were able to consolidate power much earlier than in the rest of the region, due both to the historical weakness of domestic conservative forces and to this country's isolation within the Federation of Central America. Guatemala and El Salvador correspond to a second pattern in which liberals faced greater opposition in the mid-nineteenth century and in which their ability to consolidate political power was linked to midcentury socioeconomic

TABLE 4.1   The Rise of Liberals to Power: Timing and Process

	Initiation of Reform Period	Factors Shaping Timing of Reform Period	Type of Reform Period
Costa Rica	1821	Liberals are capable of launching successful reform period at time of independence due to weakness of conservatives and isolation within Federation of Central America.	Reformist liberalism
Guatemala	1871	Return of liberals to power is linked to coffee expansion, which creates new segment of second-generation liberals opposed to conservative governments.	Radical liberalism
El Salvador	1871		
Honduras	1873	Episodes of foreign intervention strongly condition timing of reform period. Liberalism is imposed in Honduras by Guatemala and El Salvador. Reform period is delayed in Nicaragua by liberals' association with William Walker.	Aborted liberalism
Nicaragua	1893		

transformations that created an economic balance favorable to radical liberalism. Finally, in Honduras and Nicaragua, the particular timing of the reform period and the process through which liberals came to power were strongly influenced by episodes of foreign intervention.

A second classification scheme identifies broad structural conditions present at the start of the reform period in each country, establishing a baseline against which the changes of the reform period can be assessed (see table 4.2). Contrasting structural conditions provided state-building leaders with different kinds of resources and posed different sets of obstacles and opportunities for the consolidation of political power. As a consequence, domestic structural conditions shaped the type of policy option pursed by liberals at the height of the reform period: a radical policy option in Guatemala, El Salvador, and Nicaragua, and a reform policy option in Costa Rica and Honduras.

As table 4.2 suggests, the five countries differed in terms of three broad structural relationships inherited from the preliberal era. First, liberal reform leaders assumed control of significantly different state apparatuses. Although in no case was there a bureaucratic, centralized state

TABLE 4.2   Structural Characteristics at Onset of Reform Period

	State Institutions	Agrarian Economy	Dominant Class
Guatemala (1871) El Salvador (1871) Nicaragua (1893)	Decentralized state, but effective institutions present at national and local levels. National government has access to moderate resources.	Partial breakthrough to commercial agriculture via coffee expansion. Further expansion inhibited by land, labor, and capital shortages.	Incipient coffee agrarian bourgeoisie has significant local political influence. Limited influence in national government.
Costa Rica (1821) Honduras (1873)	Extremely decentralized state. Effective institutions only at local level. National government has access to very limited resources.	No breakthrough to commercial agriculture. Traditional exports continue to dominate.	Merchant-commercial class (not landed) has significant local political influence.

at the initiation of the liberal reform, the national state was more extensively developed in Guatemala, El Salvador, and Nicaragua than in Costa Rica and Honduras. As a result, in these former cases the bureaucratic obstacles to implementing far-reaching national legislation were not as significant as in Costa Rica and Honduras, where effective national government institutions were almost completely absent. In addition, liberals in Guatemala, El Salvador, and Nicaragua had more actual and potential financial resources than liberals in Costa Rica and Honduras. This, too, helped facilitate a more ambitious reform effort.

Second, in the cases of Guatemala, El Salvador, and Nicaragua, a partial breakthrough to commercial agriculture via coffee production occurred in the period before the liberal reform. The prior existence of commercial agriculture, including large coffee plantations, in these three countries encouraged liberals to implement radical policies aimed at furthering the rapid expansion of commercial agriculture. By contrast, the absence of commercial agriculture in Costa Rica and Honduras meant that liberals were less likely to pursue the dramatic reforms associated with a radical policy option.

Third, the dominant-class actors present at the beginning of the liberal reform varied. Dominant-class actors were a potential source of opposition to liberal governments, and thus their interests had to be considered—and certainly not completely contradicted—in the pursuit of liberal political consolidation. If an incipient agrarian bourgeoisie was present, as in Guatemala, El Salvador, and Nicaragua, liberal maintenance of power was facilitated by the adoption of a radical policy option. If no such class was present, liberals could explore more seriously the consequences of their policies for the peasantry, a consideration that favored the adoption of a reform policy option.

Costa Rica: A Country "Born Liberal"

In the period following independence, liberal reform projects were attempted within each individual state of the Federation of Central America. As we have seen, in most cases these projects failed in the face of elite conservative opposition and peasant revolts from below. Uniquely in the region, however, a successful liberal reform project *was* launched in Costa Rica during the Federation years. Beginning almost immediately after independence, Costa Rican political leaders initiated liberal reforms that not only were effectively implemented, but that did not fall prey to a conservative reaction following the failure of the union. Indeed, in 1838, when the Federation was dissolving and conservatives were regaining political control elsewhere in the region, Costa Rica was in the midst of a phase of full-blown liberal reform under the leadership of Braulio Carrillo.

To understand how and why Costa Rica launched a liberal reform period in the early nineteenth century, it is necessary to consider the colonial period and its legacy, including the "rural democracy" interpretation of Costa Rican exceptionalism.

A Rural Democracy?

The nature and consequences of Costa Rica's colonial legacy are major topics in the historiography of Central America. Until recently, the prevailing interpretation among historians has been that Costa Rica emerged independent with an existing "rural democracy" built around a homogenous social structure characterized by individualistic, smallholding peasants living in isolation from one another.[1] Scholars who adopt this perspective have regularly placed the fundamental origins of twentieth-century democracy in Costa Rica with the cultural values associated with this early rural democratic experience. Moreover, rather than view the changes accomplished during the liberal reform period as a possible source of democracy, they have seen the rise of agrarian capitalism and coffee exportation as temporally undermining preexisting democratic tendencies.

Proponents of the rural democracy thesis often ground their arguments in certain well-established facts concerning the historical and socioeconomic features that characterized late-colonial Costa Rica and differentiated the province from the rest of the Kingdom of Guatemala. In particular, they highlight that colonial Costa Rica lacked precious minerals, a large indigenous population to serve as a workforce, and a significant export crop. As a consequence, colonial officials took little interest in Costa Rica, and the province developed without significant Spanish oversight and in relative isolation from the rest of the region. On the one hand, the marginal status of Costa Rica within the Kingdom of Guatemala is viewed as having had an essentially negative impact, because it left Costa Rica as an impoverished backwater region within what was already a marginal Spanish colony. On the positive side, however, the province is seen as having been spared from many colonial institutions and practices that served as fetters on future development in the rest of the region.

This interpretation of the colonial legacy in Costa Rica is not in great dispute among historians. What is contested are the land tenure patterns and cultural value orientations that are argued to have gone along with Costa Rica's colonial experience. In his extremely influential study on Costa Rican history, Carlos Monge Alfaro made two interrelated arguments to show how a rural democracy accompanied colonialism in Costa Rica. First, Monge emphasized that the impoverished condition of the colony fostered a homogeneous, egalitarian land structure marked by an absence of "social classes and castes."[2] This argument followed the work of Rodrigo Facio, who maintained that "parallel to [Costa Rica's] situation of backwardness and poverty, and as its natural consequence, the colony left behind a favorable balance within society: the smallholding estate [minifundio] as the only form of territorial ownership."[3] Second, Monge stressed that Costa Rican culture was built around small farmers who possessed a "very individualistic, self-focused, rugged character" and who themselves embraced egalitarian values and beliefs.[4] North American social scientists later picked up on these notions of agrarian egalitarianism and peasant individualism by arguing that a strong yeomanry characterized early-nineteenth-century Costa Rica.[5] In short, for Monge and others, small property and peasant individualism were together "the fundamental characteristics of the rural democracy of the nineteenth century."[6]

Recent and well-documented historical research by scholars such as Lowell Gudmundson and Iván Molina Jiménez has undercut the central tenets of the rural democracy model. Above all, Gudmundson has shown that the colonial period left a social structure in which "access to agricultural land was not based primarily on private appropriation of isolated smallholdings, but rather on a mixture of nonprivate cultivation of common lands by village members, smallholding on the outskirts by villagers not resident on their plots, and estate ownership by the wealthy. . . . Clear differences of wealth and status existed within older villages, not only between elite and commoner, but also within the latter group."[7] Molina's detailed study of the colonial legacy arrives at a similar conclusion, showing how colonial Costa Rica was divided between relatively prosperous merchants and poorer smallholders and how, within the province as a whole, "the distribution of wealth and power . . . was not equal."[8] Furthermore, both Gudmundson's and Molina's elaboration of the complex and stratified rural class structure in colonial Costa Rica suggests that rural group solidarity and a collective mentality built around cohesive peasant villages were at least as important to Costa Rican culture as any "individualism" on the part of the peasantry.

The overturning of the rural democracy thesis has allowed scholars to theorize that the development of agrarian capitalism may in fact have contributed to democracy in Costa Rica. However, any valid counterinterpretation to the rural democracy thesis must still incorporate the effects of Costa Rica's unique colonial legacy—for even if proponents of the rural democracy thesis mischaracterized these effects as entailing peasant egalitarianism and individualism, the fact remains that Costa Rica did emerge independent with a distinctive colonial heritage.

The Colonial Legacy and Early Liberalism

What the weakness of colonial institutions and the general poverty that characterized pre- independence Costa Rica did bring about was, most important, a constellation of political forces conducive to an early liberal reform. Costa Rica's colonial legacy laid the groundwork for an early liberal reform in two essential ways. First, as a result of the limited introduction of colonial institutions during Spanish rule, conservative forces

and institutions were conspicuously absent at the time of independence—
an absence that enabled liberal-minded elites to implement reform agendas with little domestic opposition. Second, the historic isolation of
Costa Rica from the rest of the region allowed this state to remain aloof
within the Federation of Central America and escape the destruction and
conservative resurgence that went along with the Federation experience
elsewhere in Central America. Together, these two points allow us to understand how Costa Rica was able to launch an early liberal reform, but
each needs to be established against the historical record and in light of
existing interpretations.

Within the whole of Costa Rica, colonial institutions had their
strongest base in the capital city of Cartago, and it was here that the
closest thing to a Costa Rican conservative elite could be found. As Elizabeth Fonseca has shown, Cartago possessed by far the most *ejidal*
lands, and these lands were distributed by the municipal government in
disproportionately large amounts to top-ranking colonial officials
within the Spanish bureaucracy.[9] From this process of land allocation,
a conservative oligarchy emerged that had vested interests in colonial
institutions. Furthermore, the Church was centered in Cartago, and
clergy members were closely connected to the colonial elite of this
city.[10] However, these traditional bases of conservative support—
landed elites and the Church—were comparatively weak, even in the
colonial center of Cartago. Because Costa Rica failed to consolidate a
major export crop and remained poor throughout the colonial period,[11]
the landed upper class of Cartago was small and economically marginal
when viewed in a comparative light. Unlike in the more populous countries of Guatemala and El Salvador, in Costa Rica, with its small population, land ownership "did not bring with it a servile labor force"[12] and
was thus a far less lucrative source of wealth. In fact, only a few colonial
authorities could afford to own large tracts of private land, and even
these few individuals derived most of their wealth and power from activities outside of land ownership, especially commerce.[13] As for the
Church, although some clerics did enrich themselves through land ownership, for the most part organized religious institutions possessed few
properties and could not be considered a major economic force at the
moment of independence.[14]

Outside of Cartago, governmental and socioeconomic institutions
associated with Spanish colonialism had an even weaker hold, and after
the Bourbon reform effort a large majority of elites were fundamentally
liberal in their socioeconomic outlook.[15] This was particularly the case

MAP 4.1   Major Townships and Regions of Costa Rica

in San José, which would emerge as the center of the liberal reform effort in Costa Rica, but it also held true for the other major cities located
in the Meseta Central, including even Cartago to some degree (see map
4.1). The economic and social aspects of liberalism appear to have taken
hold especially among merchants, the wealthiest and most powerful class
in colonial Costa Rica.[16] Unlike the influential conservative merchants
of colonial Guatemala, Costa Rica's merchant class did not earn huge
fortunes from trading monopolies established by the crown. Instead, they
most likely resented colonial restrictions—such as trade limitations and
taxation policies—and certainly stood to benefit on the whole from free-
trade policies. Moreover, this group stood to gain substantially if Costa
Rica could establish a significant export crop, and a broad set of liberal
policies centered on free trade, antichurch legislation, land privatization,
and government incentives for export production represented the means

to reach this end. At the same time, it must be recognized that *political liberalism* was not a major component of the liberal program in Costa Rica. In contrast to the middle-sector groups who made up the core of liberals in early-nineteenth-century Guatemala, Costa Rica's liberal merchants were usually part of—or directly tied to—the political elite in colonial Costa Rica. Given their auspicious political position, Costa Rican liberals were not especially drawn to Enlightenment ideals stressing political freedoms and liberties.[17]

Costa Rica's weak liberal-conservative cleavage overlapped with a township division between San José and Cartago. Some Marxist analysts, most notably Rodolfo Cerdas Cruz, have argued that Cartago represented a basically feudal economy headed by an aristocracy that was in conflict with a nascent capitalist economy and bourgeoisie centered in San José.[18] However, caution should be taken not to read too much into the socioeconomic base underlying the liberal-conservative/San José–Cartago cleavage.[19] Although Cartago had a greater concentration of landed estates, commerce represented the central economic activity of most wealthy individuals in this city, as well as in San José. It is a mistake to assume that Cartago possessed a landlord class that can in some way be equated with feudal lords; likewise, it is an error to assume that commercial activity and any accompanying "bourgeois impulse" were limited to San José.

During the decade and a half following independence in 1821, San José clashed with Cartago in a manner somewhat analogous to the strife between liberal and conservative cities that characterized the other Central American provinces during this time. Yet because the vast majority of elites—including many from Cartago—were in agreement on the desirability of liberal social and economic reforms, liberals were able to triumph relatively easily. Only two civil wars, in 1823 and 1835, actually occurred between liberals and conservatives. The first erupted over the question of annexation to Mexico, with conservatives from Cartago in favor of annexation and liberals from San José opposed to it. After a series of skirmishes that ultimately drew the cities of Heredia (on the conservative side) and Alajuela (on the liberal side) into the action, the war ended with a decisive victory for liberals, and the capital of Costa Rica was transferred to San José. The second civil war, the so-called War of the League, broke out when liberal reformer Braulio Carrillo repealed legislation that called for the national capital to rotate between the four principal cities of the Meseta Central. Fearing absolute dominance by San José, Heredia and Alajuela united with conservative Cartago as the

"League" and attacked San José, but again the San José liberals emerged victorious from the battle. Following the War of the League, central power was consolidated in San José, and liberals were largely unchallenged by domestic conservatives.[20]

By itself, liberal political dominance within Costa Rica was not sufficient for a successful early liberal reform. We have already seen how the Federation of Central America tied together the fates of early-nineteenth-century liberals throughout the region, bringing a common end to their initial reformist efforts. If indeed the Federation was "little more than a series of wars and struggles, internal revolutions . . . and localist pretensions" that destroyed early liberal reform efforts, then we must recognize that absolutely crucial to the success of Costa Rican liberals was the fact that "only Costa Rica had been able to avoid for the most part these maladies."[21] Due both to its geographical isolation from Guatemala and to its status as an economically depressed backwater region, Costa Rica was forced to remain isolated from the major events of the Federation. Furthermore, after initially supporting the idea of a Central American union,[22] Costa Rican liberals deliberately distanced themselves from the Federation once it became clear that a genuine national government was not forthcoming.[23] Leading studies of the Federation have regularly emphasized the ability of Costa Rica to remain neutral in most Federation matters and avoid major entanglements and wars with her more powerful neighbors.[24] Statistical data compiled from the work of nineteenth-century historian Alejandro Marure show that Costa Rica was involved in far fewer battles and suffered significantly fewer casualties than the other states during the Federation years.[25] Even after the rise of Carrera to power in Guatemala, Costa Rica's isolation and the fact that President Carrillo was opposed to the unionist cause (and indeed was identified as a conservative by Guatemalans) enabled Costa Rica to escape the invasions from Guatemala that purged liberals and reinstalled conservatives in power in El Salvador, Honduras, and Nicaragua.

In sum, as a consequence of both the domestic dominance of liberals and Costa Rica's isolation within the Federation, early-nineteenth-century liberals were able to enact major liberal reform legislation beginning almost immediately after independence and coming to a head with the Carrillo administration in the late 1830s. A discussion of the specific form and consequences of this legislation must await the analysis of the Costa Rican liberal reform period (to be presented in chapter 6). For now, we need to explore more directly the class and state structural conditions that confronted liberal reformers.

Class and State Structures on the Eve of Liberal Reform

If Costa Rica was "born liberal," in the sense that the country emerged independent with liberals already politically dominant and immediately began a successful liberal reform period, then it is the class and state structures present at the time of independence that are relevant to our analysis. Most basically, early-nineteenth-century Costa Rica was an agrarian society of small but nucleated village settlements concentrated in and around the four major towns of the Meseta Central.[26] These "nucleated settlements" were made up of households that pursued primarily small-scale and subsistence agriculture (especially the cultivation of corn and beans) on lands directly surrounding villages. Most land was not held in private plots; rather, a large percentage was rented to cultivators, either in well-measured *ejidal* plots (especially in Cartago) or in more dispersed common lands. In all cases, villages functioned autonomously in their day-to-day affairs, without direct supervision by landlords or colonial officials, and forced labor or restrictive labor practices were extremely rare. Furthermore, large estates (either owner-cultivated or based on plantation labor) were not a central feature of the Costa Rican agricultural system. Nevertheless, within the context of generally impoverished agricultural settlements, there was substantial wealth inequality between village notables and well-established city artisans on the one hand, and common farmers and laborers on the other.

At the time of independence, the dominant class in Costa Rica was not a landed elite, for it did not derive the majority of its wealth from agricultural ownership or from extracting surpluses from peasant producers. Instead, the dominant class was fundamentally a merchant elite. This was the case even though merchants might combine their trading activities with investments in urban and rural real estate. Given that Costa Rican trade was limited by regional standards, this group was small in number and not excessively rich in comparative terms. Yet within the context of Costa Rica, locally based traders and foreign-born merchants who migrated from Panama and Spain prospered on what commercial opportunities existed in the early nineteenth century. As recent research has shown, Costa Rica emerged independent not with a stagnant economy built around yeoman farmers, but with an active (though nonetheless very poor) economy centered on commercial trade.[27] In particular, large merchants obtained wealth through the domestic consumer market for imported textiles, through the exportation of cacao, livestock, silver, and some tobacco to Nicaragua and Panama, and through the trade of food and handicrafts in the daily local market. Thus, as Gudmundson argues, "merchant status, even more than landowner-ship, was the key to local power and wealth in the village economy, even before the dance of the millions began with coffee culture."[28]

No centralized state stood above the subsistence-farming nucleated settlements and trading networks of newly independent Costa Rica. Rather, effective state institutions existed only at the level of local gov-ernment, centered in the *ayuntamientos* of Cartago, Heredia, San José, and Alajuela.[29] Prosperous merchants of a liberal orientation controlled these governmental bodies—with the partial exception of Cartago, where high-ranking colonial officials of a more conservative orientation had greater influence. Certainly the victory of liberals in the 1835 War of the League would do much to centralize state authority in San José, but before this time the *ayuntamiento* was the principal decision-making body. Consequently, the liberal reform period in Costa Rica would nec-essarily be launched from local governmental institutions, and liberals would have to build central state institutions completely from scratch.

THE SOCIOECONOMIC ROOTS OF RADICAL LIBERALISM: GUATEMALA AND EL SALVADOR

The consolidation of liberal power in Guatemala and El Salvador was tied to socioeconomic development processes that occurred before the liberal reform period, particularly the establishment of incipient forms of agrarian capitalism through coffee production. In Guatemala, coffee ex-pansion paved the way for liberal victories by creating a new segment within the dominant class—a landed coffee-planter class—that had strong socioeconomic interests in seeing the enactment of a liberal reform agenda. In El Salvador, coffee expansion facilitated the rise of liberals to power by putting increased pressure on the common land systems and encouraging a fairly broad spectrum of society to support land privati-zation.

Preliberal Political Systems

The conservative reaction against first-generation liberals was strongest in Guatemala. The 1837–39 peasant revolt headed by Rafael Carrera de-feated the liberal Gálvez administration and enabled the previously re-pressed conservative elite of Guatemala City to regain political control of the capital.[30] Beginning in 1839, conservatives moved "to restore Hispanic order" by dismantling all liberal legislation put into place during the Federation.[31] Included in the conservative program were decrees that restored the Church to its former position in society by returning ecclesiastical properties and reinstating the tithe tax and clerical control of education; repealed liberal doctrines that favored individual rights and freedoms; replaced the liberal program of assimilating Indians into Western civilization with the old colonial system based on paternalism and protection; and brought back the Consulado de Comercio (formerly the Real Consulado de Guatemala, which had been abolished by liberals in 1829). In pursuing all of this, conservatives had to move with finesse and care, for Carrera was the real power within the newly restored political system, and while sympathetic to the conservative viewpoint on many issues, he was well outside of the aristocratic elite. In fact, a full-blown conservative regime was not established during the early 1840s because Carrera permitted some liberals to remain within government as a counterbalance to conservative hegemony. In playing liberals off of conservatives, he ultimately succeeded in consolidating personal power, but not before liberals made several attempts to regain political control, including a major effort in 1848 that was put down only through Carrera's control over the rebellious peasantry of the Montaña region.

Following the defeat of the liberal initiative in 1848, Carrera consolidated a stable, highly authoritarian, and thoroughly conservative political order that endured until his death in 1865. Under this political order, most major liberal leaders were purged and forced into exile, allowing conservative Guatemalan landowners and merchants to exercise absolute and unchallenged control over the National Congress. Along with the conservative elite, the Church was returned to the exalted and powerful position it had held during the colonial period. As Woodward suggests, a "conservative citadel" was established after 1850 in which Carrera and a "coalition of merchants, planters, and priests" formed the governing membership of Guatemala.[32] Within this conservative ruling structure, Carrera exercised substantial personal power through his ability to mobilize peasant support. However, it would be wrong to view the new political order as simply dominated by the person of Rafael Carrera:

> Notwithstanding the importance of Carrera's army as the base of power for the dictator, it was the consolidation of the conservative elite of the capital that gave the regime its character and was important in establishing policies that made Guatemala the 'citadel of conservatism.' . . .

While Carrera always reserved the right to make final decisions, and frequently did so, he usually allowed a small clique of well-educated and aristocratic advisors to make and execute policy. The consolidation of this conservative elite in Guatemala and its control of the capital's society, economy, and political structure is what so clearly distinguishes the period 1850–1871 from the 1840s.[33]

Within the conservative state, the Consulado de Comercio represented the principal institutional basis through which the merchant-planter elite expressed its socioeconomic interests. The former colonial guild association served as advisor to the government and was responsible for overseeing economic development in the country. In this capacity, the Consulado worked to preserve communal and *ejidal* landholding structures, openly advocated economic protectionism, and "paid only occasional attention to the promotion of new agro-exports."[34] The decision by Guatemalan conservatives to leave national development in the hands of a semiprivate agency meant that the state did not play a central role in spurring economic development before the liberal reform. Rather, major socioeconomic changes necessarily began from within society itself, and it was from there that opposition to Guatemala's conservative citadel formed.

In El Salvador, the preliberal political order was not characterized by a well-institutionalized conservative regime. Instead, the period before the liberal reform was marked by an unstable political system that featured clashes between regionally based patronage networks for control of the national government. In this fragmented political system, not even the most ambitious liberal governments could launch a successful reform period.

Liberalism had a strong hold among the Salvadoran elite, and throughout the nineteenth century many intellectuals in San Salvador favored economic and social modernization.[35] One might therefore ask why El Salvador was not the setting of an early liberal reform period similar to that in Costa Rica. The answer is that El Salvador was deeply entangled with the Federation experiment, and ongoing political violence and the eventual conservative resurgence in Guatemala prevented Salvadoran liberal leaders from successfully implementing enduring liberal reforms. Furthermore, geographical proximity to Guatemala and a strong identification with the unionist cause left El Salvador highly vulnerable to invasions from Guatemala even after the Federation failed. As

Héctor Lindo-Fuentes points out, although the majority of the Salvadoran elite was liberal in disposition, this group was unable to establish control over national politics in the mid-nineteenth century because Guatemalan conservative leaders "were always available to fight against liberal excesses in El Salvador."[36] In short, El Salvador lacked an essential ingredient necessary for an early liberal reform: isolation from the Federation government and the conservative regime of Guatemala.

National politics was marked by factionalism in which regional elites fought battles with one another for control of governmental positions at both local and national levels. Elites often mobilized under conservative or liberal flags, and both liberal and conservative governments ruled at different points in the mid-nineteenth century. Nevertheless, patron-peasant relationships and regional pressures are more important than intra-elite ideological divisions in understanding mid-nineteenth-century conflicts. A complex patronage hierarchy that linked peasants and political bosses in a system of reciprocal obligations underpinned factionalism and instability in El Salvador.[37] Regional elites relied on indigenous and peasant communities for support in their military-political campaigns. Likewise, because El Salvador lacked a permanent army before the liberal reform, the national government had to depend on these same communities to assemble citizen militias to thwart regional challenges. In their role as the source of manpower for war-fighting, peasant communities possessed a powerful weapon for bargaining with elites and defending their interests.[38] In exchange for militia service or military support, peasant communities were able to negotiate protection against hostile policies, including agrarian reforms that might threaten their landholdings.

Before the reform period, national governments encouraged growers of potential export crops with tax exemptions, prizes for production, and freedom from military service.[39] However, domestic instability and the threat of invasion from Guatemala greatly limited liberal initiatives. The example of President Gerardo Barrios (1858–63), the most ambitious liberal administration during the mid-nineteenth century, illustrates these difficulties.[40] Barrios actively promoted military modernization, infrastructure development, and the expansion of commercial agriculture. Yet his liberal orientation and military reforms threatened Guatemala, and his land policies bypassed traditional patronage politics and upset key indigenous communities. As a result, a full-scale war broke out between Barrios and Carrera in Guatemala, and Salvadoran conservative leader Francisco Dueñas was able to mobilize Indian communities against Barrios. The combined opposition from Guatemala and local indigenous communities defeated Barrios and swept Dueñas to the presidency in 1863. Once in power, Dueñas closely aligned his administration with regional conservatives, and he rewarded indigenous allies by passing legislation that gave them additional representation.[41] This example suggests how the main obstacle to full-blown liberalism in El Salvador was not a local conservative opposition, but the lack of a coherent state capable of implementing reforms in the face of potential peasant resistance and persistent opposition from conservatives in Guatemala.

Socioeconomic Changes and the Emergence of Liberal Governments

Before the coffee boom in Guatemala, the principal export crop of the country was cochineal *(grana),* a red dye obtained from insects that feed on certain types of nopal cactus.[42] Concentrated in and around Amatitlán and Antigua, cochineal essentially took the place of indigo within the Guatemalan economy after 1830—although, unlike indigo, cochineal was produced within Guatemala itself. The limited land, labor, and capital requirements for cochineal production accorded well with the policy orientation of the reigning conservative regime and the Consulado de Comercio. Outside of maintaining a few basic roads to transport the product, cochineal required almost no state role to assist in its cultivation. The dye was effectively harvested on both plantations and family plots, but small growers accounted for the majority of production, and larger plantations did not rely on governmental institutions to mobilize a labor force. In a situation quite similar to that which existed in colonial Guatemala at the height of the indigo trade, the principal beneficiaries of cochineal production were merchants of the Consulado, who used their control over export marketing and transportation systems to siphon off most of the profits from the production and trade of the dye. Thus, rather than fostering socioeconomic changes conducive to a liberal breakthrough, "cochineal tended to reinforce Guatemala's existing commercial, capital, and transport structures."[43]

Although interest in coffee production dated from the 1840s, when wealthy planters and merchants heard about successes achieved with the crop in Costa Rica, coffee cultivation initially spread rather slowly in Guatemala, not overtaking cochineal until 1870, one year before the beginning of the liberal reform period (see table 4.3). In the cochineal-producing areas around Antigua and Amatitlán, some growers began to

TABLE 4.3   Value of Guatemala Cochineal and Coffee Exports,
1859–1871

Year	Cochineal Exports (in pesos)	Coffee Exports (in pesos)	Coffee as Percentage of Total Exports
1859	1,222,680	4,680	0.3
1860	1,274,240	15,350	1
1861	788,650	53,110	5
1862	837,986	119,830	9
1863	855,838	199,830	13
1864	688,080	192,762	12
1865	975,933	265,404	17
1866	957,132	384,936	23
1867	1,068,047	415,878	22
1868	891,513	788,035	36
1869	1,266,614	790,228	32
1870	865,414	1,132,298	44
1871	876,025	1,312,129	50

Source: Ralph Lee Woodward Jr., *Rafael Carrera and the Emergence of the Republic of Guatemala, 1821–1871* (Athens: University of Georgia Press, 1993), 379, 383.

plant coffee trees as a supplement to the dye, but before the collapse of
the cochineal market in the 1860s, most capital and labor remained tied
to the production of cochineal, and many producers were reluctant to invest large amounts of money in an uncertain coffee crop that required
four to five years of cultivation before even the first dividends could be
obtained.[44] The earliest coffee plantations were established in areas that
contained large tracts of land suitable for the production of high-quality
coffee, especially near the Pacific coastline in the departments of Retal-
huleu, Suchitepéquez, Escuintla, and Santa Rosa, and some growers experimented with the crop in the towns of Quezaltenango and San Marcos and in sections of the Alta Verapaz department (see map 4.2).[45] Even
in these areas, however, the risks involved in setting up a coffee plantation dissuaded most wealthy Guatemalans from investing in the crop,
and many original coffee planters—including several German investors—came from outside of the traditional elite.[46]

Moreover, early coffee investors faced a series of obstacles linked to
the policy orientation of the conservative national government. For one
thing, the government had established no banking house, and credit
within the country was controlled by merchants who supplied goods and
short-term loans through a crop-lien system that was highly disadvanta-

MAP 4.2   Departments of Guatemala

geous to producers. As Robert G. Williams points out, "For crops with a short growing season such as indigo or cotton, the provision of short-term crop loans was not excessively burdensome, but for long-term investments such as coffee cultivation, the system was inadequate."[47] Furthermore, Consulado merchants were often unwilling to support infrastructure and public works projects pushed for by coffee planters, fearing that such projects might cut into their monopolistic control over foreign commerce. As a result, there was a lack of public financing for the construction of roads and bridges—which left many potential coffee-producing regions isolated from the only major port used for coffee shipments, located on Lake Izabal.[48]

Even more important, the communal and *ejidal* land systems maintained by the conservative government directly obstructed the expansionist designs of early coffee planters in the key potential coffee regions located along the Pacific coastline and in the Verapaz departments.[49] J. C. Cambranes reports that in mid-nineteenth-century Guatemala, more than 70 percent of the country's best land was controlled by some one thousand peasant (usually indigenous) communities.[50] In some cases this land was legally partitioned in well-measured *ejidal* plots, but more commonly the legal claim of peasant villages to ownership was based simply on the fact that they had farmed the land "since time immemorial." In any event, "the Conservative state generally sustained the claims of communities," thereby blocking access for would-be coffee elites.[51] Furthermore, while some Indian villages were willing to lease land to aspirant coffee producers, in general they resisted encroachment by outsiders and refused to give up their lands and labor for the expansion of coffee.[52] The subsistence-farming Indian communities had little economic incentive to work voluntarily for wages on the plantations, making conservative policies oriented toward the protection of Indian communities clear obstacles for planters who sought to secure a large plantation labor force.[53] Chronic labor shortages plagued growers throughout the country, but especially in the Verapaz region, where landowners who began to experiment with coffee in the 1850s "immediately encountered a shortage of workers."[54]

Receiving little help from the conservative national government, coffee growers increasingly pressured local political authorities at the departmental level for assistance, in some cases taking full control of municipal governments in potential coffee regions. Through this local influence, coffee planters were sometimes successful in defrauding Indians of their land and persuading local officials to provide labor drafts from Indian communities. Major land invasions occurred in the Verapaz and western highland (Los Altos) regions.[55] In these areas, "coffee producers . . . became associated with the liberal opposition to the Guatemala City elite that had, in their view, failed to give sufficient support to expansion of coffee cultivation and infrastructure development."[56] The death of Carrera in 1865 (by natural causes) and the emergence of a moderate conservative, Vincente Cerna, to power led to more government consideration of public works projects to assist coffee production, but many coffee growers, such as Justo Rufino Barrios of the Verapaz region, supported the full-blown implementation of radical liberal reforms.[57]

The insurrectionary movement that brought down the Cerna administration and ushered liberals into power in 1871 was led by Miguel García Granados, one of the last liberals from the Federation days who was still politically influential within Guatemala City.[58] In 1870, following Carrera's death, García Granados was forced into exile in Mexico for his opposition to the Cerna administration. From there, he began to recruit an "Army of Liberation" and aligned himself with Justo Rufino Barrios, who was also forming an insurrectionary movement in Verapaz. Although the forces of García Granados and Barrios probably totaled only a few hundred men, they were able to seize control of several towns in the western regions without any resistance at all, owing to the fact that many municipal governments in these areas were already controlled by authorities sympathetic to liberal goals. Moreover, when the forces of García Granados and Cerna eventually met, the liberals won a decisive victory against the poorly institutionalized and unreliable conservative militia troops. Following the defeat of Cerna, García Granados was able to march into Guatemala City with a strong mandate of support from the local governments where coffee had made its greatest headway.

Elites in Guatemala City were unprepared for the sudden turn of events leading to García Granados's rise to power. However, García Granados was seen as a moderate, and his administration did not initially face major challenges from conservative forces within the capital. Yet, as we shall see, the stabilization of the moderate liberal reform strategy advocated by García Granados was not possible, and his government was but a prelude to the much more radical administration of Justo Rufino Barrios.

In El Salvador, domestic instability and pressures from Guatemala made it impossible for liberals to stabilize power in the mid-nineteenth century. However, the gradual transition from a predominantly indigo-based economy to a coffee economy during this time facilitated the eventual consolidation of power by liberals. After a period of decline, indigo production increased in the 1830s, and it continued to expand until the 1880s (see table 4.4).[59] Like cochineal in Guatemala, indigo production in El Salvador deepened traditional land tenure relations, intensifying the use of *ejidal* lands by ladino growers and reinforcing Indians' claims to communal lands.[60] The production of indigo did not represent an immediate obstacle to coffee expansion, since indigo was concentrated in the northern and eastern departments near towns such as Chalatenango, Sensuntepeque, San Vicente, and San Miguel, while much of the land suitable for coffee production was located in the western zones around towns such as Ahuachapán, Santa Ana, San Salvador, Sonsonate, and Santa Tecla (see map 4.3).[61] Consequently, it was possible for coffee to expand in the west without having much of an impact on the production of indigo.

TABLE 4.4   Value of Salvadoran Indigo and Coffee Exports,
1859–1871

Year	Indigo Exports (in pesos)	Coffee Exports (in pesos)	Coffee as Percentage of Total Exports
1859	1,605,450	18,000	0.90
1860	1,375,050	26,000	n.a.
1861	1,980,600	36,000	1.53
1862	2,186,550	53,000	n.a.
1863	n.a.[a]	n.a.	n.a.
1864	1,121,105	80,605	4.81
1865	1,237,400	138,263	5.99
1866	1,584,000	197,077	8.09
1867	1,979,850	275,220	9.50
1868	2,131,500	528,123	11.73
1869	2,477,550	507,793	13.47
1870	2,619,749	663,348	20.85
1871	2,308,317	662,421	17.38

Source: Héctor Lindo-Fuentes, Weak Foundations: The Economy of El Salvador in the Nineteenth Century, 1821–1898 (Berkeley: University of California Press, 1990), 112.
[a]n.a. = not available.

Coffee production spread gradually in El Salvador before the liberal reform period. Lands were rented to coffee growers as early as the 1850s, but surpluses for coffee exportation were not large until the 1860s, and El Salvador was not a major producer of the crop until the 1880s. Many of the earliest coffee estates were small farms established on *ejidal* lands, and many early growers engaged in other economic activities besides coffee production. For these growers, access to land was less of a problem than access to credit and labor.[62] At this early stage, coffee cultivation was promoted primarily at the local level, rather than by the national government, with certain western townships passing ordinances favorable to its cultivation.[63] Before the liberal reform, there was little indication that the expansion of coffee would facilitate a full-scale assault on all common lands in the country.

Yet by 1870, the existence of vast tracts of communal and *ejidal* land raised concerns for many liberals about the future expansion of coffee and other commercial crops. Indian communities exercised control over certain prime coffee lands, as in the departments of La Libertad and Sonsonate, and resisted attempts by ladinos to encroach on their holdings.[64] Although these communities often engaged in small-scale coffee produc-

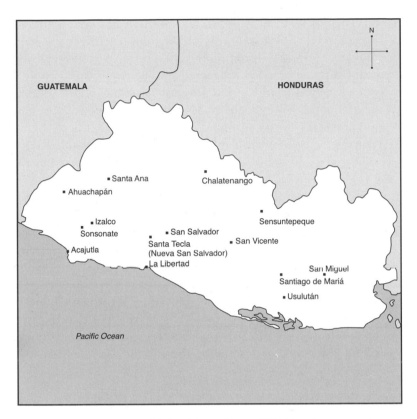

MAP 4.3   Major Townships of El Salvador

tion themselves, liberals believed that higher yields could be obtained by selling the lands to private entrepreneurs. Furthermore, liberals saw the municipalities that controlled *ejidal* lands as less than fully sympathetic to the expansion of coffee, and they viewed the local political structures that governed the communal lands as antiquated remnants of colonialism unable to efficiently promote agrarian modernization. Thus, liberals came to view the common land systems as blocking the efficient use of resources for coffee investment and production.

The solution to these problems for many actual or would-be private coffee entrepreneurs—whether small, medium, or large—involved extending the concern with introducing land privatization and pro-coffee legislation found in certain municipalities to the national level. Yet this extension was not forthcoming under the conservative administration of Francisco Dueñas (1863–71). Although by no means opposed to coffee expansion, Dueñas was unwilling to attack the traditional land system based on communal and *ejidal* lands, and he refused to carry out reforms that ran directly counter to Indian interests, since this group represented an important support base for his regime.[65] The result was a contradiction between the conservative orientation of the state and the modernizing goals of liberals similar to what was simultaneously present in Guatemala under the Cerna administration.

The consolidation of liberalism in El Salvador was possible only once liberals defeated conservatives in Guatemala, which ended the threat from the north. In 1871, Salvadoran liberals seized power in the aftermath of a war between the conservative Dueñas administration and his political opponents in Honduras.[66] Under the leadership of Salvadoran general Santiago González, a moderate liberal, Honduran troops scored a decisive victory against conservative Salvadoran forces. González formed a new government, at which point the liberal reform period was launched. Unlike in Guatemala, the old order was not directly overthrown by a liberal revolutionary movement in which coffee elites played an active supporting role. However, the existence of a nascent coffee economy did reinforce liberalism within El Salvador and created a sizable segment of liberals highly interested in destroying the common land systems.

Class and State Structures on the Eve of Liberal Reform

At the initiation of the liberal reform period, Guatemala and El Salvador had already experienced a partial transition to commercial agriculture. Coffee was an increasingly important export, surpassing cochineal in Guatemala by 1870 and rapidly gaining on indigo exports in El Salvador. At this early stage, however, it was hardly a foregone conclusion that commercial agriculture would lead to extreme land concentration and the marginalization of peasants. In both countries, large coffee estates were present, but they existed along with small coffee farms controlled by peasant farmers—the latter being responsible for a significant portion of overall production. Thus, while large coffee plantations tended to dominate in the Pacific piedmont areas of Guatemala, small coffee farms were more common in the previous cochineal districts of Antigua and Amatitlán. In El Salvador, small farmers produced significant amounts of coffee in the northern regions, while large growers were concentrated primarily in the areas of San Salvador and Santa Ana, and even here small coffee farms were common.[67] Of course, before the liberal reform, the production of coffee, whether by small or large growers, was an important enterprise for only a tiny percentage of the population. Subsistence farming, small-scale farming for local markets, and handicraft production continued to dominate the agrarian landscape, even in prime coffee regions, and much land was still held by municipalities and rented in *ejidal* form to peasant communities or was controlled directly by Indian communities. To be sure, municipal governments sometimes put pressure on these communities for access to peasant land and labor, but national legislation protected the traditional land tenure system before liberals seized power.

In conjunction with the initiation of commercial agriculture, dominant-class actors were increasingly members of a new elite associated with the large-scale production, processing, and export of coffee.[68] In Guatemala, control over land and labor was the central means to achieve membership and advancement in these privileged classes. In this country, one can trace the beginnings of an entrenched coffee elite back to a period before the liberal reform. In El Salvador, by contrast, the wealthiest and most powerful families did not yet monopolize land and labor. Instead, they typically sought diversified patterns of investment and landholding, and they often relied more on wealth generated from the processing and exporting of coffee—including coffee produced by small growers—than on profits accumulated from plantation labor. Despite these differences, both Guatemala and El Salvador saw the rise of an elite associated with coffee production, an elite that had the potential to expand its control over all aspects of the export economy.

The coffee elites of Guatemala and El Salvador exercised significant local political influence through control over municipal governments. This influence was important because local *ayuntamientos* controlled many of the means of administration and supervision in the two countries. Before 1871, however, coffee elites did not have significant influence in, much less direct control over, national states. Coffee production in Guatemala and El Salvador was launched without significant support from the national state. Although national states remained decentralized and essentially nonbureaucratic, leaving activities such as education in the hands of the Church, central governments in Guatemala and El Salvador did stand above local *ayuntamientos* and were responsible for coordinating development programs within the countries as a whole. With the liberal reform, coffee growers would seek to gain greater influence within these national state institutions—a process at which they would eventually succeed, but not until the early twentieth century.

PREMATURE AND DELAYED REFORM PERIODS: HONDURAS AND NICARAGUA

Episodes of outside intervention shaped the timing of the reform period in Honduras and Nicaragua. Liberal dominance in Honduras was not a result of the ability of domestic liberals to defeat a conservative opposition, but rather was imposed from the outside by Guatemala and El Salvador. In this sense, the liberal reform period in Honduras was *premature*—that is, it occurred before domestic conditions were conducive to liberal dominance. In Nicaragua, liberals' association with William Walker in the mid-nineteenth century discredited them and allowed for a prolonged period of conservative rule, until the last decade of the century. Thus, for Nicaragua, the liberal reform period was *delayed*—that is, it occurred much later than would have been the case in the absence of intervention.

Examining the role of foreign intervention in shaping the timing of the reform period in Honduras and Nicaragua will help prepare us to understand why these countries ultimately experienced a *similar* pattern of aborted liberalism, in which outside intervention limited the scope of transformation during the reform period itself. Nevertheless, the two cases exhibit important *contrasts* in terms of the class and state structures present on the eve of liberal reform. In a comparative light, preliberal class and state structures in Honduras resembled those of Costa Rica in significant ways, while preliberal structures in Nicaragua bore important similarities to those of Guatemala and El Salvador. These contrasting antecedent structural conditions help explain why reform leaders in Honduras and Nicaragua pursued different policy options during the liberal reform period.

The Imposition of Liberalism in Honduras

Unlike in Guatemala and El Salvador, processes of development in mid-nineteenth-century Honduras did not create a socioeconomic basis favorable to liberalism. Although the mining of precious metals in the central regions of the country was important during the colonial period, making Tegucigalpa something of a commercial center, by the conclusion of the colonial period this industry was in a state of financial crisis from which it would not recover until the 1870s.[69] The most important Honduran export in the mid-nineteenth century was cattle, raised principally in the Olancho department (see map 4.4) and sold in markets in Guate-

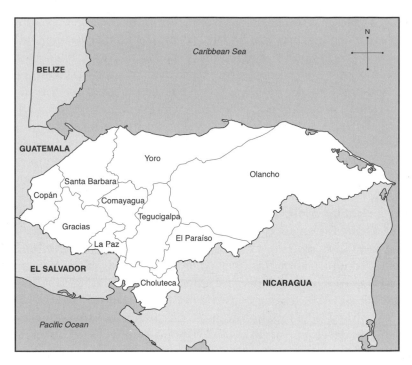

MAP 4.4   Departments of Honduras, 1869

mala and San Miguel (El Salvador). Other livestock products, such as mules, hides, and deerskins, were also exported, as were precious woods from the departments of Santa Barbara, Yoro, and Choluteca, sarsaparilla from Yoro and Olancho, limited quantities of indigo and wild cochineal from Comayagua, and tobacco from Copán and Santa Barbara.[70] Even with these economic activities, however, Honduras was the poorest country in Central America in the mid-nineteenth century, lacking a significant agro-commercial export.[71]

Demographic and geographic factors can partially explain the failure of Honduras to develop an agrarian export economy prior to the liberal reform. Like Costa Rica, Honduras was sparsely populated, lacking the more abundant labor force that permitted the formation of successful plantations in Guatemala and El Salvador. In fact, contrary to what is sometimes believed, Honduras—not Costa Rica—had the lowest population density in Central America during the nineteenth century.[72] To make matters worse, the population of Honduras was not heavily concentrated in a single region suitable for agro-export production, as was true of the Meseta Central in Costa Rica, but rather was spread through-out isolated departments that had little contact with one another. Indeed, more than 80 percent of the Honduran landscape has been categorized as mountainous,[73] a geography that separated communities from one another and posed major problems for the development of the transportation networks necessary to support an export economy.

Equally important, national and local political situations were not conducive to commercial development. At the national level, mid-nineteenth-century politics were highly unstable, marked by a series of unimpressive administrations that did little to promote development. Although the presidency changed hands many times (often through armed revolts), three nominally conservative leaders tended to dominate during this period: General Francisco Ferrera during the 1840s, Santos Guardiola during the 1850s, and General José María Medina during the 1860s.[74] Medina's administration has received the most attention from historians because he brought Honduras into a position of escalating debt after securing British loans for the construction of a hopelessly delayed interoceanic railroad. The situation at the level of municipal governments was similar: few development programs were undertaken, and almost none were successfully implemented. This was true even in Tegucigalpa, the most liberal department of the country and the central location of a merchant elite who oversaw the exportation of traditional products.

The failure of governments (whether national or local) to promote development went hand in hand with the relative absence of a clearly defined liberal-conservative cleavage in Honduras during the mid-nineteenth century. Competing caudillos did mobilize armies and carry on battles with one another in the hopes of gaining control over government. However, the ideological differences between liberals (who were known as *coquimbos, timbucos,* or "reds") and conservatives (known as *cachurecos, caladracas,* or "blues") were largely divisions over the Church and the question of a Central American union.[75] In general, the picture was one of loosely defined factions controlled by individual military chieftains who rose or fell according to their ability to mobilize armed forces, rather than by a real commitment to liberalism or conservatism.

In a comparative perspective, Honduras clearly contrasts with Guatemala and El Salvador because the nation did not experience processes of economic development that facilitated the rise of liberals to power—no incipient agrarian bourgeoisie or emergent coffee economy was present here to spur liberal revolutions. Rather, economically speaking, Honduras more closely resembled Costa Rica, whose economy also remained untransformed by commercial agriculture in the preliberal period. Yet whereas Costa Rican liberals were able to stabilize national power at the time of independence, Honduran liberals were deeply involved in Federation politics and subsequently developed into an ill-defined political faction. As a consequence, even though conservative institutions were weak in Honduras, the country lacked liberal organizations and activists capable of launching a successful reform period. Uniquely in Honduras, then, liberalism had to be imposed from the outside.

The imposition of liberalism in Honduras came shortly after liberals achieved victories in 1871 in Guatemala and El Salvador.[76] The new administrations in these countries viewed the presence of the conservative government of Medina (1863–72) as a threat to regional unity and sought to install a liberal government in its place. In 1872, following a brief war, Medina was overthrown by Guatemalan and Salvadoran forces, and Celeo Arias—a longtime liberal—was installed in power, at which point one can date the beginning of the liberal reform period in Honduras. Personal squabbling between Arias and Salvadoran president González soon broke out, however, and Arias was removed from power. For the next few years, Honduras was ruled by General Ponciano Leiva, while the governments of El Salvador and Guatemala struggled to find a "suitable" liberal leader for Honduras. In 1876, the situation finally stabilized when Marco Aurelio Soto, who had served as vice-minister of external relations in liberal Guatemala, and Ramón Rosa, Soto's cousin and chief advisor, were brought to power with the military backing of Justo Rufino Barrios in Guatemala.

The emergence of liberalism in Honduras was thus not the result of a domestic process in which liberals defeated conservatives and consolidated their rule. Rather, it was an outgrowth of liberal victories in Guatemala and El Salvador and was imposed from the outside by these nations.

William Walker, the "Thirty Years," and Coffee Expansion in Nicaragua

The timing of the rise of liberals to power in Nicaragua was also strongly conditioned by outside intervention. In this case, however, intervention took the form of a bizarre, nongovernmental invasion led by soldier of fortune William Walker, and it served to *delay* the onset of the liberal reform period by discrediting liberals who were associated with Walker. Following the Walker affair, conservatives held continuous power until the last decade of the nineteenth century, which had the key consequence that the period of conservative rule in Nicaragua overlapped with periods of full-blown liberalism in the rest of the region. These regional liberal reform efforts led Nicaraguan conservatives to go much further in promoting development than did conservatives in the other countries. In fact, under conservative rule, national legislation was initiated that promoted the commercialization of agriculture and, ironically, favored an eventual return to power by liberals.

The Walker episode developed from ongoing factional fighting between liberals based primarily in León and conservatives centered in Granada.[77] In the decade and a half following the failure of the Federation, conservatives were unable to stabilize power due to recurrent revolts by liberals, which left Nicaragua in a state of almost constant civil warfare. In 1854, following the formation of a constituent assembly and the selection of a conservative leader from Granada (Fruto Chamorro) as provisional president, an especially bloody war broke out between the two factions. As the war unfolded in the summer of 1855, conservatives prepared to forcibly take León and other liberal strongholds, and it appeared as if they might finally stabilize rule. Seemingly facing defeat, liberals contracted with U.S. "colonists" for a mercenary army to fight against the Granada/conservative faction, a service that was ultimately undertaken by Tennessee native William Walker. Walker did in fact lead an expedition that defeated the conservatives, but he quickly turned his back on the liberal conspirators, declaring himself president of the republic. The adventurer was expelled only with a concerted effort on the part of both liberal and conservative forces within Nicaragua, and with the aid of troops from Costa Rica, El Salvador, and Guatemala.

The effort to oust Walker brought competing factions within Nicaragua together and enabled them to agree on a new constitution and a relatively stable framework for a national government to be centered in Managua, a compromise city between León and Granada. Stigmatized for bringing Walker into the region, liberals were unable to maintain a posture of armed opposition to conservatives and thus agreed to recognize conservative control of the presidency, provided their faction was included in the cabinet and National Congress. In turn, conservatives made several economic concessions to liberals and began to advocate a more aggressive program of national development for the country. The result of this intraoligarchic pact was the so-called Thirty Years (1858–93) that preceded the liberal reform—a period defined by a succession of eight consecutive conservative administrations that increasingly pursued a modernization program consistent with certain aspects of the liberal agenda.[78]

A half-century of wars between liberals and conservatives had left the Nicaraguan economy in shambles by the beginning of the Thirty Years. A variety of products characterized the economy, including precious metals, timber, rubber, livestock, indigo, cheeses, sugar, cotton, tobacco, and cacao, but overall levels of exportation were low. As in Honduras before the liberal reform, Nicaragua's economy at midcentury was highly diversified, but suffered because it lacked a significant export crop.[79] Most potential coffee regions, such as the North Central Highlands around Matagalpa and Jinotega (see map 4.5), lacked roads for transportation and were isolated from major commercial centers, and thus did not enter into coffee production before important government reforms were put in place. Beginning around midcentury, limited quan-

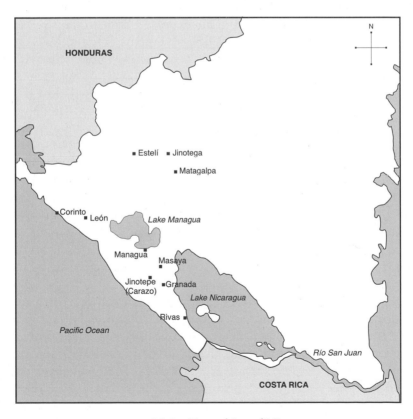

MAP 4.5   Major Townships of Nicaragua

tities of coffee were produced for exportation in the relatively compact Southern Uplands region (located in the Sierras de Managua and the Carazo Plateau of Jinotepe, near Granada), where the crop could be transported more easily to commercial centers with ox-driven carts. Even in this area, however, the arrival of William Walker and political instability severely curtailed coffee production before 1860.[80]

The Thirty Years provided the necessary political stability for state development and agrarian capitalism under conservative leadership. Already during the administration of Tomás Martínez (1859–67), measures were taken to weaken government monopolies, promote free trade, and establish stronger national control over municipalities.[81] Martínez and subsequent conservative administrations also implemented several anticlerical reforms typically associated with liberals—such as the abolition of the tithe, the expansion of secular education, and eventually the expulsion of a Jesuit order.[82] Most important, in 1877 President Pedro Joaquín Chamorro signed an agrarian reform law designed to rapidly privatize land in the North Central Highlands.[83] Prior to the 1877 legislation, most land in this region was held by Indian communities who enjoyed common property rights. The new privatization law "required that those who worked *ejidal* and communal lands pay from two to five pesos per *manzana* of land to receive freehold title to those lands. If payment was not made, the land could be put up for auction. The law also provided for the sale of national lands in lots up to five hundred *manzanas* (865 acres) for potential cropland and up to two thousand *manzanas* (3,460 acres) for grazing land."[84] Conservative governments also began to assist coffee growers by offering generous cash subsidies for successful production and by helping secure a reliable labor force. In the early 1880s, the administration of Joaquín Zavala created agricultural judges who were ordered to "rundown, capture and remit fugitive laborers wherever they have deserted."[85] At this time, employers were granted rights to quash labor disorders, and citizens were ordered to assist in the repression of worker unrest.

Yet despite these substantial efforts, large coffee growers often deeply opposed the conservative order. For one thing, conservatives never pursued the establishment of a financial and banking system capable of meeting the needs of agro-commercial investors.[86] Equally important, coffee growers believed that conservatives failed to fully implement measures designed to solve the chronic labor shortages that stood in the way of the expansion of large-scale plantations.[87] For example, in the North Central Highlands, which was targeted for coffee production because of its dense population, the resistance of indigenous communities—which flared into a major armed revolt in 1881—dissuaded many investors from taking advantage of the government legislation.[88] In the view of many coffee planters, the conservative government simply failed to effectively enforce labor codes designed to coercively compel Indians to work on coffee estates.[89]

Before the liberal reform period, coffee production spread in the North Central Highlands area around Matagalpa and Jinotega, but it did so very gradually, only partially penetrating the region by 1892.[90] Conservative legislation singled out this area for privatization, but the number of land claims issued here was limited in comparison with the subsequent Zelaya era.[91] Most likely, small growers accounted for the majority of coffee production, as resistance by indigenous groups and isolation from commercial areas prevented the spread of large plantations. It is not known what direct effect conservative policies had on promoting coffee in the Southern Lowlands region, the center of coffee production during the nineteenth century. Conservative presidents probably offered substantial incentives to ranchers, merchants, and hacienda owners near the Carazo Plateau and the conservative stronghold of Granada. These incentives likely enabled many small-scale peasant families to secure access to land, but they also appear to have led to the proliferation of relatively large estates of fifty *manzanas* or more.[92] By contrast, in the Sierras de Managua, "where local elites from Managua and foreign investors came to dominate the production," it is possible that the *ayuntamiento* of Managua—rather than the national government—took the lead in promoting coffee expansion.[93] The Sierras de Managua were the single most important coffee-producing region in the country, and the spread of large estates in this area helped create a new liberal constituency centered in Managua that was interested in pursuing an aggressive reform program. These new liberals found a leader in José Santos Zelaya, the son of a wealthy coffee planter from Managua and holder of a martial reputation developed while working for Justo Rufino Barrios in Guatemala.

In his bid to seize state power, Zelaya organized support not only from traditional liberals in León, but also from the Managua coffee elite that sought to emulate the radical liberal reforms of Guatemala and El Salvador.[94] Furthermore, once Zelaya's intentions became clear, many conservatives essentially transformed themselves into liberals and allied themselves with the movement. Although elite support was crucial to Zelaya's success, ultimately he had to defeat President Roberto Sacasa and subsequent conservative challengers on the battlefield. In this effort, he was assisted by several hundred volunteer troops from Honduras, enabling him to overwhelm the poorly organized government forces. The rise of Zelaya to power in 1893 marked the end of the Thirty Years and the beginning of the liberal reform period. Nevertheless, much of the old conservative elite from Granada remained intact, and its continuing presence would play a major role in the politics leading to a renewed bout of U.S. intervention in 1909.

Class and State Structures on the Eve of Liberal Reform

The constellation of structural conditions inherited by liberals at the beginning of the reform period differed greatly in Honduras and Nicaragua. Consequently, it is necessary to discuss the two cases separately, paying special attention to how they compare with the other countries of Central America.

In preliberal Honduras, most land was held as *ejidos* or in the more vaguely defined *común* form, including the majority of land in areas suitable for agro-commercial production. During the mid-nineteenth century, some government efforts were made to register lands, which led not only to an increase in the number of private plots, but also to an expansion of *ejidal* lands. Thus, whereas traditional land systems were simply being defended elsewhere in Central America, in Honduras they were actually *expanding* before the liberal reform.[95] Within this land system, most individuals lived in small, subsistence-farming villages located in highland sites that were isolated from one another. José Francisco Guevara-Escudero has characterized mid-nineteenth-century Honduras as a nation of multiple "hermit societies" to highlight the physical separation between most villages (due to a sparse population, mountainous terrain, and lack of roads).[96] Given the "hermitlike" character of Honduran villages, it is perhaps ironic that Costa Rica—where nucleated settlements were concentrated in a single region—has often been viewed as the Central American country that possessed an early "rural democracy." While it would be wrong to view either Costa Rica or Honduras as a rural democracy in the preliberal period, many of the features associated with this interpretation (e.g., isolation between settlers, the presence of a yeomanry, extreme poverty) seem to describe Honduras better than Costa Rica in the period before the introduction of commercial agriculture.

The majority of Hondurans lived very poorly, but the economy did not suffer from outright stagnation. The pastoral-based economy offered a variety of activities, and the trade of livestock products provided a livelihood for many individuals. In fact, the inaccessibility of Honduras's highland communities dissuaded foreign merchants from trying to take control of local trade, allowing indigenous merchants to proliferate. For this reason, and again similarly to Costa Rica, the most important dominant class of Honduras was a merchant class that oversaw the exportation of cattle, hides, sarsaparilla, tobacco, and other products.[97] In some cases, these individuals were also large cattle ranchers, but in no way were they equivalent to the plantation owners of Guatemala or the agrarian-commercial producers of El Salvador. Thus, Honduras—like Costa Rica—lacked a landed elite in the sense of a dominant class that derived wealth from estate ownership and the extraction of surplus produced by peasants or plantation workers.

State development was stunted in preliberal Honduras. Unlike in Guatemala and El Salvador, where public and quasi-public institutions were used to promote national development, the Honduran central state played virtually no role in the lives of the vast majority of citizens. Local *ayuntamientos,* functioning autonomously from the central state, continued to be the main source of administration, but even these institutions were only weakly linked to much of the population. Indeed, of all the Central American countries, the challenges of forming bureaucracies that were linked to, or in some way penetrated, village settlements were greatest in Honduras, due to the sheer isolation of most communities. Added to this difficulty was the fact that village highlanders often resisted penetration of their communities by outsiders. The result was that both central and local government institutions failed to make contact with local communities, which existed in an essentially "stateless" environment before the liberal reform period.

In Nicaragua, the socioeconomic environment that liberals inherited from the Thirty Years period broadly resembles the pattern we have noted for Guatemala and El Salvador.[98] As in these cases, coffee production made headway before the liberal reform, and it clearly represented the future of the economy. At the beginning of the liberal reform in 1893, coffee exports from Nicaragua were roughly equal to those from Guatemala in 1871 and more extensive than those from El Salvador in 1871.[99] In fact, probably to a greater extent than in either preliberal Guatemala or El Salvador, large-scale plantations that relied on wage labor already dominated the coffee landscape. The importance of capitalist-sized plantations is revealed in records on the distribution of common lands, which show a strong bias for large planters in the key coffee departments, and from conservative land and labor laws, whose language suggests strong support for plantation owners.[100]

The dominant class at the time of the liberal reform was increasingly characterized by these large coffee growers, even as non-landed merchants from the townships and cattle ranchers from the countryside continued to generate wealth from traditional exports and commerce activities. The Nicaraguan coffee elite most closely resembled the planter class of Guatemala, which derived wealth from control over land and labor rather than from processing and financing.[101] As with Guatemalan planters, a major difficulty facing Nicaraguan growers was worker shortages and the problem of converting indigenous communities into reliable sources of plantation labor without provoking revolts.[102] Yet there was something distinctive about the Nicaraguan elite. Unlike the coffee landlords of Guatemala or the emergent coffee bourgeoisie of El Salvador, Nicaragua's landed elite was deeply divided into liberal and conservative movements. For in Nicaragua, conservatives had actively pursued pro-coffee legislation, and coffee plantation owners of the Carazo Plateau were often members of the old conservative elite from Granada. Thus, even though consensus was achieved on many overarching ideological matters, liberal and conservative factions remained bitterly opposed at the beginning of the reform period.

Before the mid-1850s, the rivalry between Granada and León prevented the stabilization of national state power, leaving municipal governments as the only viable source of political authority within the country. During the Thirty Years, however, the national state in Managua expanded at the expense of municipal authorities. Through presidentially appointed political bosses, conservative governments came to monitor local authorities and constrain their ability to act autonomously.[103] Furthermore, the national government became the site of most legislation initiatives and the ultimate enforcer of law in the country. Underlying this centralization of power in Managua was the pact of 1856 between elites from León and Granada. Yet only so long as this pact was accepted by all major players could national government leaders hope to check the aspirations of city-based elites.

CONCLUSION

Central American liberals came to power in diverse ways and at different points in world-historical time. In Costa Rica, liberals were able to stabilize power in the early nineteenth century, even in the absence of significant agrarian-commercial development. In this country, a combination of isolation within the Federation of Central America and the historical weakness of conservatives permitted an early liberal reform period. In Guatemala and El Salvador, the expansion of commercial agriculture in the mid-nineteenth century promoted the return of liberals to power. In Guatemala, coffee production facilitated the 1871 "revolution" by creating a new segment of liberal elites capable of defeating a well-established conservative opposition. In El Salvador, the spread of coffee production helped foster consensus concerning land privatization among an already largely liberal elite that was historically thwarted by conservative resistance from Guatemala. Finally, the emergence of a stable liberal government was premature in Honduras and delayed in Nicaragua. In Honduras, liberals were imposed in power by Guatemala and El Salvador before commercial agriculture was launched; in Nicaragua, liberals were discredited by their association with William Walker and unable to regain control of government until the end of the nineteenth century despite significant agrarian development.

Because liberals in Central America consolidated power in diverse ways and at different times, the five countries were marked by different kinds of state and class structures at the initiation of the reform period. These contrasting structural conditions offer insight into the situational environment that influenced policy choices during the reform period itself. Two basic patterns can be usefully distinguished: a more centralized state and more developed agrarian economy in Guatemala, El Salvador, and Nicaragua, and a less developed state and agrarian economy in Costa Rica and Honduras. The existence of a more developed state apparatus and economy of Guatemala, El Salvador, and Nicaragua will help explain why liberal-oriented reformers in these countries pursued a radical policy option. By contrast, the less developed state and economy of Honduras and Costa Rica will help explain why liberals in these two countries pursued a reform policy option.

PART III

The Liberal Reform Period

CHAPTER 5

Radical Liberalism: Guatemala and El Salvador

Within Central America, the transformations produced during the liberal reform period were most extensive in Guatemala and El Salvador. In these cases, moderate leaderships proved unable to stabilize their rule, giving way to radical liberal leaders who embarked on aggressive modernization programs. The legislation initially implemented by Justo Rufino Barrios in Guatemala and Rafael Zaldívar in El Salvador, and carried to completion by subsequent liberal leaders, dramatically expanded commercial agriculture, leading in both countries to a sevenfold increase in coffee exports between the mid-1870s and the conclusion of the liberal reform period.[1] Moreover, major transformations of preexisting state and class structures had crystallized by the conclusion of the reform period. Larger, more centralized states, complete with bureaucratic institutions—especially powerful military and security branches—that extensively penetrated national territory replaced weakly centralized and nonbureaucratic apparatuses. And liberal legislation that promoted land privatization and the creation of plantation labor forces uprooted preliberal land systems based on communal ownership and the protection of ecclesiastical properties. Along with these changes, elite coffee planters and processors acquired significant leverage within the strengthened states of Guatemala and El Salvador, even as rural class relations became highly polarized and coffee elites found themselves faced with an increasingly marginalized and potentially confrontational peasantry.

The radicalism of the Guatemalan and Salvadoran liberal reforms has not escaped the attention of historians and social scientists. Yet existing analyses often provide an inadequate basis for comparing the dynamics and consequences of these reform episodes. Single-country monographs and case-study articles present highly nuanced pictures of the specific elements of the two reform periods, but because they focus on Guatemala or El Salvador individually, they lack consistent criteria for comparing the two reform periods.[2] By contrast, theoretically oriented (specifically, Marxist) analyses do conceptualize key similarities between Guatemala and El Salvador during the liberal reform period.[3] However, these studies are too apt to assume that the liberal reform period immediately brought an elite class of coffee planters to political power and allowed this class to use the state as the basis for transforming society. In truth, the political arena for most of the reform period was dominated by personal dictators who were concerned above all with consolidating and augmenting personal power. These dictators (most particularly Barrios and Zaldívar) enacted radical policy options because, given prevailing socioeconomic and political conditions, this kind of reform best enabled them to increase individual political power and secure overall liberal political control. Only as an outgrowth of politically motivated policies did coffee elites as a class come to exercise significant—and even then by no means absolute or "instrumental"—power within the state. Hence, the tendency has been to translate the *effects* of political processes initiated during the liberal reform into the *causes* of such processes and thereby misconceive the role of coffee elites during the liberal reform period in Guatemala and El Salvador.

RADICAL STABILIZATION AND THE FAILURE OF MODERATE LEADERSHIPS

Observers present in 1871 to watch the return of liberals to power in Guatemala and El Salvador could scarcely have anticipated the extent of changes that would occur in the following decades. In Guatemala, the immediate result of the so-called Revolution of 1871 was the ascent of old-style liberal reformer Miguel García Granados (1871–73) to the presidency. Although any liberal president posed threats to established institutions, conservatives must have found comfort in the political moderation of the aging García Granados, who in fact sought an accommodation with his old rivals. As Wayne M. Clegern points out, "García Granados wanted a moderate result from the Revolution of 1871. A master politician under the old regime, he knew thoroughly the personalities, circumstances, and traditions of Guatemalan governance. . . . He chose, then, what must be described as a reformist course."[4] In El Salvador, the presidency of Santiago González (1871–76) must have initially seemed to be little more than yet another phase in the oscillation of liberals and conservatives that had characterized the country since independence.[5] Indeed, when compared to the earlier liberal Salvadoran president Gerardo Barrios (1858–63), González was an ideologically moderate politician, with roots in liberal political movements going back to the early 1840s. As Alastair White suggests, González was more akin to the "idealist" liberals of the early nineteenth century—of which García Granados was one—than to the more ideologically radical liberals that would dominate the reform period beginning with the Zaldívar administration.[6]

Had moderate, first-generation liberals such as García Granados and González stabilized power, it is likely that Guatemala and El Salvador would have followed a fundamentally different path of national political development. But no such moderate stabilization proved possible. To explain why, the usual accounts that center on the direct rise of coffee planters to state power are of limited value. More useful is an analysis that focuses on the political dilemmas facing liberal leaders in the early stages of the reform period. In turbulent late-nineteenth-century Guatemala and El Salvador, leaders would rise or fall according to how successful they were at building military and bureaucratic apparatuses capable of defeating enemies and mobilizing followers. To their credit, and to the ultimate detriment of Guatemalan and Salvadoran societies as a whole, radical leaderships were most capable of pursuing these state-building activities.

García Granados and Barrios in Guatemala

After assuming the presidency in Guatemala, García Granados found himself engulfed in a situation of intra-elite squabbling over the constitutional form of the new government.[7] Positioning himself in the center as a "conservative liberal" and attempting to bring the old and the new together, García Granados permitted an active debate between progressive conservatives (including leading Church members), moderate liberals, and radical liberals. Although real issues animated this debate, García Granados's preoccupation with constitutional reform and political accommodation distracted attention away from the more fundamental task of stabilizing state power. The cautious reforms his administration pursued in the months after seizing power, perhaps most notably establishing freedom of the press and replacing the Consulado de Comercio with a public development agency known as Fomento,[8] did little to consolidate control in the vast territories outside of Guatemala City.

As García Granados futilely struggled to forge an elite consensus within the capital, Rufino Barrios, now serving as military commander of the western district centered at Quezaltenango, consciously distanced himself from parliamentary affairs and went about the task of organizing an army and solidifying his own power base. According to Jorge Mario García Laguardia, Barrios essentially organized his own "small state" in the western zone and made himself a virtual military dictator in the area by establishing "individual authority at the expense of the central government."[9]

Through these activities, Barrios was well positioned to force the hand of García Granados in a more radical direction, a possibility he wasted no time in realizing with regard to the Church.[10] A mere six weeks after the liberal seizure of power, while García Granados attempted to cautiously cooperate with religious officials in hopes of peacefully disengaging the Church from the state, Barrios privately ordered the expulsion of the Jesuit order in Quezaltenango, leaving García Granados no choice but to move on ecclesiastical matters. When the acting archbishop called for a cancellation of Barrios's action, "García Granados played for time until he could learn the circumstances and then concluded, despite his irritation at the unauthorized act, that he must support Barrios' decision. He needed the general's military vigor and his following and thus had to accept in some degree his radicalism."[11]

More important, García Granados soon found himself having to rely on Barrios's military-building capacities to quell increasingly common uprisings within society. Only months after seizing power, García Granados was forced to call upon Barrios to put down a major conservative revolt in the Santa Rosa–Chiquimula area—an uprising that local officials were unable to stop.[12] Then, as Guatemala entered into war with Honduras and García Granados was led to the front lines in 1872 and 1873, he twice appointed Barrios as interim president, no doubt in recognition of the fact that Barrios was the individual most capable of maintaining liberal power in his absence.

As acting president in 1872 and 1873, Barrios initiated reforms that completely reversed García Granados's plan to seek a compromise with religious authorities. Legislation was enacted that banned religious orders, suppressed the ecclesiastical *fuero,* and, most important, called for the nationalization of all Church properties.[13] This anti-ecclesiastical legislation facilitated future agrarian transformation by undermining Church authority in the countryside and expelling resident priests, who helped link indigenous communities with the state.[14] Furthermore, these laws polarized the broad spectrum of forces present in the García Granados government, eventually forcing out more moderate elements. "Anticlerical measures caused some cooperative Conservatives and moderate Liberals to leave the ruling alliance; the Liberal coalition became narrower and more repressive."[15]

By 1873, then, it was clear that Rufino Barrios was the real force within Guatemala. For it had been he—not the moderate García Granados—who had proved most capable of consolidating and increasing liberal state power. As new, seemingly endless uprisings continued to develop within the country,[16] a weary García Granados—ready to retire from political affairs—called for presidential elections "to decide if he or Barrios was in charge."[17] Barrios—anticlimactically, in light of his dominance within the national government—won the elections handily, merely serving to confirm his de facto position.

Possibilities for Moderate Stabilization in El Salvador

Whereas the stabilization of a radical liberal government in Guatemala went hand in hand with the state-building efforts of Barrios, even while a moderate government was formally in power, radical consolidation occurred more gradually and in a less dramatic fashion in El Salvador. Here radical stabilization began only *after* Zaldívar assumed the presidency in 1876, not during the administration of moderate leader Santiago González. In fact, when Zaldívar came to power, there were strong reasons to believe that he would follow the moderate path adopted by González.

González had a better opportunity to consolidate power than had been true of García Granados in Guatemala.[18] Conservative forces were substantially weaker in El Salvador, reducing the likelihood of both internal governmental divisions and revolts from within society. Rufino Barrios himself admitted that the moderate García Granados government in Guatemala "was not able to fulfill its mission because of the state of instability within the Republic created by the presence of armed factions opposed to the government."[19] But in El Salvador during the liberal reform, "there was no serious political opposition from the proclerical forces of the Right nor, until the end of the period, from the rising popular forces of the left."[20] Hence, no domestic opposition group—including coffee planters—brought down the González administration in 1876 (nominally headed by President Andrés Valle at the time). Instead, the failure of moderate liberalism in El Salvador came only through intraregional war. The occasion was a personal dispute between Rufino Barrios and González that led the Guatemalan strongman to invade El Salvador.[21] The superior war-fighting capacities of the Guatemalan state allowed for a quick—though financially burdensome—victory, which ousted González (and Valle) from power, thus repeating an earlier pattern in which political dynamics in El Salvador were shaped by Guatemalan intervention. With Barrios dictating the terms for peace, an elite group of Salvadoran politicians—the so-called junta of notables—assembled at Chalchuapa in May 1876 to select a new president. But it was Barrios who ultimately made the decision, choosing Dr. Rafael Zaldívar upon the recommendation of Costa Rican liberal leader Tomás Guardia.

Although a medical doctor by profession, Zaldívar had served as a top-ranking minister and legislator in the conservative Dueñas administration.[22] Now, in 1876, he identified himself as neither a liberal nor a conservative, and there was certainly no reason to believe he was ideologically predisposed to pursue a radical set of bureaucratic and agrarian transformations. Yet a series of political dilemmas led him down precisely such a path. In the first place, Zaldívar had not come to power with the support of liberal organizations and activists.[23] As a consequence, he faced repeated opposition from liberal elites, who felt they were more worthy and legitimate rulers. In addition, the presence of Barrios in Guatemala fostered an ongoing state of national insecurity. Even though Zaldívar had been handpicked by Barrios, this meant little in nineteenth-century Central America when shifting alliances and war-fighting among neighboring countries were the order of the day. Thus, Zaldívar necessarily had to prepare for challenges both at home and abroad, a process that led him, in meeting the exigencies of maintaining political control, to deepen state penetration of society and expand military power. To make matters worse, González's war effort against Barrios had drained scarce resources and left the state in a serious financial crisis.[24] To be sure, potential resources were still there—in the form of taxes on imports, which were ultimately fueled by agro-exports. But in 1876 the indigo economy was in serious decline, and coffee production had yet to fully compensate for this loss.

All of these factors would set Zaldívar on a radical course in which he would first pursue reforms to strengthen the military and then nurture agro-commercial interests in an effort to build a support base and increase overall state revenues. The result would be a liberal reform period every bit as thoroughgoing as in Guatemala.

EPISODES OF FULL-BLOWN LIBERALISM

The governments of Barrios and Zaldívar were state-building administrations in which personal dictators responded to antecedent socioeconomic conditions and ongoing political crises by rapidly expanding bureaucratic and military capabilities. State-building reforms enabled the two presidents to maintain power in the face of persistent resistance from elite enemies and their peasant followers. Expansion of the state also had a key economic effect: it provided a bureaucratic infrastructure for the promotion of commercial agriculture. Not until larger, more powerful states had been constructed could liberals in Guatemala and El Salvador effectively implement radical policy options.

The Barrios Dictatorship and State-Building Reforms

The phrase "the landlords in power," taken from the title of a chapter in a major study on the liberal reform in Guatemala, reflects the scholarly tendency to mistakenly view the Guatemalan political system as directly controlled by coffee planters during the Barrios government.[25] In fact, Barrios oversaw a personal dictatorship in which nearly all major government decisions were made by Justo Rufino Barrios himself.[26] Although a legislative-constitutional assembly existed, it was nothing more than a clientalistic outlet through which Barrios could extend patronage (in the form of assembly seats) to his elite allies, who were treated as dispensable cronies and forced to function in great fear of offending the self-proclaimed *dictador*. Moreover, top-ranking government positions (in the National Congress and in the state ministries) were not monopolized by coffee-planter friends of Barrios, but rather occupied by a heterogeneous group of full-time government bureaucrats, merchants, industry owners, army officials, and landed elites.[27] Within this political setting, Barrios's "first preoccupation was to maintain himself in power"[28]—a preoccupation that mediated all of his reformist tendencies. David Kauck has sketched the overall issues quite clearly:

> It is easy to overstate the extent to which the agrarian reforms of the "radicals" [i.e., radical liberals] were simply an expression of planters' interests. In Guatemala, political power became concentrated in a civil-military bureaucracy under the control of a personal dictator. Although the Barrios regime was clearly responsive to planters' concerns, *the planters themselves did not rule*. By overemphasizing the degree to

which planters as a class were able to influence state policy it is easy to lose sight of: (1) the fact that some of the "radical" agrarian policies had more to do with Barrios' efforts to consolidate power than with planters' concerns, and (2) the extent to which the personalistic character of the state conditioned the execution of agrarian reform policies.

Government assistance to coffee producers was offered in a manner that was designed to cement bonds of personal dependence on the president and his lieutenants. . . . Few of the benefits of the Barrios program took the form of public goods offered to all members of the planter aristocracy as a block. Instead the Barrios program offered various divisible goods and services which were allocated preferentially, as selective incentives to specific individuals who had personal ties to the Liberal government.[29]

Once we recognize that the Barrios state was a personal dictatorship with relative autonomy from coffee elites, we can make sense of the course of full-blown liberalism in Guatemala. Thus, Barrios's earliest reforms centered on strengthening the state at the expense of the Church and conservatives precisely because these actors posed the greatest threat to his rule. In contrast to what some scholars have asserted, anti-ecclesiastical legislation was not carried out in order to put "huge extensions of rural land in state hands" that could then be sold to private coffee growers.[30] Rather, the studies of Thomas R. Herrick and David McCreery show that surprisingly little land was available for nationalization, almost none of it rural.[31] Anti-ecclesiastical reforms served to increase state authority and allowed Barrios to convert churches, monasteries, and convents into public institutions such as military academies, jails, and government office buildings. In addition, Barrios could distribute the resources gained from the sale of Church real estate and possessions as patronage to his political friends.[32]

Military modernization was a central concern of Barrios from the beginning. Michael McClintock points out that "before 1871 Guatemala could not truly be said even to have a national army . . . Guatemala's army—or armies—were largely ad hoc affairs . . . they were still effectively local militias, or ill-armed mobs."[33] In 1873, Barrios moved to create a professional officer corps by contacting a Spanish military mission to set up and staff a modern military academy and training school.[34] Moreover, the new liberal government

moved to put the militia on a more or less regular footing. After 1871 it becomes possible to differentiate the regular army, which in peacetime rarely numbered more than 2,000–4,000 men, garrisoned in the urban centers and on the frontiers, from the militia. In theory the latter included all ladino males between the ages of eighteen and fifty who were not otherwise exempt. Whereas the army's principal task was national defense, the militia, although it acted as a reserve for the army and might be called up in time of war, served in the absence of a regular rural police force as the state's chief instrument of control and repression in the countryside.[35]

The professionalization and expansion of the military under Barrios promoted the interests of coffee growers by providing them with a coercive apparatus to maintain order in the countryside.[36] Yet military reforms were also consistent with Barrios's agenda of securing and enhancing personal power. In fact, Barrios did not hesitate to use the military in ways that clashed with planters' interests when it furthered his own political interests. McCreery goes so far as to say that coffee elites often "detested military recruiting and militia service for their workers" because these measures exacerbated chronic labor shortages.[37]

A strengthened army and militia provided Barrios with a security apparatus to put down domestic and foreign opposition movements seeking his overthrow. At home, the militia assisted Barrios in monitoring the rural population and tying segments of this population to the state in the form of either voluntary employment or forced participation. Abroad, Barrios used the leverage of his enhanced fighting forces to ensure that friendly governments ruled in El Salvador and Honduras. Barrios's interest in appropriating resources from society and channeling them into financially burdensome wars with Central American neighbors sometimes brought him into conflict with coffee planters, especially when he imposed forced loans on the elite or when wars disrupted production by triggering financial crises.[38]

Barrios oversaw many state infrastructure developments, utilizing the new government agency Fomento and drawing on resources from a land tax decreed in December 1873.[39] Infrastructure development facilitated the state's penetration of society, expanding its presence into formerly isolated areas, including through forced labor drafts to build roads, ports, and bridges.[40] Likewise, some infrastructure projects that improved communication, such as the creation of the first telegraph lines beginning in 1873, enhanced state control over the countryside by permitting the efficient mobilization of the military and militia in isolated regions.[41]

To build a centralized, vertically integrated state that more thoroughly penetrated national territory, Barrios worked to undermine the political power of municipal governments. Reforms were implemented that increased the authority of departmental governors (known as *jefes políticos*) at the expense of local officials.[42] *Jefes políticos* were usually ladino military men who "served at the pleasure of the President."[43] As Herrick suggests, "Barrios selected his *jefes políticos* with great care in order to prevent the possibility of uprisings. . . . Once the *jefes políticos* had been strictly regulated and their loyalty toward the president verified, they generally followed the economic program of the president."[44] Likewise, Barrios significantly weakened the political power of local indigenous leaders and institutions. Before he came to power, ethnic communities could use autonomous town councils *(municipalidades indígenas)* to appeal to the national government. With the Municipal Law of 1879, however, Barrios gave *jefes políticos* control over these institutions and thus "reduced the municipalidad indígena to the status of an auxiliary government."[45] Furthermore, new municipalities were founded, often on land that formerly had been controlled by indigenous communities, and Barrios expanded his local control by filling these new offices with close political allies.

In sum, the state-building reforms of Barrios were not carried out simply on behalf of coffee planters, and they did not initially lead to direct control over the state by planters. Instead, the Barrios state was highly personalistic, and state centralization led to the expansion of a relatively autonomous military-bureaucratic apparatus on which coffee planters became increasingly dependent.

Land Reforms in Guatemala

A coffee planter himself, Barrios was well aware of the interests, demands, and potential oppositional role of coffee elites. And he embraced a liberal ideology that offered normative justification for the transformation of land tenure relations in ways to promote coffee production. It is thus not surprising that his administration oversaw the promotion of large coffee plantations through land privatization. However, the calculated manner in which Barrios implemented land policies shows that neither planter interests nor liberal ideology completely dictated agrarian change in Guatemala. This can be seen by considering the two major land reforms carried out by Barrios—the privatization of state-owned lands and the abolition of *censo* lands—as well as his policies to regulate a plantation labor force.

Beginning in 1873, the liberal government permitted the private acquisition of state-owned communal lands (known as *terrenos baldíos*) by export producers in the western piedmont region of Costa Cuca and El Palmar.[46] Although these *terrenos baldíos* were identified by the government as "idle," in fact they were commonly settled by subsistence-cultivating peasants who lacked property titles, and in some cases were already occupied by nontitled coffee planters. Because settlers' rights to these lands were based merely on the old colonial and conservative practice of respecting traditional communal landholding relations, Barrios was able to move swiftly toward land privatization. In 1873 alone, 200,000 acres of land were divided into individual plots of 110 to 550 acres, which were put up for auction at the price of five hundred pesos per 110 acres (if lands were already being used for the production of coffee or other export crops, the price was only two hundred pesos per 110 acres). By 1880, similar policies of privatizing *baldíos* had been applied to the Verapaz departments and in some western highland regions.[47] Between 1871 and 1883, nearly a million acres of communal land were distributed as private plots, bringing roughly one-quarter million pesos into the state treasury.[48]

By setting prices for land acquisition out of reach of small producers, the 1873 decree and subsequent legislation had the clear intention of promoting large plantations. As Robert G. Williams states, "The requirement of making payments to the national government effectively excluded peasants from acquiring lands in the zones suitable for commercial agriculture."[49] McCreery arrives at a similar conclusion: "The price ensured the development of the [Costa Cuca] area in large fincas rather than small or medium-sized properties. Tracts that were already under cultivation at the time of the decree could be bought out by the processor at a reduced price, but . . . the Indians tended to be shut out. Their centuries-old corn plantings gave them no special claim, and few could afford the prices set by the state."[50]

The other major element of Barrios's land reform, the abolition of long-term leases of *ejidal* lands (known as *censo* lands), also worked to promote large plantations at the expense of small-scale producers.[51] In 1877, Barrios simply abolished the legal mechanism that sustained these lands and encouraged full privatization of select municipal territories. In theory, former leaseholders could purchase the lands they occupied. However, occupants were given only six months to make such a purchase, and the price of the lands was set at ten to fifteen times the annual rent they had previously paid. The result was that land prices were generally "greater than the resources of the typical Indian and of the majority of ladino cultivators."[52]

Despite its far-reaching consequences, Barrios's land reform was actually applied quite selectively, based on careful political considerations. Political officials working for Barrios, rather than private capitalists, were often the principal beneficiaries of land privatization. "A number of new family fortunes were founded solely on the basis of personal contacts with Barrios or his *jefes políticos*."[53] Peasants were sometimes granted land in exchange for militia service. Those who were selectively chosen for land grants could then be "called upon to support the Liberal government, hold municipal offices, and help suppress rebellions in neighboring Indian communities."[54]

Furthermore, Barrios did not move to privatize lands in areas where community resistance was most likely. The abolition of the *censo* lands was not decreed until 1877 because Barrios feared a mass uprising of the sort that had brought down Gálvez in 1838. And in densely populated highland regions, land privatization was cautiously and incompletely executed, in accordance with the degree to which Barrios felt he could maintain political stability. "Usually when villages complained that they had inadequate land for planting, Barrios received their petitions with respect, and he frequently granted villages land in areas unsuitable for coffee cultivation."[55] In fact, he not only recognized communities' rights to *ejidal* lands, but sometimes added land to the *ejidos* if villagers requested it.[56] Within certain municipalities, he went so far as to occasionally transfer lands claimed by large growers to small-producer communities. In part as a consequence of Barrios's political maneuvering, rebellions declined dramatically during the initial two decades of the liberal reform period. Specifically, revolts stemming from socioeconomic grievances were rare during Barrios's tenure.[57]

A key implication of Barrios's selectively implemented land reform was that Guatemala did not experience a wholesale transition to private property. Instead, the political needs of Barrios ensured that, whatever the laws he dictated may have said, the expansion of coffee "did not immediately threaten the survival of most communities."[58] In the western highlands and eastern departments, land was generally distributed in small parcels to peasants or left untouched in *ejidal* or communal form.[59] Even in the western piedmont region and Verapaz departments, where large private coffee plantations did come to dominate, the majority of land continued to be devoted to basic food products.[60]

The survival of common lands provided an outlet for peasants who sought to avoid serving as plantation laborers. Even for those individuals who lost their land to large plantations, the presence of an agricultural frontier allowed for reintegration into other subsistence-farming communities.[61] Within the communities themselves, there was little incentive for peasants to voluntarily work as plantation laborers, both because the communities had limited cash requirements and because plantation work required that peasants sacrifice independence and cultural integration to work under harsh conditions and face health hazards on the Pacific coastline plantations.[62] Hence, coffee planters had to look to the Barrios government to provide a reliable peasant base to serve as plantation laborers.

Labor Reforms in Guatemala

In line with a radical policy option, Barrios turned to extra-economic coercion to mobilize a rural labor force. In effect, he revived and extended old colonial systems of forced labor that had fallen dormant during the conservative period.[63] In November 1876, Barrios ordered his *jefes políticos* to reinstate the colonial practice of providing landed elites with labor drafts, known as *mandamientos*. The text of his circular stated simply, "From the Indian towns of your jurisdiction provide owners with the number of workers they need, be it fifty or a hundred, according to the importance of their operation."[64] In April 1877, the liberal government issued a general decree on agricultural labor that defined different categories of workers, spelled out employer and worker obligations, and systematized *mandamientos*. Among other things, this legislation subjected workers to serflike conditions by requiring that they carry a copy of their contract for inspection by *jefes políticos* or planters seeking to locate idle laborers and runaways.

During Barrios's presidency, the recruitment of forced labor through the *mandamiento* system was used, but increasingly it was secondary to the practice of debt peonage. A stipulation of the 1877 law gave employers the right to release from *mandamientos* all workers who were indebted to them. In effect, this provision allowed workers to avoid labor drafts by indebting themselves to a plantation owner, and it enabled planters to secure a reliable workforce by keeping their workers in debt. In some cases, peasants would voluntarily enter into debt contracts to escape the labor drafts. In other cases, employers might pay off the outstanding debts of peasants, thereby forcing them into debt peonage. In either case, Barrios's enactment of coercive *mandamientos* provided planters with workers primarily by offering inducements for the rural population to contract individual debt-labor obligations.

Even with these policies, however, planters of the Pacific piedmont routinely faced labor shortages during harvest time. A fierce competition developed among individual coffee planters and between planters and private labor contractors for control of seasonal workers from the highlands.[65] Abuses were common, and local government authorities and *jefes políticos* were often called upon to resolve conflicts between competing owners. There is evidence that these officials themselves were often deeply, and corruptly, involved in the trafficking of workers.[66] Conflicts were probably sometimes resolved through bribes, and it is known that authorities illegally sold workers that were designated for road duty or military service. Hence, as was true with land expropriation, it appears that access to labor was not equally available to all planters, but rather was often based on connections with political officials of the Barrios government.

As for disputes between workers and planters—over matters such as wages, working conditions, and contracts—liberal government authorities by no means sided universally with the planters.[67] If employers violated the codes on working conditions outlined in the 1877 labor law, they could be, and sometimes were, subjected to sanctions from the *jefes políticos*. Plantation owners in fact complained bitterly that government officials too often sided with Indians in disputes.

In short, although Barrios's labor reforms served coffee-planter interests, they also weakened the local power of such elites by making them permanently dependent on the state to recruit a seasonal workforce from the central highlands. The relationship between peasants and landlords became bitterly antagonistic, with the ever-present possibility that direct class conflict would break out, and landlords were forced to rely on the national government for security against lower-class revolts—even if it meant sacrificing additional control over the coffee economy to an increasingly militaristic state.

Zaldívar and State-Building Reforms

Many scholars of El Salvador have also equated the rise of liberals to power with the consolidation of state power by a coffee oligarchy.[68] Yet there is no evidence to suggest that a coffee elite had direct control over the state during the presidency of Rafael Zaldívar. Rather, Zaldívar—who was not a coffee planter—had an antagonistic relationship with many families of the elite, including those involved in coffee processing. Instead of an expression of coffee-elite hegemony, then, the Zaldívar administration might be best viewed as a personal dictatorship similar to that of Barrios in Guatemala.[69]

Whatever Zaldívar may have preferred ideologically, the political environment that he encountered in 1876 called for the enactment of state-strengthening reforms. His immediate problem involved stabilizing power in the face of a depleted state treasury and an indigenous population that was readily available for antigovernment mobilization by competing elites (including well-known liberals). To increase state revenues, Zaldívar had few available options. "Government income was limited to very few sources: customs duties, the liquor monopoly, stamped paper, the mails and telegraph service, and various other small items. There was no property or income tax, so that taxation was wholly and indirectly placed on the shoulders of the consumer. Among the tax sources available, the import trade was the most attractive; it was easy to control for revenue purposes, and its growth rate was greater than that of any other economic activity in the country except exports."[70] Despite the fact that taxes on imported goods often fell heavily on the wealthy classes, who sought expensive luxury goods from other countries, import tariffs were raised to higher levels during Zaldívar's administration, jumping to 50 percent in 1876 (from 20 percent in 1870) and reaching over 70 percent by 1880.[71] By the mid-1880s, import duties constituted roughly 60 percent of total government revenue, a percentage that was relatively constant well into the twentieth century.[72]

Much of this state revenue was employed in a manner fully consistent with the political needs of Zaldívar—namely, financing an institutionalized military, which laid the groundwork for enhanced security and greater state control of society. The formation of a permanent national army was ordered in October 1876, almost immediately after Zaldívar assumed power. An earlier attempt at organizing a permanent army had occurred under the liberal administration of Gerardo Barrios (1858–63), but this force had been defeated and completely destroyed by Guatemalan forces in 1863.[73] The 1876 decree called for the creation of a permanent army of 1,427 members and specified the number of troops, officers, and generals to be present in each of the country's departments.[74] The 1877 national budget allocated 381,000 pesos to the Ministry of War out of a total budget of 1,309,580 pesos, a figure that probably only partially measures total government expenditures on the military.[75] Throughout the period of Zaldivarismo, the state designated roughly 30 percent of total revenues for the Ministry of War, which, given expanding government revenue, led to an absolute increase in resources devoted to the military. Zaldívar also moved to regulate and expand the rural presence of the militia. An 1879 decree, which bears major similarities to Rufino Barrios's reform of the militia, ordered all men between the ages of eighteen and forty-five who did not meet certain exemption requirements to serve in the militia.[76]

Patricia Alvarenga has noted that before Zaldívar's reform, "the army's main function had been to participate in the conflicts between Central American nations and in the battles between dominant factions that vied for power. In both kinds of struggles, alliances with specific [indigenous] communities had been the only way to have access to a contingent of armed men."[77] Indian towns were especially convenient for mobilization by elite groups because they possessed a relatively cohesive corporate structure, allowing for the quick organization of a fighting contingent. For indigenous groups, participation in the army had traditionally served as a means to gain some leverage within the state and win representation at the level of national government. Zaldívar did away with this traditional system of military recruitment based on negotiation with indigenous groups. "For the first time the State could count on a national army that did not depend on alliances with corporate communities."[78] In fact, the military became a means of undermining the internal coherence of traditional community groups: "Incorporation into the army became a coercive mechanism that dismantled community identities. . . . The military apparatus strove to dissolve ethnic and group linkages between recruits."[79] Hence, if and when government leaders chose to implement reforms that ran counter to Indian interests, indigenous communities could no longer adequately defend themselves against the national state.[80]

Zaldívar was responsible for other key state-expanding reforms, such as the creation of the first national bank and land registry in El Salvador and the further strengthening of the state at the expense of the Church.[81] Nevertheless, he had only limited success at creating a cohesive national state that penetrated and controlled municipal governments. Zaldívar only partially established a patronage network that linked key departmental authorities to his dictatorship, and he failed to promote infrastructure developments and departmental restructuring of the type that enabled Barrios to assert state control throughout large portions of society. As a consequence, the national government was initially unable to directly implement Zaldívar's land reform policies, which helped produce a highly disorganized pattern of agrarian transformation in El Salvador.

Land and Labor Reforms in El Salvador

The centerpiece of the agrarian legislation initiated by the Zaldívar administration was the full-scale privatization of all *ejidal* and communal lands. These reforms are central to every major interpretation of nineteenth-century Salvadoran history, and even the most cautious analysts agree that their long-run consequences were enormous. The total amount of land held in *ejidal* or communal form at the time of the reforms will never be known, but the most reasonable estimates place it at about one-third of the area of the entire country and an even higher proportion of the arable land.[82] Whatever the exact total, the legislation amounted to one of the most extensive land reforms in Latin American history.

In February 1881, Zaldívar decreed that the communal land system was abolished, following experiments by municipal-level authorities to transform the function of the common land system.[83] Community leaders were instructed to distribute private titles to individual residents for the land they actively cultivated (in the event that cultivation by an individual could not be established, the land was to be divided into equal plots among community residents). The text of the decree justified the move on the grounds that the communal lands "impede the development of agriculture, obstruct the circulation of wealth, and weaken family ties and the independence of the individual."[84] A year later, in March 1882, the *ejidal* land system was abolished.[85] The government also explicitly justified this reform by arguing that the *ejidal* system was one of the "principal obstacles" to the development of agricultural industry. The 1882 decree required that residents apply for freehold titles from municipal authorities within six months and pay a fee for ownership that amounted to six times the annual rent they had previously paid for use of their *ejidal* plots. If residents failed to meet these requirements, they would lose rights to the land, and all unregistered or unclaimed lands would then be put up for public auction.

These privatization reforms have usually been interpreted as a means of transferring land from small-scale community producers to large-scale coffee producers.[86] The recent work of Aldo A. Lauria-Santiago, however, has shattered this interpretation and paved the way for a fundamentally different understanding of the reforms.[87] First, as we have already suggested, a wide spectrum of commercial farmers and rural and urban merchants constituted the main opposition to the common land systems, not a narrow bloc of coffee planters.[88] Diverse liberal actors saw the *ejidal* and common lands as wasteful and resented special privileges given to Indians, whom they viewed as unproductive and unfairly privileged by the state. Second, in El Salvador *ejidal* lands had become an impediment for many social groups, including many peasants. Thus, among small and medium-sized *ejidal* users the privatization reforms were sometimes welcomed as a positive step, perceived as a means to enhance personal security and overcome administrative barriers associated with the traditional land system.[89]

Third, land policy was implemented in a fashion that encouraged both large estates and small farms dedicated to commercial agriculture. Even if liberals were unconcerned with the personal well-being of Indian producers, they felt that small farmers had a role to play in advancing the nation as a whole. As Lauria-Santiago writes, "Liberal legislators and state administrators sought to create a layer of entrepreneurial farmers with secure access to land. . . . Enterprising peasants and farmers, it was hoped, in pursuit of their own interests, would promote the national interest as well—one defined clearly in agrarian and commercial terms."[90] Accordingly, the price of acquiring private title to land was within the means of most producers, and land records show that small producers usually did successfully gain title to their land.[91] In fact, authorities were often willing to grant *ejidal* owners extensions beyond the period for privatization stipulated in the legislation, and they sometimes allowed poor peasants to secure private title for less than the required amount.[92] Although large estates were nowhere discouraged, a preference for them was clear only with the privatization of unclaimed state lands (i.e., *baldíos*); the government routinely granted large tracts of such land in order to facilitate plantation ownership.[93]

It is essential to recognize that many smaller-scale *ejidal* producers perceived privatization favorably, for it would not have been politically feasible for Zaldívar to implement land reform legislation in the face of their outright opposition—even with the existence of an expanded coercive apparatus. Given the interests of *ejidal* holders, however, the privatization of these lands seemingly made perfect political sense: the reforms increased overall levels of production and won the support of wealthy elites without drawing significant opposition from small-scale community producers.

Residents of the communal lands were more likely than *ejidal* users to oppose privatization. The communal lands tended to be controlled by ethnic communities that had less interest in securing freehold titles and were more capable of carrying out active resistance. Resistance was especially common in the western coffee zone, where Indian communities invaded coffee estates, attacked agricultural administrators responsible for distributing lands, and occasionally led revolts.[94] In addition to economic issues, this resistance was fueled by an attempt to retain cultural integrity: "Indians believed that their lands were part of a social order inherited from the colony and legitimated by tradition; abolition of their communities was a challenge to their identity and corporate organization."[95] It is probable that part of the motivation behind land privatization for Zaldívar and other liberals was precisely to undermine Indian identity and tradition. In any case, the military reforms enacted by Zaldívar greatly enhanced the capacity of the state to privatize communal lands.[96]

Municipal governments and local officials were left in charge of the actual division and distribution of lands and kept all revenues from land sales. The result was a decentralized and highly convoluted process of land privatization that followed a distinct rhythm in different regions and brought about enormous confusion throughout the country. Privatization moved rapidly in some areas, but in other places the reforms had still not been fully implemented at the end of the nineteenth century.[97] The fact that an agrarian reform of this scope could be implemented at all reveals that the national state exercised a certain degree of local leverage throughout diverse regions of the country. National officials closely supervised the reform and actively worked to resolve disputes and prevent conflicts.[98] The state also was heavily engaged in direct promotional efforts to stimulate export production. After 1879, the government began supplying planters with free coffee trees and technical advice for growing the crop. Tens of thousands of trees were given to producers, sharply lowering the start-up costs for any landholder who wished to experiment with coffee production.[99]

Before 1880, a frequent complaint of growers was the *falta de brazos* (lack of workers). Although the government never imposed labor drafts to solve this problem, as occurred in Guatemala, state coercion played at least a moderately important role in Salvadoran labor policy. Zaldívar himself established a system of agricultural judges in all major townships to keep lists of plantation laborers, capture workers who failed to meet contractual obligations, and persecute vagrant workers. He also sent some peasants to labor on public works projects and private farms. These state-enforced systems of labor coercion were later abolished, but long-standing vagrancy laws and other legislation to regulate labor contracts and debts were increasingly enforced in the prime coffee regions, where labor shortages were most acute. In many areas, such as Santa Ana, seasonal labor from Guatemala and non-coffee-producing areas of El Salvador was used, and women often constituted a sizable portion of laborers. Myriad efforts were made to force individuals into labor contracts, but not until land concentration began to increase during the early twentieth century did nucleated villages of workers under the direct control of landlords emerge near the larger plantations.[100] At this point, landless peasants were often forced to participate in the coffee economy as permanent workers on large plantations:

> Through the use of force, squatting was held in check and the landless who did not move to less controlled areas became dependent on coffee growers for survival. . . . On larger plantations, nucleated villages of workers sprang up under the direct control of the landowner. Unlike colonos on the haciendas of the past, the workers in these nucleated villages were not allowed access to land to grow crops but were given rations by the grower and paid a money wage in return for labor year-round on the estate. Policemen were usually stationed in these settlements to keep order.[101]

Thus, although less extensive than in Guatemala, state coercion was one element of rural policy vis-à-vis workers in El Salvador.

STRUCTURAL CONSEQUENCES OF RADICAL LIBERAL POLICIES

In 1885, Rafael Zaldívar failed to cooperate with Justo Rufino Barrios in a renewed effort to establish a Central American union, leading the Guatemalan strongman to invade El Salvador. The war ultimately spelled the demise of both dictators. Barrios was killed on the battlefield, while the weakening of Salvadoran forces brought on by the war enabled a heterogeneous liberal alliance led by coffee planter Francisco Menéndez to overthrow Zaldívar.[102]

Although the fall of Barrios and Zaldívar marked the conclusion of full-blown liberalism in Guatemala and El Salvador, the basic transformative agenda enacted by these leaders remained intact. Subsequent liberal leaders continued to follow their general policy direction. The specific configuration of structural conditions that define radical liberalism can thus be understood as ultimately stemming from political choices made by Barrios and Zaldívar during full-blown liberalism.

State Militarization and Class Polarization

The implementation of radical policy options in Guatemala and El Salvador set in motion mutually constitutive processes of state militarization and class polarization: the polarization of class structures could not have occurred without the expansion of the military, and militarization of the state was driven in part by the presence of increasingly polarized class structures. It is fruitless to attempt to establish causal primacy between these two processes, for both were so interrelated and reciprocal that they are separable only at the level of analysis.

Increased state militarization in Guatemala occurred in a context in which coffee dominated the economy. Coffee exports had tripled during Barrios's period of rule, and by the early twentieth century Guatemala was among the world's leading coffee exporters (see fig. 5.1). Drawing on an 1890 census, Williams has shown that large plantations overwhelmingly dominated the coffee landscape, despite significant regional variation.[103] By the late nineteenth century, 52.7 percent of all coffee farms were already large-scale capitalist plantations. This figure reflects a predominance of large estates more extensive than in any other Central American country during the liberal reform period.

The sustained growth of coffee production in Guatemala was dependent on the ability of the state to regulate the coercive labor market and keep peasant protest in check.[104] Military officials were responsible for carrying out the day-to-day operations of the state, including overseeing the well-being of the coffee economy and the forced labor system. In 1890, state revenue devoted to the Ministry of War reached a peak of nearly 60 percent of the total budget; it has been estimated that by the early twentieth century, the Guatemalan army numbered six thousand men.[105] During his twenty-two-year dictatorship, Manuel Estrada Cabrera (1898–1920) filled top-ranking state offices and departmental governments with military officers, inflated the officer corps through mass promotions, granted special prerogatives to military bureaucrats, and allowed military officials "to engage in a series of abuses which secured a healthy income for the callous officers while at the same time effectively silencing political opposition."[106] In short, the domestic coffee economy was hardly a self-regulating market that operated independently of the state. Rather, one North American visitor in 1908 observed that so many

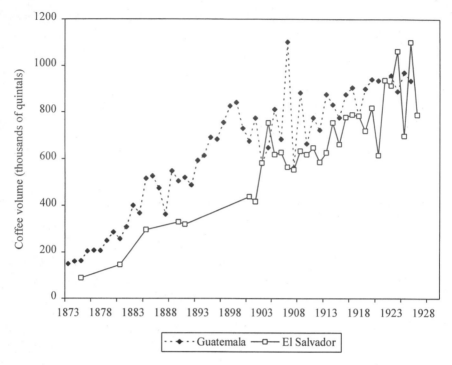

FIGURE 5.1   Coffee Exports of Guatemala (1873–1926) and El Salvador (1875–1927). *Source:* Robert G. Williams, *States and Social Evolution: Coffee and the Rise of National Governments in Central America* (Chapel Hill: University of North Carolina Press, 1994), 266–69; Héctor Lindo-Fuentes, *Weak Foundations: The Economy of El Salvador in the Nineteenth Century, 1821–1898* (Berkeley: University of California Press, 1990), 112–13.

soldiers were present in the countryside that Guatemala resembled a penal colony,[107] and another contemporary analyst described the country as a "military despotism" in which the "administration firmly maintains its authority through a large standing army and police force, and promptly and mercilessly checks the slightest manifestation of popular dissatisfaction."[108]

Just as the smooth operation of the coffee economy was dependent on the military, this institution was in turn dependent on profits from the coffee economy. For example, to finance a bloated military, Estrada Cabrera relied heavily on import taxes, which were ultimately a reflection of levels of coffee exportation.[109] Moreover, the government extended land grants to army officers to bolster the military's compliance, thereby using economic incentives available in the coffee economy to finance state militarization and troop loyalty. Furthermore, the coercive labor system itself became a major source of financial aggrandizement for military officers, who judiciously manipulated labor supplies for personal gain. State officials became so closely tied to coffee production that it was difficult for any president—including Estrada Cabrera—to diversify the economy or alter the basic coercive structures originally established by Rufino Barrios.

In the first decades of the twentieth century, however, some diversification did occur with the creation of foreign-controlled banana plantations along the isolated Caribbean coastal zone near Puerto Barrios.[110] United Fruit Company developed operations after contracting with President Estrada Cabrera to complete the construction of the Northern Railway linking Guatemala City with Puerto Barrios (a project that had been initiated by Barrios himself two decades earlier). Through a series of government concessions in which Estrada Cabrera offered land, financial support, and tax breaks in exchange for railroad construction, United Fruit gained control over the depressed eastern coastal region and began to export bananas. Although bananas accounted for a significant portion of total exports by 1920, the fruit never surpassed coffee as the principal export of the country. Moreover, banana production took place in isolation from the structural transformations occurring in the populous western countryside, and it had little effect on the development of the increasingly militarized state. Radical liberalism in Guatemala was thus driven by the locally controlled coffee economy, despite the presence of United Fruit Company and the banana industry in the east.

In El Salvador, the consolidation of radical liberalism also occurred in the context of a rapidly expanding coffee economy: coffee export volume quadrupled between 1875 and 1890; at the turn of the century, coffee constituted about 75 percent of all export revenue; and by the conclusion of the reform period in 1927, Salvadoran coffee exports roughly equaled those of Guatemala (see fig. 5.1).[111] In fact, because El Salvador lacked any banana enclave, the country was the most dependent on coffee in the region in the early twentieth century.

Historians are only now beginning to understand the drawn-out and often highly disorganized process through which *ejidal* and communal lands were divided into private plots during the reform period.[112] Zaldívar himself was forced to grant *ejidal* owners at least three extensions for purchasing their land,[113] and subsequent presidents do not appear to have been any more successful at rapidly abolishing the common land system. Lauria-Santiago has shown that the majority of *ejidal* users and communal occupants eventually gained title to lands and successfully converted themselves into private landowning peasants, albeit of diverse levels of wealth. Based on this evidence, he argues that "the privatization of *baldíos, ejidos,* and communal lands facilitated the development of commercial agriculture, but this did not mean that land was quickly concentrated in the hands of the export elite. On the contrary, privatization increased the number of property owners and created a large, differentiated class of landowning peasants and farmers. This contradicts the view that the land concentration of the late twentieth century was a direct inheritance from the colonial period or the late nineteenth-century liberal era."[114]

Like Lauria-Santiago's work, this analysis stresses the long-term importance of agrarian structures that had crystallized by the late 1920s, a time that corresponds with the conclusion of the liberal reform period as defined here. Yet, unlike Lauria-Santiago, this study locates the historical causes of those agrarian structures with the radical policy option initiated by liberals in the early 1880s. Specifically, based on evidence from other cases, we have every reason to believe that had land privatization been pursued more cautiously and selectively, such that large tracts of *ejidal* and communal land had been left intact, El Salvador would have emerged from the liberal reform period with a more equitable distribution of land and power in the countryside. Even simply protecting the *baldíos* from monopolization by speculators would have provided a safety valve for peasants and greatly attenuated land concentration. Hence, although privatization did not immediately place most peasants in a situation of great land scarcity, it clearly planted the seeds for severe class polarization in the future, whether or not liberals intentionally sought this outcome. Lauria-Santiago in fact presents much evidence consistent with this conclusion, arguing that the division of lands "froze peasants into differentiated layers, intensifying important differences among them and relegating poorer peasants to plots that would not guarantee their heirs a continued subsistence."[115] In sum, without the radical, full-scale privatization of all common lands—itself not an inevitable outcome independent of the political choices of liberals—El Salvador might not have developed a polarized agrarian class structure.

As in Guatemala, coffee landholding followed distinct patterns across different regions of El Salvador. In northern zones of the country, where conditions were least suitable for growing high-quality coffee, small-scale production was common. In the more eastern areas around

San Miguel and San Vicente, where indigo had been grown on a variety of different-sized farms, coffee production was characterized by a mixture of small, medium, and large estates. In some departments in the key western coffee-producing region, such as Santa Ana and Ahuachapán—where coffee production was under way before Zaldívar's legislation—small-scale production was an important component of overall output rates.[116]

Nevertheless, at the conclusion of the reform period, the general pattern for the nation as a whole was the dominance of the large plantation estate. At the time of the first coffee census in 1939, 37 percent of coffee farms were large capitalist *fincas* with more than one hundred *manzanas* (1 *manzana* equals 1.73 acres) of land.[117] And the census shows that a mere 263 large estate growers and 192 integrated producers (of a total of 11,545 growers) controlled 53.7 percent of all coffee lands.[118]

Even though large estates constituted a smaller portion of total coffee estates in El Salvador than in Guatemala, land concentration and class polarization were actually *more* developed in El Salvador by the 1920s. Three sets of considerations allow us to see why. First, unlike in Guatemala, El Salvador's land reform ultimately served to completely remove an agricultural frontier where land-poor peasants could retreat to avoid incorporation into the coffee economy. Peasant communities that, because of one circumstance or another, lost access to land had few options but to become part of an expanding pool of reserve laborers. Second, even though tiny El Salvador is less than one-fifth the size of Guatemala (8,100 square miles compared to 42,000 square miles), in 1920 El Salvador's population was nearly equal to that of Guatemala (1.17 million compared to 1.27 million), meaning that El Salvador's population density was almost five times greater than that of Guatemala.[119] This extremely high population density reinforced a nationwide scramble for land that began in the 1880s and brought on a degree of land concentration unparalleled in Central America.

Finally, class relations in El Salvador were more polarized because they directly pitted an agrarian proletariat with a high capacity for collective action against large coffee planters. Due to land concentration, large coffee growers in El Salvador did not, by the 1920s, have problems securing a reliable workforce.[120] Salvadoran growers simply allowed the market to regulate the supply of workers such that during harvests landless or land-poor peasants would show up at an estate seeking employment. Thus, in El Salvador, there was no need to link peasants to coffee estates as workers living in semifeudal bonds of dependence, as in Guatemala; the Salvadoran coffee economy developed a purer form of agrarian capitalism based almost entirely on free wage labor. Yet precisely because Salvadoran workers were not tied to estates in bonds of dependence in which coffee planters subjected workers to close and constant supervision, the possibility for class-based organization among peasants was much greater in El Salvador. Although both Guatemalan and Salvadoran plantation laborers became wage-based cultivators, a situation that produced a high potential for class conflict in both countries, Salvadoran laborers had a greater capacity to act on grievances than did their Guatemalan counterparts—for they were less subject to direct supervision by landlords and the state.[121]

The creation of this polarized coffee economy was made possible by, and worked to further expand, high levels of state militarization. The military grew at a moderate rate during the first decades of the liberal reform, reaching a peak in the late nineteenth century. In 1892 the army included roughly forty-five hundred members, spread throughout the country's sixteen departments, with a notable concentration of troops in the capital.[122] For the same year, the total number of militia reserve forces has been estimated to be sixty thousand men.[123] In general, however, "the military did not perform well when it was in charge of daily surveillance of the countryside. Training of the armed forces was directed toward preparing soldiers for battle, not toward pursuing offending peasants."[124] There were several attempts in the late nineteenth century to impose order in key coffee regions through rural police forces, but these efforts do not appear to have been successful.[125]

The key military innovation that established a more permanent presence in the lives of peasants and plantation workers was the creation of the National Guard in 1912, which dramatically expanded during the Meléndez-Quiñónez family dynasty (1913–27). In comparison with previous efforts to create a rural police force, the National Guard was significantly larger and better financed, and it was almost completely concentrated in the western coffee region.[126] The first Guard patrols were established in the western coffee departments, and by the 1920s posts had been set up across the country, with over four hundred Guardsmen stationed in important towns of the coffee region. The National Guard was intended to provide a national coercive apparatus to oversee order in the countryside. But it was also "on the front-line of state centralization" and played a crucial role in helping the powerful Meléndez-Quiñónez family maintain stable political rule. In particular, the National Guard became closely linked to patronage politics and helped "bring local elites into the fold of centralized politics."[127] From 1918 to 1923, when relations between President Jorge Meléndez and key military officers became strained, the national government also relied heavily on a paramilitary organization, the Liga Roja, to mobilize support and ensure stability at the local level. This division between the professional army and alternative security apparatuses, already present during the liberal reform period, would have important consequences for the way in which military authoritarianism was ultimately established in El Salvador in the mid-twentieth century.

Relations between the State and the Dominant Class

Finally, we turn to questions about the organization of national governments and coffee elites, and the relationship between the two. In addressing the functioning of national governments, it is useful to sketch in broad strokes an overall picture. We may begin by noting that national decision-making power throughout the reform period in Guatemala and El Salvador was concentrated in the presidency, and liberal personal dictators—at times involving family-based clans—invariably controlled this position.[128] Legislative and other high-level governmental positions outside of the presidency were no doubt coveted by elites, in part because these offices provided an outlet for wealth through corrupt abuse of official duties. Nevertheless, national legislatures functioned largely as rubber-stamp bodies to confirm the decisions made by chief executives. Furthermore, although the liberal ideological obsession with the formal procedures of a constitutional republic ensured that presidential and legislative officeholding technically involved elections (see table 5.1), these elections were controlled by the elite allies of the prevailing dictator, and they served merely to legitimize the acting president and to confirm his preferred selections for officeholders. The actual transfer of presidential office—when it entailed something more than a particular president simply handpicking a successor—grew out of factional struggles among liberal elites and often involved small-scale armed revolts (perhaps supported by a Central American neighbor). With the rise of a new president, legislators and top ministers were reshuffled to reflect the new liberal faction.

The politics of these dictatorships followed the classic patrimonial model in which maintenance of personal rule was the preeminent concern. Patronage—distributed in the form of officeholding, tolerance of official corruption, and financial payoffs—was a principal means through

TABLE 5.1   Liberal Presidents in Guatemala and El Salvador

President	Term of Office	Reason for Leaving Office	Coffee Investments
Guatemala			
García Granados, Miguel	1871–73	Election loss	
Barrios, Justo Rufino	1873–85	Killed in battle	P, B
Barillas, Manuel Lisandro	1885–92	Election loss	P, B
Reyna Barrios, José María	1892–98	Assassinated	
Estrada Cabrera, Manuel	1898–1920	Overthrown	
Orellano, José María	1921–26	Died in office	
El Salvador			
González, Santiago	1871–76	Defeated in external war	
Zaldívar, Rafael	1876–85	Overthrown	
Menéndez, Francisco	1885–90	Overthrown	P
Ezeta, Carlos	1890–94	Overthrown	
Gutiérrez, Rafael Antonio	1894–98	Overthrown	
Regalado, Tomás	1898–1903	Pressured election loss	P, B, X
Escalón, Pedro José	1903–7	Election loss	P, B, X
Figueroa, Fernando	1907–11	Pressured election loss	
Araujo, Manuel Enrique	1911–13	Assassinated	
Meléndez, Carlos	1913–14	End of official term	P, B
Quiñónez Molina, Alfonso	1914–15	End of official term	P, B, X
Meléndez, Carlos	1915–18	End of official term	P, B
Quiñónez Molina, Alfonso	1918–19	End of official term	P, B, X
Meléndez, Jorge	1919–23	End of official term	
Quiñónez Molina, Alfonso	1923–27	End of official term	P, B, X

Sources: Robert G. Williams, *States and Social Evolution: Coffee and the Rise of National Governments in Central America* (Chapel Hill: University of North Carolina Press, 1994), 212–14; Chester Lloyd Jones, *Guatemala: Past and Present* (Minneapolis: University of Minnesota Press, 1940), chap. 6; José F. Figeac, *Recordatorio histórico de la República de El Salvador* (San Salvador: Talleres Gráficos Cisneros, 1952); Phillip F. Flemion, *Historical Dictionary of El Salvador* (Metuchen, N.J.: Scarecrow Press, 1972); Mario Rodríguez, *Central America* (Englewood Cliffs, N.J: Prentice-Hall, 1965).

Note: I have excluded from this table provisional presidents and figurehead chief executives who served less than one year. These individuals are Alejandro Sinibaldi (1885) and Carlos Herrera (1920–21) in Guatemala; and Manuel Méndez (1872), Andrés Valle (1876), Angel Guirola (1884), Fernando Figueroa (1885), and José Rosales (1885) in El Salvador.

Key: P = coffee planter; B = *beneficio* owner; X = coffee exporter.

which dictators attempted to cultivate a support base and maintain loyalty among government and state employees. In addition, liberals also typically relied on coercion, including expatriation or execution for opposing elite actors implicated in antigovernment activities. The constant fear of being overthrown led presidents to elevate military and security branches within the state and to distribute patronage in significant amounts to army and security officers. At the same time, standard practices of patrimonial politics, such as encouraging divisions among army officers, were used against the military by all liberal presidents, with varying degrees of success.

The coffee elite of these countries can, following Jeffery Paige, be appropriately characterized as an agrarian bourgeoisie, a class marked by "a fundamental dualism—between its landed or *agrarian* and manufacturing or *agro-industrial* fractions."[129] The Salvadoran agro-industrial/commercial faction (i.e., the faction that derived wealth through the processing and marketing of coffee) was stronger than its Guatemalan counterpart, whereas the Salvadoran agrarian faction (i.e., the faction that derived wealth as large coffee planters and harvesters) was comparatively weaker. El Salvador's coffee elite tended to be less land-intensive and less controlling of labor but more technologically advanced and more efficient than the Guatemalan coffee elite.[130] Nevertheless, compared to the elites of other Central American countries, both the agrarian and the industrial factions of the coffee elite in Guatemala and El Salvador were quite powerful.

Liberal personal dictatorships in Guatemala and El Salvador did not represent an ideal governmental form for the expression of coffee-elite interests. For example, during the administration of Manuel Estrada Cabrera (1898–1920) in Guatemala, the politics of personalism ensured that state officials were often corrupt allies of Estrada Cabrera rather than the efficient, neutral bureaucrats that coffee planters may have preferred. Estrada Cabrera often simply ignored corruption by bureaucrats, even when it was at the expense of coffee elites. It was a common practice for departmental authorities—often military officers—to use labor drafts as a political "club" against coffee elites by forcing them to purchase labor allocations "at exorbitant prices from the profiteering bureaucrats."[131] Indeed, Estrada Cabrera did not hesitate to "undermine the economic base" of opponents among the coffee oligarchy by seizing their properties and redistributing them to political allies.[132] Similar remarks could be made about the Meléndez-Quiñónez dynasty (1913–1927) in El Salvador, where the personalistic rule of family dictators also isolated important segments of the coffee elite. Under the guidance of Carlos Meléndez, Jorge Meléndez, and Alfonso Quiñónez, El Salvador saw the development of a centralized patronage system in which political organizations preserved family rule in the face of opposition from elites linked to the coffee economy and their allies in the professional military.[133]

Throughout the liberal reform period, the presidency remained a personalistic office, and no president acted as an executive servant of coffee elites. Nevertheless, coffee elites in both Guatemala and El Salvador occupied the presidency for significant periods of time, and high-ranking state officials were often direct participants in the coffee economy. *Jefes políticos* and other departmental authorities sometimes secured coffee plantations or investments in coffee commerce as an extension of patronage from liberal dictators or by abusing their offices for personal gain.[134] Likewise, some high-ranking military officials were capable of transforming themselves into members of the coffee elite.[135] Even when not directly participating in the coffee economy, state officials were ultimately dependent on revenues derived (legally or illegally) from coffee profits, linking them to coffee planters and processors. These forms of political leverage by the coffee elite acted as powerful constraints on the ability of future presidents to implement reforms that directly challenged dominant-class interests.

CONCLUSION

Histories of Guatemala and El Salvador often portray the liberal reform period as a time when elite coffee planters seized control of government and enacted reforms designed to promote large plantations and secure a labor force by creating a vast class of landless peasants. Yet we have seen that such accounts too easily reduce the logic of the liberal reform to the socioeconomic interests of an assumed coffee elite. As a corrective, this chapter analyzed the liberal reform period from the perspective of the dictatorships that headed the reform effort, and it treated these dictatorships on their own terms—that is, as governmental organs dominated by individuals representing a narrow political faction rather than actual or incipient coffee interests.

By treating liberal governments in this fashion, we have learned that the power considerations of ruling dictators often drove policy choices. Given the political dilemmas faced by leaders such as Barrios and Zaldívar, and given existing structural conditions inherited from the conservative era, liberalism in these countries followed a radical course in which a penetrating assault on preexisting land structures was carried out. Yet neither Guatemala nor El Salvador witnessed the immediate and complete marginalization of the peasantry that some histories imply. In Guatemala, substantial amounts of *ejidal* and *baldío* land remained intact throughout the reform period because more extensive privatization would have threatened the political stability of Barrios and subsequent liberal dictators. Likewise, in El Salvador, liberal governments starting with Zaldívar made significant efforts to grant smallholders access to private titles and win their support as national and municipal lands were divided into farms of diverse sizes.

This revised understanding has repeatedly underscored that state-building was a crucial goal of liberals *independently* of commercial agricultural modernization. The earliest reforms of Barrios and Zaldívar, and arguably their most important, entailed military modernization and army-building. These activities were carried out primarily to ensure the political survival of Barrios and Zaldívar, and they were reinforced by subsequent liberals for similar reasons. State-building reforms had crucial supplementary effects, including, most notably, enhancing government capacity to pursue commercial agriculture. However, whereas many analysts have assumed that commercial agriculture drove processes of state-building in a unidirectional manner, we have emphasized the reverse relationship: state-building was often an essential *prerequisite* for agrarian transformation. This focus has called attention to changes in the Guatemalan and Salvadoran state apparatuses, which were as important as the more commonly acknowledged changes in class and agrarian structures. The force of this point will become fully apparent when we explore the prominent role of the military in the politics of Guatemala and El Salvador after the liberal reform period.

CHAPTER 6

Reformist Liberalism: Costa Rica

In Costa Rica, the absence of preexisting commercial agriculture and the weakness of the national state made it politically logical for reformers to attempt a less ambitious, more gradual transformative program than in Guatemala and El Salvador. This program ultimately took the shape of a *reform* policy option, in which small farms were gradually extended across the country and in which the state played a supportive—but noncoercive—role in solving land and labor problems for producers of coffee and other export crops. The implementation of this policy option was an extraordinarily drawn-out process during the nineteenth century, beginning gradually at both local and national levels and, at the national level, seeing two phases of full-blown liberalism—during the administrations of Braulio Carrillo (1838–42) and Tomás Guardia (1870–82).

Although less extensive in transformative scope than the radical policy options pursued in Guatemala and El Salvador, the reform policy option that was successfully implemented in Costa Rica led to the establishment of new structural conditions every bit as consequential for future national political development. In some ways, in fact, Costa Rica's pattern of reformist liberalism paralleled Guatemala's and El Salvador's pattern of radical liberalism. Like these other countries, Costa Rica witnessed a transition to agrarian capitalism through land privatization and massive coffee-export expansion. Similarly, beginning under the administration of Braulio Carrillo and coming to a head during the rule of Tomás Guardia, the liberal reform period saw a centralization of the state and the emergence of an agrarian bourgeoisie in the coffee sector that enjoyed significant political leverage within this strengthened state. Yet in other crucial respects, Costa Rica diverged from Guatemala and El Salvador. Most important, Costa Rica's reformist liberalism led to neither the creation of a powerful military-coercive branch that commanded a prominent position in the state nor a rural economy marked by polarized class structures and a high potential for lower-class agrarian revolts.

Given the sheer length of the liberal period in Costa Rica, it is useful to distinguish two phases of reform. The first phase (1821–70) corresponds with the emergence of a coffee economy, the administration of Braulio Carrillo, and the development of a distinctly limited role for the military. The second phase (1870–1914) corresponds with the state-building administration of Tomás Guardia and the creation of a competitive political system.

THE FIRST PHASE OF LIBERALISM: SMALLHOLDERS, THE MILITARY, AND THE COFFEE ECONOMY

Liberals in Costa Rica carried out a moderately paced program of agrarian development and state-building. Through a series of land provisions, small farms were initially established near the major townships of the Meseta Central and then peacefully extended to more-remote regions as population growth and rising land prices forced peasants to seek out opportunities on the agricultural frontier. In due course, liberals also pursued bureaucratic and administrative expansion, but without radically militarizing the state. By the late nineteenth century, Costa Rica had traveled well down a path that would culminate in the establishment of an enduring democratic regime.

The Emergence of a Coffee Economy

In 1821, at the beginning of the liberal reform, the small population of Costa Rica (less than 70,000)[1] was concentrated in and around the Meseta Central, and it was here that the lands most suitable for the production of high-quality coffee were located. At this time, lands were not usually privately owned but rather held as vast tracts of underutilized public territory in frontier areas *(terrenos baldíos* and *tierras públicas)* or rented to users by local governments when the lands directly surrounded towns *(tierras de legua)*. In addition, many indigenous communities continued to control communal land.

Almost immediately after independence, the municipal governments of the Meseta Central, led by the liberal-dominated *ayuntamiento* of San José, began to encourage coffee and other export crop production. In the early 1820s, the San José government launched programs offering potential export growers idle *baldíos* at no cost and other public lands at low cost, as well as distributing free coffee seedlings and investigating which lands were most appropriate for coffee production. The other municipalities of Heredia, Alajuela, and Cartago soon followed suit in these activities.[2] In the 1820s and early 1830s, national-level legislation was put into place to reinforce and expand these local efforts, reflecting "the appearance of an economic liberalism" in the incipient Costa Rican state.[3] In 1825 the national government removed the tithe on coffee and other potential export crops; in 1828 it awarded up to 110 acres of extra land to growers who managed to establish permanent crops on underutilized lands; and in 1832 it passed legislation offering direct subsidies for successful coffee growers.[4]

By the late 1830s, the commercialization of agriculture was well under way in the Meseta Central. From 1822 until 1839, roughly seventy thousand hectares of *baldíos* had been distributed as private property (for the entire period of 1584–1821, only about ninety thousand hectares of these lands had been distributed).[5] Records of Costa Rican exports in 1833 show that coffee was already being exported in modest quantities to cities such as Valparaiso, Liverpool, and New York.[6] By the 1840s, coffee represented roughly 80 percent of all exports from Costa Rica.[7] The department of San José dominated production within the country and probably accounted for nearly all exports, although coffee was produced in the other municipalities of the Meseta Central, often for local consumption.[8]

In these initial efforts to stimulate commercial agriculture, government leaders (both locally and nationally) sought to encourage the use of land by small producers, rather than privilege the development of large-scale estates. From the outset, land privatization in Costa Rica "gave preference to those who already occupied a particular plot of land."[9] For example, Silvia Castro Sánchez shows that government prices for private land ownership were generally set within the means of occupants, and Robert G. Williams notes that authorities took steps to make the bureaucratic process of receiving freehold title to land as accommodating to residents as possible.[10] Early records of land ownership clearly reveal the importance of the smallholding estate in the emerging coffee economy. For example, Carolyn Hall's data show that in the 1840s, only 11 of 89 documented coffee estates in the Meseta Central controlled more than 50 *manzanas* (1 *manzana* equals 1.73 acres). And the estate on which the most coffee trees were planted (70,000 trees) was itself not particularly large in land area, covering less than 60 *manzanas*.[11] Likewise, Iván Molina Jiménez's data on the 1830–50 period in San José reveal that coffee *fincas* occupying 50 or more *manzanas* constituted only 6 percent of all estates and those over 100 *manzanas* only 1 percent, whereas a full 70 percent of estates were small farms of less than 10 *manzanas*.[12]

Even though small farms dominated, prime coffee lands immediately surrounding San José, Heredia, Alajuela, and Cartago became increasingly scarce by the mid-nineteenth century, and land prices in these areas reached the point where even modest farms were valuable.[13] With the subdivision of lands through inheritance, and with high land prices, peasants were increasingly unable to secure sufficient land in the Meseta Central. In this sense, the Meseta Central resembled El Salvador, where smallholding eventually locked peasants into plots that could not provide intergenerational security. In addition, by the 1840s, wealthy speculators and other "land-grabbers" in Costa Rica were seeking to purchase peasant lands and establish large plantations like those that developed in El Salvador.[14]

However, capitalist entrepreneurs were not successful at buying up peasant farms and converting them into large estates in Costa Rica.[15] Small farms remained intact in the Meseta Central throughout the liberal reform period. The main reason is that the national government provided a safety valve for settlers who sought to migrate to outlying areas.[16] In the mid-nineteenth century, the government actively encouraged peasants to migrate to frontier areas and convert *baldíos* into small private farms. After 1839, it simplified the procedures for acquiring these lands and made them widely available at little or no cost to occupants.[17] In 1848, a national decree extended the practices used to form smallholdings in the Meseta Central to other regions, and additional legislation was soon initiated that lowered costs for *tierras de leguas* in the Meseta Central itself. In order to prevent speculators from monopolizing the *baldíos*—as occurred in El Salvador—the government limited the amount of land that could be sold to any individual.[18]

Small estates proliferated west of Alajuela as privatization reforms encouraged new settlements in the area. As late as the 1930s, 68 percent of the coffee trees in the Alajuela province were held by family-sized peasant producers, whereas only 10 percent of trees were owned by large capitalist operations.[19] To the east in the Cartago province, larger estates were developed, but this region was not an important coffee-producing area. As for communal lands controlled by indigenous communities, these territories remained largely intact until the last decades of the nineteenth century. Although several decrees and laws provided for their parceling out, in practice the expropriation of "the communal lands of the various Indian groups was not a very important or characteristic feature of Costa Rica during the last century."[20] In short, the smallholding estate prevailed in all major coffee regions. Generalizing for the entire period from 1840 to 1935, Ciro F. S. Cardoso writes that "there was an absolute predominance of small farms, in terms both of numbers and of the total area of land occupied."[21]

This smallholder economy was associated with a distinct dominant class. Unlike the coffee oligarchy of late-nineteenth-century Guatemala, whose wealth and power were based on estate ownership, "landowning per se was not [the Costa Rican elite's] defining characteristic or basis for power."[22] Instead, the Costa Rican dominant class was a coffee elite by virtue of its control over the commercial aspects of coffee production, specifically the financing, processing, and marketing of the crop. As Jeffery M. Paige argues, "the Costa Rican elite emerged as an elite of processors and exporters rather than growers. The agrarian fraction of the elite was therefore weaker in Costa Rica than anywhere else in Central America, with the possible exception of Nicaragua."[23]

It is of course true that the wealthier members of Costa Rican society were better positioned to take advantage of land privatization. Costa Rica's merchant elite acquired some large landholdings,[24] and some concentration of wealth accompanied the transition to commercial agriculture, especially in San José.[25] However, "in any comparative context, early Costa Rican land-tenure patterns with coffee were little concentrated."[26] The Costa Rican countryside simply did not display highly polarized class structures in which an entrenched landed elite was pitted against a semifeudal plantation-based peasantry (as emerged in Guatemala) or in which an agrarian-commercial elite was faced with an increasingly land-starved rural proletariat (as emerged in El Salvador). Instead, the Costa Rican countryside featured comparatively harmonious agrarian relations built around small farmers who carried out their day-to-day affairs in relative isolation from any visibly exploitative coffee elite.

Carrillo and the Costa Rican Military

The meager financial resources of the state and the absence of a landlord class made the initial adoption of a reform policy option—as opposed to a radical policy option—extremely likely in Costa Rica. This likelihood was reinforced by the lack of a significant indigenous population from which to draft a plantation labor force. Nevertheless, by the mid-nineteenth century, coffee had expanded to the point where liberals could have moved in the direction of a radical policy option, including through activities such as encouraging the spread of large plantations in the Meseta Central and closing off the agrarian frontier to landless and land-poor peasants. But these radicalizing activities did not happen in Costa Rica. To see why, we need to explore the Carrillo dictatorship (1838–42), which helped lock in a reform policy option through state-building and especially military-building measures.

Braulio Carrillo enjoys a reputation as the "architect of the state" in Costa Rica because his administration expanded bureaucratic operations and stabilized policy inclinations toward the promotion of export agriculture.[27] Most of his reforms were fairly standard liberal measures designed to enhance governmental authority within society.[28] Thus, through the Law of Foundations and Guarantees, promulgated in March 1841, Carrillo restructured territorial departments, outlined a new hierarchy of roles for government authorities, and, in effect, established a centralized, vertically integrated state bureaucracy in which he occupied the ultimate power position as lifelong dictator.[29] This legislation, along with the codification of civil and criminal laws, laid the groundwork for a state capable of performing the "nightwatchman" duties necessary for capitalist development—for example, guaranteeing the protection of persons and property and the enforcement of contracts.[30] Furthermore, Carrillo reformed public monopolies controlling products such as alcohol and tobacco, which increased overall state revenues in the late 1830s and early 1840s.[31]

Carrillo's military reforms were crucial to long-term political development in Costa Rica because they modernized security forces without massively militarizing the state. In 1841, the government enacted laws that expanded the policing powers of the departmental *jefes políticos,* augmented the size of rural police forces, reformed the national militia, and established the first coherent urban police force in San José.[32] However, the Carrillo government did not create a permanent, professional army to oversee order in the countryside and promote regime stability. In fact, in areas outside of San José, where elites were more likely to oppose his administration, Carrillo actually dissolved existing military forces. Only a small portion of the national budget was military-related, and the (nonprofessional) army remained quite small throughout the mid-nineteenth century (surely fewer than 500 men).[33] Hence, while Carrillo did carry out some important military reforms, these efforts added up to only the "embryonic" development of the Costa Rican military;[34] and they paled in comparison with the military reforms of liberal governments in Guatemala and El Salvador, where huge standing armies with many hundreds of troops were developed.

Carrillo's moderation in military expansion was not an inevitable outgrowth of the smallholder agrarian economy. In Guatemala and El Salvador, small farms were also common at the beginning of the reform period, yet state centralization was accompanied by extensive militarization. A better explanation for Carrillo's policies highlights the relatively limited political threats facing his administration. Carrillo relied heavily on the support of the wealthy San José merchant elite in staging the 1838 coup that overthrew Manuel Aguilar Chacon. Once Carrillo returned to office, however, his main concern was with maintaining personal power; and his dictatorial style was legendary, to the point that various elites opposed his rule.[35] Nevertheless, he was not confronted with powerful domestic actors who outright rejected a liberal program of development. In mid-nineteenth-century Costa Rica, there was no reactionary coalition of conservative merchants and priests; Carrillo's political enemies were liberals themselves who opposed the dictator because of personal disputes or regionally based antagonisms.[36] Furthermore, in Costa Rica, the absence of significant indigenous communities meant that opposition elites lacked the manpower base customarily used to build resistance movements in other Central American countries. Because Carrillo did not face opposition armies that mobilized large numbers of followers, a huge standing army was not necessary to protect his rule. Rather, he had little political incentive to promote extensive militarization, especially since such a move might have played into the hands of high-ranking generals not loyal to his administration.

Lacking a significant military apparatus, the Carrillo administration was not positioned to oversee the rapid privatization of common lands or policies that promoted coercive labor. Instead, the government continued to gradually extend private landholdings to small farmers, and the state never experimented with forced labor policies, despite massive labor shortages in the Meseta Central.[37] An agricultural system developed in which networks of household members, relatives, and neighbors provided most of the labor on small farms. Some outside wage labor was used on both small farms and larger estates during harvest season, but congenial relations prevailed between workers and employers, with workers being treated as "hired help" not easily replaceable in the competitive labor market.[38] In this agrarian context, "the Costa Rican military appears to have made no positive contribution to the coffee economy."[39]

Nevertheless, despite its small size and limited presence in society, the military did have an important destabilizing role to play in elite politics of the mid-nineteenth century. From the fall of Carrillo in 1842 until the rise of Tomás Guardia in 1870, the national government was controlled by a series of civilian dictators who represented major families of the merchant-based coffee elite and who were often destabilized or overthrown by military officers.[40] Table 6.1 illustrates three key features of this political system: individuals with coffee investments almost continuously occupied the presidency; these presidents were formally brought to power through restricted elections[41] or at least had their presidency "confirmed" by such elections; and military intervention on behalf of civilian factions or families to overthrow a reigning president was the most common means of executive transfer. There is debate about the relationship between the military and the coffee elite during this time. Some scholars suggest that the military was an obstacle to dominant-class interests because it fostered political instability and curtailed economic growth.[42] By contrast, others argue that the military was little more than a tool used by dominant classes to further their political interests.[43] In fact, both views are misleading, because they assume that there was a real differentiation between the dominant class and the military. In truth, top-ranking generals and officers were themselves often members of particular factions within this class.[44] Hence, while the small Costa Rican military could be conceived alternately as an economic obstacle for the dominant class as a whole or as a political tool for particular factions within the dominant class, it makes more sense to see the military, and especially its leadership, as simply one component of the divisive politics that characterized the Costa Rican dominant class in the mid-nineteenth century.

The Absence of Foreign Investment

One additional factor necessary for the success of Costa Rica's transition to commercial agriculture needs to be briefly examined: the absence of foreign investment in the economy. To understand the importance of this factor, we must consider the role of precious metals in stimulating coffee production in the early nineteenth century.

Even before the emergence of coffee as an export crop, some capital was accumulated through the extraction of precious metals from the mines of Monte del Aguacate, which had been discovered in 1815.[45] According to Carlos Araya Pochet, profits from mining operations were

TABLE 6.1 Coffee Investments and Mode of Office Transfer for Costa Rican Presidents, 1824–1917

President	Term of Office	Mode of Acquiring Office	Mode of Leaving Office	Coffee Investments
First phase of liberalism				
Mora Fernández, Juan	1824–33	Noncompetive election	End of term	—
Gallegos, José Rafael	1833–35	Elected indirectly by Congress	Resignation	P
Carrillo, Braulio	1835–37	Noncompetitive election	Election loss	P
Aguilar, Manuel	1837	Elected indirectly by provinces	Military coup	P, X
Carrillo, Braulio	1838–42	Coup	Overthrown	P
Morazán, Francisco Maria	1842	Revolt	Overthrown	—
Alfaro, José María	1842–44	Noncompetitive election	End of term	X, B
Oreamuno, Francisco María	1844	Noncompetitive election	Resignation	P
Moya Murillo, Rafael	1844–45	Provisional president	Resignation	P
Gallegos, José Rafael	1845–46	Provisional president	Coup	P
Alfaro, José Maria	1846–47	Elected indirectly by Congress	End of term	X, B
Castro Madriz, José María	1847–49	Noncompetitive election	Resignation	P, X
Mora Porras, Juan Rafael	1849–59	Revolt	Overthrown	P, B, X
Montealegre, José María	1859–63	Revolt	End of term	P, B, X

Jiménez, Jesús	1863–66	Noncompetitive election	End of term	—
Castro Madriz, José María	1866–68	Noncompetitive election	Military pressure	P, X
Jiménez, Jesús	1868–70	Military pressure	Coup	—
Caranza, Bruno	1870	Coup	Military pressure	P
Second phase of liberalism				
Guardia, Tomás	1870–82	Military pressure	Dies in office	X
Fernández, Próspero	1882–85	Noncompetitive election	Dies in office	P, X
Soto, Bernardo	1885–89	Noncompetitive election	Revolt	—
Rodríguez, José Joaquín	1890–94	Semicompetitive election	End of term	—
Yglesias, Rafael	1894–1902	Noncompetitive election	End of term	—
Esquivel, Ascensión	1902–6	Semicompetitive election	End of term	X
González Víquez, Cleto	1906–10	Noncompetitive election	End of term	P
Jiménez Oreamuno, Ricardo	1910–14	Competitive election	End of term	X, B
González Flores, Alfredo	1914–17	Semicompetitive election	Coup	P

Sources: James L. Busey, "The Presidents of Costa Rica," *The Americas* 18 (July 1961): 64–68; Robert G. Williams, *States and Social Evolution: Coffee and the Rise of National Governments in Central America* (Chapel Hill: University of North Carolina Press, 1994), 217.

Note: I have excluded some minor provisional presidents and most figurehead executives.

Key: P = coffee planter; B = *beneficio* owner; X = coffee exporter.

"indispensable for the development of the Costa Rican economy," and they played a crucial role in "the consolidation of a dominant class" capable of spearheading coffee investment.[46] In sharp contrast, however, José Luis Vega Carballo suggests that levels of gold and silver production from these mines were always low, and he argues that the economic *failure* of Costa Rica's mining industry in fact contributed to coffee expansion by forcing elites to invest their money and entrepreneurship in more profitable sectors.[47]

Leaving aside the issue of who is correct in this debate,[48] both scholars agree that a lack of foreign investment in the mining sector was crucial to the expansion of coffee in Costa Rica. For Araya, the absence of investment (despite calls for it by local authorities) enabled profits to remain in domestic hands and thereby be reinvested in a domestically controlled coffee industry.[49] For Vega, the absence of significant investment kept the mining industry in a relatively impoverished state, forcing domestic elites to seek profits in other sectors such as coffee.[50] Either way, the implication is that if foreign capital had taken control of the mining sector, the development of the coffee industry in Costa Rica would have been delayed and would have occurred in quite a different manner.

Yet no such foreign investment occurred in Costa Rica because international conditions were not conducive to economic imperialism in the Central American region during the first half of the nineteenth century. At this time, the world's leading capitalist power and Central America's main trading partner—England—was not predisposed to pursue large-scale capital investment in the region. As Robert Naylor has emphasized, from 1821 to 1851 the British government did almost nothing "to secure for British merchants a share of the newly-opened commerce of Central America." He stresses the "reluctance of British private enterprise to enter the Central American field," arguing that "with few exceptions, British investors were content to enjoy whatever trade resulted from their association with Central America without risking any direct investment in the area."[51] Likewise, Tulio Halperín Donghi has pointed out that no European power, much less the United States, had the surplus capital necessary to risk significant investment in Latin America during the first half of the nineteenth century.[52]

Given that significant foreign investment in the mining industries of Central America did eventually occur, in the late nineteenth century, it seems reasonable to conclude that the early world-historical timing of the Costa Rican liberal reform was crucial in preventing large-scale foreign investment. Without disruptions from large influxes of foreign investment, the liberal reform period was allowed to unfold in a gradual fashion during the mid-nineteenth century. Only much later, during the second phase of liberalism in Costa Rica, when world-historical conditions favored economic intervention, did foreign capital investment—especially in the banana industry—begin to play a large role in the Costa Rican economy. By this stage, however, the prosperous coffee sector was firmly controlled by domestic actors, such that not even massive investment could undermine the work already completed by liberals.

THE SECOND PHASE OF LIBERALISM: GUARDIA AND THE BIRTH OF COMPETITIVE POLITICS

Beginning in 1870, Costa Rica entered a second phase of liberalism when Tomás Guardia seized the presidency and initiated major state-building reforms. Under Guardia's rule, the state's autonomy from dominant classes was established through professionalization of the military, which put an end to a previous pattern in which competing elite families appealed to allies in the top ranks of the army to destabilize rival governments and win access to the presidency. By the conclusion of the reform period in 1914, the commercial elite had regained much of its political preeminence, but in a very different setting than before—namely, within the confines of a semicompetitive political system. As we shall see, the advent of competitive politics carried its own contradictions, with substantial implications for future political development.

Military Professionalization under Guardia

The Guardia administration (1870–82) ranks among the most famous governments in Costa Rica because of its implementation of a broad range of liberal reforms, including anti-ecclesiastical legislation, infrastructure development, and state centralization and bureaucratization.[53] For our purposes, however, Guardia's most important accomplishments rest with the establishment of the state's autonomy and the separation of the military from dominant-class authority.[54] To understand how Guardia achieved these tasks, we need to examine the politics surrounding his rise to power in 1870.

In the late 1860s, Jesús Jiménez, a representative of an elite faction based in Cartago, was president of Costa Rica.[55] During his rule a variety of actors were strongly opposed to him, among them several families from the San José coffee elite. Because military coups played an essential role in most presidential transfers, Jiménez went to some lengths to re-structure the military leadership—including removing the two most influential generals in Costa Rica, both of whom were allied with the op-position Montealegre family.[56] As a consequence, when the Monteale-gres sought to overthrow Jiménez, they could not rely on their traditional allies in the military and were forced to call on an independent-minded general, Tomás Guardia, to work on their behalf. Drawing on his sub-stantial support among the officer corps, Guardia led a successful coup on April 27, 1870. Once Jiménez was removed, however, Guardia re-fused to permit any member of the Montealegre family to take the pres-idency.[57] Moreover, after it was agreed that Bruno Carranza would serve as president, Guardia quickly used his position in the military to force the resignation of Carranza and proceeded to make himself president of Costa Rica—the first major military leader who served as chief executive in Costa Rican history.

The Montealegres or some other elite coffee family might have initi-ated a countercoup to oust Guardia, but the dictator proved quite skill-ful at consolidating a power base independent of the dominant classes. In this regard, the professionalization of the military—something per-haps only a popular general such as Guardia could have achieved—was especially crucial. With the help of Lorenzo Montúfar, his minister of war (and later a famous Guatemalan liberal historian),[58] Guardia used in-creased military spending to fight corruption and boost morale among officers as well as to expand the size of militia forces available for fight-ing external wars.[59] Whereas in the years before 1870 only 10 to 15 per-cent of the national budget was devoted to the Department of War, the figure averaged more than 20 percent during the Guardia administra-tion.[60] Most important, the military was "depoliticized" and reorga-nized as a professional fighting force designed to defend Costa Rica from external threats (especially Guatemala). In effect, by establishing new military codes, employing elite Prussian officers to train troops, regular-izing and increasing salaries, developing new training facilities and mili-tary schools, and restructuring the military leadership, Guardia suc-ceeded in transforming the military from a political extension of the dominant class into an autonomous, professional organization.[61]

Guardia's military reforms were a key ingredient in his ability to rule as a personal dictator from 1870 until his death (by natural causes) in 1882. In turn, prolonged political stability facilitated the creation of an expanded public revenue base and a more bureaucratic state that more thoroughly penetrated society.[62] Simple statistics tell part of the story. Whereas from 1866 to 1870 state revenues held steady at about one million pesos annually, by the end of the Guardia period the figure had tripled, to around three million pesos.[63] "At the same time that revenues multiplied, the number of public employees increased. In 1875 there were a total of 1,683 employees, in 1881 they climbed to 2,118, and they increased to 2,310 the following year."[64] Furthermore, in 1881 Guardia reformed the central ministries, increasing staff sizes and expanding the duties of the secretariat. And his administration did more than any previous one in carrying out infrastructure projects, ranging from constructing ports and highways to paving city streets, installing running water and street lighting, and erecting municipal buildings for city halls, jails, schools, and military barracks.[65]

Education Reform and the Advent of Competitive Politics

Differentiation between the national state and the commercial coffee elite was pushed further under the dictatorships of General Próspero Fernández (1882–85) and General Bernardo Soto (1885–89). Guardia's efforts to professionalize and depoliticize the military had already succeeded, enabling these generals to moderate defense spending without provoking a coup. And reduced defense spending worked to further constrain the ability of the military to intervene in national politics. According to Orlando Salazar Mora, "the most important achievement of this period [1882–89] was the diminution and near liquidation of military intervention in politics."[66] Following the education reform of 1885, much of the capital left over from the reduced military budget was used to support public education.[67] As figure 6.1 illustrates, state spending on education increased dramatically in the mid-1880s, in close proportion to decreases in military spending. By the conclusion of the reform period in 1914, education and military spending were about even, at 15 percent of the national budget. From a comparative perspective, Costa Rica's commitment to education appears quite striking. In El Salvador, for example, at most 5 percent of the national budget was devoted to education during the nineteenth century.[68] And whereas literacy in Guatemala during the early twentieth century was less than 20 percent, in Costa Rica literacy increased from 11 percent in 1864 to 31 percent in 1892, and then to 76 percent in 1927.[69]

Government leaders had an interest in promoting education to the degree that it facilitated nation-building and a deeper penetration of so-

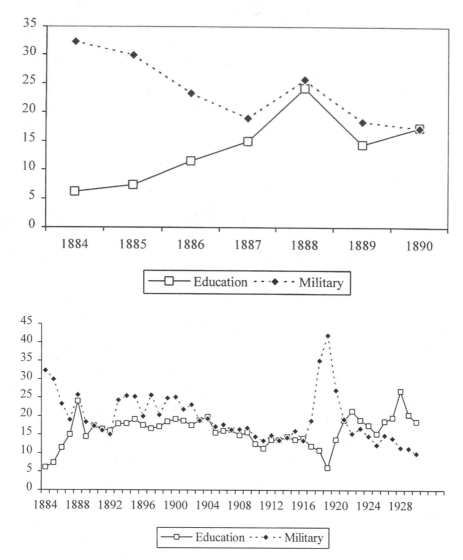

FIGURE 6.1 Education and Military Spending as a Percentage of the National Budget in Costa Rica, 1884–1890 and 1884–1930. *Source:* Astrid Fischel, *Consenso y represión: Una interpretación socio-política de la educación costarricense* (San José: Editorial Costa Rica, 1990), table 1.

ciety by the state.[70] One might therefore see the promotion of education as a policy choice that was imposed on a reluctant dominant class by presidents or bureaucratic policymakers who enjoyed substantial insulation from society. Yet evidence suggests that much of the Costa Rican elite itself supported (or was at least indifferent to) the 1885 reform and the public spending provisions it entailed. This reaction was likely a product of Costa Rica's nonpolarized agrarian economy. Specifically, the relatively nonconfrontational relations that existed between commercial elites and small-farmer producers may have permitted upper-class toleration of education programs that benefited a broad spectrum of society. In Costa Rica, even the elite could view education as a means of producing a better national "citizenry."

Yet if Costa Rica's nonpolarized agrarian economy permitted elite acceptance of spending on teachers and schools, the absence of a clear lower-class threat also worked against dominant-class cohesion and accentuated political divisions within the elite. Intra-elite bickering—long a feature of Costa Rican politics—came to a head with the 1889 electoral campaign. This election occurred against a backdrop of growing Church hostility toward liberals following the expulsion of a popular bishop and the enactment of anticlerical reforms promoting public education, civil marriages and divorces, and the secularization of cemeteries.[71] In its opposition to President Bernardo Soto, the Church was able to mobilize significant popular support, especially among artisan workers and lower rural classes.[72] The Church was joined by a political movement led by José Joaquín Rodríguez, which attracted support from several wealthy families that resented the increasing loss of dominant-class control over public agencies after 1870.[73] These forces came together as the Democratic Constitutional Party, in opposition to Soto's Progressive Liberal Party.

In an earlier period, no doubt, this crisis would have been resolved through some appeal to the armed forces. But in 1889, after two decades of restructuring of relations between the military and the dominant class, no such appeal was possible. Hence, the parties looked to popular mobilization as an alternative means to resolve the conflict, and the Constitutional Party—through the Church—used such mobilization quite effectively. Not only did popular protest force Soto to relinquish office, but it gave the Liberals little choice but to carry out a semicompetitive presidential election in 1889. This election was not democratic by today's standard: the suffrage excluded women and was restricted by literacy and wealth requirements (which left about 20 percent of the population as eligible voters), and the election was still conducted indirectly and without secret ballots.[74] Nevertheless, it can be classified as semicompetitive in the sense that there was genuine competition between the two parties and a significant level of mass participation, and because the election results were ultimately respected by all sides. The victory in fact went to Rodríguez of the opposition Constitutional Party, who won 377 electoral votes out of a total of 467.

From 1889 until the conclusion of the reform period, all Costa Rican presidents attained office through elections and left at the end of an officially elected term. Several scholars have pointed out that Costa Rica was not a democracy during this period because of important political irregularities, including electoral fraud through the misrepresentation of the popular vote in the electoral college, restrictions on the suffrage through literacy and property requirements, the absence of a secret ballot, and the occasional suspension of all constitutional guarantees.[75] Nevertheless, it is misleading to characterize the country as having a full-blown authoritarian regime. In addition to the election of 1889, the presidential elections of 1902, 1909, and 1913 were relatively competitive affairs between opposing political parties. And when we recall that even established European democracies of the early twentieth century placed important restrictions on the suffrage and were typically marked by electoral irregularities,[76] it seems appropriate to classify Costa Rica as having a semicompetitive political regime in the early twentieth century.

Recognition of the competitive (if not fully democratic) nature of the Costa Rican political system allows us to round out our analysis of the evolution of relations between the state and the dominant class. After having lost direct control over the state during the dictatorship of Guardia, the Costa Rican coffee elite was able to regain major political leverage with the advent of competitive politics. Individuals with significant coffee investments controlled the presidency from 1902 until the end of the reform period, after a long hiatus of rule by generals (1870–89) and by non-coffee elites (1889–1902) (see table 6.1). In effect, competitive politics replaced military plotting and scheming as the means through which Costa Rica's divided elite carried out political struggle.

In Guatemala and El Salvador, of course, the coffee elite also exercised leverage within the state at the end of the reform period. However, this leverage was not rooted in electoral politics among a divided elite, but rather in a mutually dependent alliance between liberal dictators who relied on profits from the coffee economy to sustain their rule and a homogeneous dominant class that relied on a militarized state for protection against class-based revolts from below. Only in Costa Rica, where class relations were less polarized and where the state was less militarized, could economically dominant actors actually look to lower classes for the purposes of electoral mobilization. Only in Costa Rica, in short, could coffee elites actually seek out more democratic forms of government.

Here, finally, is the key to the consequences of Guardia's reforms and the overall political implications of the second phase of liberalism. Guardia's efforts to centralize the state and professionalize the military closed off any possibility that Costa Rica might follow the path of Guatemala and El Salvador. After his reforms, an old pattern in which dominant-class factions ruled the state, and in which disputes among competing factions were resolved through military intervention, could not be sustained. In the post-Guardia period, if the divided coffee elite sought to exercise control over government—as opposed to permitting arbitrary rule by personal dictators—it had to agree to resolve internal divisions through electoral competition. Such a compromise carried the seeds for future episodes of democratization, as competing elite actors increasingly looked to lower classes for electoral mobilization in the course of political struggles.

Foreign Capital and the Banana Industry

As we have seen, the early timing of Costa Rica's reform period contributed to the absence of large-scale foreign capital investment in the mining sector, enabling the domestically controlled coffee economy to consolidate. Yet Costa Rica's lengthy reform period eventually overlapped with a world-historical environment in which foreign capital investment was much more pervasive. Beginning around 1880, a new geopolitical context emerged in which U.S. foreign capital investment and political domination in Latin America were increasingly strong possibilities.[77] In Costa Rica, mining had evaporated as a potentially profitable sector by this time, and the coffee economy was already firmly in domestic hands. But the country possessed substantial lands suitable for the development of the region's other major export crop—bananas—and a foreign enclave could develop in this sector.

The Costa Rican banana industry was from its origins closely tied to American investment, developing out of a railroad contract with an American businessman. In 1871, President Guardia contracted with Henry Meiggs Keith to build a 150-kilometer railroad line connecting

San José to the isolated Atlantic Coast rain-forest region.[78] The railroad was intended to facilitate the creation of an Atlantic port at Limón, which was needed to effectively market coffee in Europe and the eastern United States. Laying railway tracks in the heavily forested, disease-ridden area proved to be extremely difficult, however. During the long construction process, which ended up taking nineteen years, Minor C. Keith took over his uncle's contract and secured significant concessions from the Costa Rican government. Most notably, in August 1884 President Guardia granted Minor Keith control over the lines already constructed and eight hundred thousand acres of national lands in the area.[79]

Keith entered the commercial banana business as a subsidiary activity in order to make the interminable railway project profitable before construction was complete. After experimenting with small shipments of bananas from Limón, Keith became convinced that the industry could yield large profits. In the late 1870s, he oversaw the first banana exports from Limón to New York and New Orleans. Banana exports began to take off in the 1880s, with around a million stems going to the United States in 1890 (see fig. 6.2). From 1890 to 1900, the quantity of bananas exported more than tripled. By 1913, exports reached a peak of over 11 million stems, the Limón area supplying almost 90 percent.[80] In the early twentieth century, the annual value of banana exports roughly equaled

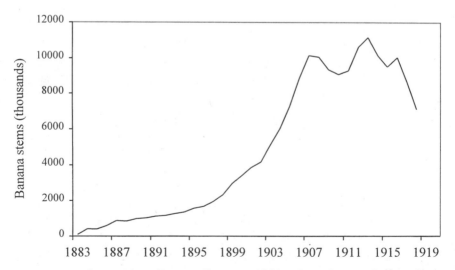

FIGURE 6.2   Costa Rican Banana Exports, 1883–1918. *Source:* Jeffrey Casey Gaspar, *Limón, 1880–1940: Un estudio de la industria bananera en Costa Rica* (San José: Editorial Costa Rica, 1979), 322.

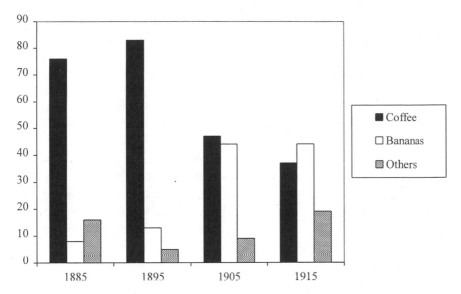

FIGURE 6.3   Percentage of Coffee, Banana, and Other Exports in Costa Rica, 1885–1915. *Source:* José Luis Vega Carballo, *Hacia una interpretación del desarrollo costarricense: Ensayo sociológico,* 5th ed. (San José: Editorial Porvenir, 1986), 236.

that of coffee exports (see fig. 6.3). Keith and a partner founded the United Fruit Company in 1899, which monopolized the banana trade and proved remarkably adept at shutting out competition from other American companies.[81]

United Fruit Company never produced all of the bananas it exported, and in fact its control over production gradually declined, with private producers growing 54 percent of its banana exports in 1905 and 63 percent in 1907.[82] Before 1900, the vast majority of banana growers were small farmers who had originally been imported from Jamaica as railroad workers. Keith allowed these individuals to use small plots of the huge tracts of land he controlled, and eventually many of them settled permanently as small private cultivators, though they remained dependent on Keith for continued access to land. In addition to small growers, large plantations using wage labor—plantations that pre-dated the formation of United Fruit—were also present, accounting for a larger share of banana production than all small growers put together.

By the early twentieth century, then, a major foreign-capital-dominated enclave had developed within the Costa Rican economy. One U.S.

company—United Fruit Company—was responsible for a huge portion of total national exports. The national state of Costa Rica exercised virtually no control over United Fruit, permitting the company to function autonomously along the eastern coast. Although United Fruit had brought some development to Limón, and the Pacific railway line facilitated coffee exports, the national state itself generated almost no revenues from the banana trade. In 1915, when banana exporting was at its height, government taxes on bananas amounted to only 3.2 percent of public revenue.[83]

As was the case with the banana economy in Guatemala, however, the isolation of this industry meant that it had little distorting effect on the class and state structures that emerged with coffee expansion in the rest of the country. As one observer of Costa Rica notes, "the banana industry did not produce a marked structural transformation, because it was economically untangled from the national economy."[84] It is likely that U.S. capitalists associated with the banana sector would have wielded much greater influence in the overall national economy and the state were it not for the fact that Costa Rica had already established a prosperous, domestically controlled coffee economy. In effect, because the creation of the foreign-controlled banana industry *followed* that of the coffee industry, key structural changes in the state and economy had already been consolidated; the foreign presence was confined to an isolated area, having no substantial impact on national development. Thus, the state and class structural characteristics associated with reformist liberalism prevailed throughout most of the country even as the banana industry developed into a major export enclave.

Conclusion: The Roots of Democracy in Costa Rica

The foundation of Costa Rican democracy does not lie in a distinct yeoman peasantry and culture that dates back to the colonial period. Nor was an existing rural democratic society ever undermined by the spread of commercial agriculture in the nineteenth century. Nevertheless, social structural features associated with the colonial period did contribute to Costa Rican democracy. In particular, the weakness of the national state, the absence of a significant indigenous population, and the lack of a preexisting commercial economy conditioned the initial decision of liberals to pursue a gradual transition to commercial agriculture through the promotion of small farms.

Once this transition had been initiated, however, nothing inherent in the agrarian structure of society ensured that liberals would continue to promote the smallholder model in the mid-nineteenth century. By this time, the economy and population had developed to the point where liberals could have encouraged the spread of large and labor-intensive plantations in the prime coffee regions of the Meseta Central. Political factors explain why they did not. In Costa Rica, reformers such as Braulio Carrillo were not confronted with antiliberal opposition movements that mobilized hundreds of followers, and hence they were not predisposed to build massive armed forces that regulated the agrarian economy and radiated throughout the state and society. In turn, the absence of a significant and professionalized military made it unlikely that liberals would move toward a radical policy option, because they lacked the coercive instruments necessary to implement such policies. Without a significant military apparatus, Costa Rican liberals were locked into a reform policy option. By the time of Guardia's military reform, which professionalized the armed forces and facilitated the development of competitive politics, the smallholder pattern had been consolidated throughout the country.

In the final analysis, then, the roots of Costa Rican democracy have as much to do with the way in which the state was developed, especially the military, as with the manner in which the coffee economy was consolidated.

CHAPTER 7

Aborted Liberalism: Honduras and Nicaragua

L ike their counterparts in Guatemala, El Salvador, and Costa Rica, liberals in Honduras and Nicaragua sought to build modern state machineries and establish prosperous export economies. The first major liberal leaders of these countries, Marco Aurelio Soto in Honduras (1876–83) and José Santos Zelaya in Nicaragua (1893–1909), were every bit as committed to these goals as individuals such as Barrios, Zaldívar, and Guardia. Despite the intentions of Honduran and Nicaraguan liberals, however, their reform projects were the least successful in the region at actually achieving basic institutional and economic transformations. At the conclusion of the reform period, the state remained relatively decentralized and lacked autonomous power, and the agrarian economy—while having undergone a transition to commercial agriculture—was still comparatively underdeveloped and marked by an extremely weak local dominant class.

Much of the explanation for the comparatively limited extent of reform in Honduras and Nicaragua rests with U.S. intervention, which served to distort and minimize domestic changes. In Honduras, such intervention was rooted in massive foreign investment from the United States. Beginning with the mining industry and later extending to banana plantations, U.S. companies established control over the most important sectors of the domestic economy. Through this economic influence, U.S. capitalists wielded tremendous political power within the Honduran government, eventually to the point that U.S. companies assumed many of the tasks that one would normally associate with a national state. In the face of this foreign presence, the policy reforms sought by liberals had trouble getting off the ground and were relatively unsuccessful at state-building, and were of secondary importance in commercializing agriculture. Indeed, the transition to commercial agriculture in Honduras was carried out largely by foreign actors, and the state became little more than an instrument for American investors to use in pursuing their own goals.

Nicaragua also experienced U.S. intervention during the reform period, but only after major and potentially far-reaching domestic changes had already been partly enacted. In this case, intervention took the form of a direct U.S. military occupation that suddenly put a stop to an ongoing radical liberal program. Through a marine landing, the United States established a form of neocolonial control over the Nicaraguan political system, using previously defunct conservative elites to govern on its behalf. Business interests from the United States followed on the heels of the U.S. invasion, ultimately establishing control over the key financial sectors of the Nicaraguan economy. The ultimate consequence was that liberal policy programs were not fully implemented in Nicaragua, and preliberal state and class structures carried over to the postliberal period.

Thus, the liberal reform periods in Honduras and Nicaragua were strongly conditioned by foreign intervention, leading these two countries to follow a shared pattern of aborted liberalism. Prior to U.S. intervention, however, the two countries were quite distinct, as liberals sought to enact fundamentally different reform programs. In Honduras, where political conditions resembled those found in early-nineteenth-century Costa Rica, President Soto and subsequent liberals sought to implement a *reform* policy option. By contrast, in Nicaragua, where conditions more closely resembled those present in Guatemala and El Salvador before the reform period, liberals under the leadership of President Zelaya initiated programs consistent with a *radical* policy option. Hence, in the absence of foreign intervention, Honduras might well have followed the pattern of reformist liberalism that characterized Costa Rica, whereas Nicaragua might have experienced the pattern of radical liberalism that characterized Guatemala and El Salvador. Only as a consequence of foreign intervention and the lack of success in implementing policy options did the countries follow a single pattern of aborted liberalism.

A Reform Policy Option in Honduras

In the historiography on the Honduran liberal reform, much scholarly effort has been devoted to specifying the reasons why liberals were unable to promote—despite their widely acknowledged efforts to do so—significant economic development and state-building. Historians engaged in this discussion have sometimes used the Guatemalan liberal reform as a basis for assessing Honduras, attempting to identify the factors that differentiated Honduras from Guatemala and made reform difficult or impossible in the former case. From these efforts, a certain received wisdom has come to characterize the historiography on Honduras's "frustrated" liberal reform.[1] First, it is argued that the weakness of landed elites worked against a successful reform. In the words of Héctor Pérez Brignoli, "Without a consolidated base of oligarchic strength, the [Honduran] Liberal Reform . . . could not result in anything more than yearnings and promises."[2] Second, the weakness of the national state is also often seen as having inhibited successful reform. For example, Charles Brand writes that "the physical size and structure of government was . . . an important factor affecting development. It was too small to effectively engage in, let alone support, developmental efforts."[3] Finally, demographic and geographic obstacles are viewed as having worked against a successful reform period. For example, the sparse population of Honduras is understood to have provided a poor basis for plantation labor.[4]

Despite the well-established place of this received wisdom in the historiography, evidence from a broader comparison forces us to question its validity. Indeed, what is most striking about the standard reasons given for the difficulties of the Honduran liberal reform is that they are precisely factors that help account for Costa Rica's gradual but quite successful liberal reform period. The presence of a weak landed elite, the lack of a coherent national state, and demographic obstacles—these conditions contributed to a successful period of reformist liberalism in Costa Rica. Hence, without examining the specific context of the Honduran liberal reform, we have no reason to suppose that the same conditions should not have favored a similar outcome in Honduras.

Soto's State-Building Efforts

Marco Aurelio Soto and his chief collaborator, Ramón Rosa, embraced an ideological program for the development of Honduras that closely corresponded with the version of liberal reform carried out by Braulio Carrillo in Costa Rica.[5] Such parallels were rooted in the similar political situations present in Honduras at the beginning of the reform period in 1876 and in Costa Rica in the late 1830s. Soto, like Carrillo, was not confronted by a well-established conservative elite that was fundamentally opposed to liberal policies.[6] As Juan Arancibia has pointed out, in Honduras there was not "a powerful landholding church that forcefully opposed the reformers."[7] Rather, already weakened by the anti-ecclesiastical reforms initiated by Francisco Morazán decades earlier, the Church was unable to pose any significant challenge to the liberal reforms of the 1870s and 1880s, including even the secularization of education, cemeteries, and matrimony.[8] Likewise, the landed oligarchy was comparatively small and offered little opposition to liberal reforms. In fact, Soto and Rosa viewed this class as a key ally necessary for the success of their goals, not a political opponent that stood in the way of their reform agenda.[9] And, outside of the Church and the precapitalist oligarchy, there were "not additional potential enemies to the reform."[10]

All of this does not mean that Soto was completely free from political opposition. The imposition of Soto in power by Guatemala stabilized liberal control over the presidency, but it did not end a decades-old pattern in which rival elites sought to win state power by mobilizing makeshift militias and carrying out armed revolts. To meet the exigencies of this unstable political environment, Soto's first move as president was to order the confiscation of all arms possessed by local forces. The government reported having collected over fifteen hundred weapons in less than three months.[11] The need to achieve political stability also led Soto to reorganize, modernize, and expand the militia, including putting large percentages of the national budget toward defense.[12] After an October 1878 decree, all Honduran men between eighteen and thirty-five years of age were required to serve in the state militia (with some exceptions, including export crop producers). The secretary of war projected that twenty thousand individuals would be available by 1879 for the defense of the republic.[13] Also under Soto's administration, the first national police force in Honduran history was formed in Tegucigalpa.[14]

These reforms have something in common with those pursued during episodes of full-blown liberalism in Guatemala and El Salvador. Nevertheless, they most closely resemble the modest initiatives of Carrillo in Costa Rica. Like Carrillo—and unlike Barrios and Zaldívar—Soto increased the size of available defenses, but he did not establish a permanent army in Honduras.[15] Nor did he use the military as the principal means of extending the reach of the state in society. Soto's state-building efforts were often unrelated to the military, involving instead the establishment of a legal and material groundwork to support agrarian capitalist development. Thus, for example, Soto revamped the legal system and developed new civil and penal codes, established a national money house and banking system, modernized the post office, installed the first telegraph in the country, and expanded the construction of roads.[16] Carrillo had earlier pursued similar measures in Costa Rica, financing them with profits ultimately derived from coffee expansion; Soto and Rosa relied primarily on increasing the tax on alcohol, tobacco, and cattle exports to pay for their reforms (the state budget nearly tripled from 1875 to 1880).[17] At the same time, the Honduran reformers were careful to avoid discouraging potential export crop investors. In fact, legislation was passed abolishing the use of forced loans, and Soto and Rosa regularly made appeals explicitly designed to encourage local investment.[18]

By the early 1880s, the state-building efforts of Soto had created a degree of political stability unprecedented in nineteenth-century Honduras. With the final defeat of Soto's principal political enemies—former president José María Medina and indigenous leader Calixto Vásquez[19]—the state was capable of assuming a more permanent presence in society. As Guillermo Molina Chocano has put it, "the Honduran state attained the appearance of a modern national entity and of a stable national regime, consistent with the [liberal] historical era."[20] Soto believed that these changes would provide a foundation for economic development, a goal that he vigorously pursued through agrarian reforms designed to expand commercial agriculture.

Soto's Agrarian Reforms

Within a year of coming to power, the Soto administration carried out a sweeping agricultural reform. Both Soto and Rosa were quite aware of the successes achieved with commercial agriculture (especially coffee) by governments elsewhere in the region, including the Carrillo government in Costa Rica.[21] Their own agrarian reform, in fact, bore important similarities to the reform policy option pursued by Costa Rican liberals. The Honduran reformers sought to use the small farm as a basic unit of agricultural modernization. Thus, while Soto held a very negative opinion of communal and *ejidal* lands, he did not seek to replace such lands with large private plantations. Rather, he sought to create what he once referred to as "family plots" *(lotes de familia)*—that is, small plots that would be formed by distributing communal and *ejidal* land to individual families. As he once wrote: "The objective of . . . 'family plots' is primarily to benefit the poor class of our nation, which is the most numerous one. But, at the same time, it seeks to resolve, in accordance with science, the question of the *ejidos*, the cause of so many maladies, disturbances, conflicts, and disgraces, as well as the backwardness of our incipient agricultural industry. To convert communal property, absurd and useless, into patrimonial private property is, in my judgment, a solution of immense usefulness for Honduras."[22]

The key agricultural reforms of Soto and Rosa were embodied in the Decree for the Development of Agriculture of April 29, 1877.[23] The liberal government committed itself to making lands available at low or no cost to any individual who planted coffee, sugar cane, or other specified export crops. Despite Soto's acknowledged dislike of the traditional land system, the reform legislation "did not directly attack the rights of communities and municipalities to hold and distribute land; rather it encouraged them to make use of existing holdings, maintaining the same land tenure relationships as before."[24] Hence, within Central America, the Honduran reform legislation was the least destructive to the common and *ejidal* land systems. As in Costa Rica (and initially El Salvador), the national government was too weak to oversee land distribution itself, leaving much of this task to the municipalities and focusing its efforts instead on promotional tasks for small growers. Individuals cultivating export crops had to own only a very modest quantity of land in order to meet the Honduran government's definition of "agricultural farmer" *(agricultor)* and thereby receive special benefits from the national government. For example, families who cultivated five or more *manzanas* of coffee were considered agricultural farmers and thus were exempted from military service. Likewise, the government offered a variety of generous incentives to encourage the proliferation of export products, including making available at no cost basic agricultural inputs such as tools, seeds, and fertilizer, and providing easy credit and materials for housing construction.[25]

The overlap between agrarian policies in Honduras and Costa Rica also extends to the realm of labor policy. Although the wording of Soto and Rosa's labor regulations was influenced by their experience working for Barrios in Guatemala, the policies they advocated lacked the repressive component of the Guatemalan legislation. As Molina points out, the Honduran government "did not introduce a program of forced labor similar to the *mandamientos* of the colonial period, which Barrios drafted for the indigenous masses of Guatemala."[26] Rather, Honduran authorities advocated primarily a noncoercive, regulatory role to govern worker-employer relations, in which local authorities would enforce labor agreements and make sure employers paid workers on time.[27]

The geography of Honduras made it difficult for coffee—the dominant export crop of Central America—to gain a foothold in the country. Although Honduras possessed substantial land suitable for growing high-quality coffee, this land was scattered in isolated pockets through-out the country. Hence, the construction of roads and the provision of services to integrate a coffee economy were especially challenging. During Soto's administration, coffee production began in the departments of Santa Barbara, Comayagua, and Choluteca, but some ten years after the passage of the 1877 agrarian legislation, coffee exports accounted for only 2.7 percent of total exports.[28] Evidence such as this has been used to argue that a domestically led transition to agrarian capitalism was impossible in Honduras.[29] However, we must remember that coffee exportation began only gradually in Costa Rica, taking almost two decades after the initiation of the reform period to bring in significant export revenue. Furthermore, Honduras had good opportunities to commercialize agriculture through agro-exports besides coffee. Most notable in this regard was banana production.

During the course of the Soto administration, bananas received increased governmental attention as farmers from the isolated North Coast began producing the fruit for export. By the 1880s, several land grants had been made to small-scale Honduran farmers in the North Coast, where the burgeoning banana industry was located, especially around Tela.[30] At this early stage, the production of bananas was carried out by domestic actors, primarily small farmers, who sold the crop in local competitive markets to U.S. exporters shipping to cities such as New Orleans and Mobile.[31] "Expansion of cultivation on the North Coast still gave little indication of the future monopolization of the banana industry by increasingly fewer U.S. interests. Actual production was still controlled by local residents . . . , and none of the foreign shippers or planters controlled any area."[32] There is some scholarly debate over the role of the indigenous, merchant-based dominant class in early Honduran banana production.[33] The most extensively documented work suggests that the dominant class in Honduras was quite interested in the banana market, even to the point that major resources were siphoned away from the coffee economy. According to Darío Euraque, "to initiate and cultivate a coffee plantation in Honduras was very costly, especially when compared with the task of setting up and cultivating a banana plantation."[34] As a result, "the emergence of bananas beginning in 1870 channeled commercial capital toward banana cultivation and not toward the cultivation of coffee."[35] Led by small local growers, banana production accounted for over one-quarter of total exports in 1887–88, more than double the share of cattle, Honduras's traditional export.[36]

How the promising banana industry was transformed from a locally controlled sector of the economy dominated by small landholders into a foreign-capital enclave marked by large plantations will be explored below. For now, the important point to note is that, in the late nineteenth century, Honduras was seemingly experiencing a pattern of reformist liberalism quite similar to that of Costa Rica in the early nineteenth century.

THE DOMINATION OF FOREIGN CAPITAL IN HONDURAS

The successful implementation of a reform policy option in Costa Rica had depended on the absence of large-scale foreign capital investment. In the mining sector, Costa Rica sidestepped the potential perils of foreign investment largely because of the timing of the country's reform period: massive foreign capital investment simply was not a world-historical possibility in the early nineteenth century. Later in the nineteenth century, when world-historical conditions had changed, Costa Rica's banana sector did come under the influence of foreign investors, but by this time the coffee sector was already firmly controlled by national actors, preventing full-scale economic domination by foreign capital and allowing the national state to remain under domestic control.

By contrast, the liberal reform period in Honduras *was* launched in a world-historical environment of pervasive foreign investment. The advanced industrial nations increasingly penetrated less developed nations, in part for the purpose of extracting natural resources and other primary goods. In this international context, foreign capital investment poured into the Honduran mining sector and later the banana industry, completely overwhelming the domestic economy.

The Mining Industry

Shortly after coming to power, Soto became convinced that the reopening of abandoned mines from the colonial period (in towns such as San José de Yuscarán, Santa Lucía, Valle de Angeles, and Tegucigalpa) could revitalize the Honduran economy.[37] Although he challenged local capitalists in newspaper editorials to take advantage of the historic opportunities offered by gold and silver extraction, the main thrust of his efforts involved attracting American and European capitalists, not the locally based dominant class of merchants. Soto believed that local capital was simply too weak and technologically backward to stimulate mining on its own. Hence, he looked to foreigners to lead the way, offering a series of generous concessions for investment.

For investors willing to restart mining in the key Rosario mine in San Juancito, Soto provided a twenty-year exemption from export taxes and all other national and municipal taxes.[38] These concessions attracted Washington S. Valentine and other New York investors and led to the formation of the New York and Honduras Rosario Mining Company. Soon after, the concession policy offered to Valentine was standardized to apply to any significant mining company (foreign or domestic) willing to reopen Honduran mines. Soto also pursued other major promotional activities for mining interests, including labor recruitment, administrative and legal streamlining, and even awarding several investors full ownership of mines at no cost provided they at least organized one company and made some effort to exploit the mines. By the time Soto was forced from office in 1883,[39] there were several competing foreign mining companies operating in Honduras.

Soto's successor, President Luis Bográn, accelerated the trend of using government concessions to obtain foreign investment, consolidating a pattern of full governmental cooperation with foreign entrepreneurs. During the eight-year period from 1883 to 1890, the government offered some 145 concessions to mining companies, of which roughly half were from the United States or Europe.[40] Stimulated by government concessions, mining came to play a huge role in the economy. In 1887–88, precious metals and minerals constituted over 50 percent of total exports from Honduras, almost twice the share of bananas.[41] Yet although dozens of companies were started during the boom period, very few of them were profitable, and only the Valentine family's New York and Honduras Rosario Mining Company could be considered a true success. In 1887–88, Rosario was in fact responsible for over 85 percent of all mining exports. Hence, a single New York–based company accounted for roughly 45 percent of the value of all Honduran exports![42]

The most obvious political consequence derived from Rosario's near-monopoly control over precious metal mining was that Washington Valentine, head of the Rosario company, became a significant political actor within Honduras. Valentine developed a close relationship with President Bográn and extensively courted central government members by distributing gifts, throwing lavish parties, and flooding the government with information stressing the economic importance of Rosario.[43] Valentine often appealed directly to the president to resolve conflicts between his company and local people in the San Juancito area. Bográn nearly always granted his requests, even when they came at the direct expense of local mining enterprises and the local population. Valentine repaid such favors through a variety of direct political kickbacks, including helping to finance Bográn's 1887 reelection campaign.

More important than the individual political influence of Valentine, however, was the general effect of the foreign-controlled mining sector on the state and the economy. With the Bográn administration, maintaining executive control had become partially dependent on relationships with U.S. investors, and much state activity involved catering to the needs of foreign capitalists. By the time of Bográn's reelection in 1887, it was clear that government programs to stimulate domestic agricultural production were on the back burner and secondary to accommodating the foreign-controlled mining sector. The irony of state promotion of mining is that even while the industry distracted attention from domestic agriculture, it contributed little to the economic development of Honduras. As Kenneth Finney notes, the capital-intensive nature of the industry meant that few Hondurans actually worked in the mines, and the (relatively high) wages paid to miners did little to stimulate the local economy.[44] Given the limited supply of precious metals in Honduran mines and the impoverished state of agriculture, foreign companies had no incentive to reinvest profits in other sectors of the economy. In addition, mining contributed almost nothing to development of the state, because "state revenues did not secure any tax base from even the few companies that eventually initiated mineral exploitation nor from those which actually profited from operational ventures, like the Rosario Mining Co."[45]

Yet we should not overstate the degree to which the mining sector stunted the development of agriculture and the state during the liberal reform period. Although the Rosario company maintained profitable and growing operations until well into the twentieth century, by the 1890s mineral resources had been exhausted from most areas, with lucrative activities largely confined to the Tegucigalpa and Choluteca departments.[46] Government concessions in the mining sector fell noticeably in the 1890s.[47] While foreign investment in the mining sector temporarily directed attention away from agriculture, it did not permanently undermine the development of Honduras's agrarian economy and state apparatus. Perhaps the most important consequence of the late-nineteenth-century mining boom in Honduras was the governmental precedent it established: relying on foreign capital to develop the nation and offering extremely generous concessions to foreign investors. Future Honduran administrations followed these precedents closely in the even more significant banana industry.

The Banana Industry

Banana exportation took off during the last decade of the nineteenth century and the first two decades of the twentieth century. Figure 7.1 shows the steady increase of banana exports during this period, with the fruit far surpassing mineral exports by the conclusion of the reform period in 1919. During the first two decades of the twentieth century, bananas constituted around one-half of all exports from Honduras.[48] Although in the 1920s an even greater surge in banana exports would occur (by 1930 they brought in over forty million pesos and represented almost 90 per cent of all exports),[49] the reform period itself had seen the initial transition to commercial agriculture and the country's incorporation into the international market through banana exportation.[50]

Honduras's incorporation into the international market was closely linked to foreign-capital domination of the banana sector. Direct U.S. in-

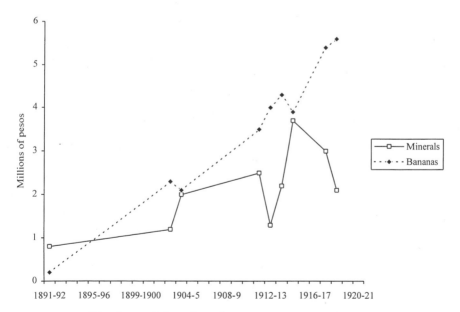

FIGURE 7.1 Honduran Mineral and Banana Exports, 1891–1919. *Source:* Vilma Laínez and Víctor Meza, "El enclave bananero en la historia de Honduras," *Estudios Sociales Centroamericanos* 5 (May–August 1973): 145.

vestment in Honduras expanded dramatically after 1908, reaching a peak shortly before the depression of 1930.[51] Figures are not readily available on the exact percentage of U.S. control over Honduran banana exports, but at the conclusion of the reform period, the number might well have approached 100 percent.[52] Indeed, Arancibia reports that in 1923, when Honduras was the world's leading banana exporter, one company—United Fruit Company—accounted for 70 percent of all Honduran banana exports.[53] Although United consolidated many of its holdings only after the reform period (in the early 1920s), this fact is highly suggestive of the monopoly control that a few foreign companies exercised over the entire Honduran banana economy.

Foreign control of the banana industry grew out of liberal governments' concessions to wealthy financiers and investors. Although Honduran citizens were in no way excluded from these concessions, in practice the vast majority went to foreigners, especially North Americans.[54] The reason is simple: the Honduran elite lacked the investment capital and entrepreneurship of their northern counterparts. Of course, Honduran liberals did not simply give away control of the dynamic export sector to foreigners. Rather, they attempted to link concessions with capital-intensive infrastructure projects that would spur broader development in the country. Most notable were "land-for-railroad-construction" concessions offered by the government; others included the right to build and control docks, electric-power facilities, and sanitary infrastructure. From 1900 to 1920, at least forty-seven large-scale concessions were made to the major banana companies in exchange for infrastructure-development contracts.[55]

This concessionary policy in the banana sector, in conjunction with the presence of U.S. investors willing and able to take advantage of such concessions, underpinned aborted liberalism in Honduras. Successive liberal administrations abandoned a domestic development strategy built around a reform policy option and instead looked to foreign capital to more rapidly develop the nation. American investors, initially welcomed by the Honduran government, fully exploited available possibilities for capital accumulation in the banana industry and moved on to pursue a much broader set of economic activities.[56] The result was that "the banana companies closed development possibilities for other sectors of the Honduran economy and condemned the country to permanently spin in the orbit of the enclave."[57]

One example of how this process worked was the Vacarro Brothers Company, the first major U.S. banana company in Honduras. The Vacarros, three Italian American brothers from New Orleans, set up business in 1899 after their nephew arranged a government land concession in the La Ceiba region.[58] They were subsequently awarded other major concessions for carrying out small infrastructure projects that almost exclusively benefited their company and gave them control over the means of communication and transportation in La Ceiba. In turn, "the Vacarro Company was capable of monopolizing the purchasing of fruit and, consequently, of establishing the prices and deciding arbitrarily about banana production in the region."[59] In less than two decades, the Vacarro Brothers Company became not only a huge banana exporter, but a major conglomerate enterprise with investments in sugar and coconut plantations, railroads, steamship lines, a soap factory, a brewery, a distillery, a shoe factory, a hospital, and a bank.

The example of Samuel Zemurray (apparently known in the trade simply as Sam the Banana Man) is particularly instructive about the politics of aborted liberalism in Honduras.[60] In this case, the Honduran government initially awarded a railroad concession to William F. Streich of Philadelphia. After building a five-mile line from Cuyamel to Vera Cruz, Streich rented five thousand hectares of land on both sides of the Cuyamel River, intending to use it to plant bananas. However, lacking sufficient funds, he instead sold his lease to Zemurray, who at this time had some financial backing from United Fruit Company. United Fruit soon disposed of its investment, but Zemurray prospered nonetheless, establishing the Cuyamel Fruit Company in 1911. Like the Vacarro Brothers Company, Cuyamel had benefited from several concessions linked to infrastructure developments and expanded into a major enterprise, eventually controlling a light and power company, an electric plant, a public utilities corporation, a telephone and telegraph company, and other key communication outlets for the city of San Pedro Sula and other northern towns.[61]

More than any other single individual, Samuel Zemurray symbolizes the profound political influence that U.S. capitalists wielded within Honduras by the end of the reform period. Nowhere can this influence be seen more clearly than in Zemurray's role in the overthrow of Honduran president Miguel Dávila in 1911.[62] Dávila was supported by the mineral giant Washington Valentine, who used his influence to dictate the government's fiscal and concessionary policies in ways that clashed with fruit interests, including by convincing Dávila to go along with an arrangement in which J. P. Morgan and other New York bankers would refund an old British railway debt if the Honduran government ceded control over the country's customs houses to the U.S. financiers not connected to fruit interests.[63] In late 1909, Zemurray and the banana companies decided to dispose of President Dávila by promoting and financing a revolutionary force led by ex-president Manuel Bonilla. Zemurray alone contributed a hundred thousand dollars to Bonilla's forces, and it soon became "public information that the fruit companies were staking Bonilla, hoping to receive large concessions in return."[64] Despite the substantial efforts of Valentine to win U.S. governmental support for Dávila, President William Howard Taft and Secretary of State Philander Knox assumed (correctly) that if they refrained from supporting Dávila and allowed Bonilla's "revolution" to take its course, then a grateful Bonilla would win Honduran governmental support for a treaty on Nicaragua that was then before the Senate. In February 1911 Bonilla took control of Puerto Cortés, and Dávila was soon forced to resign, "saying he would turn his office over to anyone the United States suggested."[65] In October 1911, Bonilla was duly elected president. Although Bonilla died in March 1913, he managed to make three railroad concessions, a port concession, and a ten-thousand-hectare land lease to Zemurray. Further, he annulled a major railroad concession given to Valentine by Dávila in Puerto Cortés, and he made huge land-for-railroad concessions to subsidiaries of United Fruit Company, which began to assume a much more prominent role in Honduras. Thus, the investment of the banana companies in the revolution of 1911 had surely paid off. This was especially true for Samuel Zemurray, who was no doubt the most powerful man in Honduras at the end of the liberal reform period.

The Weakness of the State and the Dominant Class

In its structure and functions, the state that existed at the conclusion of the liberal reform remained in key respects indistinguishable from the feeble apparatus that had characterized preliberal Honduras. The national bureaucracy failed to penetrate most areas of Honduras, and the majority of the population continued to have little relationship with any administrative-coercive organization. On the one hand, this meant that the actual demands made on most people's lives for resources and loyalty to a national authority were quite limited. On the other hand, rudimentary state services such as education, electricity, and public roads were not available to the majority of Hondurans.

Behind such a limited state role in society—that is, a thoroughly "disembedded" state[66]—rested a bureaucratic apparatus that was meager in size and administratively incompetent.[67] During any single administration, the civil service operated within the contours of an extreme spoils system in which political loyalty and affiliation were the vehicles for administrative advancement. But unexpected transfers of presidential power were common, and a change of administration—often by armed revolt—typically led to a reshuffling of state personnel. Not even the national army maintained any real corporate integrity; it represented scarcely more than the followers of the particular political leader who happened to be in power. As Steve C. Ropp writes, "no military *institution* existed in Honduras during the 19th and early 20th centuries. While there was always the semblance of structure, the military did not develop to the extent that any real institutionalization occurred."[68]

The dominant class that characterized Honduras at the close of the reform period was not a landed elite in any standard sense of the term.[69] As Edelberto Torres-Rivas suggested three decades ago, Honduras did not consolidate a "landed oligarchy," as did Guatemala and El Salvador, because the country "was integrated into the world market with an export product that was controlled by foreigners."[70] Nor was the Honduran elite a wealthy merchant-based dominant class equivalent to what existed in late-nineteenth-century Costa Rica. For, unlike the Costa Rican elite, which was able to derive significant revenue from coffee processing and exporting, the Honduran elite never gained control over the marketing of bananas.[71] From the beginning, U.S. shipping companies used their monopoly over transportation to dominate the commercial aspects of the banana industry. Furthermore, unlike Costa Rican merchants, who could develop fortunes by controlling the processing of coffee beans, Hondurans had no opportunities for processing the ready-to-eat banana fruit before shipment.

The Honduran dominant class was primarily a commercial elite only partially transformed from the preliberal era. Although characterizations of this class as a "comprador" bourgeoisie that sold out to foreign capital may be exaggerated, the Honduran dominant class was often closely connected to activities in the foreign-controlled sectors of the economy. With the rise of precious metal mining in the 1880s, a small sector of national proprietors accumulated capital by serving as merchants for the expanding foreign industries. By the early twentieth century, this group had begun to invest in the expanding domestic market for manufactured goods.[72] With the rise of banana corporations, commercial activity increased in the northern areas of the country, especially in the growing city of San Pedro Sula. Here and elsewhere, a small group of elite Hondurans accumulated wealth through retail investments, real estate, housing, transportation companies, and activities directly associated with the banana companies such as legal service and lobbying.[73] It was this commercial-oriented elite—not a landed oligarchy—that represented the Honduran dominant class at the end of the liberal reform period.

Two further characteristics differentiate the Honduran commercial elite from the coffee elites of Guatemala and El Salvador. First, the Honduran elite did not exercise significant leverage within the state. Rather, the state was formally controlled by local politicians from Tegucigalpa who were closely linked to U.S. banana interests; indeed, U.S. banana companies were the most politically important actors within the state. Second, by virtue of its weak commercial status, the Honduran elite did not stand in any directly conflictual relationship with lower rural classes. In fact, the rural structure was not conducive to class-based revolts in which lower rural groups acted in concert against landlords or state agents. Honduran campesino families continued to function largely independently from one another, mitigating the likelihood of sustained collective action. Furthermore, because the Honduran elite was not a traditional landed oligarchy and the national state was not deeply embedded within society, there was no clear target for peasant farmers to direct their grievances against; if they perceived exploitation, their exploiters were not easily identifiable.

Of course, a very different agrarian and political structure prevailed in the North Coast banana plantations. Here cultivators drew income from wage labor rather than land, and here a wealthy class of foreign corporate plantation owners was present. However, this type of agricultural setting—a plantation economy marked by wealthy companies that employ resident wage laborers—tends to be characterized by strong working-class organizations and reform labor movements, not revolutionary organizations and explosive lower-class revolts.[74] Indeed, class antagonisms in this setting were centered on economic rather than political issues and on the distribution of income from property rather than the ownership of property itself. Even in the foreign banana enclave, then, class relations were not highly polarized as they were in Guatemala and El Salvador.

A RADICAL POLICY OPTION IN NICARAGUA

If U.S. economic intervention undermined a reform policy option in Honduras, then overt political intervention by the United States aborted a potentially successful—if historically delayed—radical policy option in Nicaragua. Before the events that led to the fall of reform leader José Santos Zelaya in 1909, Nicaraguan liberals were in the midst of implementing legislation remarkably similar to that carried out in Guatemala and El Salvador. Thus, for Nicaragua, we must come to terms with how and why a potential case of *radical* liberalism was aborted.

The Zelaya Dictatorship and State-Building Reforms

Like studies of Guatemala and El Salvador, leading analyses of the Nicaraguan liberal reform period have assumed that the national state headed by the Zelaya government (1893–1909) was simply an instrument of coffee elites.[75] However, the coffee elite was in fact deeply divided throughout the reform period, and Zelaya was able to use these divisions to set up a system of highly personalistic rule. Factionalism among the coffee elite in Nicaragua has roots in the bizarre William Walker affair, which discredited liberals, delayed the start of the liberal reform period until 1893, and allowed Nicaraguan conservatives to become more influential in the coffee economy than was the case in the rest of Central America. Hence, whereas in other Central American countries coffee elites were identified as liberals, in Nicaragua many coffee growers (especially in the Carazo Plateau) held allegiance to the Conservative Party and were unwilling to cooperate with the liberals. This political division made it impossible for Zelaya to rule on behalf of the dominant class as a whole, and it eventually led him to repress Conservative Party coffee growers who did not show loyalty to his dictatorship.

By 1896, Zelaya in fact wielded so much personal power that debate exists over whether he was a brutal tyrant or a more benevolent, modernizing dictator.[76] From a comparative perspective this debate seems somewhat misplaced, however, for Zelaya acted in a manner no different from that of other liberal dictators who carried out actions for the purposes of maintaining and expanding personal political power. Most notably, Zelaya responded to persistent threats from armed opposition movements sponsored by conservatives and rival liberal factions with military-building reforms similar to those of Barrios and Zaldívar in Guatemala and El Salvador.[77]

The conservative era had not seen the creation of a professional army or formal military apparatus. To improve available defenses, Zelaya first carried out a standard set of liberal military-related reforms, such as decrees ordering that all arms held by civilians be surrendered to authorities and threatening the use of extreme force against anyone who attempted to disrupt public order.[78] In October 1894 he signed the "Martial Law of Public Security," which created *jefes políticos* to maintain "peace and security" in each department and granted the president power to suspend the constitution through a "state of siege."[79] Most important, at the end of 1895, Zelaya ordered the creation of a new National Army, specifying the distribution of infantry, brigadiers, divisions, and so forth across the various newly created "military zones" of the country.[80] The exact size of the army and other coercive forces throughout the reform period is not known, but most likely the permanent active forces constituted around one to three thousand men in times of peace and potentially many more when the militia was activated for war.[81] Expenditures on the military were very high, even in peacetime, as Zelaya placed great emphasis on military modernization, weapons procurement, and martial programs in general. The sheer firepower of Zelaya's forces made the Nicaraguan military arguably the strongest in the region during the first decade of the twentieth century.

The creation of a powerful coercive apparatus under Zelaya was not exclusively or primarily intended to serve coffee planters. Instead, the military reforms were designed to enhance governmental security at home and abroad: the army was effectively used both to uphold internal order against domestic enemies, such as the Church and conservatives,[82] and to allow Zelaya to pursue an expansionist agenda in the region, often in the name of recreating a Central American union. Beyond this, the military took on a multifaceted role within society. Benjamin I. Teplitz writes that after Zelaya's reforms, "the military played a more complex and expanded role in society. Among its major duties were the quelling of revolts, engaging in tests of strength with other Central American powers, withstanding European threats and incursions and expanding national sovereignty. The armed forces also functioned to arrest labor fugitives, maintain political loyalties, dispense patronage, protect social status and to raise revenues by selling draft exemptions. At least by 1900, the Liberals' martial emphasis resulted in the militarization of much of Nicaraguan society."[83]

Liberals also moved to establish an administrative-bureaucratic apparatus that would far surpass earlier conservative efforts at state-building. Though data on the number of personnel that made up the administrative bureaucracy are not available, its expansion during the Zelaya years is revealed by the many new tasks that the liberal state assumed. In the financial realm, where the liberals had inherited a monetary crisis from the conservative era, the government took steps to centralize and rationalize budgetary accounting and revenue collection, including by distributing paper money and organizing a National Monetary System and a National Financial System.[84] State-sponsored or state-financed infrastructure projects also ballooned during the reform period: the construction of new railroad tracks almost doubled; more than two thousand miles of telegraph and telephone lines were built (again, about doubling the previous total); mail delivery increased at an annual rate of 22 percent; and cargo transportation similarly witnessed a huge advance.[85] As Oscar René Vargas writes, "Imagine the quantity of salaried workers necessary to expand . . . every service sector of the state: workers who install telephone and telegraph lines, public employees who distribute the mail, persons who have to train in the operation of telegraphs, technicians who can repair telephones and telegraph lines, administrative personnel throughout all of the public sectors, and so forth."[86] In addition, the Zelaya period saw a great expansion of state functions at the expense of corporate groups within society: "The state gradually absorbed functions that civil society, above all the Church, had traditionally exercised, including services of public education and support, civil registration of births and deaths, and marriage."[87]

The political concomitant of this more active and socially embedded state was a national government that more thoroughly penetrated local governmental structures.[88] Conservatives had long sought to exercise greater control over *ayuntamientos,* but not until the Zelaya administration did a national government fully succeed at the task. Zelaya's personally appointed *jefes políticos* were responsible for a myriad of duties "which caused them to intervene in municipal autonomy: overseeing the collection of road taxes, the conscription of laborers, the safety of mines, the sub-division of communal lands and the gathering of vital statistics."[89] Through martial law, the *jefes* were granted substantial military and civil forces that gave them the coercive capability to actually carry out the government's mandate. This was especially true after liberal dissidents in León revolted in 1896, which led Zelaya to squash local autonomy through massive state centralization. Municipalities were monitored by national police units, departmental councils were abolished, conservative judges were removed, new elections were called to reelect mayors and councilmen, and local organizing was censured through federal license requirements. Teplitz highlights the key result: "Although civil wars would rage anew and ultimately would be successful against Zelaya, never again would a municipality, *per se,* challenge the sovereignty of the national Liberal government."[90]

Land and Labor Reforms

Coffee expansion began during the Thirty Years, when farms of various sizes spread along the gently sloped hills of the Carazo Plateau and the mountains of the Sierras de Managua within the Southern Uplands. By the time Zelaya came to power, coffee was already the country's leading export, and a significant infrastructure was in place to service the coffee economy.[91] Nevertheless, a radical policy option was not initiated until Zelaya's land and labor reforms. This legislation featured a major governmental effort to promote large-scale plantations throughout all of the country's coffee regions and attempts to coercively secure workers to service the plantations. In pursuing these policies, Zelaya sought to promote the overall well-being of coffee planters,[92] but he selectively applied the reforms to favor those members of the dominant class who supported his administration politically.

In 1895, the liberal government took steps to undermine the communal land system in which indigenous people collectively owned large tracts of land. Especially in the North Central Highlands around towns such Matagalpa and Jinotega, where previous land legislation had been least effective, this land system stood in the way of coffee production. The government first declared that all members of ethnic communities were obligated to grant one another permission before land use could commence. According to Teplitz, "only one Indian in each community had to be tricked or made drunk and told to sign a sales agreement for the liquidation of his village to start."[93] Over the next several years, myriad legislation began to replace the communal and *ejidal* land systems with individual forms of land ownership, further undermining indigenous communities.[94] Finally, in 1906, title to all communal and *ejidal* land was simply abolished. The legislation was explicitly biased to ensure that large estate owners would obtain much of the divided collective lands. Moreover, the law was implemented by "men from outside the Indian society" who sought to service the interests of non-ethnic claimants.[95]

During the Zelaya period, known land sales, grants, and leases totaled over 3.25 million acres, with a relatively small number of families receiving much of the total.[96] Land distribution for coffee planting continued in the Southern Uplands around Managua and Granada, but it also extended to the North Central Highlands. A 1909 coffee census showed that the northern departments of Matagalpa, Jinotega, Nueva Segovia, and Estelí had 29 percent of the coffee trees in the country.[97] In Matagalpa, land claims increased almost fourfold under Zelaya, and the

Matagalpan Indian community lost roughly 10 percent of its land to coffee expansion.[98] The extension of coffee production to Matagalpa and other northern towns may well have reflected the increased ability and willingness of the liberal government to use state coercion to defeat the resistance of indigenous opposition.[99]

Before the overthrow of Zelaya, the overall contours of the Nicaraguan economy were beginning to develop striking resemblances to the coffee republics of Guatemala and El Salvador. Most important, the large coffee estate was the principal unit of agricultural production. Drawing on the 1909 coffee census, Robert G. Williams has shown that large plantations dominated to a greater degree than in any other Central American republic except Guatemala. Specifically, "capitalist farms (those requiring hired labor for permanent maintenance and picking) had 81 percent of the trees in the census sample."[100] Of course, there was regional differentiation within the country, with some departments having a relatively greater concentration of smaller holdings. For example, in the department of Masaya, peasant farms and family-sized units controlled over 60 percent of all coffee trees. Smaller units were also more common in the North Central Highlands area, which had been incorporated into the coffee trade under Zelaya. These variations can be explained by geographic and demographic factors, as well as factors such as the ability of the indigenous communities to resist or adapt to the advances of capitalist agriculture.[101]

While Zelaya's land policy was clearly intended to promote coffee-planter interests, it was implemented in a highly political fashion. Because "the Zelayistas sought to use the land law to control the elite," a large majority of all distributed lands went to liberal supporters.[102] Teplitz's sample of thirty-six different persons in 1900 reveals that over 70 percent of government-approved transactions involved families who were allied with Zelaya in the civil war of 1896. Many leading conservative families involved in coffee production are conspicuously absent from the list of land sales.[103] In addition, political favorites enjoyed other benefits such as lax enforcement of a regulation that limited the amount of land any single individual could receive. "Centralized control [of land distribution] benefited Liberal supporters. Foes learned the government's control of land could exclude them as readily as it did the lower class."[104]

Like land policy, labor reforms also served to polarize class relations in the countryside. An 1894 labor law required that all male and female agricultural wage laborers over fourteen years old register with agricultural judges stationed throughout the country's departments.[105] Laborers were also required to carry a work card, showing their employment status and their indebtedness. A vagrancy regulation mandated that all insolvent persons find employment or face imprisonment. Agricultural judges, working with *jefes políticos,* were charged with "prosecuting, capturing, and remitting to work" individuals who failed to comply with the regulations. The law also obligated estate owners to put down any form of labor unrest on their plantations. In turn, coffee planters were guaranteed ample labor, even in time of war.

Fugitives who broke their contracts or ignored the regulations remained a major problem for growers, as rural workers could fairly easily escape to neighboring departments or areas where the military was not present.[106] In addition, because workers were customarily paid at the beginning of their contract, they had an incentive to sign agreements with multiple estate owners, compounding the problem. In 1899, the Zelaya administration "attempted to defeat the fugitive problem by bolstering their corps of agricultural justices, and forming a special force of agricultural guards."[107] A further extension of the military was put into place, with army forces, the civil guard, a mountain guard, and a cavalry guard now all working to catch fugitives for estate owners. In 1901, a new agricultural labor law was passed, forcing any individual of at least sixteen years of age who possessed less than five hundred pesos in cash or property to immediately obtain a *libreta* (work card) from the agricultural judge.[108] "Thereby, the liberals attempted to compel most of the nation over sixteen years of age to join a manual labor pool."[109] Persons who failed to comply faced fines and were put to work on public projects. In short, a variety of legal and coercive instruments—vagrancy laws, work cards, military conscription, public service drafts, and outright military force—began to solve some of the severe labor problems present in liberal Nicaragua.

Taken together, the labor and land policies enacted in Nicaragua were perhaps the most thoroughgoing in the region. Zelaya's labor policy was especially similar to that put into place by Barrios in Guatemala, where a forced labor draft system was also installed (a somewhat less harsh and more market-based system developed in El Salvador). By contrast, Nicaraguan land policy was closer to that carried out in El Salvador, where all communal and *ejidal* lands were simply abolished (a somewhat less encompassing attack occurred in Guatemala). Hence, based on the legislative efforts of Zelaya and the Nicaraguan liberals, we have every reason to imagine that this country would have developed in a manner similar to the radical liberal cases of Guatemala and El Salvador. Yet ultimately, Nicaragua—like Honduras—was not able to complete its process of liberal transformation.

FOREIGN INTERVENTION IN NICARAGUA

Aborted liberalism in Nicaragua occurred as a result of U.S. political intervention beginning in 1909, which led to the overthrow of Zelaya and the creation of an informal protectorate. Although many accounts of the intervention in Nicaragua have stressed U.S. concerns about investment opportunities in Central America and the Caribbean, the decision to intervene appears to have been most immediately motivated by political considerations. Furthermore, the decisive causes of the intervention had as much to do with ongoing political events within Nicaragua and the overall political project pursued by Zelaya as with changing socioeconomic realities in Nicaragua.

The Fall of Zelaya

Zelaya became an enemy of the United States not simply or primarily because U.S. policymakers believed that the dictator was hostile to U.S. capitalists and investment in Nicaragua. Rather, U.S. government leaders turned against Zelaya when they came to see him as working against their geopolitical goal of having friendly, stable governments in power in a region that they had historically treated as the "backyard" of the United States. Zelaya had been accommodating to foreign capitalists, offering generous concessions to U.S. businessmen, so much so that his critics accused him of having sold out Nicaragua to Yankee investors.[110] However, Zelaya's regional expansionist designs and unwillingness to recognize ultimate U.S. authority and hegemony in the region led the State Department to oppose him. Not only was Zelaya identified as the main cause of a 1906 war that engulfed the entire region, but after the United States stepped in to stop the fighting, Zelaya denounced the Roosevelt administration for interfering in Central American affairs.[111] And after the Panama Canal was built in 1903, Zelaya infuriated the United States by making overtures to Germany and Japan to build a second canal through Nicaragua without U.S. participation. Finally, in 1908, Zelaya negotiated significant loans from a British financial syndicate to construct a railway against the wishes of the State Department.[112]

Growing U.S. opposition to Zelaya was closely linked to the transformation of U.S. foreign policy taking place at the beginning of the twentieth century. Although the "big stick" of President Theodore Roosevelt has been associated with an aggressive foreign policy, in fact the "dollar diplomacy" of President Taft and Secretary of State Knox proved to be much more interventionist in Central America.[113] Drawing on the belief that capital investment and wise fiscal management would produce political "good" in less advantaged nations, Taft and Knox normatively justified seizing the financial institutions of their poorer neighbors so that they could ultimately protect them from threats of revolutions, instability, and other catastrophes. Knox believed that in order to allow U.S. investors to do "good"—both for themselves and for the nation in question—the use of force was sometimes necessary to support the role of the constructive dollar.

Yet this conducive international context was not enough to bring on intervention in Nicaragua; political conditions there were also an essential ingredient. In 1909, a revolt broke out on the isolated Mosquito Coast of eastern Nicaragua. The uprising was led by General Juan José Estrada, a disillusioned liberal appointed by Zelaya as governor of Bluefields. Estrada made an alliance with leading conservative families in return for assurance that he would be selected president once the revolt succeeded. Among the conservative financiers and participants were several prominent Granada families, including major coffee families such as that of Emiliano Chamorro.[114] In addition, a small number of Americans living in the area joined the revolutionary forces and played an important role in funding the effort. Nevertheless, the revolt initially appeared to be not much different than any of the several uprisings that had broken out during Zelaya's sixteen-year rule. Zelaya easily crushed the incipient rebellion by simply arresting the conservative leadership.

Yet things were different in 1909, for the United States was now seeking to remove Zelaya. In 1908, the U.S. minister to Nicaragua reported that Zelaya was "all to the bad," and felt that the Conservative Party, led by Chamorro, would better serve U.S. interests in the region.[115] Although Secretary Knox shared this view and sent four hundred marines to the area to monitor events, he did not formally intervene on behalf of the rebels until an appropriate pretext was established. Such a pretext arose when Zelaya's forces captured two Americans laying mines in the San Juan River that were intended to blow up ships carrying Zelaya's army forces. Zelaya ordered the execution of the Americans. Knox responded by declaring the action "an outrage" and stating that the Zelaya government "has been a blot upon the history of Nicaragua and a discouragement to a group of republics whose aspirations need only the opportunity of free and honest government." Knox went on to say that "the Government of the United States is convinced that the revolution represents the ideals and the will of a majority of Nicaraguan people."[116] The "revolution" had actually been dying, despite the presence of U.S. marines, but now it gained new strength. The newly installed Taft administration was determined to use U.S. forces to support the rebel cause. Zelaya recognized that the end had come—he simply could not sustain his government in the face of outright U.S. hostility—and he resigned and went into exile.

Before leaving Nicaragua, however, Zelaya made certain that the Nicaraguan congress appointed a liberal candidate, José Madriz, to the presidency. This was unacceptable to Knox, and the U.S. government continued to back the rebels led by Estrada and Chamorro. After initially resisting and calling for British intervention, Madriz soon also realized the situation was impossible, and he took refuge in exile in August 1910. The liberal government then quickly collapsed. With turmoil reigning in Managua, the conservative vanguard entered the capital and announced that elections would be held to determine a new president.

U.S. Occupation and Neocolonialism

For the next two decades, Nicaragua functioned as a neo-colony of the United States. In the political sphere, the U.S. State Department (through a marine landing) worked to prop up sympathetic governments that would support American interests. In the economic sphere, U.S. capitalists quickly came to dominate the country's financial and fiscal institutions. The crucial consequence was that the policies enacted by Zelaya did not have an enduring impact on the development of the state and the economy.[117]

Stabilizing the political situation in Nicaragua was initially not an easy task for U.S. policymakers. Factional fighting among Nicaraguan elites left the United States scrambling to find a suitable leader.[118] By the summer of 1912, pro-Zelaya liberals led by Benjamín Zeledón had organized a major assault against the U.S.-backed government of Adolfo Díaz. In response to Díaz's request for help, Taft sent the first of several U.S. marine contingents. The U.S. force, which soon reached twenty-seven hundred men, forcibly occupied León and extended its control along the railway line to Granada. In November 1912 the liberal forces were routed, and Zeledón was captured and killed; around a thousand Nicaraguans perished in the revolts of this time.[119] In subsequent years conservative rule was stabilized, and the size of the U.S. occupation force in Nicaragua was reduced. However, a token contingent of a hundred marines remained in the country until 1925 to discourage further liberal uprisings and promote governmental stability.

During this period of renewed conservative rule, all Nicaraguan presidents acted as agents for promoting U.S. hegemony.[120] The U.S. minister in Managua worked closely with the Nicaraguan government and was immediately informed about any significant domestic development. Moreover, U.S. officials played a major role in making sure that each presidential transfer (nominally through elections) was a stable affair that brought an acceptable conservative candidate to power. To ensure their continued rule, Nicaragua's conservative presidents jailed anti-U.S. demonstrators, shut down the anti-U.S. press, and supported U.S. interests in the international community. The Dawson Agreements of 1910 set up a U.S.-dominated commission to resolve disputes involving contracts and concessions granted by Zelaya and provided a U.S.-financed loan to the Nicaraguan government. In 1914 conservatives signed the Bryan-Chamorro Treaty, which gave the United States perpetual canal rights across Nicaragua.

Even more important were the fiscal and financial controls granted to the United States. In order to secure U.S. loans, the Nicaraguan government relinquished control of the customs houses to the State Department, and it turned over the national railway and the national bank to U.S. investors. Eventually, the fiscal mess facing the conservatives led them to grant to a high commission appointed by the State Department the right to approve and supervise the national budget, to fix customs duties, and to oversee the payment of all governmental bonds. Moreover, U.S. investors dominated the coffee trade, through their control over loans and access to credit and through the creation of a merchant company to export coffee.[121] By 1917, almost half of the Nicaraguan budget was being spent on servicing the national debt.

In sum, in a few short years the United States had replaced the liberal government of Zelaya with a new conservative government that served as an instrument for maintaining basically colonial control over Nicaragua. This neocolonial system had substantial implications for the way in which state and class structures developed in the country.

The Weakness of the State and the Dominant Class

U.S. intervention stunted socioeconomic development to the point that Nicaragua most closely resembled Honduras—not Guatemala or El Sal-

vador—in terms of state and class structural features in the years immediately following the reform period. After the fall of Zelaya, the steady
growth of coffee exports that had taken place during the liberal reform
ceased, with the period from 1911 to 1920 witnessing no increase in
annual export volume.[122] Although some U.S. capitalists still profited
through their control over key productive sectors, the domestically controlled economy had collapsed. Economic stagnation found its political
parallel in declining state expenditures and initiatives. As John A. Booth
points out, Nicaragua's extraordinary public indebtedness after 1909
"contributed to a continual inability to supply many basic public services, not to mention the incapacity to continue the infrastructural development programs of the Zelaya era. Public services declined and economic development stagnated."[123] In the twenty years following the fall
of Zelaya, as Knut Walter tell us, "there was no expansion of the railway
network nor construction of roads north or east from the central departments."[124] Not only did massive debt and U.S. financial domination
of the state make the initiation of development projects difficult, but successive conservative governments seemed uninterested in pursuing such
projects in the first place. In the context of neocolonialism, then, the state
became little more than an instrument through which U.S. investors exercised financial control over Nicaragua and U.S. political advisors ensured that friendly governments were in power.

Furthermore, the previous movement toward the militarization of
the state and society was stopped short. Although Zelaya had succeeded
in creating a formidable military organized under the Liberal Party, this
institution rapidly fell into chaos when conservatives assumed control
over government. Conservatives had little interest in preserving or promoting the liberals' institution, since they could now rely on the U.S.
marines to maintain security. For their part, U.S. policy advisors sought
to create a climate of stability in the country conducive to investment; accordingly, they worked toward demilitarization and channeling of public resources away from coercive institutions that were not organized under their own authority. The Nicaraguan national army was eventually
disbanded during the occupation years, thereby effectively terminating
the militarization project of the Zelaya period.

As for domestic class arrangements, the aborting of Zelaya's radical
liberal project left Nicaragua with a national agrarian bourgeoisie that
was economically quite weak. In comparison with the coffee agrarian
bourgeoisie of Guatemala, the Nicaraguan elite lacked extensive control
over land and people, failing to fully consolidate an estate landholding

pattern in which large growers used coercive channels to maintain a resident labor force. In comparison with the coffee agrarian bourgeoisie of El Salvador, the Nicaraguan elite was inefficient and backward, failing to achieve high levels of production through the use of advanced technology and processing techniques.[125] As Jeffery Paige suggests, these weaknesses must be linked to U.S. intervention: "There is little doubt that the intervention stopped the rationalization and expansion of production in what later would become Nicaragua's most dynamic coffee zone. . . . The intervention also deprived the coffee elite of control over exports and finance, which passed into the hands of American banks. The backwardness of the Nicaraguan coffee elite in both production and processing is a direct result of the American intervention."[126] At the same time, the U.S. intervention prevented coffee elites from establishing substantial political power equivalent to that of the dominant classes of Guatemala and El Salvador. Although conservative elites with coffee holdings sometimes occupied government, they wielded little autonomous power next to U.S. financial interests and State Department employees. Hence, Nicaragua and Honduras stand alone in Central America as the only two cases in which dominant-class actors did not exercise significant political leverage within the state at the conclusion of the reform period.

CONCLUSION

The similar structural patterns present in Honduras and Nicaragua early in the twentieth century must be seen against the background of liberal reform periods that were in important respects extremely different. In Honduras, liberal reformers beginning with Marco Aurelio Soto did not move to massively expand the military or achieve development by rapidly overturning existing social relations. Rather, they pursued a reform policy option that sought to gradually promote commercial agriculture, primarily through small farms, without undermining previous landholding patterns. In Nicaragua, by contrast, liberal reformer José Santos Zelaya aggressively pursued military-building and the abrupt transformation of socioeconomic arrangements. Here liberals followed a radical policy option that encouraged plantation agriculture and coercive labor practices at the expense of previous landholding and communal living institutions. Given such differences between the two countries, which were clearly evident by the early twentieth century, one could hardly expect them to have followed a similar path of future development. Honduras appeared well on its way to replicating the Costa Rican pattern of reformist liberalism, while Nicaragua had made substantial headway toward completing a pattern of radical liberalism much like that of Guatemala and El Salvador.

Yet U.S. intervention, it has been argued in this chapter, caused the failure of liberal policies in Honduras and Nicaragua, leading the two countries to follow a single pattern of aborted liberalism. In Honduras, intervention took the form of massive foreign capital investment that overwhelmed the domestic economy. The gradual reform policy option pursued by Honduran liberals—like that followed by Costa Rican liberals—was inherently vulnerable to such economic intervention. But whereas Costa Rican liberals operated in a world-historical environment that preceded the emergence of large-scale foreign investment, Honduran liberals pursued their reforms at a time when the United States was actively seeking new markets abroad. During the reform period, Honduran liberals vigorously promoted foreign investment, paving the way for foreign capitalists to seize control over the most dynamic parts of the economy— eventually to the point that domestic sovereignty was called into question. In Nicaragua, by contrast, Zelaya's liberal revolution was less vulnerable to economic intervention and more susceptible to political intervention. In this case, foreign intervention grew out of an aggressive U.S. foreign policy in which the United States worked to ensure that politically supportive governments would protect its strategic interests in the region. To achieve this end, the United States used its military might to overthrow the Zelaya government, installing a friendly conservative administration in its place and thereby aborting Nicaragua's ongoing coffee revolution.

PART IV

Legacies of the Liberal Reform Period

CHAPTER 8

Aftermath: Reactions
to the Liberal Reform

In all five countries of Central America, the liberal reform period triggered strong political reactions and counterreactions, setting in motion developmental processes that ultimately culminated in the establishment of enduring national political regimes. These reactions occurred because the transformation of state and class structures during the reform period created new social actors and defined new possibilities for the expression of political opposition and support. In addition, the liberal reform period reshaped the stakes of political struggle among these actors, providing clear targets to challenge or defend. The playing out of these political struggles, along with their resolution through the creation of new regimes, represents the legacy of the liberal reform period.

It is useful to divide the legacy into two periods: aftermath and heritage. The *aftermath* is the time immediately following the liberal reform when a series of political reactions and counterreactions took place. The *heritage* corresponds with the establishment of enduring political regimes and represents the long-run legacy of the reform period. This chapter focuses on the aftermath of the liberal reform. It occurred during different chronological periods in each country: 1926–54 in Guatemala; 1927–48 in El Salvador; 1914–49 in Costa Rica; 1919–32 in Honduras; and 1909–36 in Nicaragua.

The aftermath period saw countries move from diluted versions of particular types of national political regimes to full-blown instances of those regimes. Thus, Guatemala and El Salvador evolved from political systems marked by traditional authoritarianism in which the military played a key role to full-blown examples of military authoritarianism. Costa Rica moved from a competitive electoral but nondemocratic regime to a full-blown democracy. And Honduras and Nicaragua saw neocolonial political orders evolve into sovereign national regimes characterized by traditional dictatorships. This chapter assesses the political reactions and counterreactions that drove these processes of political development.

At a general level, two key variables associated with the aftermath period can explain the connection between different kinds of liberal reform periods and the construction of different kinds of national regimes. First, whether or not major democratizing episodes occurred during the aftermath period was highly consequential. In the three countries where the liberal reform period was not undermined by foreign intervention— Guatemala, El Salvador, and Costa Rica—the initiatives of key state actors and the mobilization activities of popular-sector movements brought the issue of democracy to the forefront of national politics. The emergence of such democratizing movements made it impossible for elites to sustain the old liberal model in which traditional dictators controlled the government and in which military and coffee oligarchs held privileged positions within the state apparatus. Democratizing movements pushed national politics either in a more repressive direction, in which the military exercised institutional control over the state and ruled in a highly coercive fashion, or in a more democratic direction, in which popular-sector groups were incorporated into the political system. The structural foundation of radical liberalism made it extremely likely that Guatemala and El Salvador would follow the former, repressive path of regime development in the face of democratizing episodes, whereas reformist liberalism left Costa Rica with a structural legacy highly conducive to democratic evolution once popular-sector groups began seeking expanded political power.

In Honduras and Nicaragua, where an extensive foreign presence accompanied aborted liberalism, reestablishing national sovereignty was the most basic task of the aftermath period. In these countries, the emergence of democratizing movements was effectively closed off by a semicolonial environment in which domestic actors did not exercise full power over the state and the economy. Substantial popular mobilization did take place, but it was directed at U.S. actors, not domestic dominant classes or local authoritarian elites. Because foreign intervention stunted development in Honduras and Nicaragua, it is not surprising that the reestablishment of national sovereignty in the 1930s was accompanied by the reemergence of traditional dictatorships. During the course of these renewed traditional dictatorships, structural modernization of the state and the economy occurred, providing a foundation for the emergence of democratizing movements, especially in the mid-1940s. However, at that point in history, these movements could do little more than force a governmental transition from one traditional dictator to another.

FAILED DEMOCRATIZATION: GUATEMALA AND EL SALVADOR

In Guatemala and El Salvador, the aftermath period was launched in the late 1920s with an elite-led democratic episode in which a relatively progressive president attempted to expand the political arena by incorporating middle-sector and working-class groups into the state. In both cases, these political openings triggered the opposition of powerful actors, including coffee oligarchs and military officers. These actors were successful at closing the door on initial democratic episodes: in the early 1930s, reformist governments were toppled by military coups, and personalistic dictators who were relatively sympathetic to dominant-class interests seized power. These dictators—Jorge Ubico in Guatemala and Maximiliano Hernández Martínez in El Salvador—ruled from 1931 until 1944.

A second round of democratization began in the early 1940s. This time, urban-based, multiclass coalitions led the way, as protest movements formed almost simultaneously in Guatemala and El Salvador to oppose reigning dictatorships. These movements were successful at overthrowing the presidential dictators who had governed since 1931 (Ubico and Martínez), undermining an old political pattern in which the dominant class enjoyed special access within personalistic states. In place of personal dictatorships, relatively progressive governments initially assumed power. However, these governments threatened the military as an institution, and they ultimately triggered a strong reaction from the armed forces. In both Guatemala and El Salvador, the military overthrew the reformist governments, assumed full control of the state, and began to govern autonomously from all major societal groups. Thus, democratizing episodes driven by protest from below represented the final link in the causal chain leading to military authoritarianism in Guatemala and El Salvador.

Despite these overall similarities, there were distinctive steps in the process in Guatemala and El Salvador, including the emergence and brutal defeat of a massive peasant revolt in El Salvador in 1932 and the rise and eventual overthrow of social democratic reformers in Guatemala during the 1944–54 period. From the comparative perspective of this study, Guatemala's failed political revolution of 1944–54 is especially important, raising the key question of why a parallel process did not occur in El Salvador. I shall suggest that the proximate cause of this difference rests with contrasts in the nature of military autonomy under the Ubico and Martínez governments. However, these contrasts in military autonomy were themselves the path-dependent outcome of a long chain of causal processes going back to different agrarian relations established during the liberal reform period.

Political Openings and Political Closures, 1926–1931

Elite-led democratizing episodes occurred during the administrations of Lázaro Chacón in Guatemala (1926–30) and Pío Romero Bosque in El Salvador (1927–31). Both leaders had come to power in non-exceptional ways from the liberal ranks,[1] and initially there was little reason to believe that either president would pursue a major political realignment. However, Chacón and Romero emerged as surprisingly independent presidents, breaking with the liberal past in important ways. They reacted to expanding middle-sector groups and an incipient working class that had begun to demand political reforms and greater political inclusion in the aftermath of decades of liberal reformism and a surging international coffee market in the early twentieth century.[2]

In Guatemala, increased social protest began in 1920, when urban mobilization helped topple the twenty-two-year dictatorship of Manuel Estrada Cabrera.[3] One might reasonably date the beginning of the aftermath period with the administration of Carlos Herrera (1920–21), who drew on popular mobilization in an effort to establish more genuine political liberties in Guatemala.[4] Likewise, the administration of José María Orellana (1921–26), while at times repressive, also took steps in recognizing political rights for urban middle sectors.[5] Yet the Chacón administration was more consequential; it oversaw the formation of new workers' associations and unions and tolerated middle-class parties and political organizations seeking greater influence within government. This was the case even though Chacón was reputedly a corrupt, weak leader; many important social reforms were initiated by his cabinet and the congress, rather than by Chacón himself.[6]

The Chacón administration responded to increased social mobilization by creating the National Labor Department, by passing several pieces of legislation that protected workers' rights, by revamping the electoral process to permit a wider spectrum of party representation, and by tolerating an environment of increased political expression and discussion.[7] These actions brought about the "initial incorporation of the labor movement" into the state[8] and provided the first serious political opening for middle-sector groups in many decades. In 1927, Chacón permitted the adoption of a relatively progressive constitution that "imposed constitutional limits on the Executive's authority, provided for greater separation of powers, and elevated the principles of social welfare and individual rights."[9] However, Chacón never went so far as to allow a free election or to begin to address the needs of the vast rural majority.

Salvadoran leader Pío Romero Bosque responded to similar pressures, going even further toward incorporating new actors, such as salaried commercial and public employees and urban workers, into the state. Romero oversaw the legalization of the eight-hour day, the creation of a Labor Ministry, the promulgation of numerous provisions to protect employee rights, the expansion of legislative provisions for commercial employees, and the lifting of a long-standing state of siege.[10] He permitted extensive organization by a wide variety of opposing politicians and political parties and attempted to reorganize the military by undermining the power bases of older officers.[11] Most important, he was instrumental in setting up the first genuinely competitive elections in Salvadoran history. The presidential election of January 1931 featured six main candidates, ranging from the progressive coffee planter Arturo Araujo of the newly formed Labor Party, to Alberto Gómez Zárate of the Quiñónez family, to the military candidacy of General Maximiliano Hernández Martínez. Although Gómez Zárate was the early favorite, General Martínez joined the Araujo ticket as vice-president, and it was ultimately Araujo who emerged on top (winning 101,000 votes out of a total of 217,000, compared to Gómez Zárate's 64,000).[12] Araujo, who made promises of land reform, was able to dominate in the central and western departments, where lower rural classes associated with the coffee economy were located.[13] Initially, at least, all major actors accepted Araujo's victory, and he assumed power in the spring of 1931. Despite some irregularities,[14] this election and presidential transfer amounted to the most democratic moment in Salvadoran history before 1979.

Political openings in both Guatemala and El Salvador generated strong reactions in the form of military coups. These coups were supported by elite actors of the liberal reform period, including top military officials and members of the agrarian bourgeoisie who were threatened by the incorporation of new actors into the political system as well as by the accompanying increase in societal polarization. The coups took place during a dramatic fall in international coffee prices associated with the depression of 1930, which shook the foundations of the Guatemalan and Salvadoran economies. While political experimentation may have been tolerable for a short period during good economic times, it was unacceptable in the depths of an economic depression.

In Guatemala, Chacón was already in trouble when the Depression hit. His administration was widely viewed as corrupt, and urban social mobilization and popular unrest had reached disturbingly high levels. With the Depression, exports plummeted, revenues dwindled, and only foreign credits kept the administration afloat.[15] In late 1930, Chacón suffered a serious stroke, prompting the military to take control: under the leadership of General Manuel Orellana, a coup toppled the government. The United States quickly pressured the Guatemalan military and political-economic elite to restore political stability through elections.[16] General Jorge Ubico, a popular military official and a member of one of the leading families of the elite, emerged as the top candidate. In February 1931, he was unanimously selected president of Guatemala in an uncontested election.

In El Salvador, Araujo also had the misfortune of presiding over an economy in a state of collapse. The economic collapse led much of the elite to boycott the government, taking with them many experienced administrators responsible for running the national government and bureaucracy.[17] Araujo also isolated many high-ranking military officials and even many junior officers by being insensitive to their institutional needs (e.g., by reducing the military budget and failing to pay officers promptly).[18] Finally, the political opening associated with Araujo's election gave organizational space to workers and peasants in which they could act on pent-up grievances. Major peasant strikes and urban popular demonstrations occurred in April and May 1931. Following student demonstrations in July, martial law was activated in an attempt to restore political order.[19]

On December 2, 1931, a military coup ousted Araujo from power. Relatively unknown junior officers, acting without the support of key senior army commanders, led the coup.[20] These officers quickly formed a Military Directorate and within two days installed General Martínez as president, thus following constitutional guidelines that provided for vice-presidential succession. However, "the young officers obviously intended to employ Martínez as a figurehead in an attempt to satisfy domestic and foreign opinion, while continuing to exercise power."[21] In this sense, and in contrast to Ubico, Martínez did not come to power with a strong support base in the army. Furthermore, whereas Ubico's rise to power was viewed quite favorably by the United States, Martínez initially faced enormous pressure from the State Department to step aside.[22] Lacking key domestic and international support, Martínez appeared to stand little chance of prolonging his government beyond a few months. However, just as a presidential transfer seemed imminent, the peasant revolt of 1932 erupted, enabling General Martínez to consolidate a secure power base.

The Peasant Revolt of 1932 in El Salvador

To understand why a peasant revolt broke out in El Salvador when Martínez assumed power but no similar rural rebellion accompanied the rise of Ubico to the presidency, it is necessary to review patterns of rural organization whose origins we earlier traced in the analysis of radical liberalism. Class relations in both countries were blatantly exploitative, and peasants in key coffee-producing regions no doubt sought at times to strike out against perceived sources of oppression. However, Guatemalan rural workers found themselves in a structural position that left little opportunity to act on their frustration. Guatemala's plantation labor force did not function autonomously from plantation owners and military officials, but rather was subject to close and relatively constant supervision, undermining the potential for sustained collective action. By contrast, in El Salvador, plantation laborers *did* have substantial autonomy from landlords and state agents, enhancing the possibility of collective action. Furthermore, whereas Guatemalan peasants could avoid incorporation into the agrarian capitalist system by fleeing to isolated regions where private property had not taken hold, in densely populated El Salvador all communal lands had been abolished, and there were few opportunities to express dissatisfaction by exiting to subsistence-farming communities. In short, the events of the late 1920s and early 1930s provided a basically similar impetus for lower rural classes to rebel, but only in El Salvador were peasants structurally positioned to act on this impetus.

The history of the Salvadoran peasant insurrection of 1932, known simply as the *matanza* (massacre) because of the government response it generated, has been debated, but the basic facts are not in dispute.[23] The revolt followed on the heels of growing rural mobilization in the western departments during the Araujo government. The internally divided Salvadoran Communist Party (PCS), led by Agustín Farabundo Martí, had organized in this area since 1930, and at least some rural leaders supported Martí and the Communists. Yet most scholars agree that the 1932 revolt was primarily a spontaneous peasant rebellion led by Indian town caciques and religious organizations rather than a Communist-inspired insurrection; the PCS did not direct the actual uprising and certainly did not control it once it began, even though the Communists may have had some influence on its timing.[24] In fact, most of the top PCS leadership was in prison, and almost no preparations had been made when the rural rebellion came to a head in mid-January 1932.

The revolt was centered in the coffee-producing departments of Sonsonate and Ahuachapán. Rebels armed with antiquated rifles and machetes succeeded in capturing roughly a dozen municipalities, including the important towns of Izalco, Nahuizalco, and Juayúa; and major revolts threatened key areas around San Salvador. For the coffee elite and the military, the revolt represented the worst possible combination: Indian rebellion and Communist revolution.[25] Within days, the government was on the offensive, seeking to destroy both participants and those who sympathized with the rebellion. The National Guard was crucial to driving back the rebels, but also important were civilian vigilante groups—so-called Civic Guards—promoted by the government and often financed and organized by leading coffee elites. The overall level of repression was extraordinary, going far beyond merely defeating the rebellion. PCS supporters in the towns were identified through voting lists and were literally hunted down and killed; entire villages were wiped out. In the end, the *matanza* saw the execution of an estimated ten to thirty thousand peasants.

Despite its enormous cost in human lives, the *matanza* enabled Martínez to generate a support base. The claim that Martínez "became a heroic figure to the masses" after the revolt[26] may be exaggerated, but it is true that, as Kenneth Grieb suggests, "successful suppression of the rebellion won the Martínez government broad support," especially among middle-sector groups in San Salvador.[27] Furthermore, the massacre helped Martínez avoid being toppled by a military coup. In the short run, the insurrection had this effect because it temporarily directed the attention of the professional army to the rural crisis. In the long run, the insurrection served Martínez's political needs by heightening the power of loyal coercive units that could be used as counterweights to the somewhat disloyal professional army. In particular, the revolt led to the expansion of the National Police, the National Guard, and paramilitary forces such as the Civic Guards—all units in which Martínez enjoyed considerable support.[28]

Authoritarian Liberalism Restored, 1931–1944

The governments of Ubico (1931–44) and Martínez (1931–44) were the culmination of reactions to political openings in the late 1920s. Under these governments, Guatemala and El Salvador experienced full reversals of earlier efforts at incorporating new urban groups into the state: patterns of reform and mobilization quickly gave way to extreme political demobilization.

Internal security concerns preoccupied Ubico and Martínez throughout their rule, and both identified labor organizations and urban civic associations—legalized under Chacón and Romero—as key potential sources of opposition. The Ubico administration used the Guatemalan military and police to crack down on workers, intellectuals, and organized professional sectors.[29] Especially after a plot to assassinate Ubico was discovered in 1934, the government implemented strict political control in urban Guatemala, monitoring all social gatherings and the press and even regulating discourse by banning words that implied class struggle.[30] Likewise, the Martínez government officially discouraged the organization of labor unions and suppressed voluntary associations, claiming they were subversive. In the wake of the 1932 revolt, San Salvador was closely monitored, and occasional efforts by urban middle-sector groups at mobilizing against the government "were met with swift repression."[31]

The degree of personalism under Ubico's government is reminiscent of the administration of Justo Rufino Barrios. Ubico was in fact the godson of Barrios, and he consciously modeled his administration after his *padrino*. Grieb points out that Ubico "sought to concentrate all decisionmaking power in his own hands. The Legislature became primarily a rubber stamp, selected under carefully controlled balloting. The President personally designated its members, and the governmental apparatus assured their 'election.' . . . The result was an extreme concentration of power—in reality Ubico *was* Guatemala during his tenure in office, heading a personal and paternalistic government which was capable of rapid and decisive action."[32] Despite his close connections to the coffee elite, "Ubico's efforts did not entirely coincide with the predilections and attitudes of the oligarchy."[33] For example, he promoted agricultural diversification, overseeing a rapid expansion of corn and rice cultivation, which cut against the coffee elite's interest in maintaining significant fallow land.[34] Ubico also remade labor legislation in ways that may or may not have accorded with dominant-class preferences. Beginning in 1934, the debt peonage system was abolished and replaced with a vagrancy law that considered as vagrants all men who did not meet an income requirement or did not possess a modest amount of personal land.[35] Whether the termination of debt peonage actually accorded with dominant-class interests is in dispute.[36] Nevertheless, it caused a further expansion of the military's role in overseeing labor policy and increased the dependence of coffee elites on the state for rural control.[37]

Nor was Ubico simply a token representative of the armed forces. Although the general held the armed forces in high esteem and preferred to surround himself with military men,[38] appointments to the top ranks of the military were invariably based on political loyalty to Ubico rather than on professional criteria.[39] At the same time that Ubico politicized the commanding heights of the military, "the Caudillo placed considerable emphasis on professionalizing the Army, hoping that the resultant training would insulate the officer corps from political machinations."[40] Especially through the reform of Guatemala's main military academy, Ubico oversaw the creation of "an expanding corps of well trained, professionalized officers."[41] Unlike the top military leadership, these younger officers were generally of middle-class origin and not tied politically to Ubico.[42] Hence, the Guatemalan military was divided between junior officers who functioned independently of Ubico and senior officers who were encapsulated within Ubico's patronage network.

With respect to relations between ruler and dominant class, the Martínez government in El Salvador was similar to the Ubico government. As Patricia Parkman notes, "Martínez was not simply the agent of any single sector of Salvadoran society. . . . He was a classic Latin American dictator, personally dominating the government."[43] David Luna likewise characterizes Martínez as leading a "personalistic regime" and argues that "Martínez was not a representative of dominant classes."[44] Furthermore, despite suggestions to the contrary,[45] Martínez's rule did not correspond with a situation of institutional military rule. It is true that after 1932 Martínez replaced civilian officials with military officers at all levels of government, such that there were relatively few important bureaucratic positions held by civilians.[46] However, the overwhelming personal power of Martínez represented a major check on the military's institutional hold over government.

The image of Martínez as a figurehead for the military as a whole loses credibility when one simple fact is recognized: Martínez never enjoyed broad support within the professional armed forces. Here we will recall that, unlike Ubico, Martínez came to power without significant backing in the army, and it is quite likely that only the peasant revolt of 1932 allowed him to avoid being overthrown in the initial months after assuming power. The insurrection had this effect because it led to the expansion of paramilitary security forces in the countryside and the capital that counterbalanced the regular army. In effect, after the 1932 massacre, the state security apparatus was bifurcated between paramilitary units and the professional military. In the wake of the peasant revolt, Martínez relied on the National Guard and the National Police, both of which were linked to powerful civilian vigilante groups.[47] By the mid-1930s, the professional army strongly resented what it perceived to be favoritism toward the paramilitary units.[48] According to McClintock, "in the latter years of his presidency, Martínez' grasp on power appeared to be held *despite* the army. . . . The army had not become Martínez' practorian guard, but to a large extent the paramilitary security services *had* and, after 1937, took a proportionately bigger slice of the budgetary pie than did the regular army."[49] Indeed, whereas the officer corps in Guatemala swelled in size under Ubico's rule, the Salvadoran officer corps saw little or no growth under Martínez.[50] Throughout the 1930s, there were several coup attempts against Martínez,[51] but the strongman managed to maintain power by relying on allies within the National Guard and National Police.

By the early 1940s, then, the structure of relations between the ruler and the military and the nature of divisions within the security apparatuses varied significantly in Guatemala and El Salvador. In Guatemala, the most salient division was within the army itself, in particular the split between older officers and generals who had risen to substantial influence during the Ubico years and younger, junior officers who were less tied to the dictator. Ubico had considerable support among the former group, and so long as he remained in power, the armed forces functioned relatively cohesively, providing a strong pillar for his sustained rule. Yet just beneath the surface was a major contradiction: the state was run by military leaders who lacked the autonomy to govern independently of Ubico. The removal of Ubico could thus send shock waves throughout the state apparatus and provide opportunities for junior officers less tied to the dictator to influence national politics.

The Salvadoran army was also divided between younger and older officers. But in this case the most important division was between the professional military and the quasi-public security forces. Major factions of the professional army, including factions that represented top-ranking officers, were opposed to Martínez's ongoing rule. Because the regular army had not been co-opted by Martínez, this organization's leadership would be more capable of maintaining institutional coherence in the absence of the dictator. Indeed, Martínez's personalistic power was actually an obstacle preventing the military from exercising full-blown institutional domination of the Salvadoran government and state.

Renewed Democratic Hopes, 1944

It remains for us to understand the political processes that led to the fall of Ubico and Martínez and their replacement with full-blown military-authoritarian regimes. As we will see, renewed protest movements in 1944 were a crucial impetus for such political developments. Protest movements raised new hopes for democracy, especially when they brought about the resignation of Martínez and Ubico and ushered into power provisional governments that made arrangements for competitive elections.

In April 1944, after Martínez amended the constitution to permit himself a fourth term in office, disenchanted officers from the army and air force staged a coup.[52] As had happened several times during his rule, Martínez survived the military revolt by drawing on the support of the National Guard and the National Police. This time, however, the coup was particularly bloody, costing at least two hundred lives and seeing the execution of the leading conspirators.[53] In part as a reaction to the failed coup, what Parkman aptly calls a "nonviolent insurrection" broke out in San Salvador in the spring of 1944.[54] Beginning with students at the University of San Salvador and later extending to a broader segment of middle-sector groups (such as clerks, professionals, entrepreneurs, and high school students), nonviolent civic strikes (huelgas de brazos caidos) were utilized to protest against the government. This nonviolent protest movement was led by individuals of the upper and middle classes, but it eventually encompassed much of the working class and other lower urban groups, often including young people influenced by World War II and the Allies' defense of political freedom and democracy. Because Martínez enjoyed little support within the officer corps, the army was not eager to defend the government. "Soldiers disappeared from the streets, leaving law enforcement in the hands of the police and the National Guard."[55] But Martínez had personal reservations about using the police and National Guard to violently repress the urban protest movement (in marked contrast to his reaction to the peasant revolt of 1932). With the Salvadoran government deeply divided and unable or unwilling to stop the civic protest movement, the U.S. ambassador persuaded Martínez to resign on May 9, 1944. Before retiring to Honduras (where he was later assassinated), Martínez made sure power was transferred to Vice-President Andrés Ignacio Menéndez.

After Martínez's fall, democracy seemed to be on the political horizon in El Salvador. Provisional president Menéndez lifted the state of siege, issued a general amnesty for political prisoners, and abolished Martínez's personal secret police force.[56] Presidential elections were scheduled for January 1945, and political organizational and party-building activities escalated. A progressive candidate, Arturo Romero—who favored sweeping socioeconomic changes, civilian rule, and a reform of the military—attracted wide support. Arturo Romero was, in effect, the Salvadoran equivalent of the famous Guatemalan reform leader Juan José Arévalo.[57]

Yet whereas Arévalo went on to win relatively free elections in Guatemala, Romero and his allies were not permitted similar opportunities in El Salvador. Once the obstacle of Martínez was removed, public demonstrations and talk of civilian rule became unacceptable to senior representatives of the army, and this institution soon found itself in conflict with President Menéndez.[58] On October 21, 1944, Colonel Osmín Aguirre y Salinas carried out a coup d'état that "put an end to El Salvador's democratic opening."[59] Though technically led by a single individual, the coup was actually planned and orchestrated by much of the military leadership and drew support from throughout the armed forces. With broad military backing, Colonel Aguirre brought full closure to the political opening: the army repressed labor organizations, the short-lived civilian parties, and the student radicals. Although strikes and demonstrations by urban middle-sector groups were launched to protest this turn of events, the military maintained a surprising degree of unity, even in the face of an armed invasion led by Romero.[60] Unable to take advantage of splits in the military, the civilian resistance soon declined. To formalize its control over national politics, the army held show elections for president in March 1945, bringing General Salvador Castaneda Castro to power in a virtually uncontested race.

Under General Castaneda, the stage was set for many decades of institutional military rule in El Salvador. Casteneda helped resolve the division between paramilitary and professional military forces by giving control over all security forces to the Ministry of War. In the past, the Ministry of Government had supervised the paramilitary forces, while the Ministry of War had been under the direction of the professional army. This division had inhibited institutional military rule in El Salvador by counterbalancing the professional military with the paramilitary forces and allowing Martínez to rule without the support of the professional military. With the new change, "less opportunity would exist for the inter-ministerial maneuvering enabling independent-minded police directors, or Ministers of Government to override the regular military hierarchy, which controlled the Ministry of War. The opportunity for an astute president to play off the security forces against the regular army—a technique Martínez had developed in his latter years of power—would also be reduced. Civilian militias too, vanished with the fall of the Martínez regime."[61] Moreover, beginning in 1948, the division between younger, more professionally trained officers and older, more politicized officers greatly declined in significance.[62] In this year, a group of younger officers located at Fort Zapote overthrew General Castaneda in the so-called Majors' Coup. With this event, the professional military, as represented by professional junior officers, seized institutional control of the Salvadoran state and government.

Meanwhile, in Guatemala, in part as a reaction to events in El Salvador, a multiclass opposition movement formed in June 1944 to force Ubico from office.[63] The movement joined together students from the University of San Carlos, members of the middle classes (especially lawyers and other professionals) disillusioned with the economy under Ubico, and even factions of the coffee elite that had grown tired of the personalistic government. Although Ubico initially responded with coercion, many top government officials did not have the stomach to violently repress professionals and the urban middle class. It soon became clear even to loyal Ubico allies in the army that the government could not control the popular mobilization in a politically acceptable fashion. On July 1, 1944, less than two months after the fall of Martínez, Ubico resigned in the face of political pressure.[64]

Nominally, a three-man junta led by General Federico Ponce Vaides governed Guatemala after Ubico stepped down. However, *ubiquista* generals "constituted the real repository of the presidency, with the junta officers as figureheads. . . . It quickly became apparent that the Generals, oligarchs, and perhaps Ubico himself, were still in control, and the governmental transfer to the Ponce regime resembled a changing of the guard rather than a significant alteration of the power structure."[65] Although the new government announced that elections would be held, which led to substantial urban mobilization in support of democracy, the Guatemalan military had no more intention of permitting a fair election than the Salvadoran military had. Like the Aguirre government in El Salvador, the Ponce government in Guatemala soon "began to suppress the opposition ruthlessly."[66]

The key difference between Guatemala and El Salvador was not only that the Guatemalan military failed to defeat the urban protest movement, as the Salvadoran military did, but junior officers actually allied with the democratic forces. Here the contrasts noted above between Guatemala and El Salvador with respect to relations between the ruler and the military come into play. In El Salvador, where the professional armed forces were often isolated under Martínez, the 1944 opening provided a pretext for this institution to finally begin governing on its own, without having to play a secondary role beneath the privileged paramilitary units. In this context, the Salvadoran army remained cohesive in the face of urban movements for democracy and responded with sustained repression until the opposition was defeated. By contrast, the Ponce government in Guatemala was controlled by highly politicized army men who were not clearly differentiated from Ubico, and thus the fall of Ubico did little to settle the long-standing grievances of junior officers in the army. When civilian protests for democracy mounted, not only were these officers unwilling to repress the democratic movement, but they came to view the civilians as an acceptable alternative to the Ubico power bloc.

Now, finally, we can understand why the reform period that occurred after 1944 was much more extensive in Guatemala than in El Salvador. Whereas Salvadoran generals sustained themselves in power until urban protest waned in the mid-1940s, in Guatemala junior army officers allied with the civilian opposition and led a military coup that forced Ponce and the *ubiquista* generals from office in October 1944. The different reactions of the militaries in Guatemala and El Salvador were rooted in the particular internal military cleavages that had developed under Ubico and Martínez, which in turn had their origins in agrarian structures established in the nineteenth century. In El Salvador, agrarian class structures inherited from the liberal period led to a massive peasant revolt, which ultimately helped produce a major division between military and paramilitary units in the security system. Because the paramilitary forces had been nurtured by Martínez, his removal allowed the professional military to finally seize full control of the state. By contrast, in Guatemala, agrarian structures were less conducive to peasant revolts in the early twentieth century, and here the most important division was between junior officers and Ubico loyalists. Junior officers had to turn to the democratizing movement in an effort to gain the upper hand against politicized officers carried over from the Ubico period. Notwithstanding the key role of social mobilization, then, the 1944 coup in Guatemala was very much a conflict between two different factions of the military, and it did not substantially weaken the Guatemalan military's overall position within the state.[67] After the coup, an interim military-civilian junta was appointed to rule the country until elections could be held in March 1945. With the backing of junior officers, civilian reformer Juan José Arévalo won these elections, marking the beginning of a new reform episode in Guatemala.

The Reform Period of 1944–1954 in Guatemala

The role of the United States in undermining the 1944–54 reform in Guatemala has dominated much of the historiography on Guatemala. It has now been thoroughly documented that the Eisenhower administration considered the reform project to be a communist threat and actively used the CIA to destabilize and overthrow the Guatemalan reformers. Although early analysts debated whether the reformers represented a genuine communist threat to the United States,[68] the overwhelming consensus is now that President Arévalo (1945–50) and his successor, Jacobo Arbenz (1950–54), were committed to private property, democracy, and improving social welfare, even if they may have permitted communists to organize and hold government offices. The irony of the U.S. intervention in 1954 is that the Arbenz government was carrying out reforms congruent with what the Kennedy administration (1960–63) would later advocate for Latin America through the "Alliance for Progress" foreign policy. Whether U.S. intervention was motivated by economic or security factors has also been a favorite topic of debate among analysts. Proponents of the economic interpretation point to connections between United Fruit Company and key officials in the Eisenhower administration,[69] while those emphasizing the security explanation argue that, even in the absence of economic factors, Cold War anticommunist concerns would have led to U.S. intervention.[70]

For our purposes, the more important controversy concerns the relative importance of domestic factors versus external factors in explaining the failure of the 1944–54 reform period. Whereas previous debates are motivated by the assumption that U.S. intervention was decisive to this failure, recent work suggests that domestic factors were at least as important as U.S. intervention in blocking successful reform in Guatemala.[71] Indeed, these studies suggest that the 1944–54 reform period might have failed *even in the absence of U.S. intervention.* In this section, I build the case for this argument, suggesting that preexisting patterns of state militarization and class polarization had put Guatemala on a trajectory of development that made it extremely likely that military authoritarianism would develop even without the interventionist activities of the United States. At the core of this argument is the claim that the Guatemalan military was poised to seize power if any government—even a government headed by a respected general such as Jacobo Arbenz—attempted to alter class structures in the countryside in ways that empowered lower rural classes.

The Arévalo administration, which ruled from 1945 to 1950, was a reformist civilian government that enacted modest changes without fundamentally upsetting the explosive rural socioeconomic order.[72] Arévalo focused primarily on improving conditions in the urban sector, achieving important gains for city workers: a 1947 labor code encouraged formation of unions, recognized labor rights, and promoted worker interests by setting a minimum wage and establishing a tribunal to arbitrate disputes. The absence of equivalent rural legislation was in part the product of serious divisions among the revolutionary parties that controlled the congress, and in part a result of Arévalo's concern with mollifying hard-line factions within the armed forces.[73] The one action he did take to improve the lives of rural workers—the abolition of a vagrancy law signed by Ubico to ensure rural workers for the coffee harvest—drew the wrath of the coffee elite and nearly led to his overthrow. Hence, even without significant agrarian reform, Arévalo's actions provoked hostility from the oligarchy, conservative political parties, and key factions within the military.

Whether a democratic regime built around the moderate urban reformism favored by Arévalo could eventually have been stabilized cannot be known, because in 1950 elections brought the more radically progressive Arbenz administration to power. These elections were easily the freest in Guatemalan history before the 1990s, though they were not fully democratic by today's standard.[74] Once in power, Arbenz launched a major agrarian reform intended to increase productivity and more equally distribute land. The agrarian reform legislation was the centerpiece of the 1944–54 revolution, and it was this effort to transform agrarian structures that ultimately triggered a military reaction. As Jim Handy suggests, "It was in the countryside that the revolution prompted the most vehement opposition, and it was primarily because of the administration's activities in the countryside that relations between it and the military became strained. It was this opposition that was most important in forcing Arbenz's [ouster]."[75]

The Agrarian Reform Law passed in June 1952 was not revolutionary in comparison with land reforms initiated in other Latin American countries such as Mexico and Peru. It targeted for expropriation only idle state-owned farms and uncultivated private plantations of more than two hundred acres. Smaller landholdings and all cultivated holdings were unaffected.[76] Given the extreme land concentration that existed in Guatemala, however,[77] a huge number of peasant families stood to benefit substantially under even this moderate reform. By June 1954, roughly 750,000 *manzanas* of land had been expropriated from some eight hundred private *fincas*. As a result, "close to 100,000 peasant families may have received land in some form under the reform, directly benefiting as many as 500,000 people out of a population of close to 3 million."[78]

The Arbenz administration permitted increased mobilization by lower-class rural groups and allowed radical groups such as the Communist Party to organize in the countryside and assist with the agrarian reform. In turn, such actions enabled enemies of the government—including United Fruit Company—to proclaim that Arbenz was controlled by communists. By 1954, not only was Guatemala diplomatically isolated (the threat of a U.S. invasion force assisted and organized by the CIA loomed large), but key domestic actors had become indifferent toward the reform experiment or worked actively in the opposition. Crucially, much of the urban middle class—the original core of the democratizing movement—had ceased to support the government. Toward the end of the Arbenz administration, only peasants and rural workers were willing to actively defend the reform project.[79]

In the end, it was a small invasion force trained by the CIA and headed by Carlos Castillo Armas that forced Arbenz to resign, terminating the reform experiment. By itself, Armas's tiny, unimpressive liberation force could never have overthrown Arbenz if the Guatemalan military had chosen to defend the government. However, Arbenz's efforts to transform the agrarian sector had isolated the military, which caused the failure of the reform period. As Handy writes, "it was the military command's inaction in the face of intervention and, finally, its refusal to defend Guatemala unless Arbenz resigned that signaled the end of the revolution. The military's actions in the tension-filled days of June 1954 cannot be divorced from the revolution occurring in the countryside with the implementation of the Agrarian Reform Law."[80]

Although Arbenz restructured the politicized military inherited from Ubico, including placing loyal junior officers in key government positions, he failed to fully purge senior officers hostile to the reform effort. Throughout his rule, Arbenz was forced to negotiate the support of these still-powerful officers.[81] This proved impossible once the land reform was initiated. The military's privileged position in the state had historically been tied to the countryside, where it exercised bureaucratic and coercive control over the coffee economy. With the land reform, explicit steps were taken to increase the influence of other state agencies and nonstate actors in rural areas at the expense of the military. "Representatives of a whole range of activities began to penetrate rural areas: agricultural extension workers, cultural missions, forestry guards, labor inspectors, teachers, and political party and labor organizers. They all to some degree challenged the dominance of the military in rural areas."[82] Moreover, the reform threatened the military's monopolistic hold over the means of coercion in the countryside. Armed peasant leagues and agricultural workers' unions were organized, even as military-supervised militias were undermined to the point that army leaders feared they would be unable to defend the nation adequately in the event of war.[83] In sum, the agrarian reform amounted to nothing short of an assault on the military in the eyes of many powerful officers.

Ambivalent officers turned against the government, and most of the military leadership became convinced that Arbenz was controlled by communists; the army moved to repress peasant organizations and assist landlords in disputes with these groups.[84] In June 1954, with the Armas expeditionary force poised to invade and the U.S. State Department calling for Arbenz's resignation, top officers promised Arbenz that if he resigned, they would defeat Armas's movement. Still believing that the revolution could continue, Arbenz stepped down. However, divisions immediately developed within the military leadership, and the faction sympathetic to Arbenz was forced out of the ruling bloc. With the help of the CIA, those officers willing to make a deal with Armas assumed control. Shortly thereafter, Armas entered Guatemala from El Salvador and assumed the presidency.

Although U.S. intervention may have sped up the process, the overthrow of Arbenz and the defeat of the reform project in Guatemala did not depend on the occurrence of such intervention. Given the unwillingness of the military to tolerate land reform, a severe reaction from the military was unavoidable once the agrarian legislation had been launched. A more debatable question, indeed, is whether Guatemala could have maintained democracy had the government chosen not to pursue land reform in the first place. Based on the history of the Arévalo administration, we know that the Guatemalan military was willing to permit—and sometimes even encourage—substantial urban reform that benefited workers and professionals. On this basis, I believe, one could reasonably argue that Guatemala would have sustained a democratic regime had the reform process not threatened agrarian structures and the fundamental interests of the armed forces. Yet, at the same time, such a democracy would have surely faced—sooner or later—major challenges from peasant movements, precisely because it left the agrarian question unanswered. Whether these pressures would have then destabilized the democratic regime and brought about military authoritarianism cannot easily be known.

In point of fact, though, Guatemala ended up like El Salvador, with the military commanding institutional rule over the country. It did so because, as in El Salvador, highly polarized agrarian class structures and a militarized state apparatus had been developed during the liberal reform period. This structural foundation did not make the emergence of military authoritarianism inevitable. But it did so strongly condition political development that not even the dramatic reform period of 1944–54 was able to blow a radical liberal development trajectory off course.

Pathway to Democracy: Costa Rica

In Costa Rica, competition between factions of the political-economic elite was a central dynamic of the aftermath period, driving patterns of reform and reaction from 1914 until 1949. Eventually, the different factions of the elite accepted democracy—with all its uncertainty—as the best and most reliable basis for preserving their interests. However, they arrived at this decision only after gradually and painfully discovering that neither military rule nor semicompetitive electoral processes were viable options. Military rule was excluded as an option because the Costa Rican armed forces lacked the power to govern on their own, and because the elite was generally too divided to offer the cohesive backing that sustained militarism would have required. Thus, after Costa Rica's last military coup in 1917, the elite committed itself to peaceful, semicompetitive politics.

Less than fully democratic politics, however, also proved impossible to maintain. During the 1920s and 1930s, urban middle classes, small and medium-sized coffee growers, and urban working classes began to demand increased influence within the national political arena. By the late 1930s, political organizations and parties—most notably the Communist Party—representing these groups emerged as important social forces within the country. The political mobilization of previously excluded popular groups undermined the status quo that had been built around semicompetitive politics. It did so not because these groups threatened to directly overthrow the existing political regime, but rather because politicians found their potential support irresistible in the context of intense electoral competition. Especially in the early 1940s, elite political factions voluntarily incorporated previously excluded groups into the political arena for the purpose of mobilizing support.

The incorporation of new classes into Costa Rican politics raised the stakes of political competition between elite factions. In the past, elections were a means of resolving differences that arose between members of the same wealthy class. With the inclusion of new class actors, however, elections became an arena through which basic socioeconomic and interclass issues could be addressed. In this new context, fraudulent electoral practices were no longer tolerable to the losing side. The contradictions of this semicompetitive political system were ultimately resolved through the creation of a fully democratic regime, but not before the less than fully democratic election of 1948 triggered a civil war and brought factions of the elite into armed conflict.

González Flores, Tinoco, and Costa Rica's Last Military Coup

Although President Alfredo González Flores (1914–17) came to power as a virtual unknown through highly fraudulent electoral means, he led a notably progressive administration that represented nothing less than the "first twentieth-century attempt at reforming the liberal state."[85] González Flores's proposed reform package included a direct tax system aimed principally at the wealthy, a tax increase on coffee exports, and the creation of agricultural boards to grant credit to peasants. These measures were intended to head off a serious fiscal crisis, but they immediately drew the opposition of the political-economic elite of Costa Rica. González Flores's difficulties were exacerbated by a lack of significant political backing among middle-sector groups and the lower classes. Although historians would later credit him with being a progressive statesman, González Flores was extremely isolated during his term in office.

In January 1917, Colonel Federico Tinoco and his brother Joaquín led the last successful military coup in Costa Rican history, removing González Flores from office and establishing a personal dictatorship.[86] Most likely, Tinoco acted with the open support of the elite; indeed, the coup was possible in the first place precisely because the Costa Rican elite presented an unusually united stance in its opposition to González Flores.[87] Unanimous elite support for the coup soon dissipated, however, and Tinoco could not sustain himself in power for more than a brief period. He maintained control of the small Costa Rican army, likely through bloated military expenditures,[88] but domestic instability, international isolation, and a poor economy were enough to turn the wealthy classes against his administration. Armed uprisings led by Julio Acosta and Jorge Volio soon broke out, and middle-sector groups—especially students and teachers—protested against the government. The Wilson administration refused to recognize Tinoco, leading to speculation about a possible U.S. invasion to reinstate González Flores (most people, including Tinoco, thought it was imminent). In August 1919, Tinoco resigned and turned power over to Juan Bautista Quirós, who, along with the traditional political-economic elite, called for new competitive elections.

Beginning with the December 1919 presidential elections, the competitive political system that characterized the reform period was reinstated.[89] Scholars have justly criticized the idea that Costa Rica was a "democracy" before 1949 by pointing to major irregularities in the electoral system. For example, fraud was still widely practiced during elections, especially the annulment of votes by local political bosses; and elections suffered from other problems, such as being accompanied by violence (as in 1924) or serious constitutional irregularities (as in 1932). Nevertheless, about half of all presidents between 1914 and 1948 were selected in competitive elections.[90] The overall trend during this time was toward more competitive politics. In 1928, President Ricardo Jiménez Oreamuno passed laws that established the secret franchise, electoral identification cards, and a Grand Electoral Council to oversee elections.[91] The 1920s and 1930s saw increased political mobilization and participation by small and medium-sized coffee producers, as well as urban middle sectors and the working classes.[92] By the late 1930s, the Communist Party was having growing electoral success, as city workers became a major voting constituency that could not easily be ignored. In addition, the Center for the Study of National Problems, which was a forerunner of the Social Democratic Party, attracted substantial middle- and upper-middle-class support. This expanded political arena helped shape a "right-left" political division and led to the appearance of more permanent political parties that reflected programmatic differences.

Reform and Reaction in the 1940s

The tension between enhanced popular mobilization and the existence of a semicompetitive political system came to a head during the reformist administration of Rafael Angel Calderón Guardia (1940–44).[93] Calderón initiated a democratic episode by incorporating the working class (through the Communist Party) into the governing coalition and enacting important social security legislation that laid the foundation for a future welfare state. In doing so, he made it impossible for competing factions to peacefully accept the results of fraudulent electoral contests.

Calderón was a member of the National Republican Party, which controlled the presidency from 1932 to 1948, and he was elected with significant oligarchic support. Nevertheless, Calderón was genuinely committed to improving social welfare in Costa Rica, introducing a social security reform package less than a year after coming to power. In November 1941, Congress passed the legislation, which was modeled after Chile's Workers' Insurance Fund Law. There is no evidence that this reform was a reaction to pressures from labor groups or the Communist Party.[94] Nor is there any evidence that the Costa Rican oligarchy initially opposed the law. At the time, most of the oligarchy was remarkably unaware of the potential political significance of social security insurance.[95]

However, the actual implementation of the legislation soon changed matters. By early 1942, Calderón's commitment to social security had cost him significant oligarchic support.[96] Furthermore, a series of other events—controversial political appointments, a steady inflationary trend, and harsh property-confiscation and relocation policies for German nationals and descendants living in Costa Rica—turned much of the elite against Calderón.[97] To make matters worse, Calderón failed to forge an alliance with social democrats from the Center for the Study of National Problems. "This was clearly a major political miscalculation because they [the Center's members] were eager to gain entry into the reformist apparatus of the state and could have easily been coopted in what would have been a logical alliance between reformists."[98] Ironically, then, the most obvious support base for Calderón—social democratic leaders—became a highly articulate part of the opposition. By mid-1942, the government was left with few organized support groups other than the Catholic Church.[99]

To avoid virtual political isolation, Calderón broke with tradition and turned to the Communist Party for support mobilization. The bizarre alliance that formed in the spring of 1943 united an elitist president with a socialist organization and brought together bitter rivals in the Communist Party and the Church. The party was an attractive option to Calderón because it mobilized a substantial number of urban workers and banana-plantation laborers and had become an electoral force by the mid-1930s.[100] Furthermore, the Communists gained credibility by advocating a moderate, nonviolent reform program, and they were increasingly seen as viable after the United States allied with the Soviet Union.[101] Unlike the earlier reformist government of González Flores, therefore, Calderón was able to draw on a powerful support base rooted in urban sectors. It is worth noting that in contrast to urban workers, the rural sector "was largely uninterested in mobilizing alongside the reform alliance,"[102] opting instead to support the conservative elite and eventually the antireform candidacy of León Cortés in the 1944 elections.[103]

In conjunction with the inclusion of the Communist Party in the governing coalition, Calderón enacted additional provisions on social guarantees and labor regulation. Urban workers were especially big winners with the legislation, which created health-care and income-maintenance programs, provided for maternity, sickness, old-age, and disability benefits, gave workers the legal right to strike and form unions, recognized the need for state protection of workers, and established a minimum wage. As Mark Rosenberg has noted, Calderón's reforms are "remarkable if viewed in the general Central American context: Calderón's presidency (1940–44) coincided with the personalist, antireformist dictatorships of Anastasio Somoza in Nicaragua, Tiburcio Carías in Honduras, Maximiliano Hernández in El Salvador, and Jorge Ubico in Guatemala."[104]

At the time of the presidential election of 1944, most political actors were only beginning to realize that the political incorporation of working- and middle-class groups meant that elections were now events in which one class coalition could deny another control over the commanding heights of state power. The 1944 election pitted Calderón's handpicked successor, Teodoro Picado Michalski—who had the support of the Church and the Communists—against ex-president Cortés, who represented Calderón's enemies within the oligarchy. Picado won the election; Cortés's Democratic Party cried fraud. There is little question that fraud was committed by the *calderonistas,* but it is likely that Picado would have still prevailed in its absence.[105] At any rate, Picado managed to serve out his term from 1944 until 1948, marking the last time in Costa Rican history that a presidential candidate came to power through a nondemocratic election.

Opposition to the Picado government was not limited to factions of the traditional economic elite. In March 1945, two intellectual opposition groups based in the middle classes—the Center for the Study of National Problems and Democratic Action—joined together to form the Social Democratic Party (PSD). While the PSD advocated many of the reforms legislated by Calderón and Picado, party members were suspicious of the Communists and generally believed that the government alliance was opportunistic and not genuinely committed to social reform.[106] In the 1946 midterm elections, the Social Democrats, Cortés's Democratic Party, and another party of the elite—the National Union Party, headed by Otilio Ulate Blanco—all independently opposed the government alliance. Despite the substantial opposition, the *calderonista* parties maintained control of the legislature. The election results revealed that the Communists were very influential and that the opposition parties would not have defeated the government party even if they had been united.[107]

After the midterm elections, the opposition did unite, first to undermine the government's legitimacy, and later in an effort to win the presidency in the 1948 elections.[108] In 1946 and 1947, numerous oppositional activities were carried out: Cortés attempted to persuade President Picado to break with the Communist Party, Ulate drew on his role as a newspaper publisher to denounce the government, and José Figueres Ferrer of the Social Democratic Party began planning an armed overthrow of the government.[109] But the most important activity was a massive antigovernment strike staged by the opposition in July 1947, shortly after the government enacted a redistributive tax reform. Beginning as a political demonstration, the event escalated into a highly successful commercial strike ostensibly aimed at pressuring the government to provide electoral guarantees for the opposition in the upcoming elections. The strike ultimately forced the hand of the government: in August 1947 it agreed that Ulate, designated as the opposition's presidential candidate, could appoint the members of a new three-person Electoral Tribunal that would serve as the final arbiter in the 1948 elections. As Deborah Yashar notes, "the opposition had gained control over the electoral process, which had historically provided the opportunity to oversee and commit fraud."[110]

Thus, in early 1948, the government and its opponents were headed for a showdown in the upcoming presidential elections. Because of the class issues raised by the government–opposition division, the elections posed real dilemmas for both sides. For the opposition, the electoral status quo built around the manipulation of voting results by political bosses loyal to the government was now unacceptable. Indeed, the opposition would have rather completely destroyed competitive politics than permitted the government to use electoral fraud to maintain itself in power. For the government, however, fraud was increasingly difficult to practice, and the opposition's control of the Electoral Tribunal meant that the government was not assured an electoral victory, even if it was the legitimate winner. So long as the electoral process was not fully democratic, then, one side or the other was destined to be disillusioned with the outcome and denounce the results as fraudulent. Crying fraud was, of course, a time-honored tradition in Costa Rica. But things were different in 1948: the stakes of the election were so high that factions on both sides were willing to fight a war to prevent the other side from taking power.

If the increased stakes of electoral politics that accompanied the incorporation of new groups help explain why a war might break out between the government and the opposition, the question still remains why the winning side in such a war would ever agree to a democratic compromise. As we shall see, the winning side would likely play by the rules of democracy only if it were satisfied that the losers did not pose a serious electoral threat. Hence, the victorious coalition would have to demobilize or delegitimate the losing coalition before a democratic compromise could take place. Furthermore, because neither the government coalition nor the opposition coalition was a unitary actor, the winning side would necessarily have to reach a compromise among its constitutive units, a process that could be facilitated by an encompassing democratic agreement.

The 1948 Civil War and the Democratic Compromise

In February 1948, the Electoral Tribunal announced that opposition candidate Ulate had defeated Calderón, the government's candidate, by a total of 54,004 votes to 44,197 votes. However, the tribunal declared that the government parties had maintained a majority in the legislature. The split decision pleased no one: both sides denounced the electoral process as fraudulent. To make matters worse, the Electoral Tribunal almost immediately fell apart when its acting president left to join opposition forces planning an armed attack against the government and another member expressed a lack of confidence in the results. Objective efforts to assess the true election results have generated inconclusive findings.[111] The government was especially unwilling to accept the outcome, because it meant that Ulate would assume the presidency. Fortunately for the government, the final responsibility for ratifying the tribunal's declaration rested with the legislature, and this body was controlled by *calderonistas*.

Not surprisingly, the government-controlled Congress annulled the presidential election results within a month, while accepting the legislative results—thereby convincing the opposition forces that the *calderonistas* would never allow them to take power through elections. On March 8, José Figueres of the PSD (Social Democratic Party) initiated the forty-day long Costa Rican civil war of 1948. In effect, the war pitted the opposition Social Democratic Party against the Communist Party— the two parties that actually mobilized a significant number of followers for combat.[112] Interestingly, it was the Communist Party, not the small national military, that defended the government, drawing on its urban supporters.[113] The Social Democrats relied significantly on rural support, including small coffee farmers. Although the Communist forces greatly outnumbered the opposition, they were not adequately prepared for war-fighting. By contrast, Figueres had been organizing an armed force for years. As a result, his small but well-trained forces defeated the government in a war that saw the death of an estimated one to two thousand individuals.[114]

Peace negotiations between defeated government leaders and the opposition were complicated by the fact that the opposition was itself divided after its war victory. The question of who should assume the presidency led to a power struggle between Ulate, representing the National Union Party (PUN) and much of the traditional elite, and Figueres, representing the Social Democrats.[115] Figueres had been the leader of the opposition forces in the war, but presumably the goal of the war had been to restore the 1948 election victory of Ulate. Intent on seizing power, Figueres rejected a proposal arranged between Ulate and former president Calderón that called for an interim president and new elections. Figueres used his position of power to force Ulate into a democratic compromise—sometimes referred to as the Figueres-Ulate pact of 1948, though both sides probably had intentions of eventually breaking the agreement to further their own agenda.[116] Under the compromise, Ulate's PUN and Figueres's PSD would take turns ruling in the immediate post-war period; after that, free electoral competition would determine who governed in Costa Rica. Although this agreement laid the groundwork for a future democracy, it also ensured that an anti-*calderonista* party would initially control the government. Specifically, the agreement appointed Figueres to lead a revolutionary junta for eighteen months and provided that Ulate would serve a presidential term following this period.

The Figueres-Ulate "agreement" temporarily settled the issue of internal divisions within the anti-*calderonista* alliance, even though some in the PUN opposition still schemed to overthrow President Figueres. But the agreement did not resolve the question of what role the *calderonista* alliance would play in Costa Rican politics. Both the Social Democrats and the PUN agreed that the defeated government forces, especially the Communists, could not be permitted to reemerge as a major electoral force under the new democratic system. Because Ulate and his oligarchic supporters "lacked arms or access to an army," however,[117] the task of demobilizing and delegitimating the government reform coalition—the final step in the democratization process—was left to Figueres and the Social Democrats.

During his eighteen-month junta, Figueres ruled from behind closed doors in a highly repressive and controlling fashion, exercising martial law, strictly limiting the press, and attacking all enemies, including the Costa Rican coffee elite.[118] Figueres oversaw the defeat of the Communists and affiliated labor unions by dissolving major unions, imprisoning labor leaders, and outlawing the Communist Party. Moreover, he ensured the long-term isolation of these groups by skillfully appropriating the role of national reformer. "Since 1948, the PSD, which became the Partido Liberación Nacional (PLN) in 1951, has taken credit for many of the reforms legislated between 1941 and 1948, before it came to power."[119] Despite the authoritarian nature of the Figueres junta, a new constitution was drafted in 1949, providing the basis for a democratic regime. It eliminated all literacy and property restrictions, and women and minorities were given the right to vote. The constitution also set up a fully independent Supreme Electoral Tribunal to oversee elections and prevent electoral fraud. The tribunal indeed became the key institution to ensure democracy: it was left in charge of campaign finance, political advertisements, executive neutrality in elections, compliance with electoral laws, validating election results, and "defending the freedom to vote" should it become necessary.[120]

No discussion of Costa Rica in 1948–49 would be complete without mentioning that the Figueres junta abolished the armed forces and prohibited a standing army. Although this event is often remarked upon, few scholars have seriously reflected on how it was possible. Four sets of considerations can shed some light. First, the Figueres junta did not rely extensively on the institutionalized military for domestic stability, much less for regulating the agricultural economy. Figueres's personal army—which was maintained throughout the life of the junta—had won the civil war, and Figueres and his allies considered themselves strong enough to defend the government from domestic threats in the absence of a standing army. As for international threats, because Costa Rica was no match for the militaries of her neighbors, the abolition of the military might win international support for the defenseless country. Moreover—and this is the second point—Figueres had clear political incentives to abolish the military, including winning domestic support just before the constitutional convention was scheduled to meet. Most important, removing the army would deny oligarchic elites (i.e., PUN loyalists) the only real channel through which they might overthrow Figueres, since these elites did not control their own private coercive unit.[121]

Third, although the oligarchy may have had an interest in maintaining the armed forces as a check against Figueres, it did not strenuously defend the institution. Traditionally, the Costa Rican dominant class had not relied on the military for rural social control, and consequently the proposed change did not pose an immediate economic threat. Polarized rural class structures had not been created under reformist liberalism, which enabled the coffee elite to maintain its economic position without a military. Finally, the Costa Rican military could be abolished because the armed forces lacked the institutional strength to effectively defend themselves—another direct legacy of the liberal reform period. After the civil war, the professional military basically ceased to exist, and there was simply no officer class to voice opposition to the change. In April 1949, a small faction of the military did stage a revolt, but the causes of the uprising do not appear to have been related to the decree to abolish the armed forces. In any case, the revolt was defeated when its leadership failed to generate adequate support. Hence, two structural features of reformist liberalism—the absence of polarized rural class structures and the absence of a powerful military—were essential to the ability of politicians to abolish the armed forces in Costa Rica.

Although democratic consolidation was not guaranteed when Figueres took power after the 1948 civil war, the abolition of the military was a giant step in this direction. After this move, Costa Rican politicians both for and against the social democratic PLN (the successor to the PSD) had little choice but to recognize that a democratic regime was the only game in town for advancing their interests.

NEOCOLONIALISM AND POLITICAL BACKWARDNESS: HONDURAS AND NICARAGUA

U.S. neocolonialism was of decisive importance in Honduras and Nicaragua during the aftermath of the liberal reform period. The pervasive presence of the United States in the state and the economy reinforced divisions in elite politics and diminished the possibility that any particular individual, elite faction, or mass movement would launch a democratic opening. In Honduras, foreign-capital domination of the banana economy froze into place the old nineteenth-century pattern in which corrupt elections and war-fighting determined which faction of a largely nonideological elite formally controlled the presidency. In Nicaragua, politicians of the Conservative Party acted as puppet administrators for the State Department, allowing U.S. actors to oversee major state decisions and assume fiscal control over the economy. When mass opposition movements did develop in Honduras and Nicaragua, they were directed at the foreign presence and had anti-imperialistic goals. Indeed, in neocolonial Nicaragua, the U.S. presence within the state was so pervasive that anti-state mobilization necessarily involved directly challenging the United States. Thus, it is perhaps not surprising that, under the leadership of Augusto C. Sandino, Nicaragua saw the first major anti-imperialistic peasant insurgency in Central American history. In Honduras, the plantation economy was so thoroughly dominated by the United States that workers' efforts to challenge employers of necessity took the form of mobilization against U.S. businesses rather than against local dominant classes composed of Honduran businessmen.

Because political mobilization was directed at foreign occupiers and investors rather than national authorities during the early twentieth century, Honduras and Nicaragua cannot be said to have developed democratizing movements by the 1920s as in the rest of the region. In the absence of such democratizing movements, the polarization of the aftermath period triggered neither the formation of reactionary military regimes as in Guatemala and El Salvador nor the creation of a democracy as in Costa Rica. Rather, in Honduras and Nicaragua, a traditional authoritarian form of national politics developed in the 1930s that would persist much longer than in the rest of the region.

Politics of the Honduran Banana Republic

The conclusion of the liberal reform period in Honduras can be dated with the civil war of 1919 and General Rafael López Gutierrez's ascent to the presidency. As Darío A. Euraque has noted, these events "marked a turning point" in Honduran politics.[122] Unlike previous civil wars, this one occurred in a context in which competing U.S. banana companies had consolidated control of the North Coast and in which the Honduran government was unable to sustain itself without revenues from U.S.-controlled sectors of the economy. Once López Gutierrez emerged victorious from the war and assembled a new government, banana companies began to play a crucial role in financing government deficits. Whereas before 1919 revenue from local capitalists had kept the state afloat, now the "banana companies subsidized government expenditures of outgoing administrations and new administrations assuming power, usually after bloody military engagements."[123] The banana companies also extended their political influence through "a network of local associates, men who occupied very important positions in the local government."[124] Thus, the liberal reform period concluded at that point when the national state became unable to act as a corporate and sovereign entity.

By this time, the U.S. companies on the North Coast themselves functioned very much like a national state. These companies provided and controlled much of the material infrastructure of the country, including nearly all railroad lines, steamship lines, communication lines, docks, and port facilities. On the banana plantations, U.S. enterprises provided many of the basic services normally distributed by a national state through company-owned medical clinics and educational facilities. Indeed, by virtue of their control over private company security forces, the banana companies exercised a near monopoly on the legitimate use of force in areas on or near the plantations.

Yet if U.S. banana companies functioned like a second state in Honduras, then it is also true that—as in the domestic state itself—there were major divisions within this second, neocolonial state. Fierce competition among the three major banana companies in early-twentieth-century Honduras—United Fruit Company, Cuyamel Fruit Company, and Standard Fruit Company—characterized foreign-capital domination in the country. In a sense, each company had carved out its own ministate. As Charles David Kepner Jr. and Jay Henry Soothill note about these companies, "Each one controls its own district; each one transports the bananas on its own railroad to the port which is under its control, and exports them in its own ships."[125] Competition between the companies had of course as its ultimate purpose expanded control over the production and marketing of bananas, but increased leverage within the formal Honduran state was the means to this end. As a result, many banana-company initiatives were designed to influence politicians in Tegucigalpa.

During the aftermath period in Honduras, then, there were two separate but intersecting worlds of state power: a domestic one characterized by elite factionalism and violent struggles for control over the presidency, and a neocolonial one characterized by intense competition among banana companies seeking expanded economic profits. The Honduran dominant class—composed of merchant-commercial actors centered near San Pedro Sula—became an integral part of the foreign-controlled banana economy, not formally participating in the domestic "world" of state power centered in Tegucigalpa. Thus, while the Honduran dominant class was frequently involved in joint ventures with the U.S. banana companies, national politics in the capital took its course largely unaffected by these domestic elites.[126]

The Honduran working class was also better positioned to influence events in the North Coast banana sector than in Tegucigalpa. In the early 1920s, strikes were reported on the Cuyamel plantations, and major demonstrations took place in La Ceiba. Around this time, "San Pedro Sula became a center of artisan activity and left-wing meetings and organizations."[127] This political mobilization was directed primarily at the U.S. banana companies, not Honduran capitalists or politicians in Tegucigalpa. Indeed, strikes often received the support of domestic economic elites and independent banana growers, and influenced national politics at most by putting the social question on the political agenda. Hence, it was ultimately not the Honduran working class, any more than it was the Honduran dominant class, that shaped politics at the formal domestic state level. This role fell to the banana companies and their domestic *political* allies centered in Tegucigalpa.

Toward the Carías Dictatorship

Politicized competition between the banana companies, especially United Fruit Company and Cuyamel Fruit Company, stood in the way of a stable regime in Honduras. The tendency of United and Cuyamel to stake opposing presidential candidates in elections meant that any particular president was likely to face opposition from one of the companies. Furthermore, the stalemate between rival factions of the Tegucigalpa political elite—eventually represented by the National Party and the Liberal Party—hindered the consolidation of a stable regime.

These two impediments to political stability—competition between the banana companies and competition within the political elite—were closely intertwined. Divisions within the Honduran political elite partly reflected banana-company divisions, as United and Cuyamel shaped an artificial cleavage between Liberals and Nationals. If the conflict between the companies were resolved, therefore, the cleavage between competing politicians might also find a resolution: the banana interests could throw all their weight behind one party, giving it a decisive advantage in political competition. Because personalistic leaders still dominated Honduran parties, stable control of the state by one party could then lead to sustained political domination by an individual dictator who ruled in collaboration with banana interests. Changes in the nature of banana-company competition set into motion just this set of events.

Conflict between the banana companies declined in the late 1920s as United Fruit Company increasingly monopolized the industry. In the mid-1920s, United already accounted for a large majority of Honduran banana exports (and thus exports in general), and after 1929 its dominance increased still further. In that year, United acquired Samuel Zemurray's Cuyamel Fruit Company, thus absorbing its main competitor. "Through this takeover," Marvin Barahona notes, "United Fruit Company established an indisputable monopoly over the production and commercialization of Honduran bananas; the presence of Standard Fruit Company in the region of La Ceiba did not represent a true competition for the United Fruit Company."[128] Moreover, after the global depression beginning in 1929, profits in the Honduran banana industry began to contract rapidly. These economic conditions reduced the competition that United might otherwise have faced by dissuading potential investors from putting resources into Honduras.[129]

In the early 1920s, even before monopolizing the banana industry, United had made an alliance with the newly formed National Party, which was dominated by the person of General Tiburcio Carías.[130] Carías's fate ultimately became linked to the rising fortunes of United Fruit Company, even though he was unable to assume the presidency until 1932. In conjunction with the 1924 elections, a brief civil war broke out, and the U.S.-brokered peace treaty that followed prohibited Carías from participating in a new round of elections. These elections were ultimately won by Miguel Paz Barahona—a fellow National Party politician—who took the presidency with 99 percent of the vote.[131] In the

1928 presidential election, Carías lost to an independent candidate, Vicente Mejía Colindres, and he decided to recognize the outcome rather than draw the wrath of the United States by challenging the results.[132] Not until the presidential elections of 1932, then, did Carías actually take power. In this election, Carías and his National Party followers drew on the support of the Tegucigalpa political elite and the U.S. banana companies. By contrast, the Liberal Party candidate, Angel Zúñiga Huete, was backed by North Coast Honduran elites and the working class employed on the banana plantations.[133] In the end, the impact of the Depression cost the Liberals significant support, and Carías handily won the elections. During the Carías administration, Honduras regained a semi-sovereign status, even as politics ossified around a traditional-dictatorial regime type that persisted until the early 1980s.

Factional Conflict in Neocolonial Nicaragua

In Nicaragua, the fall of Zelaya in 1909 marked the end of the liberal reform period and the beginning of an extended period of U.S. intervention. The United States came to play a pervasive role in Nicaragua, though its presence could not stop the century-old pattern of war-fighting between Liberals and Conservatives. This elite-centered factional conflict shaped much of the period of U.S. occupation, including the eventual establishment of the Somoza family dynasty.[134]

From 1913 to 1923, Conservative politicians ruled with the blessing of the United States, but civil war broke out at least ten times, and martial law was almost continuously exercised.[135] During this period, Liberal politicians came to recognize that opposing the United States held no political future in Nicaragua; they eventually joined Conservatives in supporting broad U.S. interests, such that by 1920 the Liberal Party was taking an active part in elections. Although the liberal threat was removed, the U.S. presence remained fraught with difficulties, and the State Department genuinely sought to withdraw from Nicaragua. For one thing, there was much popular hostility in both the United States and Nicaragua toward the U.S. presence, especially after occupation forces were implicated in a series of crimes and abuses against Nicaraguans.[136] Furthermore, the State Department had been unable to find a stable balance between granting Nicaraguan politicians and their New York banker allies autonomy, which tended to lead these groups to drain the economy through rent-seeking behavior, and exercising tighter control over government and the economy, which tended to intensify popular opposition to North American intervention. By 1920, the State Department believed that electoral competition between Liberals and Conservatives without direct U.S. occupation would provide a better basis for political stability and the long-term protection of U.S. economic interests.

During the decade of the 1920s, however, the United States was unsuccessful at removing the marines. An effort was made to do so following the presidential elections of October 1924, which were won by Carlos Solórzano, a Liberal-backed candidate. Within a month of the marines' departure, however, Conservative forces took over Managua, and soon enough Conservative leader Emiliano Chamorro had forced Solórzano and his Liberal allies from office and assumed the presidency himself. U.S. foreign-policy makers tried to stay neutral, but factional fighting prevented any simple resolution. Major Liberal rebellions broke out, the country fell into chaos, and by early 1927 the United States was led to land an occupation force of more than five thousand marines in order to put a lid on the crisis. Hence, two years after the planned withdrawal, there were more marines present in Nicaragua than ever.

The State Department and U.S. business interests put substantial pressure on both sides to reach an agreement throughout this period, eventually with some success. Under a May 1927 truce embodied in the Espino Negro Pact, Liberals and Conservatives agreed to accept the outcome of a free, U.S.-supervised election to be held in 1928. Both sides called for their generals to lay down their arms. Crucially, the marines were to remain in the country to assist with the creation of a politically neutral, nonpartisan national guard that would supervise the 1928 elections and eventually exercise control over all policing and military functions in the country.

How the National Guard of Nicaragua went from a nonpartisan constabulary to a political instrument of the Liberal Party and eventually of the Somoza family must be told. However, we can better understand this story if we first consider the end of the U.S. occupation in Nicaragua. Doing so requires a discussion of the Sandino Revolt.

The Sandino Revolt, the National Guard, and the Rise of Somoza

Augusto César Sandino was a Liberal Party general, but when the United States orchestrated the Espino Negro Pact, he refused to sign, believing that the party was in effect selling out to the United States.[137] From the mountains of Segovia, he began to organize an army with the goal of ending the U.S. occupation in Nicaragua. Within months, the army had grown from a minor nuisance into a major problem for the marines and the U.S.-created National Guard. Although Sandino started with only 150 men, his army drew significant rural support, especially among peasants who were displaced by coffee expansion in the Northern Highlands. Eventually, Sandino commanded nearly two thousand soldiers. Using guerrilla tactics, the force proved remarkably successful at ambushing the marines and the National Guard. The war dragged on into the early 1930s with no clear end in sight.

In 1931, the U.S. secretary of state announced that the occupation force would leave Nicaragua. The loss of marine lives and the financial expense of waging war against Sandino had become highly unpopular in the United States. In addition, remaining in Nicaragua made the U.S. government look hypocritical in light of its protest against the Japanese occupation of Manchuria. With the U.S. exit, Sandino returned to Managua and agreed to negotiate with the government. This fact underscores an important point: Sandino was not leading a democratizing movement seeking a basic transformation of the political system. As John A. Booth notes, "Many have wondered why Sandino did not press on to seize power once and for all. The explanation, however, is simple. Sandino's goal was nothing more than the expulsion of the invaders; he had fulfilled his mission."[138]

Although the National Guard got off to a promising start, the continued rivalry between Nicaragua's traditional political parties ultimately led to its politicization.[139] In the elections of 1928, the Guard seemed to supervise polling effectively, and at the time there were reasons to believe that it could develop into a cohesive and professional policing force. Following his decisive electoral victory, however, José Moncada of the Liberal Party worked to convert the institution into a political force of the Liberals. Under his administration, Liberals were recruited into the Guard in disproportionately large numbers. The State Department protested, but President Moncada insisted that a nonpartisan military was impossible in Nicaragua. Once Sandino began negotiations with the government, the State Department itself gave up on developing a nonpartisan force. Under a 1932 plan, the Guard's upper-level posts were divided evenly between Liberals and Conservatives, and the top position of Jefe Director was to be chosen by the president. As Richard Millet notes, with the new plan "officers were selected because of their political ties, not because of their lack of them. This ensured that the Guardia's top ranks would be filled by men of definite political loyalties and that the Jefe Director would be a picked representative of the ruling party." In effect, the change "once again placed control of Nicaragua's armed forces in partisan, political hands."[140]

Liberals prevailed in the elections of November 1932, bringing Juan Bautista Sacasa to the presidency. Sacasa supposedly had the right to make appointments to the top Guard posts, but it may actually have been another Liberal general—ex-president Moncada—who made the selection. At any rate, "three out of five colonels and six of the eight majors appointed by Sacasa were Liberals, creating a Liberal Party domination over the Guardia from the start of Sacasa's administration."[141] Moreover, Moncada's longtime protégé, Anastasio Somoza García, was appointed Jefe Director. Somoza was favored by key U.S. interests, and they likely played an important role in making sure he got the appointment. By the time Somoza took over the National Guard, it was clear that the United States had succeeded in giving Nicaragua the best-trained and best-equipped army the nation had ever known. However, it was also clear that the Guard had become a partisan force that could be used to support a narrow spectrum of elite political interests.

By 1934, Somoza had a strong following in the Guard, and he used his position as Jefe Director to challenge the acting Liberal president, Sacasa. A series of confrontations between Somoza and Sacasa made it clear that Somoza sought the presidency himself. Sacasa appealed to the United States for help, but the U.S. government was now following a policy of nonintervention and claimed no responsibility for the Guard's actions. In 1935, Somoza began building a political machine to support his future candidacy for president. In May 1936, his troops stormed the Presidential Palace; Sacasa resigned without a fight.[142] A Somoza loyalist was temporarily installed as president until elections could be held in late 1936.

The coup against Sacasa undermined the Liberal Party's old hierarchy, as the leadership of the most important faction fell into Somoza's hands. At the same time, Somoza maintained control over the National Guard and gained access to other important state agencies. Although he ran in the 1936 elections without any significant opposition, Somoza built an electoral coalition that included urban businessmen, some urban and rural laborers, rightist middle-class groups, and some ex-Conservatives.[143] In the years to come, Somoza would maintain this coalition through an extensive patronage network that allowed him to govern without having to rely on the day-to-day coercion found in Central America's military-authoritarian regimes.

CONCLUSION

This chapter has traced paths of development from the conclusion of the liberal reform period to the moment when enduring national regimes were first created. Let us briefly review these paths, moving now from Honduras and Nicaragua to Costa Rica, and finally considering Guatemala and El Salvador.

In Honduras and Nicaragua, the structural foundation of aborted liberalism made political stabilization in the form of a democratic or a military-authoritarian regime impossible. Here the issue was how a sovereign and coherent form of traditional politics could reemerge from a political environment marked by neocolonialism and intense factional fighting between traditional political parties. In Honduras, conflict between the National Party and the Liberal Party intersected with competition between opposing banana companies, with United Fruit Company backing the Nationals and Cuyamel Fruit Company supporting the Liberals. Consequently, once United Fruit achieved a near monopoly over the banana industry, the National Party and its leader—Tiburcio Carías—were well positioned to exercise stable control over politics in Tegucigalpa. In Nicaragua, intense war-fighting between Liberals and Conservatives prevented domestic stabilization during the protectorate years. Only with the withdrawal of the marines and the U.S. effort to leave behind a domestic policing unit did regime stabilization occur: the National Guard of Nicaragua was converted into a political instrument dominated by Somoza and the Liberals. Hence, in both Honduras and Nicaragua, regime stabilization occurred when neocolonial processes enabled a particular political party and its personalistic leader to monopolize governmental control.

In Costa Rica, rivalry between elite factions took the form of peaceful electoral competition at the end of the liberal reform period—not violent war-fighting, as in Honduras and Nicaragua. The question facing this nation was whether a stable electoral regime that fell short of democracy could be maintained. Avoiding a democratic outcome proved impossible. The elite found the potential electoral support offered by newly mobilized class groups ultimately irresistible in a context of intense political competition. When in due course a faction of the elite incorporated the working class and the affiliated Communist Party into the political arena, elections suddenly became contests in which issues of basic socioeconomic distribution were at stake. Such contests were hardly an occasion in which prevailing modes of electoral fraud could be grudgingly accepted by the losing politicians. Instead, as the events of 1948 made apparent, politicians would rather wage war with one another than permit an opposing side to take office through a fraudulent process. The only viable alternative to endemic warfare in Costa Rica was the creation of a full-blown democratic regime, an outcome that came into being when politicians finally recognized that their differences could be most productively resolved through fair electoral competition.

Finally, Guatemala and El Salvador followed a path in which state militarization and rural class polarization—two structural features left behind by radical liberalism—provided little room for political stabilization in a form other than military authoritarianism. Here democratic challengers not only failed, but the threat they posed to the agrarian order led the military as an institution to assume control of national government. Even during the progressive reform period of 1944–54 in Guatemala, the armed forces' dependence on the prevailing organization of rural society was enough to trigger a military takeover at precisely that point when the government attempted to transform agrarian class relations. In El Salvador, the military was poised to govern on its own after the peasant revolt of 1932, an outcome it realized fully once urban-based revolts forced Martínez from office in the mid-1940s. Thus, in Guatemala and El Salvador, democratizing movements actually contributed to the creation of harsh military regimes, leading the armed forces to quash social mobilization and seize institutional control of the state.

Regime Heritage: Military Authoritarianism, Democracy, and Traditional Dictatorship

B y the mid-twentieth century, vastly different political regimes had been consolidated in the countries of Central America: repressive military-authoritarian regimes in Guatemala and El Salvador, a progressive democracy in Costa Rica, and traditional dictatorships in Honduras and Nicaragua. These regimes were not fleeting political expressions of particular national governments, but persistent kinds of structures that left an indelible stamp on the character of politics in Central America. This chapter analyzes these regimes as the heritage of the liberal reform period.

The analysis presents both an overall assessment of the differing regime types, and an account of the mechanisms through which they were reproduced over time. I argue that the organization of the state apparatus—as much as or more than the organization of the agrarian sector—was crucial to the reproduction of these regimes. Military authoritarianism in Guatemala and El Salvador was sustained over time primarily because the military had become an autonomous organization with the interests and capacity to maintain governmental control without support from major societal groups, including domestic dominant classes. By contrast, in Costa Rica, the absence of a significant military and the presence of state institutions designed to foster social development helped maintain democracy even as land scarcity became a real problem for many small farmers.[1] Finally, corrupt state institutions oriented toward the distribution of political patronage helped sustain traditional dictatorships in Honduras and Nicaragua despite the fact that agriculture had become increasingly modern during the twentieth century. In short, if one wishes to understand regime continuity in mid-twentieth-century Central America, the place to look is in the power structures defined by different kinds of state apparatuses.

By the end of the twentieth century, the nondemocratic regimes associated with the heritage of the liberal reform period had eroded or disappeared in Central America. In their place, new electoral forms of politics were established such that by the beginning of the twenty-first century, all five Central American countries could be considered democracies. These democracies have been compatible with a wide range of landholding structures, including the highly polarized landholding structures that still prevail in El Salvador and Guatemala. Indeed, for democracy to come into being in the 1980s and 1990s, it was not necessary for landholding structures to be transformed. Rather, it was the organization of the state apparatus that had to be uprooted. The most basic challenge of democratization in the late twentieth and early twenty-first centuries has in fact been building new state institutions that allow for genuine political competition between organized interests, even while effective governmental decision-making authority resides squarely in the hands of elected civilian politicians.

MILITARY AUTHORITARIANISM: GUATEMALA AND EL SALVADOR

A central theme in many discussions of authoritarianism in Guatemala and El Salvador is the relationship between the military, domestic dominant classes, and the United States. Most commonly, scholars understand this trio as a reactionary alliance in which the military acts as a tool for both dominant classes and the United States, providing the domestic stability sought by these groups. Yet the military was a much more powerful and autonomous actor than this characterization suggests. The military came to power in reaction to democratizing movements and the inability of the old liberal model—in which the agrarian elite enjoyed major political power—to sustain itself. If under the nineteenth-century liberal system dominant classes had to contend with the relative autonomy of personal dictators, these economic elites now found themselves dependent on a relatively autonomous military institution that was capable of implementing policies that clashed with their core interests. Similarly, despite the crucial role of the United States in leading the Guatemalan and Salvadoran militaries toward a focus on internal security through repression of perceived left-wing opponents, the relationship between the military governments and the United States was not one of consistent alliance, especially before the 1980s. Rather, Guatemalan generals often had cool relations with Washington foreign-policy makers, and the United States played a surprisingly small role in El Salvador until well into the 1970s.

State Terror in Guatemala, 1954–1986

The military-authoritarian regime that characterized Guatemala from 1954 to 1986 was one of the most repressive political systems in the history of Latin America. It has been estimated that during the thirty-two-year regime, as many as two hundred thousand people died as a result of political violence.[2] Some of these casualties were combatants directly involved in the guerrilla violence that escalated after 1978; however, most were noncombatant civilian victims of systematic state repression. According to the Commission for Historical Clarification (CEH), which was charged with impartially documenting human rights abuses during the Guatemalan civil war, the army was responsible for 85 percent of human rights violations during the 1962–96 period, while guerrilla organizations were accountable for only 3 percent of the total.

Throughout the military-authoritarian regime, perceived government opponents—such as leaders of progressive parties, teachers' associations, and peasants' unions—were subject to arbitrary arrest by security and paramilitary forces and suffered torture, harsh prison terms, and, not uncommonly, execution.[3] James Dunkerley points out that "by 1967 Guatemalans were already familiar with the phenomenon of 'disappearance' and in that year a committee of relatives of the disappeared was established—a full decade before the formation of the *Madres de la Plaza Mayo* in Argentina."[4] After 1978, the vast majority of these state-sponsored abuses were directed at Mayan rural communities in the northwestern departments, most notably in Quiché. The CEH has documented more than six hundred massacres—usually perpetrated against indigenous communities—that can be directly attributed to state forces.[5] Given this level of state violence, it almost goes without saying that political parties were severely restricted, the press was controlled, and elections were not fully competitive contests. Furthermore, many social gains made by the urban and rural popular sectors during the 1944–54 period were eliminated, and important new restrictions were introduced. Although labor unions technically remained legal, the state only recognized selected unions, such that within a year of the 1954 coup, union membership dropped from 100,000 to 27,000.[6] Indeed, "Guatemala since 1954 has had the lowest percentage of unionized workers in Latin America—between 1.2 and 3 percent of the industrial work force."[7] Likewise, in the rural sector, land expropriated under the 1952 Agrarian Reform Law was returned to its former owners, and peasants who were active in support of the land reform were among those targeted for elimination by the government of Carlos Castillo Armas.[8]

The most striking feature of elite politics from 1954 to 1986 was the extent to which military officers controlled government operations. Although personalistic military rule still prevailed under the governments of Castillo Armas (1954–57) and Miguel Ydígoras Fuentes (1958–63), by the mid-1960s militarization had been institutionalized throughout government. Under the administration of Enrique Peralta Azurdia (1963–66), "the institutionalist character of the regime was particularly marked, Peralta taking office not as president in a personal capacity but a 'Chief of State' on behalf of the armed forces as a whole."[9] By 1970, the question of executive transfer had been standardized through the use of elections every four years in which fraud and repression ensured that officers representing the official military party controlled the presidency. Civilians were afforded few or no institutional channels of access within this governmental structure. Even the wealthy elite, which in time came to include the growers and processors of important new exports such as cotton, cattle, and sugar, "lacked any independent, organized political forces within the government itself."[10] In this sense, military authoritarianism was built on the political exclusion of all major interests in Guatemalan society.

Perhaps if rural guerrilla movements had not emerged in Guatemala, the national regime would have evolved into a kind of bureaucratic authoritarianism like that simultaneously present in South America, where repressive militaries became united with technocratic policy advisors and foreign capitalists interested in promoting industrial development.[11] In these South American cases, the military initiated coherent—if varied and often socially devastating—economic projects.[12] But in Guatemala, once guerrilla forces developed in the western zones in the 1960s, the military became so narrowly focused on maintaining national security that it never formulated a clear national developmental project, leaving economic expansion almost entirely in the hands of the agro-export elite. And instead of encouraging foreign capital investment in the local economy, as in South America, the U.S. State Department became affiliated with the Guatemalan military, offering arms, equipment, and training to help the armed forces defeat the guerrillas.[13]

The emergence of guerrilla movements in Guatemala is often—and appropriately—explained in terms of local agrarian class structure.[14] Yet the expansion of these movements was also related to the militarized organization of government. As Robert G. Williams has argued, state policy toward Central American peasant movements in the 1970s and 1980s played a crucial role in determining whether these movements became large, mass-based guerrilla armies or whether they were defused and then withered away.[15] In Guatemala, the decision of military officers to respond to peasant demands in the 1970s with state terrorism legitimated the revolutionary cause and contributed to the escalation of guerrilla activity. This state reaction was predicable enough, given that the 1954 overthrow of Jacobo Arbenz had signaled a zero-toleration policy for any social transformation. Indeed, if the 1954 coup was in part an effort to defend embattled economic elites and military institutions in the countryside, by the 1970s and 1980s the armed forces had fully internalized the doctrine of national security such that the harsh repression of peasant demands became a knee-jerk response in defense of national security against what was perceived as a genuine communist threat.

The story of how guerrilla violence did and did not contribute to the fall of military authoritarianism must await an analysis of democratization in Central America (to be presented below). Here we may simply note that the end of military authoritarianism in the mid-1980s took place without a formal end to the civil war in Guatemala. In 1983, when Oscar Mejía Victores overthrew the bizarre and brutally repressive government of General Efraín Ríos Montt, a transitional period was launched in which the military began to step down even as the war raged on. In 1986, Vinicio Cerezo, a civilian candidate of the Christian Democratic Party, was permitted to win relatively free elections. Although the military continued to exercise such enormous power in Guatemala that it would be wrong to say that a democratic regime was present after 1986, the national regime no longer fit the description of military authoritarianism. Formally elected civilians and their appointees—not the institution of the military—controlled most major governmental positions after this time.

Institutional Military Rule in El Salvador, 1950–1979

In comparison with Guatemala, military control over government consolidated even more rapidly during the heritage period in El Salvador.[16] From 1950 to 1979, although particular individuals such as Oscar Osorio were influential, the armed forces as a whole—not individual military leaders—dominated the government. Legitimacy issues were addressed by the military with the regular use of restricted elections in which the military's official party typically ran in largely uncontested races. Most military presidents formally advocated some civilian inclusion in government, but during the life of the military-authoritarian regime, little progress was actually made on this front. Electoral-based military rule was so well institutionalized and provided such a consistent basis for political administration that one could argue that, with the exception of Costa Rica, El Salvador had the region's most procedurally stable regime.[17]

In the early stages of this regime, under the governments of Oscar Osorio (1950–56) and Colonel José María Lemus (1956–60), the military sought to use the state to promote industrialization oriented toward the domestic market, thus following "developmentalism" as an economic model.[18] These initial governments bore striking resemblances to the bureaucratic-authoritarian regimes that later emerged in South America. During this time, the Salvadoran military aligned with urban capitalists at the expense of the traditional oligarchy and ruled in a rather technocratic and repressive fashion designed to spur rapid economic growth. In addition, as in the bureaucratic-authoritarian cases, the most important opposition to the Salvadoran military in the 1950s emerged in the urban sector, not the countryside. Perhaps only the lack of a highly internationalized bourgeoisie and a prominent role for foreign capitalists distinguishes the Salvadoran regime in the 1950s from bureaucratic authoritarianism.

In the 1960s and early 1970s, state policy changed frequently as elections brought new administrations to power and ongoing domestic events led governments to adopt more or less repressive policies. At various points during this period, military governments experimented with discussions of land reform, greater inclusion of civilians in government, and freer legislative and presidential elections. Alternatively, at other moments, the armed forces cracked down on urban protesters and expanded the military's control in rural areas. Likewise, economic policy ranged from the promotion of urban interests and industrialization to support for rural interests and the coffee oligarchy. Nevertheless, despite these frequent changes in government orientation and policy, the persistence of stable military roles in the state fostered regime continuity in El Salvador. Military domination of the state bureaucracy ensured that real democracy was extremely limited, serious protest was systematically halted, and basic changes in the distribution of property and power in the urban and rural sectors were never actually accomplished.

As in Guatemala, the Salvadoran regime gradually evolved toward the single-minded goal of defeating guerrilla movements. In the early 1970s, still before the FMLN (Farabundo Marti Front for National Liberation) revolutionary alliance had coalesced, guerrilla opposition movements developed in the countryside. These movements emerged following the fraudulent 1972 presidential election when the military manipulated the vote count to deny José Napoleón Duarte, a popular civilian candidate, an electoral victory. After this election and a military crackdown on the University of El Salvador and urban shantytown dwellers, guerrilla warfare intensified in several areas of the country. The military responded by expanding the presence of death squads and paramilitary organizations in the countryside. The most notable case was ORDEN (the National Democratic Organization), a right-wing paramilitary/parapolitical organization that encompassed thousands of members and was openly backed by the military. ORDEN worked actively with the National Guard and the army to demobilize the countryside and prevent the further escalation of guerrilla activities. With the election of Jimmy Carter in 1976, the United States began to raise objections about human rights violations in El Salvador, leading the armed forces to renounce U.S. military assistance. By 1978, when the notoriously repressive administration of Carlos Humberto Romero was in power, paramilitary security forces had completed a transition from primarily repressing urban actors to primarily assaulting peasant organizations. It has been estimated that in that year, government forces and death squads killed an average of fifty-seven people per month.[19]

In October 1979, in the wake of the Sandinista Revolution in Nicaragua, young military officers working actively with progressive civilian leaders overthrew the Romero administration. The military-civilian junta that came to power was the first step in a long road toward civilian rule and the military's return to the barracks. As Enrique Baloyra points out, the 1979 coup marked the end of the political system that had characterized El Salvador since 1948.[20] To be sure, the coup did not initiate a full-blown democratic opening in El Salvador. The junta proved powerless in the face of conservative military intransigence and continued right-wing violence; civilian members of the government resigned within three months. In fact, in the 1980s, state-sponsored terrorism escalated significantly, and the military increased dramatically in size and social prominence.

Nevertheless, the 1979 coup did mark the end of institutional military control over government in El Salvador. In the 1980s, El Salvador was characterized by a nondemocratic, civilian regime in which formal elections were used to select top governmental officials. These elections took place in the context of a civil war in which the United States was eager to promote a stable, nonleftist civilian government. "Demonstration elections" is an apt label to describe the process, because the U.S. State Department used them to demonstrate that civilian governments enjoyed domestic legitimacy.[21] The elections were intended to impress not only the Salvadoran people but also U.S. citizens, whose tax dollars ultimately funded much of the political violence.

In short, repressive authoritarianism characterized El Salvador until at least 1990, and the importance of the 1979 transition for future democracy should not be exaggerated.[22] Yet the presence of civilian governments formally legitimated through elections in the 1980s was critical to the ability of the state to retain power in the face of the FMLN-led revolutionary movement. As Timothy Wickham-Crowley has pointed out, Latin American revolutionaries have had great difficulty mobilizing against and overthrowing electoral regimes like the one established in the 1980s in El Salvador.[23] In this sense, for better or for worse, the erosion of military control of government and the decline of military authoritarianism after 1979 had important consequences for ending revolutionary violence in El Salvador.

A DEMOCRATIC OUTCOME: COSTA RICA

Since the landslide electoral victory of José Figueres in 1953, Costa Rica's government has been controlled by politicians who have come to power through competitive, honest elections held every four years to select the president, legislators, and municipal authorities. Throughout this period, Costa Rica has functioned without an institutionalized military. The dominance of elected civilians in government and the absence of the military obviously stand in contrast to the military-authoritarian regimes of Guatemala and El Salvador. So, too, do the low absentee rates during elections in Costa Rica—usually around 20 percent—and the fact that most Costa Ricans express a very high level of support for their system of government.[24] Indeed, if the persistence of military authoritarianism in Guatemala and El Salvador rested on the ability of the military to impose its will, the endurance of democracy in Costa Rica has been grounded significantly in legitimation mechanisms and broad societal appeal.

The Party System

For most of the period since 1949, Costa Rica's party system can be best characterized as a "bipolar system," a close variant of a two-party system.[25] That is, the party system has revolved around competition between the National Liberation Party (PLN) and several different parties that make up the "opposition." Candidates from the PLN have controlled the executive in seven out of the last twelve terms, with opposition candidates winning presidential victories in 1958, 1966, 1978, 1990, and 1998. Opposition coalitions have also maintained significant influence in the legislative assembly, but not until 1990 did the opposition control an absolute majority of seats.[26] Since 1948, this party system has been relatively integrative, generally bringing opposing sides together and defusing conflict.

Multiparty-integrative political systems have characterized other Latin American countries, but Costa Rica stands alone when we consider the social class foundation of political parties. Despite its status as Latin America's most successful social democratic party, the PLN has consistently *not* included the working class and broad segments of the urban popular sector as part of its electoral coalition. Rather, the working class has generally identified with the opposition, which is supported by wealthy agricultural exporters and commercial importers.[27] The PLN draws much electoral support from rural areas of the Meseta Central, especially from small and medium-sized farmers.[28] This party-class alignment is simply bizarre by the standards of Latin America, where the peasantry has usually been a quite conservative electoral force, and where the working class has historically been a major constituency of political parties identified with social welfare projects.

The progressive ideological orientation of the political center in Costa Rica further differentiates the country's party system from the rest of Latin America. It is often noted that in two-party (or bipolar) systems, both parties have an electoral incentive to move to the center. In many South American countries, such as Colombia, Uruguay, and Venezuela, two-party competition and the resulting centrism have inhibited the development of electorally viable parties of the left. The bipolar party system of Costa Rica has been no different, encouraging the PLN and the opposition to coalesce around a similar ideological program and policy agenda. However, this ideology and policy agenda are notably left-oriented by Latin American standards. At least until the 1980s, both the PLN and the opposition were committed to the generous social programs originally advocated by Calderón. As Cynthia Chalker notes, "When in power, the opposition has not dramatically altered the role of government."[29] The creation of state institutions designed to promote social welfare has underpinned much of this continuity in policy orientation even when the PLN has been out of power. As Bruce M. Wilson points out, "the PLN filled government positions with its own supporters and granted them job security, thus guaranteeing a bureaucracy friendly to the PLN's goals and aspirations."[30] In this sense, the notably progressive orientation of political parties in Costa Rica has been rooted in the types of state agencies— not just socioeconomic structures—that have developed over the years.

The Welfare State

The decades following 1949 witnessed a vast expansion of the public sector in Costa Rica. Between 1949 and 1958, the number of state employees more than doubled; from 1950 to 1985, state employment increased eightfold, whereas the size of the private sector only tripled. Public-sector expenditures reveal a similar trend: from 1950 to 1980, absolute state expenditures increased more than tenfold. Indeed, large percentages of the economically active Costa Rican population—at times, around one out of five Costa Ricans—have been employed by the state.[31]

Much public-sector growth in Costa Rica has entailed the creation of semi-independent government agencies known as autonomous institutions.[32] These autonomous institutions carry out myriad tasks related to two overarching goals: distribution of social welfare services and promotion of capitalist development. Thus, there are autonomous institutions to administer education, health care, social assistance, rural development, and low-income housing, and there are autonomous institutions responsible for banking, tourism, state-owned production, and credit regulation. These agencies have been crucial to the maintenance of a model of development in which social and economic progress are understood as mutually reinforcing processes. As John Booth notes about the period before the 1980s, "The basic premise shaping the development of the Costa Rican economy . . . was that unfettered capitalism causes undesirable and destabilizing socioeconomic dislocations and inequalities. The state therefore constrained the free market through social guarantees, regulation of business, and public ownership of certain means of production. Furthermore, the state has sought to promote economic development through joint ventures with private capital and through public investment in production, while also attempting to redistribute income to the middle class and poor."[33]

From 1960 to 1978, this economic model underpinned one of the highest rates of growth in Latin America. During this period, Costa Rica had an average annual growth rate of 6 percent, topped only by Ecuador and Brazil within Latin America.[34] Even more remarkably, income was redistributed from the wealthy to the middle sectors to a degree that is simply unprecedented in Central American history. For example, from 1961 to 1971 the share of national income controlled by the wealthiest 20 percent of society dropped from 60 to 51 percent.[35] Furthermore, there have been substantial gains for the national citizenry: Costa Rica has by far the best performance in Central America on standard social indicators such as infant mortality, caloric intake, and life expectancy. And the country is one of the most educated in all of Latin America, with a college enrollment rate that matches some advanced industrial countries, including Switzerland and the United Kingdom.[36]

In line with other leftist parties of Latin America, PLN leaders responded to the economic depression of the 1980s with a shift toward neoliberalism. Around this time, the opposition parties—which strongly support neoliberal reformism—unified as the United Social Christian Party, which has competed well with the PLN in both presidential and legislative elections. Nevertheless, major aspects of the welfare system have endured in the neoliberal era. It is true that government has shrunk in size, some state-owned companies have been privatized, and significant financial liberalization has been achieved. Yet in Costa Rica, a social welfare orientation has been institutionalized within the state, and many autonomous institutions responsible for social development have remained intact.[37] According to Evelyne Huber, policy reforms have not worked to eliminate pension and health-care systems, but rather to strengthen their universalistic features and develop a stronger financial basis for social support in the future. Indeed, in contrast to countries such as Chile, where politicians have pursued the individualization and privatization of social welfare, Costa Rica's social policy offers an alternative to the neoliberal model for the rest of Latin America.[38] During the 1980s economic crisis, social expenditures as a percentage of GDP saw only a modest decline, with increases in spending on social assistance and housing balancing decreases in education and health.[39] Moreover, electoral processes have continued to function smoothly, and the vast majority of Costa Ricans continue to express high levels of support for the democratic system.[40] In these crucial ways, then, the progressive democratic legacy of the liberal reform period appears to be persisting as Costa Rica enters the twenty-first century.

TRADITIONAL DICTATORSHIP: HONDURAS AND NICARAGUA

A third major regime outcome, traditional dictatorship, was present in Honduras from 1932 until 1982 and in Nicaragua from 1936 until 1979. These traditional dictatorships combined highly personalistic control over the state with the corrupt use of patronage for generating support to a degree that was unparalleled in mid-twentieth-century Central America. At the level of elite politics, the Honduran and Nicaraguan regimes featured a personalistic pattern of governance in which individual authority and influence took precedence over formal rules and legally institutionalized patterns of behavior. Within this setting, the establishment of patron-client relations became a dominant means through which rulers controlled subordinates and governed society. Although ruling dictators sometimes used elections to generate legitimacy and mobilize popular support, these regimes were decidedly not democratic, for important controls on political organizing and expression were always maintained. Yet neither can these regimes be classified as military-authoritarian like those of Guatemala and El Salvador, for the military *as an institution* never governed in Honduras and Nicaragua during the heritage period. Personalistic rule by an individual member of the military—as sometimes did occur in Honduras and Nicaragua—should not be mistaken for the legalized and institutional form of militarism that developed in Guatemala and El Salvador.

Traditional dictatorships are not unique to Honduras and Nicaragua, having characterized much of Central America during the nineteenth and early twentieth centuries. But the traditional dictatorships of Honduras and Nicaragua are distinctive in that they managed to persist past the mid-twentieth century, failing to give way to a more modern regime type as in Guatemala, El Salvador, and Costa Rica. To understand the persistence of traditional dictatorship in Honduras and Nicaragua, it is useful to contrast the administrations of Tiburcio Carías (1933–49) in Honduras and Anastasio Somoza García (1936–56) in Nicaragua, on the one hand, with the dictatorships of Jorge Ubico (1931–44) in Guatemala and Maximiliano Hernández Martínez (1931–44) in El Salvador, on the other. Despite many important similarities between all four of these dictatorships, including patterns of authoritarianism that generated common democratic challenges in the mid-1940s, the aborted development of the military in Honduras and Nicaragua during the liberal reform period left these two countries without the structural basis for the establishment of full-blown military authoritarianism.

Differences between the Carías and Somoza governments themselves can help explain subsequent contrasts in the evolution of traditional dictatorial rule in Honduras and Nicaragua after the mid-1940s. Specifically, Somoza's control over the National Guard and his relatively broad coalitional support base enabled him to extend personal rule beyond a key crisis period in 1944 and eventually transfer power to his sons, thereby establishing Latin America's most prominent twentieth-century family dynasty. By contrast, in Honduras, Carías lacked a coercive institution equivalent to the National Guard, and he could count on only a narrow social support base. As a result, he was forced to step down following the 1944 crisis, after which a series of dictators controlled the Honduran government in a relatively non-institutionalized manner.

Carías and Somoza García

Scholars of Central America sometimes refer to the period from the mid-1930s to the mid-1940s as the "decade of the dictators" to highlight the nearly simultaneous personal rule of Ubico in Guatemala, Martínez in El Salvador, Carías in Honduras, and Somoza García in Nicaragua.[41] Despite the major similarities shared by these governments, including personalistic and clientalistic rule as well as strong ties to the United States, there are nevertheless important distinctions to be made. First, the Carías and Somoza administrations were distinctive in their relations with dominant-class actors when compared to Ubico and Martínez.[42] In Guatemala and El Salvador, radical liberalism had created an entrenched class of coffee elites and powerful military forces capable of acting autonomously from political elites. A central issue for Ubico and Martínez was therefore maintaining personal authority in the face of powerful economic elites and a well-developed officer corps. By contrast, in Honduras and Nicaragua, aborted liberalism left behind an extremely weak agrarian bourgeoisie and military institutions that were either weak or, in the case of the National Guard in Nicaragua, a personal instrument of the ruling dictator. Hence, Carías and Somoza did not have to contend with threats from dominant classes and military officers in the way that Ubico and Martínez did. In addition, during the 1920s and 1930s, electoral competition between rival political parties was more developed in Honduras and Nicaragua, with the consequence that existing political parties could be used more centrally as tools by Carías and Somoza to distribute patronage and maintain clientalistic networks linking them to regional elites.[43] Specifically, Carías used the National Party extensively in maintaining his rule in the face of challenges from rivals of the Liberal Party, while Somoza used the Liberal Party to deflect opposition from Conservatives and dissident Liberals.

There were also important differences between the Carías and Somoza governments themselves, which will help us make sense (below) of the varying evolution of traditional dictatorship in Honduras and Nicaragua. For one thing, the dictators had somewhat different relations with organized labor. In Honduras, after the major labor unrest of the 1920s and early 1930s, Carías took steps to eliminate worker organizations. Here organized labor was viewed as a threat and was strictly controlled.[44] In Nicaragua, by contrast, Somoza attempted to incorporate workers as a part of his coalitional support base. At least before 1948, Somoza was reasonably successful at gaining labor's support on his own terms.[45] Security forces also played different roles in the two governments. For Somoza, the National Guard was an essential pillar of political support. He actively promoted the institution, to the point that it often appeared as if the Guard were "a separate military caste, loyal only to their own leader, not to the nation as a whole."[46] By contrast, Carías did not rely on an institutionalized military force as a support base, perhaps because he feared officers might overthrow him.[47] Although Carías took steps to develop the Honduran air force, the military remained extremely marginal until at least the late 1950s.[48]

Though neither Carías nor Somoza enjoyed a base of true legitimacy, both used their respective parties to build extensive urban and rural clientalistic networks that enabled them to mobilize support when necessary. Creating party patronage networks often entailed the expansion of state bureaucracies to link worker and peasant groups to the national government (a process that was more successful in Nicaragua). Because the liberal reform period in Honduras and Nicaragua had been aborted by outside intervention, it was, ironically, the backward dictatorships of Carías and Somoza that oversaw the first successful efforts to permanently extend the reach of the national state into society.[49] The centralization of state power in the 1930s and 1940s in turn provided a foundation for nationally oriented democratizing movements.

Democratizing Movements and the Crises of 1944

In 1944, the very year when mobilization from below forced Ubico and Martínez from power in Guatemala and El Salvador, democratizing movements emerged in opposition to the Carías and Somoza governments. As in Guatemala and El Salvador, these movements were strongly supported by student and middle-sector groups who were influenced by the democratic ideals associated with World War II. In Honduras, the main demonstrations against Carías developed in the urban centers of Tegucigalpa and San Pedro Sula and were "led largely by students, professionals, and the wives of prominent liberal dissidents."[50] In Nicaragua, in late June 1944, students in Managua began to demand democracy and liberty for both Nicaragua and Guatemala, and they were soon joined by Conservative and dissident Liberal politicians.[51]

Carías and Somoza initially responded to this political pressure in somewhat different ways. After the fall of Ubico in Guatemala, which bolstered opposition hopes throughout the region, Carías turned to heavy-handed coercion. "On 6 July 1944, five days after General Jorge Ubico abandoned power in Guatemala, Carías's local henchmen in San Pedro Sula challenged a demonstration with a brutality that resulted in the massacre of more than fifty people."[52] By contrast, Somoza responded in a relatively peaceful manner, turning his back on the protest even when middle-sector groups such as shopkeepers began to join the opposition. Yet despite this difference, both presidents were led—like Ubico and Martínez before them—to attempt to defuse the crisis by promising to step down. Under pressure from the United States, Carías took steps to find a suitable candidate to replace him in the next round of presidential elections in 1948. Likewise, in July 1944, Somoza announced that he would not seek the presidential nomination for the next term in 1947.

Thus, democratizing movements developed in Honduras and Nicaragua that were remarkably *similar* to those simultaneously present in Guatemala and El Salvador. As a result, the presence of these movements is of limited utility in explaining the important political *divergence* that occurred after the mid-1940s. For in Honduras and Nicaragua, the only real transition that occurred after the 1944 crisis was a *government* transition, from one traditional dictatorship to another—not a fundamental *regime* transition, from one basic type of political system to another. Indeed, one can meaningfully date the heritage period in Honduras and Nicaragua with the beginning of the Carías and Somoza governments, because no major regime change followed these administrations. Nevertheless, given that democratizing episodes did develop during the heritage period in Honduras and Nicaragua, it is worth asking why these countries did not break down into military-authoritarian regimes, as in Guatemala and El Salvador.

Military authoritarianism emerged from political crises in Guatemala and El Salvador because, most basically, military officers had both a political incentive to launch coups and the institutional capacity to rule on their own in the aftermath of such coups. Neither of these conditions was present in Honduras and Nicaragua. As an outgrowth of aborted liberalism, military officers were not linked to a highly polarized agrarian export economy, and they were not directly threatened by democratizing movements as were the armed forces of Guatemala and El Salvador. Furthermore, the Honduran military in the 1940s remained a feeble apparatus, far too weak to institutionally control government; the National Guard in Nicaragua, while a much more potent force, was still a praetorian outfit that possessed little autonomy from Somoza himself. Hence, Honduras and Nicaragua lacked a structural basis for military authoritarianism.

Although Carías and Somoza did not run in the elections that were held in 1948 in Honduras and in 1947 in Nicaragua, their handpicked successors—National Party candidate Juan Manuel Gálvez in Honduras and Liberal Party candidate Leonardo Argüello in Nicaragua—prevailed with the help of fraudulent electoral practices. This governmental change was of greater consequence for the political longevity of Carías than of Somoza. After the 1948 election, Carías gradually lost control of the National Party and lost political influence within the government. He was unable to fully control Gálvez, and though he managed to have himself nominated as the National Party candidate for the elections of 1954, he was defeated. Thus, despite substantial efforts to regain political power, Carías could not maintain personal rule. By contrast, less than a month after Argüello formally assumed the presidency, Somoza used the National Guard to overthrow the new government, for it had become clear that Argüello could not be fully controlled. To replace him, a Somoza puppet was initially installed by the National Congress. By 1951, Anastasio Somoza García was president once again.

What explains the differing ability of Carías and Somoza to maintain their rule? Here the contrasts between these two dictatorships noted above come into play. First, the fact that Somoza had the National Guard available as a personal tool was absolutely critical to his ability to sustain himself. Through this institution, Somoza could reinsert himself or some puppet against the wishes of political rivals. Carías had no such coercive instrument available (recall that he consciously chose not to develop the army). Thus, when Carías formally left the presidency, only his (gradually weakening) control over the National Party could be used to influence the government, which proved insufficient for maintaining personal rule. Second, the coalitional support bases of Carías and Somoza are important, and specifically the fact that Somoza did a better job of building a support alliance system than Carías. Because Somoza had significant labor support at the time of the 1944 crisis, he was able to count on their quiescence, a fact that helps explain why he did not have to respond with high levels of coercion. By contrast, Carías was much more isolated in 1944, and he was led to use significant force against the opposition. These tactics eroded his reputation and the reputation of the National Party, which had important implications for Carías's ability to sustain himself in power in any electoral contest.[53]

Patterns of Regime Evolution

Because Somoza was able to maintain power and Carías was not, the specific forms of traditional dictatorship present in Nicaragua and Honduras differed in the post–World War II era. Most notably, personal rule was more thoroughly institutionalized in Nicaragua, as the Somoza family oversaw one of the most enduring dictatorships in Latin American history. In Honduras, by contrast, personalistic control over the state was present, but there was a regular oscillation between competing dictators.

Probably the most striking feature of the Honduran political system from the 1950s until the early 1980s was the backwardness of government, especially the lack of formal rules and institutionalized practices for regulating presidential leaders, government activity, and state-society relations. Mark B. Rosenberg offers an excellent characterization:

> Noninstitutionalized government is the norm; persons take precedence over rules. The public system of rules is subject to continual abuse, neglect, and whim in accordance with momentary needs. . . . Personal rule in Honduras is a dynamic world of political will and action that is determined by personal authority and power instead of by institutions. It

is a system of relations based on shifting coalitions that links rulers and would-be rulers with patrons, associates, clients, supporters, and rivals. . . . Leadership tends to respond to particularistic interests of the moment; there is no tradition of public interest that can be defined beyond the narrow interests of the personal ruler and his coalition in power.[54]

Some observers might be inclined to describe the Honduran regime in the post-Carías era as military-authoritarian, especially given that military officers often occupied the presidency. Yet the military as an institution never governed in Honduras.[55] The most prominent dictator of the period was Colonel Oswaldo López Arellano, who ruled as president almost continuously from 1963 to 1975. Rather than ruling on behalf of the military as an institutional whole, however, López Arellano sustained himself by relying on civilians of the same National Party machine that Carías had earlier used to support his dictatorship. It was this civilian party apparatus, not the military, that underpinned traditional dictatorship in Honduras through the mid-1970s. Indeed, if we wish to understand military politics in Honduras before the 1980s, we must recognize that the military was simply too underdeveloped and internally divided to rule the country through an institutionalized and collegiate command structure similar to what characterized Guatemala and El Salvador. The truth is that Honduran military leaders invariably failed when they attempted to replace personalism with more institutionalized forms of military rule.

Furthermore, Honduran dictators were far more oriented toward buying off societal loyalty through reform than toward pursuing the harsh repression of political opponents that marked Guatemala and El Salvador. We can see this clearly with the state's orientation toward agrarian reform. Both the civilian government of Ramón Villeda Morales (1957–63) and the final López Arellano government (1972–75) enacted major agrarian reforms in the face of peasant demands for increased access to land. As a result, "between 1962 and 1979 various Honduran governments distributed 207,433 hectares of land to 46,890 landless and land-poor families. This amounted to 8 percent of the country's farmland and by 1980 had affected about 12 percent of rural families."[56] As Donald E. Schulz and Deborah Sundloff Schulz point out, "No other Central American land reform prior to the 1980s accomplished nearly as much."[57] As for state repression, although the Honduran government was involved in human rights abuses, the pre-1980s level of repression was mild when compared to that in Guatemala and El Salvador. "In Honduras, the body count was in the low hundreds rather than the tens of thousands. Massive repression was considered neither necessary nor desirable."[58] Indeed, almost all of the worst abuses and repression occurred after the early 1980s, when an elected civilian regime was already in power. One simply cannot sustain the argument that the Honduran regime was equivalent to those present in Guatemala and El Salvador before the 1980s.

The situation was somewhat different in Nicaragua, where the Somoza family managed to hold power until the Sandinista Revolution of 1979. In 1956, when Somoza García was assassinated, his sons were well positioned to govern the country on their own.[59] Somoza's elder son, Luis Somoza Debayle, was constitutionally designated to assume the presidency from his position as president of the Congress, while Somoza's younger son, Anastasio Somoza Debayle, was chief of the National Guard. Until his own death in 1967, Luis Somoza directly or indirectly ruled the country—sometimes in relatively progressive ways, including permitting increased political freedoms and promoting social reforms.[60] The repression and violence often associated with the Somoza family was actually more of an exception than a rule until Anastasio Somoza Debayle assumed the presidency in 1967; Nicaraguans even gave significant support to Somoza Debayle until he plundered international aid resources in the aftermath of the devastating earthquake of 1972. Before the mid-1970s, the following description of the Somoza regime is accurate: "As authoritarian regimes go, this one ceded to its political enemies and critics a relatively large amount of space to act in public life."[61] Only in the mid-1970s, when a broad-based opposition began to demand political change, did the Somoza regime begin to fit the extremely repressive and violent image with which we now often associate it.

The ability of the Somozas to hold power until 1979, even when not formally occupying the presidency, was linked to their control of the National Guard. Whereas in Honduras the military could be used by aspiring officers to overthrow unpopular leaders, in Nicaragua the option of a military coup was not available to opponents of the Somoza government. Although politicians from the opposition Conservative Party, such as Pedro Joaquín Chamorro, did sometimes call on Guard members to overthrow Somoza Debayle, they were not ultimately successful.[62] The National Guard also played a key part in the distribution of patronage to Somoza loyalists, which was arguably more important to regime continuity than day-to-day repression. Through its control over numerous state activities—including customs control, railway operation, policing, tax collection, and postal and telecommunications service—the Guard diverted public resources into private hands and literally bought loyalty for the Somoza family. In addition, the National Guard itself became a source of patronage, as top-ranking Guard positions were given to Somoza loyalists and as the government won support from lower-ranking members by permitting corruption for personal gain.[63]

The National Guard's lack of institutional autonomy from the Somoza family helps explain why there was no military coup in the mid-1970s when the old regime faced serious pressure from a broad-based revolutionary opposition led by the Sandinista Front for National Liberation (FSLN). Although personal dictatorships like those of the Somoza family are inherently vulnerable to overthrow by revolutionaries, not all such dictatorships inevitably succumb to social revolution.[64] In cases where armed forces are able to act autonomously from ruling dictators, military leaders have avoided revolutionary breakdowns by orchestrating coups or siding with moderates in the opposition. Yet in Nicaragua, the National Guard lacked the autonomy to pursue such regime-saving strategies, instead fighting to the end to preserve Somoza family rule. In short, the distinctively personalistic nature of the Somoza regime, along with the inability of the National Guard to act autonomously from Somoza, helps explain why Nicaragua underwent a social revolutionary transformation in 1979. Other countries that experienced serious revolutionary challenges in the 1970s and 1980s, specifically Guatemala and El Salvador, had regimes that were far less vulnerable to social revolutionary overthrow. Still other countries—namely, Costa Rica and Honduras—did not experience serious revolutionary violence, for reasons that we will now explore.

REVOLUTION AND DEMOCRACY

Central America began to receive significant scholarly and nonscholarly attention only when revolutionary and political crises developed in the 1970s and 1980s—events that temporarily transformed the region from a backwater into a significant player in international politics.[65] Since that time, students of revolution have been particularly interested in the region because of national variations in the way in which revolutionary violence has occurred. In addition, scholars of democratization have recently focused renewed attention on Central America. In understanding these major contemporary happenings, a focus on the regime heritage of liberalism provides an invaluable lens of analysis.

Revolutionary Violence

Although the Central American crisis of the 1970s and 1980s affected all of the region's countries, it was specifically Guatemala, El Salvador, and Nicaragua that witnessed major social revolutionary movements, including, most dramatically, the successful Sandinista Revolution in 1979 in Nicaragua. In contrast, Costa Rica and Honduras weathered the crisis period without seeing the emergence of significant guerrilla movements or civil violence. The general causes of the economic and political crises in the region rest with the contraction of the global economy in the 1970s and its debilitating effects on the Central American agricultural-export economies. But economic downturn threatened political stability everywhere in Central America, and therefore it cannot explain variations in the revolutionary violence and mass social upheaval found in the region. To understand these variations, we need to focus centrally on state policy toward social protest in the early 1970s. In turn, to understand differences in state policy, we must again call attention to the major regime types analyzed in this chapter.

Shocks from the world economy, first from 1973 to 1975 and then from late 1977 until well into the 1980s, sent the agricultural economies of Central America into severe crises. In response, peasants across the region attempted to gain access to more land, workers sought increased wages, and wealthy elites sought to protect properties and investments. The important contrast between Central American countries was not primarily the degree of economic crisis, nor primarily the level of initial protest that accompanied the crisis. Rather, the key difference was in the way in which the state responded to initial social pressures generated by the crisis. As Williams notes, "In Nicaragua, El Salvador, and Guatemala, national governments attempted to contain the pressures from below by terrorizing the poor. . . . In contrast, . . . the governments of Honduras and Costa Rica did not side with the elites in a single-minded way, but made some concessions to the poor in land and wage disputes."[66] As we have seen, the military governments of Guatemala and El Salvador in the mid-1970s, as well as the Somoza Debayle government in Nicaragua after 1972, moved toward political closure and repression in the face of mobilization from below. By contrast, the Honduran government offered concessions in the form of meaningful land reform in response to peasant demands in the early 1970s, and the Costa Rican government maintained a generous system of rural social provision throughout the crisis period. This basic difference between state retrenchment with escalating revolutionary violence in Guatemala, El Salvador, and Nicaragua, and state accommodation and relative social stability in Honduras and Nicaragua is crucial to the better comparative interpretations of the crisis.[67]

From the perspective of this study, this difference is intriguing because the ordering of cases into the two patterns corresponds with the policy options that were pursued during the liberal reform period: Guatemala, El Salvador, and Nicaragua adopted harsh, radical policy options in the late nineteenth century and responded with state terror to crises in the late twentieth century; by contrast, Costa Rica and Honduras adopted moderate, reform policy options in the nineteenth century and responded to the crisis period with accommodating policies rather than repression. Such parallels are understandable when we recognize that the different state policies pursued during the 1970s crisis period grew out of political regime structures whose origins rest with the liberal reform period.[68] Thus, in what were the radical liberalism cases of Guatemala and El Salvador, coercively oriented military regimes responded, not surprisingly, with high levels of violence when national economies collapsed during the depression of the 1970s. By contrast, in the reformist liberalism case of Costa Rica, where a progressive democratic regime had been established, government authorities favored a more peaceful resolution to the crisis period. More difficult to explain are the two aborted liberalism cases of Honduras and Nicaragua, which were characterized by very different state responses to rural mobilization during the crisis period but which shared the same traditional-dictatorial regime type. Part of this difference in state actions can be attributed to the failure of Honduran guerrilla movements, unlike those in Nicaragua, to generate significant peasant support, which made it politically feasible for Honduran authorities to pursue land reform. In turn, the differing success of guerrilla movements in the two countries is likely rooted in contrasting agrarian structures. Already by the early twentieth century, Nicaragua had more polarized rural relations than Honduras—for Nicaragua had experienced an aborted coffee revolution, not an aborted experiment at creating small farms, as had Honduras. With the introduction of new crops in the mid-twentieth century and the creation of the Central American Common Market in 1960, the proportion of land used for export production in Nicaragua far surpassed that in Honduras. As a result, by the late 1970s, Nicaragua had a significantly higher level of land concentra-

tion than Honduras, which fueled greater support for guerrilla movements and contributed to a harsh state response to rural protest.[69]

But also important to understanding contrasting levels of peasant
mobilization and state responses in Honduras and Nicaragua are political regime differences. In Nicaragua, the highly personalistic nature of
the regime, in which one individual and his family could correctly be
viewed as controlling national politics, facilitated a broad-based opposition movement that spanned multiple social classes. Furthermore, because the National Guard was so closely tied to Somoza, it lacked the capacity to disobey his orders when called on to repress social protest. By
contrast, the Honduran regime featured important mechanisms—elections and military coups—that allowed for the removal of unpopular
presidents, such that the regime never appeared to be a personal dynasty
equivalent to Somoza rule in Nicaragua. In fact, the regular transfer of
presidents and the occasional use of elections sometimes gave the regime
the appearance of a democracy, which mitigated the potential for antigovernment mobilization. Honduran presidents were not likely to call for
highly repressive policies precisely because some popular support was
necessary to sustain themselves in power.[70] And even if a government did
call for repression, the Honduran armed forces had enough autonomy to
be capable of ignoring orders and forcing a presidential transfer via a military coup.

In sum, harsh state responses to initial social protest in the 1970s had
much to do with the development of revolutionary crises in Guatemala,
El Salvador, and Nicaragua. By contrast, more accommodating state
strategies in Honduras and Costa Rica helped thwart potential societal
upheavals. In this section, I have argued that regime differences provide
insight into the origins of these differing state responses. Although these
regime differences are not the full story in explaining patterns of violence
in the region, their importance does suggest the relevance of the liberal
legacy for politics in late-twentieth-century Central America.

Transition to Democracy

In the midst of the Central American crisis, civilian-led regimes were established in Guatemala (1985), El Salvador (1984), Honduras (1982),
and Nicaragua (1990), while Costa Rica maintained its long-standing
democracy. Civilian rule was an important step toward democracy, and,
as of the late 1990s, all five Central American countries had formally
democratic regimes.[71]

Although democratization has substantially eroded the regime heritage analyzed in this chapter, a focus on these earlier regimes still provides a useful perspective for explaining the transition to democracy.[72] In particular, such a focus can fruitfully supplement two alternative interpretations of democratization in Central America. The first of these interpretations, which is advocated by scholars such as Samuel P. Huntington, sees democratization as significantly a product of U.S. pressure for civilian rule and free elections.[73] In this interpretation, some combination of U.S. economic, political, diplomatic, and military pressure on authoritarian leaders was critical to democratization in the region. A second interpretation argues that democracy was the (perhaps unintended) result of revolutionary pressures from below. This view sees revolutionary movements as forcing the hand of reluctant military and authoritarian leaders, giving them no choice but to step aside and thereby pave the way for civilian democrats to assume power. As Jeffery M. Paige provocatively puts it, Central America represents "a radically new route to democracy—through socialist revolution from below."[74]

Both these explanations have much to contribute, but, taken in isolation, they are not adequate. The United States–centered explanation overlooks the often profoundly negative impact that the United States had vis-à-vis democratic interests in Central America. For much of the 1980s, the United States played a central role in economically, politically, diplomatically, and militarily promoting Central American organizations with some of the worst human rights violations in Latin American history. The United States was directly or indirectly linked with death squads, paramilitary units, and counterrevolutionary organizations that helped oversee the repression and killing of thousands of civilians in the region.[75] Whatever one might think of the long-term consequences of the counterrevolutionary and anticommunist agendas that motivated U.S. policy, it is hard to deny that their short-term consequences were severely negative for human welfare in the region. Hence, in important senses, the United States was a cause of many highly authoritarian features of Central American politics.

Explanations that trace democracy to revolutionary pressures from below also suffer from limitations. The revolutionaries in Guatemala and El Salvador were not struggling for formal democracy per se. Rather, these forces had primarily socioeconomic goals, and their secondary political goals were—if the truth be told—not always fully supportive of formal democracy.[76] Hence, there is a strong sense in which formal democracy developed in Guatemala and El Salvador *in spite of* the goals of both socialist revolutionaries and regime elites. This conclusion is supported by Honduras's relatively peaceful transition to democracy. Although the Honduran transition parallels those of the other countries in many ways, revolutionary pressures and a revolutionary crisis were absent, demonstrating that social revolution was in no way necessary for Central American democracy. In addition, the Nicaraguan Revolution of 1979, an important case for the "revolution from below" interpretation, did not lead immediately to democracy. Rather, a democratic regime developed in 1990 only after there were significant pressures from below led by *counter*revolutionaries. These counterrevolutionaries (the Nicaraguan contras) were hardly the progressive revolutionary forces envisaged by supporters of the democracy-from-below thesis. In this light, we see that the antisocialist counterrevolution in Nicaragua—despite its many devastating consequences for social welfare in that country—may have actually contributed to formal political democracy.

In my view, adequately explaining the transition to democracy in Central America requires treating the old regime as the primary unit of analysis and situating the old regime's institutions at the intersection of cross-pressures from the United States and actual or potential revolutionary opponents. From such a framework, three patterns of late-twentieth-century democratization can be identified for the region. Guatemala and El Salvador represent a pattern of "democratization via social revolutionary defeat," in which endangered military regimes used a transition to civilian rule to defeat social revolutionary movements. In this pattern, revolutionary movements played the essential role of destabilizing military-authoritarian regimes and making it impossible for the military to maintain rule in the absence of devastating social violence. However, the United States was also a critical factor: it promoted transitions to civilian rule and electoral democracy as a means of defusing revolutionary crises, a strategy that was ultimately successful. It is possible that, without U.S. pressure, Guatemala and El Salvador would have remained embroiled in warfare, or, perhaps, that guerrilla movements would have seized power and established one-party revolutionary states. Thus, both revolutionaries and the United States were important to democratization in Guatemala and El Salvador: revolutionaries made the authoritarian status quo impossible to maintain, and the United States successfully pushed for a civilian (and eventually democratic) solution to prevent a social revolution.

Nicaragua's transition to democracy in 1990 followed a path of "democratization via counterrevolutionary insurgency," a variation on the above pattern. In this case, the obstacle to formal democracy was the Sandinista regime, a progressive if occasionally flawed and less than fully democratic revolutionary government.[77] We cannot be certain what regime would have emerged in the absence of the U.S.-supported counterrevolutionary opposition. Some version of revolutionary one-party rule might have persisted in Nicaragua. Alternatively, in the absence of U.S. intervention, the Sandinistas might have democratized Nicaragua on their own, thus following Paige's pattern of democracy through social revolution from below. As it historically turned out, however, the United States did intervene, and the Sandinistas maintained an authoritarian national regime structure (although with progressive and often democratic mass political institutions) while consolidating revolutionary power in the 1980s. Counterrevolutionary tactics were not sufficient to defeat the Sandinistas, and consequently the United States moved to force the Sandinistas from power via electoral processes. In particular, the United States promoted democracy in Nicaragua by forcing the Sandinistas to hold an election in which the U.S.-backed opposition could win. Hence, Nicaragua's transition to democracy was closely linked to broader U.S. counterrevolutionary efforts.

Finally, Honduras represents a pattern of "democratization via revolutionary preemption." Here the United States pressured a fragile regime to move toward democracy in large part to preempt potential domestic revolutionary movements and to legitimate the Honduran political system while using the country as a base for counterrevolutionary activities elsewhere in the region.[78] In 1980, the United States insisted that the relatively progressive Honduran military government of the time give way to a civilian government brought to power through competitive elections. The United States sought to promote the image of democracy in Honduras in conjunction with using Honduras and Costa Rica as a launching pad for CIA-backed operations against the Sandinistas in Nicaragua. Thus, while regular elections were held throughout the 1980s, the United States also pumped millions of dollars of aid into the Honduran military. As a consequence, Honduras witnessed a substantial growth of the military and, at the beginning of the twenty-first century, faced many of the military-civilian problems that plagued the newly installed democracies in Guatemala and El Salvador.

The new democracies of Central America are not simply puppets of the United States, even if that country continues to represent a "hovering giant" monitoring the region.[79] In fact, in comparison with many South American countries, a fairly impressive spectrum of different forces—including former revolutionary organizations in Guatemala, El Salvador, and Nicaragua and a long-standing social democratic party in Costa Rica—make up the political landscape in Central America. At the same time, however, there is little support for Jeffery Paige's argument that the chances for democratic consolidation are better in Central America than elsewhere in Latin America. Although the Central American transitions were often accompanied by revolutionary violence, Paige's claim that "the institutions of the old order are gone for good" as a result of socialist revolutionary pressures is not correct.[80] The military and the coffee elite remain alive and well in Guatemala, and the decentralized and often corrupt traditional political parties of Honduras and Nicaragua continue to persist. Instead of having been wiped out, then, institutions of the old regime have carried over to the current period and continue to represent important obstacles to democratic consolidation.

CONCLUSION

The development and persistence of differing national political regimes defined the heritage of liberalism in Central America. These regimes were marked by sharp contrasts in the nature of the ruling governmental elite and the nature of the state's relations with society. In Guatemala and El Salvador, the permanent state apparatus and the government became fused through highly institutionalized military rule. Even by Latin American standards, these military-authoritarian systems were notable for the extreme level of repression that was employed to achieve political stability. Things could hardly have been more different in Costa Rica, where a peaceful and democratic regime was established. This democracy featured not only free and fair elections and broad civil liberties and rights, but also a progressive political orientation in which all major political actors were committed to social welfare policies. Finally, the mid-twentieth-century political systems of Honduras and Nicaragua warrant special attention because they were two of the last historical instances of a dictatorial regime type that used to be widespread throughout Latin America. The traditional dictatorships of Honduras and Nicaragua are indeed exceptional because they managed to persist well into the twentieth century, when elsewhere in Latin America this kind of regime had usually disappeared many decades earlier.

Although the late twentieth century saw the erosion of these regime outcomes in most countries, they nevertheless influenced the way in which subsequent political processes occurred. The presence of institutional military rule in Guatemala and El Salvador predisposed the governments of these countries to repress social demands in the 1970s, which had the effect of exacerbating social crises and facilitating the emergence of powerful revolutionary movements in the 1980s. Moreover, the antecedent military-authoritarian regimes of these countries helped produce a distinct path of democratization in which U.S. actors pressured military leaders to step down in the face of stalemated revolutionary violence. Antecedent regimes also offer insight into late-twentieth-century events in Honduras and Nicaragua. The traditional dictatorship of Nicaragua must be invoked to explain the Sandinista Revolution, for the Somoza dictatorship featured characteristics—such as extreme personalism and the inability of the armed forces to act autonomously—that are generalized causes of revolutions. Likewise, the distinctive nature of the Honduran dictatorship, in which informal channels existed for removing unpopular leaders, is essential to explaining the absence of major guerrilla movements and state repression in this country. Finally, of course, the fact that Costa Rica was a socially progressive democracy strongly conditioned this country's peaceful response to the Central American crisis. The presence of this antecedent democratic regime in fact made the question of regime change irrelevant when the worldwide wave of democracy swept through the region in the 1980s and 1990s.

CHAPTER 10

Conclusion: Path Dependence and Political Change

The concept of path dependence is built around the idea that crucial choice points may establish certain directions of change and foreclose others in a way that shapes development over long periods of time. The analysis of this book has elaborated this basic idea toward the goal of developing a new explanation of political change in Central America. The book has argued that the liberal reform period of the nineteenth and early twentieth centuries was a critical juncture, and that actor choices and structural transformations during this period had a profound effect on the subsequent evolution of politics in the region, including through the establishment of enduring national political regimes. Although the liberal reform period did not make it inevitable that countries would develop particular kinds of regimes, the period so strongly shaped political development that not even major attempts to rupture the liberal legacy were successful. Without exception across the Central American region, national regimes consistent with the structural foundation of the liberal reform period had been created by the mid-twentieth century.

This argument was developed through the comparison of all five Central American countries. The systematic juxtaposition of aggregate variables across these countries provided a means of adjudicating among rival explanations of political development. Such cross-country comparisons also helped frame new concepts and new lines of argumentation not previously offered in analyses of Central America. In addition to comparisons across cases, the argument relied heavily on the close examination of disaggregated processes within each particular country. A central challenge was to determine whether the cross-national argument could be sustained when assessed in light of the highly detailed historical processes and events occurring in each of the five countries. The book's overall analysis was thus informed by a methodological approach that combined systematic cross-case comparison with detailed within-case analysis.

THE HISTORICAL ARGUMENT

The liberal reform period of the nineteenth and early twentieth centuries was a watershed in Central American history. In all five countries, this period saw liberal elites enact reforms that greatly expanded commercial agriculture and more fully incorporated local economies into the international market. In their quest for state and agrarian modernization, however, liberals pursued different policy options, and with different degrees of success. As a consequence, the structural transformations completed during the reform period varied across the region, setting countries on distinct paths of long-term development that led to sharply contrasting regime outcomes by the mid-twentieth century.

At the height of the reform period in Guatemala and El Salvador, during the 1870s and 1880s, liberal dictators faced major challenges from political opponents, including conservatives, the Church, and rival liberal elites. In this unstable political environment, rulers attempted to maintain personalistic control over government by increasing state penetration of society and enhancing governmental coercive capacities through the creation of permanent army forces. The enlargement and militarization of the state in turn facilitated the pursuit of aggressive agrarian policies designed to stimulate export agriculture. In these two countries, liberals carried out mixtures of highly encompassing land privatization reforms and coercive labor policies that led to the rapid expansion of coffee production and to fundamental changes in the economy and the state. Under the pattern of radical liberalism that had crystallized by the 1920s, severe land concentration and class polarization marked the agrarian sector, elite coffee producers and processors exercised significant influence within the state, and the military assumed a commanding role in overseeing both the state and the coffee economy. These structural patterns persisted over time not because of any consensus of the majority, but because agrarian and state elites had sufficient power to maintain them in the absence of societal support.

In the period following the liberal reform, Guatemala and El Salvador saw the emergence of democratizing movements that sought to challenge the structural patterns of radical liberalism. These democratic movements were led by progressive presidents who responded to and actively promoted the mobilization of popular-sector groups in an effort to bring a broader array of actors and issues into the national political arena. Especially when agrarian interests were involved, democratizing movements posed a direct threat to the entrenched militaries of Guatemala and El Salvador, whose officers were often closely tied to the economic elite. Despite an explosive peasant revolt in El Salvador in 1932 and a major social reform period in Guatemala during 1944–54, democratizing movements in both countries proved unable to overturn the radical liberal order, and their efforts, ironically, served to polarize politics to the point where political stabilization could not stop short of harsh authoritarianism. Thus, in both Guatemala and El Salvador, reformist governments and movements were defeated, army officers seized control of government, and long periods of authoritarianism were inaugurated that were characterized by institutional and highly autonomous military rule.

In Costa Rica, where the reform period was launched at the time of independence, liberals were not faced with the kinds of political threats that led reformers elsewhere to build large standing armies and extend the reach of the state in society through the rapid expansion of export agriculture. Rather, Costa Rican liberals found it politically expedient to pursue a gradual and selective agrarian transformation. The pattern of reformist liberalism that had developed by the early twentieth century saw neither the creation of a powerful military-coercive branch that commanded a prominent position in the state nor an associated rural economy marked by polarized class structures and a high potential for lower-class agrarian revolts. Instead, by the conclusion of the reform period, Costa Rica had an agrarian export economy built around small and medium-sized coffee farmers and a state apparatus that gave as much attention to education as to military-building.

Nevertheless, Costa Rica was not a full democracy at the end of the liberal period. Meaningful elections were held regularly, but they were confined to factions of a politically divided coffee elite. As a result, as in Guatemala and El Salvador, democratizing movements appeared in Costa Rica as groups sought access to the restricted political arena in the aftermath of the reform period. In the context of Costa Rica's nonpolarized agrarian society, however, elites viewed these movements less as threats to the rural economy and more as potential electoral resources that could be exploited in ongoing political contests. Thus, in response to the needs of electoral competition, elite factions actively mobilized democratic challengers and incorporated them into national politics.

This logic of electoral competition and support mobilization paved the way for Costa Rica's contemporary democratic regime by convincing most elite actors that full democracy was preferable to the political instability that inevitably accompanied a restricted electoral system.

Finally, in Honduras and Nicaragua, the liberal reform periods were aborted by foreign intervention in the early twentieth century. In Honduras, U.S. banana companies took control of the export economy and came to exert a powerful influence over national politics, thwarting liberal efforts to promote a Costa Rica–like process of modernization. In Nicaragua, the landing of U.S. marine forces undermined a radical liberal experiment and turned the local government into a semicolonial apparatus controlled by U.S. policymakers. As a result of this shared pattern of aborted liberalism, Honduras and Nicaragua emerged from the reform period with states that were relatively decentralized and that lacked autonomous power, and agrarian economies that were comparatively underdeveloped and marked by extremely weak local dominant classes.

Once the semicolonial U.S. presence was terminated in the 1930s, Honduras and Nicaragua were able to stabilize sovereign national regimes. However, aborted liberalism left these countries without the centralized states, economic modernization, and politicized agrarian elites that helped foster national-level democratizing movements elsewhere in the region. In the absence of democratizing pressures, political stabilization took the form of neither democracy nor military authoritarianism. Instead, a traditional kind of authoritarian rule emerged in which corrupt personalism reigned more prominently than either free electoral competition or harsh military rule.

In sum, under radical liberalism in Guatemala and El Salvador and reformist liberalism in Costa Rica, state consolidation and socioeconomic modernization took place to a significant degree during the liberal reform period, breeding democratizing challenges in the early and mid-twentieth century. The presence of these democratizing movements was a necessary condition for a modern political regime, whether it was a harsh military regime (as in Guatemala and El Salvador) or a progressive democracy (as in Costa Rica). By contrast, the aborted liberalism cases of Honduras and Nicaragua lacked the requisite state and socioeconomic modernization to develop powerful democratizing movements in the early twentieth century. In the absence of such movements, traditional dictatorships of the kind that were typical in the nineteenth century managed to persist well into the twentieth.

COMPARATIVE PERSPECTIVES
ON PATH DEPENDENCE

Comparative-historical studies that develop path-dependent arguments now occupy a central place in the literature on national regime change. There is a great diversity among these works, with analysts offering explanations for regime outcomes as distinct as totalitarianism, neopatrimonialism, and social democracy, and across regional contexts as different as Europe, Asia, and Latin America. Nevertheless, these studies are united in their refusal to adopt a narrow focus on the short-term causes of regime change. Likewise, they all reject the notion that political development must be seen as an incremental process. Instead, all argue that adequate explanation requires analyzing critical junctures when historically contingent selection processes lead to abrupt changes and set countries on enduring paths of development.

Despite the proliferation of path-dependent studies, there has been little effort to synthesize their diverse findings. Currently, we lack systematic knowledge about how different arguments offered in this literature are related and whether they are consistent with one another. The failure to integrate different studies has been an obstacle to cumulative knowledge. Here I take stock of the accumulation of knowledge by discussing my findings about liberalism and regime change in Central America in relation to other path-dependent arguments. The discussion below examines several analyses, but it is framed around three well-known studies: Barrington Moore Jr.'s *Social Origins of Dictatorship and Democracy: Lord and Peasant in the Making of the Modern World*; Gregory M. Luebbert's *Liberalism, Fascism, or Social Democracy: Social Classes and the Political Origins of Regimes in Interwar Europe*; and Ruth Berins Collier and David Collier's *Shaping the Political Arena: Critical Junctures, the Labor Movement, and Regime Dynamics in Latin America*.[1] As figure 10.1 suggests, each of these works follows the logical structure of path-dependent analysis, but each offers quite different explanations of political change.

Lords and Peasants in Regime Change

Barrington Moore's classic work is sometimes summarized in terms of static variables, but in fact the analysis follows a kind of path-dependent argument in which the sequencing of processes over time is of crucial importance. Specifically, Moore seeks to locate key branching points that

	Antecedent conditions	Critical juncture	Structural persistence	Reactive sequence	Outcome
Moore	Extent of bourgeois impulse	→ Adoption of coalitional ally by bourgeoisie	→ Production and reproduction of social class power	→ Revolutionary surge toward modernization	→ Democracy, communism, or fascism
Luebbert	Extent of middle-class divisions	→ Decision of liberals to ally with labor	→ Development of working-class organizations and movements	→ Demands of labor and responses of parties	→ Liberal democracy, social democracy, or fascism
Collier and Collier	Political position of oligarchy	→ Policies for shaping and legitimating the labor movement	→ Production and reproduction of different types of labor incorporation	→ Reactions of labor and oligarchy to incorporation	→ Type of party system heritage

FIGURE 10.1   Path-Dependent Explanations of Regime Change

brought on three routes from preindustrial society to the modern world: bourgeois revolutions leading to liberal democracy, revolutions from above leading to fascism, and revolutions from below leading to communism.

The starting point for Moore's argument is antecedent differences among countries in the level of "bourgeois impulse" that developed during agricultural modernization, a level that ranged from strong in the democratic cases (Britain, France, the United States), to moderate in countries where fascism was established (Germany, Japan), to weak in the communist cases (Russia, China). Unfortunately, Moore never clearly defined the concept of bourgeois impulse, perhaps because he considered it merely an antecedent condition whose causal effect was mediated by more fundamental variables—namely, the patterns of alliance and conflict that developed between landed elites, the bourgeoisie, and peasants in preindustrial society. For Moore, "the varied political roles played by the landed upper classes and the peasantry" was the critical juncture that gave rise to contrasting paths of societal modernization.[2]

The key branching point at which the democratic cases split off from the nondemocratic cases concerns the alliance patterns that developed between the bourgeoisie and landed elites. In countries that followed the democratic route, the bourgeoisie was able to avoid an alliance with landed elites, and consequently the emergent axis of societal class conflict was between bourgeois and landed factions of the elite. According to Moore, this intra-elite conflict was ultimately resolved by "bourgeois revolutions" in which the bourgeoisie either formed an alliance with the peasantry and overthrew a landed aristocracy with its labor-repressive system of agriculture (France and the southern United States), or led a political revolution in a context where market agriculture already prevailed (Britain). Despite other differences, therefore, the similar ability of the bourgeoisie to avoid an alliance with landed elites set countries on similar paths toward democracy.[3]

By contrast, in the nondemocratic cases, an alliance between the bourgeoisie and the landed elite was developed in the premodern period, closing off democracy as an historical route to the modern world. In these cases, the central axis of class conflict was within the agrarian sector, specifically between landed elites and the peasantry. In the countries that became fascist dictatorships, landed elites were more powerful than the bourgeoisie, facilitating the creation of coercive labor structures in the countryside that undercut the peasantry's potential to carry out large-scale revolts from below. In the absence of such peasant revolts, bourgeois and landed interests promoted "revolutions from above" in which highly repressive fascist regimes were consolidated.[4] On the other hand, in the countries that became communist dictatorships, landed elites were weaker, and peasant structures allowed for large-scale revolts from below. In these cases, peasant revolts underpinned "revolutions from below" that overthrew reigning bourgeois–landed elite alliances and brought on the consolidation of communist regimes.[5]

The applicability of these patterns to Central America has been evaluated in several recent works, including excellent studies by Jeffery Paige, Lowell Gudmundson, and Dietrich Rueschemeyer, Evelyne Huber Stephens, and John D. Stephens.[6] As Paige notes, Moore's categories of landed elite and bourgeoisie do not fit the Central American context perfectly, because the coffee elite often combined commercial bourgeois and landed-agrarian aspects.[7] The combination of landed elites and the bourgeoisie into a single class—an agrarian bourgeoisie—makes it difficult to apply Moore's argument to Central America. In particular, the possibility of a clear branching point marked by the presence or absence of an alliance between the bourgeoisie and landed elites was precluded by the joint development of these class factions.

Nevertheless, if one adopts a more narrow reading of Moore's work, the evidence presented above provides support for his hypotheses. Most notably, Guatemala and El Salvador, although not fully fascist regimes, broadly conform with Moore's hypothesis that an antipeasant alliance of labor-repressive landlords and the bourgeoisie causes reactionary authoritarianism. In these two countries, the agrarian bourgeoisie was marked by both strong agrarian and strong bourgeois factions, and this class actor actively sought to maintain labor-repressive agriculture in the countryside. The coups that inaugurated full-scale military-authoritarian regimes in Guatemala and El Salvador, in which military officers overthrew civilian leaders and used the state to set up a system of harsh repression, are somewhat similar to Moore's vision of "revolution from above" leading to fascism. The major drawback of Moore's approach with respect to Guatemala and El Salvador is that it overlooks the autonomous role of the armed forces. In these countries, the military was no mere reflection of the agrarian bourgeoisie, but an autonomous organization that interacted with and shaped class-based politics. The military figured at least as prominently as the agrarian bourgeoisie in the creation and endurance of military authoritarianism. And differences in the organization of the military in Guatemala and El Salvador can explain why El Salvador did not experience a social and democratic reform period equivalent to what occurred in Guatemala from 1944 to 1954. When extended to Central America, therefore, Moore's analysis needs to add the military to the class trilogy of bourgeoisie, landed elites, and peasants.

In Costa Rica, where agriculture was commercialized in the form of small coffee farms, nothing equivalent to a strong bourgeois–landed elite alliance in support of repressive agriculture developed in the course of agrarian modernization. Rather, the agrarian bourgeoisie was dominated by commercial elites that resembled Moore's triumphant bourgeoisie freed from an alliance with landed elites. As Moore would expect, the commercial elite of Costa Rica actively shaped competitive politics, establishing significant electoral competition in the late nineteenth century, which eventually gave way to a fully democratic regime. In this fundamental way, then, the case of Costa Rica supports Moore's hypothesis. Yet the creation of full democracy was not accomplished by the bourgeoisie alone, as Moore's work suggests, but instead required significant mobilization from below on the part of middle and lower classes. As a result, perhaps even more than Moore's study, the work of Rueschemeyer, Stephens, and Stephens is supported by the Costa Rican case.[8] These authors emphasize that the bourgeoisie often leads the initial charge for democracy but rarely allows the political arena to expand to include subordinate groups in the absence of pressure from below. Rueschemeyer, Stephens, and Stephens specifically suggest that full democracy usually requires sustained pressure from working classes in alliance with other groups, including perhaps middle classes. Such pressures from below were indeed present in Costa Rica in the 1940s, broadly conforming to the class coalitional explanation of Rueschemeyer, Stephens, and Stephens. At the same time, however, a narrow focus on class dynamics can lead one to lose sight of the main story of Costa Rican democratization, which, as we have seen, concerned elite politics and processes of electoral mobilization from above. Balance of class power frameworks such as the one outlined by Rueschemeyer, Stephens, and Stephens present a vision of democratization in which pressures from subordinate groups force the hand of elites unwilling to expand the political arena through their own initiative. In important respects, however, Costa Rica paralleled countries such as nineteenth-century England and Chile, where divisions within elite classes fueled the active mobilization of lower classes in a context of political competition.[9] In Costa Rica, then, elite factions responded to democratization pressures not by reluctantly incorporating undesired groups to thwart a societal crisis, but by actively mobilizing these groups for the purpose of generating support in the political arena.

Interesting efforts have been made to analyze the Sandinista Revolution in Nicaragua in light of Moore's pattern of peasant revolution leading to communism.[10] In fact, however, a full-blown communist regime was never established in Nicaragua, and a weak variant of socialism prevailed for only less than a decade.[11] It makes more sense to evaluate Nicaragua, along with Honduras, in light of a fourth pattern explicitly developed by Moore in his discussion of India.[12] In this pattern, countries are marked by a weak bourgeois impulse, the failure to fully modernize agriculture, and the emergence of backward political systems that do not represent a clear break with the past. This notion of a distorted transition to commercial agriculture leading to traditional political systems broadly corresponds with the cases of Honduras and Nicaragua. In fact, although Moore never directly theorized the role of transnational relations, he implied that India's failed breakthrough to modernity and the accompanying traditional features of India were significantly caused by the British presence.[13] This notion of modernity being blocked by colonialism and of traditional forms of politics persisting in the aftermath of colonialism broadly corresponds with the pattern of aborted liberalism in Central America.

Finally, one additional set of differences between this study of Central America and Moore's work needs to be underlined. This analysis identifies a branching point that comes *before* Moore's major agrarian class groups were fully constituted as historical actors. Specifically, the decision of liberals to pursue a particular type of agricultural modernization, not the class coalitions that were forged once agriculture was already modernized, is the most important critical juncture in Central American political development. Moore's analysis is relatively insensitive to the choices of state leaders about agricultural modernization because, in his view, agricultural modernization is fundamentally driven by class struggles that occur outside of the realm of state power. Yet in Central America it was precisely political decisions concerning the agrarian sector—as embodied in state policy—that put countries on similar or different routes of modernization. Class coalitional formation of the kind emphasized by Moore became centrally important only later in the twentieth century, when countries were already on well-established paths of development; and even then the pivotal coalitional classes were often middle sectors and peasantry, not the agrarian elite or the industrial bourgeoisie. Hence, whereas Moore virtually ignores politics and the state during agrarian commercialization, this study has argued that these variables were of decisive importance for political development in Central America.

Liberalism and Regime Change

Gregory Luebbert's work on the origins of different regimes in interwar Europe—liberal democracy, social democracy, and fascism—shares with Moore's study a concern with social classes and a belief that the coalitions formed among these classes represent critical junctures in European political development. However, Luebbert holds that social classes must ultimately act through political organizations and movements, and thus he focuses much attention on how class interests are expressed in the political arena, including through the activities of liberal political movements. His study suggests that the choices of liberal political movements in Europe—as in Central America—were of great significance for the development of contrasting regime outcomes.

Luebbert's argument is set in motion by contrasts across European cases in the political cohesion of middle classes, as reflected in religious, regional, linguistic, and urban-rural divisions.[14] Since the middle class was a natural constituency for liberal political movements in Europe, these antecedent divisions shaped the extent of liberal political power. In Britain, France, and Switzerland, the countries that maintained liberal democracy between the wars, middle classes were cohesive and liberals were politically hegemonic prior to World War I. This early liberal hegemony was important because it influenced liberal decisions about allying with labor; specifically, liberals were secure enough to grant concessions to working classes and form liberal-labor coalitions. In turn, these "lib-lab" coalitions led to the political subordination of labor and the structural development of weak trade unions and worker organizations. The crucial consequence was that, during the crises of the interwar period, the working class was neither ideologically predisposed to mount significant challenges to the prevailing economic and political order nor organizationally capable of doing so. Rather, socialist and working-class parties were weak, and liberals could preserve democratic stability by forging center-right coalitions that avoided building significant welfare states between the wars.

Elsewhere in Europe, the failure of liberals to ally with labor before World War I paved the way for social democracy or fascism. In these countries, middle classes were divided, which denied liberals the political hegemony and security that underpinned lib-lab coalitions in the liberal democratic cases. Unconstrained by liberal tutelage, strong labor movements and powerful socialist parties developed in the first decades of the twentieth century. The demands and mobilization of these movements ensured the collapse of liberal socioeconomic orders between the wars, but whether this collapse took the form of fascism or social democracy depended on the reaction of political parties representing farmers. When farmers' parties made alliances with workers' parties, as in Sweden, Norway, and Denmark, powerful "red-green" coalitions developed in parliament, and governments responded to workers' demands during the interwar crisis with social welfare legislation. By contrast, when farmers allied with urban middle classes rather than workers, as in Germany, Italy, and Spain, "brown-green" coalitions developed that gave support to far-right parties committed to defeating the working class though harsh repression. Hence, social democracy and fascism were founded on the failure of lib-labism and on the subsequent development of red-green or brown-green alliances.

Luebbert's argument about regime development in interwar Europe contrasts with Moore's explanation in certain basic ways. For one thing, Luebbert is centrally concerned with coalitions between political parties in the context of parliamentary democracy in the late nineteenth and early twentieth centuries, whereas Moore is concerned with alliances between aggregate social classes that developed in the preindustrial era and that existed outside of formal governmental settings. Furthermore, for Luebbert, the fundamental critical juncture is the relationship that develops between parties of the middle and working classes, whereas for Moore the bourgeois–landed elite relationship is the critical juncture. Indeed, Luebbert does not believe that landed elites were important for European politics by the early twentieth century, and he presents powerful evidence to undercut Moore's assertion that fascism was brought into being with the direct support of landed elites.[15] On the other hand, one might argue that the level of middle-class cohesion emphasized by Luebbert was a product of Moore's earlier critical juncture when the bourgeoisie either formed or avoided an alliance with landed elites.

The analysis of Central America presented in this work parallels Luebbert's in that it focuses on the choices of liberals during a critical juncture period. However, the liberals who led the reform period in Central America were not based in well-developed middle classes, and they did not share with their European counterparts a concern with participating in parliamentary democracy. Nor were Central American liberals confronted with significant working-class movements and socialist parties equivalent to what existed in Europe. Probably the most relevant Central American case for Luebbert's study is Costa Rica, where a hybrid version of liberal and social democracy was consolidated after World War II. This regime outcome can be assessed in relation to Luebbert's political coalitional argument. In the 1940s, lib-labism failed in Costa Rica because it was Calderón and the political party of the coffee elite that made an alliance with labor. Rather than lib-labism, a kind of "brown-green" alliance developed before and after the civil war of 1948 that united middle classes with interests representing the countryside, including farmers and the commercial export elite. As Luebbert would expect, this coalition defeated Calderón and worked to destroy the most radical elements of the Costa Rican labor movement. Yet in contrast to Luebbert's theory, the brown-green alliance in Costa Rica did not mobilize around fascist or reactionary politics. The reason is that the Costa Rican middle class remained social democratic in orientation throughout this period, and the National Liberation Party that emerged after the civil war proved capable of establishing political dominance by drawing on rural support from small and medium-sized farmers. Hence, in a strange turn of events, Costa Rican democracy was founded on a brown-green alliance of the type that facilitated fascism in Europe between the wars.

Perhaps clearer parallels between Central America and Europe can be drawn by considering Andrew C. Gould's recent path-dependent analysis of the origins of liberal dominance in Europe.[16] Gould's study examines the period before Luebbert's, asking why liberals achieved political dominance in some European countries but not in others. In this sense, Gould's book can be seen as exploring the causes of differences in the antecedent conditions analyzed by Luebbert (i.e., the extent of middle-class divisions). A central component of Gould's explanation focuses on the policies of liberals toward religious authorities and the responses of the clergy and peasants to these policies. According to Gould, in countries where liberals attacked Church authorities, they isolated the clergy and failed to win support from peasants and provincial middle classes. The consequence was that liberal parties were defeated and had difficulty sustaining a constitutional democracy. When viewed in relation to nineteenth-century Central America, Gould's analysis provides insight into the failure of liberals during the Federation of Central America. Specifically, antichurch liberal policy in Guatemala—the center of the Federation—along with the failure of liberals to build alliances with peasants, helps explain why conservatives were able to defeat the liberal-dominated Federation in the 1830s. The subsequent liberal ideology that developed in

Central America during the mid-nineteenth century was not liberal from a West European perspective. Rather, when considered in light of Gould's work on Europe, liberalism failed in Central America in the early nineteenth century and evolved into an authoritarian movement that embodied only certain distorted features of its original European source.

Political Development in South America and Mexico

Ruth Berins Collier and David Collier use evidence from seven South American countries and Mexico to argue, as does Luebbert, that the emergence of labor movements and the ways in which other actors positioned themselves vis-à-vis labor had a crucial impact on national politics. Collier and Collier are particularly interested in exploring the effects of different patterns of labor incorporation— that is, differences in the way in which the state shaped and legitimated an institutionalized labor movement. They argue that labor-incorporation periods were critical junctures that set countries on distinct paths of development and had major implications for the organization of the electoral arena.

The way in which state actors incorporated labor movements was conditioned by the political strength of the oligarchy at a time when governments representing middle-sector groups initiated reform programs to transform existing oligarchic states.[17] In countries where the oligarchy enjoyed a very strong political position, such as Brazil and Chile, these reformist governments sought to create a legalized labor movement that was depoliticized, controlled, and penetrated by the state. By contrast, in countries where the oligarchy was weak in the political arena, such as Venezuela and Mexico, reformist governments actively mobilized the labor movement for electoral support, established strong links between union and party, and incorporated the peasantry along with the labor movement. Finally, in those countries where the oligarchy was of an intermediate strength, such as Uruguay, Colombia, Peru, and Argentina, the terms on which governments incorporated labor fell between these two extremes.

Different policies toward labor led to four specific types of labor incorporation: state incorporation (Brazil and Chile), radical populism (Mexico and Venezuela), labor populism (Peru and Argentina), and electoral mobilization by a traditional party (Uruguay and Colombia). These different patterns triggered contrasting reactions and counterreactions in the aftermath of labor incorporation. For example, the pattern of state incorporation led to the radicalization of the working class and aborted populist experiments, whereas the pattern of radical populism brought about the development of a conservative governing coalition that included labor. Eventually, through a complex set of intermediate steps, relatively enduring party-system regimes were established in all eight countries: multiparty polarizing systems (Brazil and Chile), integrative party systems (Mexico and Venezuela), systems of political stalemate (Peru and Argentina), and systems marked by electoral stability and social conflict (Uruguay and Colombia).

Collier and Collier's work converges with Luebbert's around the idea that choices made by political parties in positioning themselves toward labor were of tremendous long-term consequence. For example, just as Luebbert argues that the failure of liberals to form an alliance with labor before World War I brought on substantial worker radicalization that escaped liberal control in the interwar years, Collier and Collier argue that the failure of middle-class-led governments to promote labor politicization during incorporation periods led to substantial labor radicalization that escaped state control in the aftermath of the incorporation period.[18] At the same time, however, the nature of the coalitions forged with labor varied considerably in Latin America and Europe, as did the political and socioeconomic contexts that shaped actor decisions. The closest parallel to Luebbert's lib-lab coalition in Collier and Collier's work is probably the pattern of labor populism for Peru and Argentina, in which labor incorporation was accompanied by electoral mobilization and the linkage of unions to a political party. But in the context of Latin America, where actors associated with a previous oligarchic period were still quite strong, this union–party alliance produced substantial polarization and conflict rather than political continuity and liberal hegemony, as in Europe. The work of Barrington Moore is helpful in understanding this difference, for the class-structure variables emphasized by Moore—such as the strength of landed elites—were decisive in producing the more severe oligarchic reaction that accompanied labor incorporation in Latin America in comparison with Europe. The lingering strength of landed elites in Latin American simply prevented any easy transition to a governing coalition that centrally included the labor movement.

In the Central American countries, the organized labor movement generally has not played the pivotal role that it did in Mexico and South America, making it difficult to apply Collier and Collier's framework to this region. There are straightforward reasons for this difference. First, due to the comparatively limited growth of the manufacturing and urban sectors during the liberal reform period in Central America, unions and the labor movement never developed the strong capacity for collective action found in the more advanced Latin America countries, and consequently worker organization and protests never took on the political significance that they did in these more advanced countries. Second, with the exception of Costa Rica, the electoral arena was closed for most of the twentieth century in Central America, stunting the development of coherent party systems around which competitive politics could develop. As a result of these differences, labor incorporation in Central America was not associated with outcomes similar to those that emerged in South America and Mexico.

The argument about the liberal reform period presented here emphasizes an historical episode that occurred before labor-incorporation periods. This emphasis raises the question of whether a prior episode of liberal state-building and export expansion also critically influenced long-run development in South America and Mexico. Collier and Collier themselves note that late-nineteenth-century export expansion was crucial in setting in motion the processes and actors analyzed in their study.[19] For example, the political strength of the oligarchy—the antecedent variable that launches Collier and Collier's argument—was likely shaped by the way in which this earlier period played itself out across South America and Mexico. Hence, one might hypothesize that the kinds of changes analyzed in this book can help explain differences in what Collier and Collier treat as antecedent conditions among their eight Latin American countries.

Evelyne Huber Stephens's path-dependent work on South America provides some evidence in support of this hypothesis.[20] She argues that the type of national export economy established in nineteenth-century South America was a critical juncture that shaped the kinds of democratic systems that emerged before 1930. In countries with labor-intensive agriculture, such as Brazil, Colombia, and Ecuador, stable but highly restricted forms of democracy emerged. By contrast, in countries with non-labor-intensive agriculture, such as Uruguay and Argentina, stable and more fully democratic systems were established. Finally, in countries where mineral-based economies predominated, such as Chile, Peru, Venezuela, and Bolivia, highly unstable democracies appeared. Whether or not these differences in national export economies were associated with the choices of liberal political elites during well-specified reform periods is not explicitly addressed by Huber Stephens. Nor does she directly explore questions about how state structures were transformed during this period. Nevertheless, her work shows that different patterns of national development in South America can be traced all the way back to differences in the nature of agricultural modernization in the nineteenth century.

The possibility that multiple critical junctures shape development trajectories, such as the export-expansion period and the labor-incorporation period in South America, is central to other path-dependent studies, including the work of Seymour Martin Lipset and Stein Rokkan on party-system formation in Europe and Timothy R. Scully's analysis of party-system evolution in Chile.[21] Lipset and Rokkan's approach to analyzing multiple critical junctures is to treat them as separate branching points on a tree in which countries gradually diverge from one another in the course of national development. Thus, for Lipset and Rokkan, no single critical juncture explains party-system outcomes in Europe; rather, only by looking at how countries experienced several critical junctures can one understand how they arrived at particular outcomes. Scully's approach to studying multiple critical junctures is somewhat different. He focuses on how each critical juncture "freezes" the political system for a substantial period of time but is then supplanted by a new critical juncture that redefines the political landscape. Hence, in contrast to Lipset and Rokkan, Scully treats the outcome immediately following each critical juncture as important in itself, independent of subsequent critical junctures. In this sense, Scully's imagery is not so much branching points on a tree as a model of punctuated evolution, in which sudden changes inaugurate substantial periods of stability.

The notion that liberal processes of reform may represent an antecedent critical juncture before Collier and Collier's labor-incorporation periods suggests an image of path dependence more similar to that of Scully than of Lipset and Rokkan. In other words, the different ways in which state and class structures were transformed during the export boom in nineteenth-century South America and Mexico may have initially defined the nature of national politics in the region. Labor-incorporation periods may have then reshaped the evolution of national politics, setting countries on new trajectories of development. If this is true, the outcomes produced by each critical juncture can be meaningfully analyzed independently of one another.

LESSONS FOR NEOLIBERAL REFORM

At the dawn of the twenty-first century, the liberal reform period is a distant historical epoch of state-building and economic development not often discussed in conversations about Central American politics. Although an economic model of "neoliberalism" had taken hold in the region, as it did elsewhere in the developing world, the connections between the programs embraced by neoliberal reformers and those advocated a century earlier by liberal reformers were not always easy to see. For the two movements had developed under very different world-historical circumstances. Liberals of the nineteenth century had emerged in a postcolonial environment in which entry into the global market through primary product exportation offered real opportunities for economic advancement, and where obstacles to achieving such gains included established domestic actors from the colonial era such as the Church and merchant guilds. By contrast, neoliberals confronted a quite different global context, one in which continued reliance on primary product exports did not promise the achievement of rapid growth, and one in which vastly more powerful nations and their international institutions demanded that reformers not depart from the dominant neoliberal model despite its potential costs to large segments of the domestic population.[22]

Yet the neoliberals that appeared in the late twentieth century carried the name they did because of their important parallels with nineteenth-century liberals. Like the liberals before them, neoliberals embraced a rhetoric stressing the benevolence of the market, even as they found it necessary to employ the state and often expand its power in order to move in a more market-oriented direction. If neoliberal reformers have had to relearn that the creation of free markets may depend on state capacity, and that market creation may serve to empower—not undermine—state organizations, it is not for a lack of historical precedents during the liberal reform period. The accomplishments of liberals at transforming the market, for better or for worse, very much depended on the kinds of state apparatuses and structures they could harness to support their economic and political projects.

Should neoliberal reformers seek to learn from the past successes and failures of liberals, the patterns of radical, reformist, and aborted liberalism suggest some important lessons. Under radical liberalism in Guatemala and El Salvador, market reforms were carried out at an extremely rapid pace, targeting much of the agrarian economy for privatization, with little consideration given to those groups that had been protected under previous, less market-oriented arrangements. Although this radical strategy did serve to promote agrarian development in the short run, it also created class and state structures that provided a foundation for highly repressive political systems in the future. If reactionary authoritarianism was historically a product of radical market policies, it is surely also possible that neoliberal reforms—when implemented in a rapid, all-encompassing fashion—carry the potential to create a new kind of class polarization and state control that could underpin highly repressive political systems in the decades to come.

A glance back at the history of aborted liberalism in Honduras and Nicaragua reminds us of the decisive role that foreign intervention can play in shaping political outcomes in Central America. Like their liberal predecessors, neoliberals are potentially vulnerable to failure due to outside intervention, especially through foreign investment that overwhelms the domestic economy. Contemporary neoliberals have had to perform delicate balancing acts between meeting international demands for market adjustment, on the one hand, and preserving national sovereignty and domestic control of the economy, on the other. Although the neoliberal reform model is objectionable on many valid counts, the history of Honduras and Nicaragua also teaches us that developing countries can ill afford to completely avoid economic restructuring. In the late nineteenth and early twentieth centuries, the failure of liberals in Honduras and Nicaragua to transform class and state structures produced political and economic backwardness for many decades to come. Now, a century later, the adoption of market reforms may be the only way to avoid a similar kind of political and economic underdevelopment.

Costa Rica's pattern of reformist liberalism offers a vision of how the gradual and selective implementation of market reforms might provide a long-term basis for economic growth under politically acceptable conditions. During the nineteenth century, reformist liberalism had this consequence because it created comparatively harmonious agrarian relations, avoiding the highly polarized class structures of Guatemala and El Salvador. Equally important, reformist liberalism enabled the state to assume a more positive role in the promotion of human welfare, avoiding a kind of militarization in which the control of societal groups was paramount for state actors. The history of Costa Rica suggests that contemporary neoliberal leaders must indeed use the state to support the market through regulatory and promotional activities in order to avoid an outcome like that in Honduras and Nicaragua. However, neoliberals must do so in a gradual manner, with much attention being devoted to the short- and long-term consequences of market policies for the development of state institutions and the lived conditions of societal majorities. Such moderate reformism will not solve all of the many problems facing countries such as those of Central America. But it probably represents the best temporary solution for achieving national development in a highly constraining global context where few real alternatives exist.

Whether countries follow a contemporary example of reformist liberalism or some other pattern is contingent on many factors, including the political choices of key elites. But the fact that governments are implementing neoliberal reforms in a democratic context provides some ground for optimism. The liberals who headed the nineteenth-century reform period were authoritarian in their ideology, embracing neither political liberties and freedoms nor formal democratic electoral procedures. By contrast, the current generation of liberals in Central America has been willing—at least so far—to play by the rules of formal democracy. While formal democracy does not necessarily entail enhanced socioeconomic equality or even high levels of political participation, it does necessarily ensure protection from arbitrary state abuse and a certain level of governmental accountability—conditions that have historically been absent in most of Central America. Should real alternatives to neoliberalism become available, these existing democratic institutions could be very important instruments for advancing mobilization in support of progressive political movements and policies. In this sense, the maintenance of contemporary democracy in Central America may be requisite for movement toward more substantive democratic outcomes in the future.

NOTES

CHAPTER ONE: EXPLAINING POLITICAL DEVELOPMENT
IN CENTRAL AMERICA

1. See Paul Pierson, "Increasing Returns, Path Dependence, and the Study of Politics," *American Political Science Review* 94 (June 2000): 251–67; and James Mahoney, "Path Dependence in Historical Sociology," *Theory and Society* 29 (August 2000): 507–48.

2. Douglas C. North, *Institutions, Institutional Change, and Economic Performance* (Cambridge: Cambridge University Press, 1990), 100; Sheri Berman, "Path Dependency and Political Action: Reexamining Responses to the Depression," *Comparative Politics* 30 (1998): 380. William Sewell asserts that path dependence means "that what has happened at an earlier point in time will affect the possible outcomes of a sequence of events occurring at a later point in time." This definition—which has been widely employed—suffers from similar shortcomings. See William H. Sewell Jr., "Three Temporalities: Toward an Eventful Sociology," in Terrence J. McDonald, ed., *The Historic Turn in the Human Sciences* (Ann Arbor: University of Michigan Press, 1996), 262–63.

3. Barrington Moore Jr., *Social Origins of Dictatorship and Democracy: Lord and Peasant in the Making of the Modern World* (Boston: Beacon Press, 1966); Gregory M. Luebbert, *Liberalism, Fascism, or Social Democracy: Social Classes and the Political Origins of Regimes in Interwar Europe* (New York: Oxford University Press, 1991); Ruth Berins Collier and David Collier, *Shaping the Political Arena: Critical Junctures, the Labor Movement, and Regime Dynamics in Latin America* (Princeton: Princeton University Press, 1991).

4. The concept of critical juncture was developed by Seymour Martin Lipset and Stein Rokkan in "Cleavage Structures, Party Systems, and Voter Alignments: An Introduction," in Seymour Martin Lipset and Stein Rokkan, eds., *Party Systems and Voter Alignments: Cross-National Perspectives* (New York: Free Press, 1967), 37. The most comprehensive statement on critical junctures is Collier and Collier, *Shaping the Political Arena*, chap. 1. Collier and Collier define a critical juncture as "a period of significant change, which typically occurs in distinct ways in different countries (or in other units of analysis) and which is hypothesized to produce distinct legacies" (29). I adopt a slightly different definition here.

5. Paul A. David, "Clio and the Economics of QWERTY," *American Economic Review* 75 (May 1985): 332–37. For a discussion of this literature, see W. Brian Arthur, *Increasing Returns and Path Dependence in the Economy* (Ann Arbor: University of Michigan Press, 1994). For critiques of and commentaries on this literature, see S. J. Liebowitz and Stephen E. Margolis, "Path-Dependence, Lock-In, and History," *Journal of Law, Economics, and Organization* 11 (1995): 205–26; S. J. Liebowitz and Stephen E. Margolis, "The Fable of the Keys," *Journal of Law and Economics* 33 (1990): 1–25; and Pierson, "Increasing Returns."

6. Collier and Collier, *Shaping the Political Arena*, 27.

7. On this problem of historical regress, see the discussion of Cleopatra's nose in Blaise Pascal, *"Pensées" and Other Writings*, trans. Honor Levi (New York: Oxford University Press, 1995).

8. See Pierson, "Increasing Returns," 263; and Arthur, *Increasing Returns*.

9. Margaret Levi, "A Model, a Method, and a Map: Rational Choice in Comparative and Historical Analysis," in Mark Irving Lichbach and Alan S. Zuckerman, eds., *Comparative Politics: Rationality, Culture, and Structure* (Princeton: Princeton University Press, 1997), 28.

10. See Arthur Stinchcombe, *Constructing Social Theories* (New York: Harcourt, Brace & World, 1968), 101–3; Stephen D. Krasner, "Sovereignty: An Institutional Analysis," *Comparative Political Studies* 21 (1988): 80–85; and Collier and Collier, *Shaping the Political Arena*, 35–36.

11. Stinchcombe, *Constructing Social Theories*, 103–4.

12. North, *Institutions*, 94; Arthur, *Increasing Returns*, chap. 7. See also Walter W. Powell, "Expanding the Scope of Institutional Analysis," in Walter W. Powell and Paul J. DiMaggio, eds., *The New Institutionalism in Organizational Analysis* (Chicago: University of Chicago Press, 1991).

13. Robert K. Merton, *Social Theory and Social Structure: Toward the Codification of Theory and Research* (Glencoe, Ill.: Free Press, 1949), 23–24; Francesca M. Cancian, "Varieties of Functional Analysis," in David L. Sills, ed., *International Encyclopedia of the Social Sciences* (New York: Macmillan, 1968), 30; Stinchcombe, *Constructing Social Theories*, 80–91.

14. See Anthony Obershall and Eric M. Leifer, "Efficiency and Social Institutions: Uses and Misuses of Economic Reasoning in Sociology," *Annual Review of Sociology* 12 (1986): 245–46; Randall Collins, *Four Sociological Traditions* (New York: Oxford University Press, 1994), 123; and Dietrich Rueschemeyer, *Power and the Division of Labour* (Stanford: Stanford University Press, 1986).

15. See John Dowling and Jeffrey Pfeffer, "Organizational Legitimacy: Social Values and Organizational Behavior," *Pacific Sociological Review* 18 (1975): 122–36; Juan J. Linz, *The Breakdown of Democratic Regimes* (Baltimore: Johns Hopkins University Press, 1978), 16–23; and W. Richard Scott, "Unpacking Institutional Arguments," in Powell and DiMaggio, *New Institutionalism*, 169–70.

16. The concepts of "aftermath," "heritage," and "legacy" discussed in this

section and throughout this work are from Collier and Collier, *Shaping the Political Arena*.

17. Andrew Abbott, "From Causes to Events: Notes on Narrative Positivism," *Sociological Methods and Research* 20 (1992): 445.

18. Daniel H. Levine, "Paradigm Lost: Dependence to Democracy," *World Politics* 40 (1988): 177–94; Nancy Bermeo, "Rethinking Regime Change," *Comparative Politics* 22 (1990): 273–92; Terry Lynn Karl, "Dilemmas of Democratization in Latin America," *Comparative Politics* 23 (1990): 269–84; Terry Lynn Karl and Philippe C. Schmitter, "Modes of Transition in Latin America, Southern and Eastern Europe," *International Social Science Journal* 128 (1991): 269–84; Karen L. Remmer, "New Wine or Old Bottlenecks? The Study of Latin American Democracy," *Comparative Politics* 23 (1991): 479–93; Herbert Kitschelt, "Political Regime Change: Structure and Process-Driven Explanations?" *American Political Science Review* 86 (1992): 1028–34; Gerardo L. Munck, "Democratic Transitions in Comparative Perspective," *Comparative Politics* 26 (1994): 355–75; James Mahoney and Richard Snyder, "Rethinking Agency and Structure in the Study of Regime Change," *Studies in Comparative International Development* 34 (1999): 3–32.

19. These explanations figure prominently in the fine studies by Stephen Schlesinger and Stephen Kinzer, *Bitter Fruit: The Untold Story of the American Coup in Guatemala* (Garden City, N.Y.: Anchor Books, 1982); Jacobo Schifter, *La fase oculta de la Guerra Civil en Costa Rica* (San José: EDUCA, 1979); and Knut Walter, *The Regime of Anastasio Somoza, 1936–1956* (Chapel Hill: University of North Carolina Press, 1993), chap. 2.

20. Lowell Gudmundson and Héctor Lindo-Fuentes, *Central America, 1821–1871: Liberalism before Liberal Reform* (Tuscaloosa: University of Alabama Press, 1995), 3.

21. Honduras is ignored or discussed primarily as a deviant case in three outstanding comparative-historical works on the region: Robert G. Williams, *States and Social Evolution: Coffee and the Rise of National Governments in Central America* (Chapel Hill: University of North Carolina Press, 1994); Jeffery M. Paige, *Coffee and Power: Revolution and the Rise of Democracy in Central America* (Cambridge: Harvard University Press, 1997); and Deborah J. Yashar, *Demanding Democracy: Reform and Reaction in Costa Rica and Guatemala, 1870s–1950s* (Stanford: Stanford University Press, 1997). On the tendency to use Guatemala as a model for the region as a whole, see Enrique A. Baloyra-Herp, "Reactionary Despotism in Central America," *Journal of Latin American Studies* 15, pt. 2 (1983): 295–319; Robert H. Holden, "Constructing the Limits of State Violence in Central America: Towards a New Research Agenda," *Journal of Latin American Studies* 28 (May 1996): 435–59; and Ralph Lee Woodward Jr., "The Rise and Decline of Liberalism in Central America: Historical Perspectives on the Contemporary Crisis," *Journal of Interamerican Studies and World Affairs* 26 (August 1984): 291–312.

22. John Weeks, "An Interpretation of the Central American Crisis," *Latin American Research Review* 21, no. 3 (1986): 31–54; Baloyra-Herp, "Reactionary Despotism in Central America"; Victor Bulmer-Thomas, *The Political Economy of Central America since 1920* (Cambridge: Cambridge University Press, 1987).

23. Ralph Lee Woodward Jr., *Central America: A Nation Divided,* 2d ed. (New York: Oxford University Press, 1985).

24. James Dunkerley, *Power in the Isthmus: A Political History of Modern Central America* (London: Verso, 1988); Lowell Gudmundson, "Lord and Peasant in the Making of Modern Central America," in Evelyne Huber and Frank Safford, eds., *Agrarian Structure and Political Power* (Pittsburgh: University of Pittsburgh Press, 1995); Paige, *Coffee and Power;* R. G. Williams, *States and Social Evolution.*

25. The comparative-historical study of Central America that comes closest to my concerns with the state is R. G. Williams, *States and Social Evolution.*

26. Gudmundson and Lindo-Fuentes, *Central America, 1821–1871,* 7–8.

27. Dunkerley, *Power in the Isthmus;* Paige, *Coffee and Power;* Yashar, *Demanding Democracy.*

28. Of the leaders who headed the phase of full-blown liberalism, Barrios and Guardia can be considered members of the coffee agrarian bourgeoisie, and Carrillo and Zelaya were at least minor coffee planters. Many of the other presidents during the liberal reform in Central America were also members of the agrarian bourgeoisie—though in no case did members of the export oligarchy directly occupy the presidency for a majority of the years that constituted the liberal reform period in a given country (for details, see table 6.1 in R. G. Williams, *States and Social Evolution,* 212–19). The oligarchic class as a whole did not control the liberal state: personalistic rule by a member of an economic elite is not equal to dominant-class control over the state. Indeed, one might expect personalistic dictators from the oligarchy to use their control over the state to "prey" on competing economic elites and rule contrary to the economic interests of the oligarchy as a whole. A genuine ideological commitment to overall societal development, as well as friendship networks, militated against this possibility in Central America.

29. See R. G. Williams, *States and Social Evolution,* chap. 1; and Michael J. Jiménez, "'From Plantation to Cup': Coffee and Capitalism in the United States, 1830–1930," in William Roseberry, Lowell Gudmundson, and Mario Samper Kutschbach, eds., *Coffee, Society, and Power in Latin America* (Baltimore: Johns Hopkins University Press, 1995), 38–64.

30. Edelberto Torres-Rivas, *Interpretación del desarrollo social centroamericano: Procesos y estructuras de una sociedad dependiente,* 2d ed. (San José: EDUCA, 1971), 57.

31. These variants include both simplistic dependency accounts and world-systems theories. On simplistic dependency theory, see André Gunder Frank,

Capitalism and Underdevelopment in Latin America (New York: Monthly Review Press, 1967). On the literature that critiques this position, see the relevant citations in Gabriel Palma, "Dependency: A Formal Theory of Underdevelopment or a Methodology for the Analysis of Concrete Situations of Underdevelopment?" *World Development* 6 (1978): 881–924. On world-systems theory, see Immanuel Wallerstein's ongoing work, beginning with *The Modern World-System I: Capitalist Agriculture and the Origins of the European World Economy* (New York: Academic Press, 1974). For telling critiques, see Robert Brenner, "The Origins of Capitalist Development: A Critique of Neo-Smithian Marxism," *New Left Review* 104 (July–August 1977): 25–92; Theda Skocpol, "Wallerstein's World Capitalist System: A Theoretical and Historical Critique," *American Journal of Sociology* 82 (March 1977): 1075–90; and Maurice Zeitlin, *The Civil Wars in Chile (or The Bourgeois Revolutions That Never Were)* (Princeton: Princeton University Press, 1984), chap. 5.

32. The classic work from this perspective is Fernando Henrique Cardoso and Enzo Faletto, *Dependency and Development in Latin America*, trans. Mariory Mattingly Urquidi (Berkeley: University of California Press, 1979). This book is an expanded English version of Cardoso and Faletto's *Dependencia y desarrollo en América Latina* (Mexico City: Siglo XXI, 1969). Edelberto Torres-Rivas's pathbreaking *Interpretación del desarrollo* remains the classic comparative work on Central America that employs the "historical-structural" methodology advocated by Cardoso and Faletto. Numerous case-study analyses also explicitly follow Cardoso and Faletto's approach.

33. On the distinction between a global capitalist system and an international states system, see Theda Skocpol, *States and Social Revolutions: A Comparative Analysis of France, Russia, and China* (Cambridge: Cambridge University Press, 1979), 22; and Hagen Koo, "The Interplay of State, Social Class, and World System in East Asian Development: The Cases of South Korea and Taiwan," in Frederic C. Deyo, ed., *The Political Economy of the New Asian Industrialism* (Ithaca: Cornell University Press, 1987), 169.

34. This is essentially the argument of Miles Wortman in his excellent book *Government and Society in Central America, 1680–1840* (New York: Columbia University Press, 1982). See also the interesting argument in Consuelo Cruz, "Identity and Persuasion: How Nations Remember Their Pasts and Make Their Futures," *World Politics* 52 (April 2000): 275–312. Unfortunately, this article came to my attention too late to be considered here.

35. David Scott Palmer, "The Politics of Authoritarianism in Spanish America," in James M. Malloy, ed., *Authoritarianism and Corporatism in Latin America* (Pittsburgh: University of Pittsburgh Press, 1977), 379–83.

36. Baloyra-Herp, "Reactionary Despotism in Central America." See also Bulmer-Thomas, *The Political Economy of Central America*.

37. Baloyra-Herp, "Reactionary Despotism," 297–308.

38. Ibid., 307.

39. Woodward, *Central America: A Nation Divided*, 215. See also Yashar, *Demanding Democracy*, 238 n. 6. One difference between my argument and Woodward's should be highlighted. Whereas Woodward suggests that the dictatorships of the 1930s and those of the late nineteenth century both basically share the pattern of what Baloyra calls oligarchic domination, my analysis suggests that this conceptualization is somewhat misleading. In particular, the revised understanding of liberal dictatorships offered in this study highlights how the so-called period of oligarchic domination in Central America was in fact characterized by personal dictatorships and complex alliances among various actors. Scholars of Latin America attempting to make a broad characterization of the late nineteenth century have taken peaceful refuge under the concept of oligarchic domination. Unfortunately, it is not a very useful concept.

40. See James Mahoney, "Nominal, Ordinal, and Narrative Appraisal in Macrocausal Analysis," *American Journal of Sociology* 104 (1999): 1154–96.

41. I discuss within-case analysis in greater depth in James Mahoney, "Strategies of Causal Inference in Small-*N* Analysis," *Sociological Methods and Research* 28 (May 2000): 387–424.

CHAPTER TWO: THE LIBERAL REFORM PERIOD AND ITS LEGACIES

1. Reinhard Bendix, *Kings or People: Power and the Mandate to Rule* (Berkeley: University of California Press, 1978), 582.

2. My thinking on European liberalism has been strongly influenced by Andrew C. Gould, *The Origins of Liberal Dominance: State, Church, and Party in Nineteenth-Century Europe* (Ann Arbor: University of Michigan Press, 1999).

3. See, for example, Louis Hartz, *The Liberal Tradition in America* (San Diego: Harcourt Brace Jovanovich, 1955).

4. On "world society" and liberal world culture, see John W. Meyer, John Boli, George M. Thomas, and Francisco O. Ramirez, "World Society and the Nation-State," *American Journal of Sociology* 103, no. 1 (July 1997): 144–87; and John W. Meyer, "The Changing Cultural Content of the Nation-State: A World Society Perspective," in George Steinmetz, ed., *State/Culture: State Formation after the Cultural Turn* (Ithaca: Cornell University Press, 1999).

5. General discussions of liberalism—within and outside of Central America—that were especially useful to me in developing this definition include Jesús Julián Amurrio, *El positivismo en Guatemala* (Guatemala: Universidad de San Carlos, 1970), 16–17, 43–44, 63–65; David Bushnell and Neill Macaulay, *The Emergence of Latin America in the Nineteenth Century*, 2d ed. (New York: Oxford University Press, 1994), 33–34, 180–92; Joseph L. Love, "Structural Change and Conceptual Response in Latin America and Romania, 1860–1950," in Joseph L. Love and Nils Jacobsen, eds., *Guiding the Invisible Hand: Economic Liberalism and the State in Latin American History* (New York: Praeger, 1988),

1–33; Charles A. Hale, *The Transformation of Liberalism in Late Nineteenth-Century Mexico* (Princeton: Princeton University Press, 1989), esp. chaps. 1, 7; A. Gould, *Origins of Liberal Dominance;* Edwin Williamson, *The Penguin History of Latin America* (London: Penguin, 1992), 283–84, 298–300; Ralph Lee Woodward Jr., "The Rise and Decline of Liberalism in Central America: Historical Perspectives on the Contemporary Crisis," *Journal of Interamerican Studies and World Affairs* 26 (August 1984): 292–94; and Ralph Lee Woodward Jr., introduction to Woodward, ed., *Positivism in Latin America, 1850–1900: Are Order and Progress Reconcilable?* (Lexington, Mass.: D. C. Heath & Company, 1971), ix–xiv.

6. Liberals did not always directly discuss Comte, and many mid-nineteenth-century liberals were probably not very familiar with his work. However, the strong influence of Comtean positivism is clearly present in liberal discussions of this time.

7. For some Central American countries—especially Guatemala—a major component of political positivism was specifically centered against indigenous peoples. Indigenous people and culture were seen as the antithesis of order and progress, and thus as obstacles to be removed. This sometimes led to an officially sanctioned policy of racism. Further, racist beliefs played at least some role in liberals' encouragement of immigration from European countries, whose whiter populations were seen as more capable of pursuing the goal of modernization.

8. See A. Gould, *Origins of Liberal Dominance.*

9. The concept of a moral economy is from James C. Scott, *The Moral Economy of the Peasant: Rebellion and Subsistence in Southeast Asia* (New Haven: Yale University Press, 1976). Its applicability to preliberal Latin American is suggested (perhaps to the point of exaggeration) by the discussion of agrarian relations in E. Bradford Burns, *The Poverty of Progress: Latin America in the Nineteenth Century* (Berkeley: University of California Press, 1980).

10. In the case of Honduras, the transition to agrarian capitalism and the accompanying incorporation into the global market occurred through banana production and exportation, a sector of the economy that was dominated by foreign-owned enterprises. The special issues raised by the role of foreign direct investment in the process of liberal reform in Honduras are discussed at length in chapter 7.

11. For example, Ciro F. S. Cardoso, "The Liberal Era, c. 1870–1930," in Leslie Bethell, ed., *Central America since Independence* (Cambridge: Cambridge University Press, 1991), 37–67; James Dunkerley, *Power in the Isthmus: A Political History of Modern Central America* (London: Verso, 1988), chaps. 1–2; Edelberto Torres-Rivas, *Interpretación del desarrollo social centroamericano: Procesos y estructuras de una sociedad dependiente,* 2d ed. (San José: EDUCA, 1971), chap. 2; and Ralph Lee Woodward Jr., *Central America: A Nation Divided,* 2d ed. (New York: Oxford University Press, 1985), 155.

12. This is particularly true in single-country monographs and articles. For

Guatemala, see Augusto Cazali Àvila, "El desarrollo del cultivo del café y su influencia en el régimen del trabajo agrícola: Época de la reforma liberal (1871–1885)," *Anuario de Estudios Centroamericanos* 2 (May 1976): 36; for El Salvador, Héctor Lindo-Fuentes, *Weak Foundations: The Economy of El Salvador in the Nineteenth Century, 1821–1898* (Berkeley: University of California Press, 1990), 125; for Costa Rica, Eugenio Rodríguez, *Don Tomás Guardia y el Estado liberal,* 2d ed. (San José: EUNED, 1989); for Honduras, Guillermo Molina Chocano, *Estado liberal y desarrollo capitalista en Honduras* (Tegucigalpa: Banco Central de Honduras, 1976), ix; and for Nicaragua, Oscar René Vargas, *La revolución que inició el progreso (Nicaragua, 1893–1909)* (Managua: Ecotextura, 1990).

13. See Jeffery M. Paige, *Coffee and Power: Revolution and the Rise of Democracy in Central America* (Cambridge: Harvard University Press, 1997), chap. 2.

14. See Paige, *Coffee and Power.*

15. Dietrich Rueschemeyer and Peter B. Evans, "The State and Economic Transformation: Toward an Analysis of the Conditions Underlying Effective Intervention," in Peter B. Evans, Dietrich Rueschemeyer, and Theda Skocpol, eds., *Bringing the State Back In* (Cambridge: Cambridge University Press, 1985), 52.

16. Here I follow Rueschemeyer, Stephens, and Stephens in arguing that state consolidation was a necessary condition for movement toward democracy in Latin America; see Dietrich Rueschemeyer, Evelyne Huber Stephens, and John D. Stephens, *Capitalist Development and Democracy* (Chicago: University of Chicago Press, 1992), 159, 163.

17. As Rueschemeyer, Stephens, and Stephens point out, "Some autonomy of the state from the dominant classes, from the bourgeoisie and especially— where it still exists—from the landlord class, is a necessary condition for democracy to be possible and meaningful." Ibid., 64.

18. Robert Fishman, "Rethinking Regime and State: Southern Europe's Transition to Democracy," *World Politics* 42 (April 1990): 428.

19. On this distinction, see Ruth Berins Collier and David Collier, *Shaping the Political Arena: Critical Junctures, the Labor Movement, and Regime Dynamics in Latin America* (Princeton: Princeton University Press, 1991), 782, 789; and Fishman, "Rethinking Regime and State," 428. Both Collier and Collier and Fishman adopt a Weberian understanding of the state. For an effort to differentiate regime from a Marxist understanding of the state, see Fernando Henrique Cardoso, "On the Characterization of Authoritarian Regimes in Latin America," in David Collier, ed., *The New Authoritarianism in Latin America* (Princeton: Princeton University Press, 1979). The most comprehensive statement on different types of regimes is Juan Linz, "Totalitarian and Authoritarian Regimes," in Fred Greenstein and Nelson Polsby, eds., *Handbook of Political Science,* vol. 3 (Reading, Mass.: Addison-Wesley, 1975).

20. See Samuel Huntington, *The Third Wave: Democratization in the Late Twentieth Century* (Norman: University of Oklahoma Press, 1991).

21. The strongest statement of this position is Lowell Gudmundson and Héctor Lindo-Fuentes, *Central America, 1821–1871: Liberalism before Liberal Reform* (Tuscaloosa: University of Alabama Press, 1995). For good review essays on the revisionist literature, see David Kaimowitz, "New Perspectives on Central American History, 1838–1945," *Latin American Research Review* 31, no. 1 (1996): 201–10; Jeffrey L. Gould and Lowell Gudmundson, "Central American Historiography after the Violence," *Latin American Research Review* 32, no. 2 (1997): 244–56; and Paul Dosal, "Recent Developments in Central American Studies: A Review of Trends and Prospects," *Latin American Research Review* 34, no. 3 (1999): 225–40.

CHAPTER THREE: LIBERALS AND CONSERVATIVES BEFORE
THE REFORM PERIOD

1. See Andrew C. Gould, *The Origins of Liberal Dominance: State, Church, and Party in Nineteenth-Century Europe* (Ann Arbor: University of Michigan Press, 1999); Andrew C. Gould, "Origins of Liberal Dominance in Western Europe, 1815–1914" (manuscript, University of Notre Dame, April 1995); and Gregory M. Luebbert, *Liberalism, Fascism, or Social Democracy: Social Classes and the Political Origins of Regimes in Interwar Europe* (New York: Oxford University Press, 1991).

2. The colony was also known as the Captaincy General of Guatemala.

3. The authoritative work on the consequences of this colonial transformation in Central America is Miles L. Wortman, *Government and Society in Central America, 1680–1840* (New York: Columbia University Press, 1982). As Wortman stresses, much of the history of Central America can be viewed as "the struggle between the Hapsburg heritage of economic and political traditional society, regional autonomy, and Christian ideals and the Bourbon legacy of liberal economies, centralized authority, and 'enlightened' thought" (277).

4. Ibid., 130; Ralph Lee Woodward Jr., *Central America: A Nation Divided*, 2d ed. (New York: Oxford University Press, 1985), 62–63; Woodward, "Changes in the Nineteenth-Century Guatemalan State and Its Indian Policies," in Carol A. Smith, ed., with the assistance of Marilyn M. Moors, *Guatemalan Indians and the State, 1540–1988* (Austin: University of Texas Press, 1990), 53–55; Héctor Pérez Brignoli, *A Brief History of Central America*, trans. Ricardo B. Sawrey A. and Susana Stettri de Sawrey (Berkeley: University of California Press, 1989), 55–63.

5. Indigo, a blue dyestuff, became an important Central American export as the textile revolution advanced in eighteenth-century Europe. Until the early nineteenth century, indigo was the basis of Guatemala's economy and financed much of the Kingdom's imports. On the trade of indigo in colonial Central America, see Robert S. Smith, "Indigo Production and Trade in Colonial Guatemala," *Hispanic American Historical Review* 39 (May 1959): 181–211.

6. Troy S. Floyd, "The Guatemalan Merchants, the Government, and the *Provincianos, 1750–1800*," *Hispanic American Historical Review* 41 (February 1961): 90–110.

7. Ralph Lee Woodward Jr., "Economic and Social Origins of the Guatemalan Political Parties (1773–1823)," *Hispanic American Historical Review* 45 (November 1965): 552.

8. Ralph Lee Woodward Jr., *Class Privilege and Economic Development: The Consulado de Comercio of Guatemala, 1793–1871* (Chapel Hill: University of North Carolina Press, 1966), 5–6.

9. For a discussion of the peasantry in the late colonial period specifically in the Guatemalan province, see David McCreery, "State Power, Indigenous Communities, and Land in Nineteenth-Century Guatemala, 1820–1920," in C. A. Smith, *Guatemalan Indians and the State*, 97–100.

10. Ciro F. S. Cardoso and Héctor Pérez Brignoli, *Centroamérica y la economía occidental,1520–1930* (San José: EDUCA, 1977), 114. All translations of quotations from works in Spanish are mine.

11. On the ability of merchants to thwart the Bourbon reform effort, see Floyd, "The Guatemalan Merchants." On the formation of the Consulado, see Robert S. Smith, "Origins of the Consulado of Guatemala," *Hispanic American Historical Review* 26 (May 1946): 150–61; and Woodward, *Class Privilege and Economic Development*, 3–8.

12. See Miles Wortman, "Government Revenue and Economic Trends in Central America, 1787–1819," *Hispanic American Historical Review* 55 (May 1975): 251–86.

13. Ralph Lee Woodward Jr., "The Aftermath of Independence, 1821–c. 1870," in Leslie Bethell, ed., *Central America since Independence* (Cambridge: Cambridge University Press, 1991), 2–9.

14. Ralph Lee Woodward Jr., *Rafael Carrera and the Emergence of the Republic of Guatemala, 1821–1871* (Athens: University of Georgia Press, 1993), 20.

15. Mario Rodríguez, *The Cádiz Experiment in Central America, 1808 to 1826* (Berkeley: University of California Press, 1978), 28.

16. Woodward, "Economic and Social Origins," 559–61; Woodward, *Central America: A Nation Divided*, 93.

17. Susan Emily Strobeck, "The Political Activities of Some Members of the Aristocratic Families of Guatemala, 1821–1839" (M.A. thesis, Tulane University, 1958), 11; Woodward, "Economic and Social Origins," 559–60.

18. On the epoch of Bustamante's rule, see especially Ramón A. Salazar, *Historia de veintiún años: La independencia de Guatemala*, 2d ed., tomo 2, vol. 5 (Guatemala: Editorial del Ministerio de Educación Pública, 1956).

19. Background on the formation of the original political parties in Central America can be found in Woodward, "Economic and Social Origins," 559–64; Hubert Howe Bancroft, *History of Central America*, vol. 3 (San Francisco: The

History Company, 1887), 26–28; Dana G. Munro, *The Five Republics of Central America: Their Political and Economic Development and Their Relations with the United States* (New York: Oxford University Press, 1918), 28–29; M. Rodríguez, *The Cádiz Experiment*, 18–27; R. A. Salazar, *Historia de veintiún años*, 235–36; and Strobeck, "Political Activities," 10–11.

20. Woodward, "Economic and Social Origins," 564.

21. Woodward, "The Aftermath of Independence," 4; Woodward, *Central America: A Nation Divided*, 88–89.

22. Woodward, "Economic and Social Origins," 564–65; Strobeck, "Political Activities," chap. 2.

23. Woodward, *Rafael Carrera*, 26–27.

24. M. Rodríguez, *The Cádiz Experiment*, 236–37; Robert G. Williams, *States and Social Evolution: Coffee and the Rise of National Governments in Central America* (Chapel Hill: University of North Carolina Press, 1994), 200–201.

25. Woodward, *Rafael Carrera*, 27.

26. See Lowell Gudmundson, *Hacendados, precaristas y políticos: La ganadería y el latifundismo guanacasteco, 1800–1950* (San José: Editorial Costa Rica, 1983), 18; and Lowell Gudmundson, "Society and Politics in Central America, 1821–1871," in Lowell Gudmundson and Héctor Lindo-Fuentes, *Central America, 1821–1871: Liberalism before Liberal Reform* (Tuscaloosa: University of Alabama Press, 1995), 82ff.

27. Discussions of the period of annexation to Mexico can be found in Bancroft, *History of Central America*, 3:50–67; Alberto Herrate, *La unión de Centroamérica: Tragedia y esperanza* (Guatemala: Editorial del Ministerio de Educación Pública, 1955), 127–36; and Gordon Kenyon, "Mexican Influence in Central America, 1821–1823," *Hispanic American Historical Review* 41 (May 1961): 175–205.

28. Pérez Brignoli, *Brief History*, 66.

29. Francisco Peccorini Letona, *La voluntad del pueblo en la emancipación de El Salvador* (San Salvador: Ministerio de Educación, Dirección de Publicaciones, 1972), chap. 2.

30. Pérez Brignoli, *Brief History*, 67.

31. See A. Gould, *Origins of Liberal Dominance*.

32. Ibid.

33. A. Gould, "Origins of Liberal Dominance," 8.

34. For example, Robert S. Smith, "Financing the Central American Federation, 1821–1838," *Hispanic American Historical Review* 43 (November 1963): 483–510.

35. For example, Rodrigo Facio B., *La Federación de Centroamérica: Sus antecedentes, su vida y su disolución* (San José: Escuela Superior de Administración Pública, 1960), 7.

36. For example, Bancroft, *History of Central America*, 3:76.

37. For example, Thomas L. Karnes, *The Failure of Union: Central America, 1824–1960* (Chapel Hill: University of North Carolina Press, 1961), 90.

38. The substantial and excellent research of Ralph Lee Woodward Jr. adopts a focus on liberal-conservative cleavage during the Federation years. See, for example, his *Central America: A Nation Divided*, 92–111.

39. This point is stressed in Gudmundson and Lindo-Fuentes, *Central America, 1821–1871*.

40. For details on the politics surrounding the Constituent Assembly, see Alejandro Marure, *Bosquejo histórico de las revoluciones de Centro-América: Desde 1811 hasta 1834*, vol. 1 (Guatemala: Tipografía de "El Progreso," 1877), 59–123; Bancroft, *History of Central America*, 3:60–78; and Karnes, *The Failure of Union*, chap. 3.

41. Useful discussions of the constitution of the Federation of Central America can be found in Karnes, *The Failure of Union*, 49–56; and Pedro Joaquín Chamorro, *Historia de la Federación de la América Central, 1823–1840* (Madrid: Ediciones Cultura Hispánica, 1951), 67–91.

42. On Arce's fortuitous rise to the presidency, his alliance with conservatives, and the liberal reaction to his presidency, see Philip Flemion, "States Rights and Partisan Politics: Manuel José Arce and the Struggle for Central American Union," *Hispanic American Historical Review* 53 (November 1973): 600–618; Bancroft, *History of Central America*, 3:79–100; Karnes, *The Failure of Union*, 56–67; and Marure, *Bosquejo histórico*, 1:137–91.

43. The politics surrounding the 1826–29 period is the subject of Marure, *Bosquejo histórico*, vol. 2.

44. See R. S. Smith, "Financing the Central American Federation."

45. See Héctor Lindo-Fuentes, *Weak Foundations: The Economy of El Salvador in the Nineteenth Century, 1821–1898* (Berkeley: University of California Press, 1990), 40–60. Karnes, *The Failure of Union*, 67, offers a contrasting assessment of the damage done by warfare during the Federation. I follow Lindo-Fuentes because his assessment on this point appears to be based on better-documented research.

46. Woodward, *Rafael Carrera*, 38–39; Lorenzo Montúfar, *Reseña histórica de Centroamérica* (Guatemala: Tipografía de "El Progreso," 1878), 1:153–60.

47. See Mary P. Holleran, *Church and State in Guatemala* (New York: Columbia University Press, 1949), 100–113.

48. Woodward, *Central America: A Nation Divided*, 95.

49. Aldo A. Lauria-Santiago, *An Agrarian Republic: Commercial Agriculture and the Politics of Peasant Communities in El Salvador, 1823–1914* (Pittsburgh: University of Pittsburgh Press, 1999), 105–8.

50. Cardoso and Pérez Brignoli, *Centroamérica y la economía occidental*, 150.

51. Hazel Marylyn Bennett Ingersoll, "The War of the Mountain: A Study

of Reactionary Peasant Insurgency in Guatemala, 1837–1873" (Ph.D. diss., George Washington University, 1972), vi.

52. Ralph Lee Woodward Jr., "Social Revolution in Guatemala: The Carrera Revolt," in Mario Rodríguez et al., eds., *Applied Enlightenment: Nineteenth Century Liberalism* (New Orleans: Middle American Research Institute, Tulane University, 1972), 48–49.

53. For example, Keith L. Miceli, "Rafael Carrera: Defender and Promoter of Peasant Interests in Guatemala, 1837–1848," *The Americas* 31 (July 1974): 73–76.

54. Ingersoll, "The War of the Mountain," chap. 2; Woodward, "Social Revolution in Guatemala," 49–54. See also Juan Carlos Solórzano F., "Rafael Carrera, ¿Reacción conservadora o revolución campesina? Guatemala 1837–1873," *Anuario de Estudios Centroamericanos* 13 (1987): 5–35; and Greg Grandin, *The Blood of Guatemala: A History of Race and Nation* (Durham, N.C.: Duke University Press, 2000), chap. 3.

55. For details on the Carrera revolt, see Ingersoll, "The War of the Mountain"; Woodward, "Social Revolution in Guatemala"; and Woodward, *Rafael Carrera*, chaps. 3–4.

56. Woodward, "Social Revolution in Guatemala," 64.

57. Ibid., 66.

58. Gudmundson, "Society and Politics," 89.

59. Stone's work suggests that both conservative and liberal elites can often trace their ancestry back to a common familial background among the Spanish colonial nobility. See Samuel Z. Stone, *The Heritage of the Conquistadors: Ruling Classes in Central America from the Conquest to the Sandinistas* (Lincoln: University of Nebraska Press, 1990).

60. This conclusion is consistent with the work of Woodward. Compare, for example, the interpretation offered in his "The Rise and Decline of Liberalism in Central America: Historical Perspectives on the Contemporary Crisis," *Journal of Interamerican Studies and World Affairs* 26 (August 1984): 292–93, with the references cited in n. 16 above. See also Gudmundson, "Society and Politics," 82–90, 127.

61. Gudmundson, "Society and Politics," 90–91.

62. Frank Safford, "Bases for Political Alignment in Early Independent Spanish America," in Richard Graham, ed., *New Perspectives in Latin American History* (Austin: University of Texas Press, 1978), 71–111. See also Gudmundson, "Society and Politics," 82, who supports this interpretation.

CHAPTER FOUR: ROUTES TO LIBERAL POLITICAL DOMINANCE

1. See especially Rodrigo Facio, *Estudio sobre economía costarricense,* reprinted in *Obras de Rodrigo Facio,* vol. 1 (San José: Editorial Costa Rica, 1972), 34; Carolyn Hall, *El café y el desarrollo histórico-geográfico de Costa*

Rica (San José: Editorial Costa Rica, 1991), 25; Carlos Monge Alfaro, *Historia de Costa Rica,* 14th ed. (San José: Librería Trejos, 1976), 143–45, 156–61, 168–70, 223–26; Carlos Joaquín Sáenz, "Population Growth, Economic Progress, and Opportunities on the Land: The Case of Costa Rica," Research Paper No. 47, University of Wisconsin, Madison, June 1972, 1–2, 9–12; Mitchell A. Seligson, *Peasants of Costa Rica and the Development of Agrarian Capitalism* (Madison: University of Wisconsin Press, 1980), chaps. 1–2; and José Luis Vega Carballo, *Orden y progreso: La formación del Estado nacional en Costa Rica* (San José: Instituto Centroamericano de Administración Pública, 1981), chap. 1.

2. Monge, *Historia de Costa Rica,* 160.

3. Facio, *Estudio sobre economía costarricense,* 34.

4. Monge, *Historia de Costa Rica,* 158.

5. For example, Seligson, *Peasants of Costa Rica.*

6. Monge, *Historia de Costa Rica,* 170.

7. Lowell Gudmundson, *Costa Rica before Coffee: Society and Economy on the Eve of the Export Boom* (Baton Rouge: Louisiana State University Press, 1986), 22. In addition to this major book, Gudmundson's research results have been reported in several articles, the most important of which include Gudmundson, "Costa Rica before Coffee: Occupational Distribution, Wealth Inequality, and Élite Society in the Village Economy of the 1840s," *Journal of Latin American Studies* 15 (November 1983): 427–52; Gudmundson, "El campesino y el capitalismo agrario de Costa Rica: Una crítica de la ideología como historia," *Revista de Historia* 8 (January–July 1979): 59–81; and Gudmundson, "Nueva luz sobre la estratificación socio-económica costarricense al iniciarse la expansión cafetalera," *Revista de Historia* 4 (January–June 1977): 149–89. One of the earliest challenges to the rural democracy thesis is Edward Dennis Hernández, "Modernization and Dependency in Costa Rica during the Decade of the 1880s" (Ph.D. diss., University of California, Los Angeles, 1975), 287–88.

8. Iván Molina Jiménez, *Costa Rica (1800–1850): El legado colonial y la génesis del capitalismo* (San José: EDUCA, 1991), 176.

9. Elizabeth Fonseca, *Costa Rica colonial: La tierra y el hombre* (San José: EDUCA, 1983), 167–71.

10. See the narratives in Ricardo Blanco Segura, *Historia eclesiástica de Costa Rica, 1502–1850* (San José: Editorial Universidad Estatal a Distancia, 1983).

11. During the colonial period, Costa Rica was banned from the indigo trade and largely failed to produce an alternative export of equal stature, despite some trade connected with tobacco production and silver mining. A brief account of the failures of colonial Costa Rica to consolidate an export crop during colonialism can be found in Ciro F. S. Cardoso and Héctor Pérez Brignoli, *Centroamérica y la economía occidental, 1520–1930* (San José: EDUCA, 1977), 121–23.

12. Gudmundson, *Costa Rica before Coffee,* 57.

13. Ibid., 56–59; Víctor Hugo Acuña Ortega and Iván Molina Jiménez, *Historia económica y social de Costa Rica, 1750–1950* (San José: Editorial Porvenir, 1991), 113.

14. Lowell Gudmundson, *Hacendados, precaristas y políticos: La ganadería y el latifundismo guanacasteco, 1800–1950* (San José: Editorial Costa Rica, 1983), chap. 1.

15. On the liberal orientation of the Costa Rican elite, see Ciro F. S. Cardoso, "Características básicas de la economía latinoamericana (siglo XIX): Algunos problemas de la transición neo-colonial," *Revista de Historia* 4 (January–June 1977): 66; Gudmundson, *Hacendados, precaristas y políticos,* 18, 38; Gudmundson, *Costa Rica before Coffee,* 46–47; Lowell Gudmundson, "Society and Politics in Central America, 1821–1871," in Lowell Gudmundson and Héctor Lindo-Fuentes, *Central America, 1821–1871: Liberalism before Liberal Reform* (Tuscaloosa: University of Alabama Press, 1995), 87; and Rodolfo Cerdas Cruz, *Formación del Estado en Costa Rica,* 2d ed. (San José: EDUCA, 1978), 100–101. Although liberalism had a firm base in early-nineteenth-century Costa Rica, it must be stressed that political party affiliation was a weak indicator of one's actual political ideology: most elites were liberal in their socioeconomic outlook even when they were formally identified with conservative parties.

16. See Molina Jiménez, *Costa Rica (1800–1850),* 125–39; and Gudmundson, *Costa Rica before Coffee,* 42–47. Later this group would form the foundation for a liberal-oriented merchant-planter coffee elite. See Eugenio Sancho-Riba, "Merchant-Planters and Modernization: An Early Liberal Experiment in Costa Rica, 1849–1870" (Ph.D. diss., University of California, San Diego, 1982).

17. For a discussion, see Sancho-Riba, "Merchant-Planters and Modernization."

18. Cerdas Cruz, *Formación del Estado.*

19. For such warnings, see especially José Luis Vega Carballo, "Etapas y procesos de la evolución sociopolítica de Costa Rica," *Estudios Sociales Centroamericanos* 1 (January–April 1972): 48–50. For an overview of the interpretive debate surrounding this issue, see Iván Molina Jiménez, "El Valle Central de Costa Rica en la independencia," *Revista de Historia* 14 (July–December 1986): 85–114.

20. General background for this paragraph was drawn from Ricardo Fernández Guardia, *Historia de Costa Rica: La independencia,* 2d ed. (San José: Librería Lehmann, 1941), chaps. 4–5; Rafael Obregón Loría, *De nuestra historia patria: Hechos militares y políticos* (Alajuela, Costa Rica: Museo Histórico Cultural Juan Santamaría, 1981), 19–24, 33–35; and Cerdas Cruz, *Formación del Estado,* chap. 6.

21. Rafael Obregón Loría, *Costa Rica en la independencia y en la federación,* 2d ed. (San José: Editorial Costa Rica, 1979), 224.

22. Hubert Howe Bancroft, *History of Central America,* vol. 3 (San Francisco: The History Company, 1887), 178.

23. See Thomas L. Karnes, *The Failure of Union: Central America, 1824–1960* (Chapel Hill: University of North Carolina Press, 1961), 73–74, 84–85.

24. For example, Karnes, *The Failure of Union,* 34–35; and Alberto Herrate, *La unión de Centroamérica: Tragedia y esperanza* (Guatemala: Editorial del Ministerio de Educación Pública, 1955), 166.

25. Karnes (*The Failure of Union,* 94) compiled the following statistics for 1824–42 from Alejandro Marure, *Efemérides de los hechos notables acaecidos en la república de Centro América* (Guatemala: Tipografía Nacional, 1895), 141, 154.

	Number of Battles	Number Killed	Number of Men Wielding Executive Power
El Salvador	40	2,546	23
Honduras	27	682	20
Nicaragua	17	1,203	18
Costa Rica	5	144	11

26. This paragraph and the next one are based mostly on Gudmundson's pathbreaking research, as best represented in his *Costa Rica before Coffee.* But I also referred to Mario Samper Kutschbach, "Los productores directos en el siglo del café," *Revista de Historia* 7 (July–December 1978): 123–217; Molina Jiménez, *Costa Rica (1800–1850),* chaps. 1–3; and Ciro F. S. Cardoso, "The Formation of the Coffee Estate in Nineteenth-Century Costa Rica," in Kenneth Duncan and Ian Rutledge, eds., with the collaboration of Collin Harding, *Land and Labour in Latin America* (Cambridge: Cambridge University Press, 1977).

27. See especially Molina Jiménez, *Costa Rica (1800–1850),* 48–65.

28. Gudmundson, *Costa Rica before Coffee,* 46.

29. See Robert G. Williams, *States and Social Evolution: Coffee and the Rise of National Governments in Central America* (Chapel Hill: University of North Carolina Press, 1994), 199–200.

30. This section on Guatemala largely follows Ralph Lee Woodward Jr.'s seminal book *Rafael Carrera and the Emergence of the Republic of Guatemala, 1821–1871* (Athens: University of Georgia Press, 1993). Other sources consulted were Keith L. Miceli, "Rafael Carrera: Defender and Promoter of Peasant Interests in Guatemala, 1837–1848," *The Americas* 31 (July 1974): 72–95; and Juan Carlos Solórzano F., "Rafael Carrera, ¿Reacción conservadora o revolución campesina? Guatemala 1837–1873," *Anuario de Estudios Centroamericanos* 13 (1987): 5–35.

31. Woodward, *Rafael Carrera,* 106.

32. Ibid., 263.

33. Ibid., 254.

34. Ibid., 355.

35. On the liberal orientation of the Salvadoran elite, see, for example, Alastair White, *El Salvador* (New York: Praeger, 1973), 62.

36. Héctor Lindo-Fuentes, *Weak Foundations: The Economy of El Salvador in the Nineteenth Century, 1821–1898* (Berkeley: University of California Press, 1990), 133.

37. See Erik Ching, "Patronage, Politics, and Power in El Salvador, 1840–1940" (Ph.D. diss., University of California, Santa Barbara, 1997).

38. Patricia Alvarenga, "Reshaping the Ethics of Power: A History of Violence in Western Rural El Salvador, 1880–1932" (Ph.D. diss., University of Wisconsin, Madison, 1994), 35–38; Aldo A. Lauria-Santiago, *An Agrarian Republic: Commercial Agriculture and the Politics of Peasant Communities in El Salvador, 1823–1914* (Pittsburgh: University of Pittsburgh Press, 1999), 128–29.

39. See David Browning, *El Salvador. Landscape and Society* (Oxford: Clarendon Press, 1971), chap. 4; Rodolfo Cardenal, *Manual de historia de Centroamérica* (San Salvador: Universidad Centroamericana, n.d.), chap. 4; and David M. Kauck, "Agricultural Commercialization and State Development in Central America: The Political Economy of the Coffee Industry from 1838 to 1940" (Ph.D. diss., University of Washington, 1988), 104–5.

40. The standard work on Gerardo Barrios is Italo López Vallecillos, ed., *Gerardo Barrios y su tiempo*, 2 vols. (San Salvador: Ministerio de Educación, 1967). Useful overviews of his administration can be found in E. Bradford Burns, "The Modernization of Underdevelopment: El Salvador, 1858–1931," *Journal of Developing Areas* 18 (April 1984): 293–316; and José F. Figeac, *Recordatorio histórico de la República de El Salvador* (San Salvador: Talleres Gráficos Cisneros, 1952), 182–214.

41. Lindo-Fuentes, *Weak Foundations*, 133.

42. This paragraph draws on especially David McCreery, *Rural Guatemala, 1760–1940* (Stanford: Stanford University Press, 1994), chap. 4.

43. Ibid., 114.

44. Ibid., 162–63; R. G. Williams, *States and Social Evolution*, 53.

45. R. G. Williams, *States and Social Evolution*, 53, 113.

46. Woodward, *Rafael Carrera*, 382–85; McCreery, *Rural Guatemala*, 169. The role of German investors in promoting coffee production is stressed in J. C. Cambranes, *Coffee and Peasants: The Origins of the Modern Plantation Economy in Guatemala, 1853–1897*, English version revised by Carla Clason-Hook (Stockholm: Institute of Latin American Studies, University of Stockholm, 1985).

47. R. G. Williams, *States and Social Evolution*, 164. See also Augusto Cazali Àvila, "El desarrollo del cultivo del café y su influencia en el régimen del trabajo agrícola: Época de la reforma liberal (1871–1885)," *Anuario de Estudios Centroamericanos* 2 (May 1976): 41–42.

48. See R. G. Williams, *States and Social Evolution*, 54–55; and Woodward, *Rafael Carrera*, chap. 17.

49. On this point, see Cambranes, *Coffee and Peasants,* esp. chaps. 4–5; McCreery, *Rural Guatemala,* 163–72; and R. G. Williams, *States and Social Evolution,* 53–57, 113–15.

50. Cambranes, *Coffee and Peasants,* 88.

51. McCreery, *Rural Guatemala,* 163.

52. Ibid., 165–66; Cambranes, *Coffee and Peasants,* 71–75.

53. R. G. Williams, *States and Social Evolution,* 114–15.

54. David McCreery, "'An Odious Feudalism': *Mandamiento* Labor and Commercial Agriculture in Guatemala, 1858–1920," *Latin American Perspectives* 13 (winter 1986): 105.

55. Cambranes, *Coffee and Peasants,* 77–84, 90–96; McCreery, *Rural Guatemala,* 165–67; R. G. Williams, *States and Social Evolution,* 55, 113.

56. Woodward, *Rafael Carrera,* 382.

57. The best analysis of the Cerna administration and its role in promoting development is Wayne M. Clegern, *Origins of Liberal Dictatorship in Central America: Guatemala, 1865–1873* (Niwot: University Press of Colorado, 1994). See also Wayne M. Clegern, "Transition from Conservativism to Liberalism in Guatemala, 1865–1871," in William S. Coker, ed., *Hispanic-American Essays in Honor of Max Leon Moorhead* (Pensacola: Perdido Bay Press, 1979), 98–110.

58. Historical information in this paragraph is based on Clegern, *Origins of Liberal Dictatorship,* esp. chap. 4.

59. Lauria-Santiago, *An Agrarian Republic,* 72.

60. Ibid., chaps. 3–4.

61. Ibid., 75, 133; R. G. Williams, *States and Social Evolution,* 69–73. Williams (71) points out that indigo production did postpone the development of coffee around San Miguel by tying up land, labor, and capital.

62. Lauria-Santiago, *An Agrarian Republic,* chap. 6.

63. R. G. Williams, *States and Social Evolution,* 72–73.

64. Information for this paragraph comes from R. G. Williams, *States and Social Evolution,* 72–73.

65. Lindo-Fuentes, *Weak Foundations,* 133.

66. Rómulo E. Durón, *Bosquejo histórico de Honduras,* 2d ed., no. 1 (Tegucigalpa: Ministerio de Educación Pública, 1956), 265–66.

67. R. G. Williams, *States and Social Evolution,* 226; Lauria-Santiago, *An Agrarian Republic,* chap. 6.

68. This paragraph builds on the ideas of Jeffery M. Paige, *Coffee and Power: Revolution and the Rise of Democracy in Central America* (Cambridge: Harvard University Press, 1997).

69. Guillermo Molina Chocano, "La formación del Estado y el origen minero-mercantil de la burguesía hondureña," *Estudios Sociales Centroamericanos* 25 (January–April 1980): 58–62.

70. José Francisco Guevara-Escudero, "Nineteenth-Century Honduras: A Regional Approach to the Economic History of Honduras" (Ph.D. diss., New

York University, 1983), chap. 1; see esp. the table on p. 63 and the surrounding discussion.

71. Mario Posas and Rafael del Cid, *La construcción del sector público y del Estado nacional en Honduras, 1876–1979*, 2d ed. (San José: EDUCA, 1983), 22–23; Héctor Pérez Brignoli, "Economía y sociedad en Honduras durante el siglo XIX: Las estructuras demográficas," *Estudios Sociales Centroamericanos* 6 (September–December 1973): 52.

72. The population densities of Costa Rica and Honduras (persons per square mile) are shown in the following table, which is based on the population statistics found in Ralph Lee Woodward Jr., "The Aftermath of Independence, 1821–c. 1870," in Leslie Bethell, ed., *Central America since Independence* (Cambridge: Cambridge University Press, 1991), 8; and on the square-mileage data found in Ralph Lee Woodward Jr., *Central America: A Nation Divided*, 2d ed. (New York: Oxford University Press, 1985), 363.

Year	Costa Rica	Honduras
1820	3.2	3.1
1830	3.7	3.5
1840	4.4	4.1
1850	5.2	4.7
1860	5.9	5.3
1870	7.0	6.1

73. Guevara-Escudero, "Nineteenth-Century Honduras," 31.

74. Luis Mariñas Otero, *Honduras* (Tegucigalpa: Editorial Universitaria, 1983), 339. See also Medardo Mejía, *Historia de Honduras,* vol. 4 (Tegucigalpa: Editorial Universitaria, 1988).

75. William S. Stokes, *Honduras: An Area Study in Government* (Madison: University of Wisconsin Press, 1950), 209–10.

76. This paragraph is based on Durón, *Bosquejo histórico de Honduras,* 263–73; Victor Cáceres Lara, *Gobernantes de Honduras en el siglo 19* (Tegucigalpa: Banco Central de Honduras, 1978), chaps. 18–20; and José Angel Zúñiga Huete, *Presidentes de Honduras,* vol. 2 (Mexico City: IPGH, 1988), 9–18.

77. The Walker affair has been the subject of several historical works. See C. W. Doubleday, *Reminiscences of the "Filibuster" War in Nicaragua* (New York: G. P. Putnam's Sons, 1886); William O. Scroggs, *Filibusters and Financiers: The Story of William Walker and His Associates* (New York: Macmillan, 1916); and William Walker, *The War in Nicaragua* (Tucson: University of Arizona Press, 1985). For general discussions of elite politics in mid-nineteenth-century Nicaragua, see especially Humberto Belli, "Un ensayo de interpretación sobre las luchas políticas nicaragüenses (de la independencia hasta la Revolución Cubana)," *Revista Conservadora del Pensamiento Centroamericano* 32 (October–December 1977): 50–53; Francisco Ortega Arancibia, *Cuarenta años de historia de Nica-*

ragua (1838–1878), 4th ed. (Managua: Fondo de Promoción Cultural—BANIC, 1993); and Juan Luis Vázquez, "Luchas políticas y Estado oligárquico," in Alberto Lanuza et al., eds., *Economía y sociedad en la construcción del Estado de Nicaragua* (San José: Instituto Centroamericano de Administración Pública, 1983), chap. 1.

78. On the pact of 1856 and the constitution of 1858, see José Luis Velázquez, "La incidencia de la formación de la economía agroexportadora en el intento de formación del Estado nacional en Nicaragua (1860–1930)," *Revista Conservadora del Pensamiento Centroamericano* 32 (October–December 1977): 13–15; and Vázquez, "Luchas políticas," 142–46.

79. The best overall analysis of the preliberal economy of Nicaragua that I am familiar with is Alberto Lanuza Matamoras, "Estructuras socioeconómicas, poder y Estado en Nicaragua, de 1821 a 1875" (tesis de grado, Universidad de Costa Rica, n.d.). Most of this work was subsequently published in Alberto Lanuza, "La formación del Estado nacional en Nicaragua: Las bases económicas, comerciales y financieras entre 1821 y 1873," in Alberto Lanuza et al., eds., *Economía y sociedad en la construcción del Estado de Nicaragua* (San José: Instituto Centroamericano de Administración Pública, 1983). Less relevant but still useful is Pablo Levy, "Notas geográficas y económicas sobre la República de Nicaragua," *Revista Conservadora del Pensamiento Centroamericana* 12–13 (August–December 1965): 7–293.

80. David R. Radell, "Historical Geography of Western Nicaragua: The Spheres of Influence of León, Granada, and Managua, 1519–1965" (Ph.D. diss., University of California, Berkeley, 1969), chap. 10; Lanuza, "La formación," 75; R. G. Williams, *States and Social Evolution*, 79.

81. Sara L. Baquero, *Gobernantes de Nicaragua* (Managua: Tipografía Gordillo, 1937).

82. Manzar Foroohar, *The Catholic Church and Social Change in Nicaragua* (Albany: State University of New York Press, 1989), 9–10; Benjamin I. Teplitz, "The Political and Economic Foundations of Modernization in Nicaragua: The Administration of José Santos Zelaya, 1893–1909" (Ph.D. diss., Howard University, 1973), chap. 3.

83. On this legislation and its consequences, see Francisco Pérez Estrada, "Breve historia de la tenencia de la tierra en Nicaragua," *Revista Conservadora del Pensamiento Centroamericano* 51 (December 1964): 21–22; and R. G. Williams, *States and Social Evolution*, 83–84. See also the village case study presented in Elizabeth Dore, "Land Privatization and the Differentiation of the Peasantry: Nicaragua's Coffee Revolution, 1850–1920," *Journal of Historical Sociology* 8 (September 1995): 303–26.

84. R. G. Williams, *States and Social Evolution*, 83–84.

85. Teplitz, "Political and Economic Foundations," 183.

86. Lanuza, "La formación," 84; Teplitz, "Political and Economic Foundations," 179–82.

87. Teplitz, "Political and Economic Foundations," 182–85; Lanuza, "La formación," 22–23.

88. On the 1881 revolt, see Jaime Wheelock Román, *Raíces indígenas de la lucha anticolonialista en Nicaragua,* 2d ed. (Managua: Editorial Nueva Nicaragua, 1985), 109–18; Jeffrey L. Gould, "El trabajo forzoso y las comunidades indígenas nicaragüenses," in Héctor Pérez Brignoli and Mario Samper, eds., *El café en la historia de Centroamérica* (San José: FLASCO, 1993); and Armando Amador, *Un siglo de lucha de los trabajadores en Nicaragua* (Managua: Centro de Investigación de la Realidad de América Latina, 1990), 12–15.

89. Teplitz, "Political and Economic Foundations," 182–89.

90. R. G. Williams, *States and Social Evolution,* 84–85.

91. See Teplitz, "Political and Economic Foundations," 213–33.

92. See Julie A. Charlip, "Cultivating Coffee: Farmers, Land, and Money in Nicaragua, 1877–1930" (Ph.D. diss., University of California, Los Angeles, 1995). Charlip suggests that small farms dominated in the Carazo Plateau throughout the late nineteenth and early twentieth centuries. She also argues that large estates were relatively rare in this region. However, her classification of properties by size is somewhat biased toward this finding. In particular, she defines "large" estates as only those landholdings with at least 200 *manzanas,* "medium" estates as those landholdings with 50–199 *manzanas,* and "small" and "minifundio" estates as those with less than 50 *manzanas.* Hence, she excludes many sizable properties from her understanding of large estates and includes many sizable properties in her understanding of small estates. Her discussion of property categories by size is on pp. 181–87. It is important to note that the semantic issue of how to define different-sized estates does not detract from the overall contributions of Charlip's study, which is the best regional-level study of the coffee economy in Nicaragua currently available.

93. R. G. Williams, *States and Social Evolution,* 209. See also the comment by Williams on 324 n. 15.

94. See especially Carlos Selva, "Un poco de historia de cuando se luchaba contra Zelaya," *Revista Conservadora del Pensamiento Centroamericano* 16 (May 1967): 1–46.

95. See Pérez Brignoli, "Economía y sociedad," 55, 80; James Dunkerley, *Power in the Isthmus: A Political History of Modern Central America* (London: Verso, 1988), 19; and R. G. Williams, *States and Social Evolution,* 210–11.

96. Guevara-Escudero, "Nineteenth-Century Honduras," chap. 1.

97. See especially Guevara-Escudero, "Nineteenth-Century Honduras," 55–59.

98. This paragraph draws on R. G. Williams, *States and Social Evolution,* 79–91, 131–38.

99. Ibid., 266–67.

100. Ilva Fernández, "Nicaragua: Estructura económico social y política del régimen de Zelaya" (licenciado thesis, Universidad Centroamericana, Managua, 1978), chap. 1.

101. Ibid.
102. R. G. Williams, *States and Social Evolution*, 133.
103. Teplitz, "Political and Economic Foundations," chap. 8.

CHAPTER FIVE: RADICAL LIBERALISM

1. This estimate is based on the statistical data found in Robert G. Williams, *States and Social Evolution: Coffee and the Rise of National Governments in Central America* (Chapel Hill: University of North Carolina Press, 1994), 266–68. See also fig. 5.1 in this chapter.

2. Thus, much comparative-historical work—which draws on the case-study material—has primarily highlighted the overall *differences* between Guatemala and El Salvador during the liberal reform period. See, for example, Ciro Flamarion Santana Cardoso, "Historia económica del café en Centroamérica (siglo XIX): Estudio comparativo," *Estudios Sociales Centroamericanos* 4 (January–April 1975): 9–55; James Dunkerley, *Power in the Isthmus: A Political History of Modern Central America* (London: Verso, 1988), 26–34; Rodolfo Cardenal, *Manual de historia de Centroamérica* (San Salvador: Universidad Centroamericana, n.d.), chap. 4; and David M. Kauck, "Agricultural Commercialization and State Development in Central America: The Political Economy of the Coffee Industry from 1838 to 1940" (Ph.D. diss., University of Washington, 1988).

3. The classic work from this perspective is Edelberto Torres-Rivas, *Interpretación del desarrollo social centroamericano: Procesos y estructuras de una sociedad dependiente*, 2d ed. (San José: EDUCA, 1971), chap. 2. Further references are presented below.

4. Wayne M. Clegern, *Origins of Liberal Dictatorship in Central America: Guatemala, 1865–1873* (Niwot: University Press of Colorado, 1994), 124. See also Jorge Mario García Laguardia, *El pensamiento liberal de Guatemala (antología)* (San José: EDUCA, 1977), 42.

5. Manuel Méndez was president for a brief period in 1872. Andrés Valle—González's handpicked successor—was president during 1876.

6. Alastair White, *El Salvador* (New York: Praeger, 1973), 86–87. See also Fabio González Cabezas, *Hechos históricos de 1848 a 1885: Biografía del Mariscal Don Santiago González* (San Salvador: Talleres Gráficos Cisneros, 1930).

7. The best analysis of elite politics during 1871–73 is still the extremely well documented study by Jorge Mario García Laguardia, *La reforma liberal en Guatemala*, 3d ed. (Guatemala: Editorial Universitaria, USAC, 1985), esp. chaps. 3–4. Many of the original primary sources used for this work can be found in the document section of García Laguardia, *El pensamiento liberal*. Also useful on this period is Clegern, *Origins of Liberal Dictatorship*, chap. 5; Hubert J. Miller, *La iglesia y el Estado en tiempo de Justo Rufino Barrios* (Guatemala: Universidad de San Carlos, 1976), chaps. 3–4; and Mary P. Holleran, *Church and State in Guatemala* (New York: Columbia University Press, 1949), 147–205.

8. "Decreto, Num. 5" and "Decreto, Numero 14," in *Recopilación de las leyes emitadas por el gobierno democrático de la República de Guatemala,* vol. 1 (Guatemala: Imprenta de la "Paz," 1874), 4, 10–12.

9. García Laguardia, *La reforma liberal,* 118–19. On the ability of Barrios to form a peasant-based army during these years, see also J. C. Cambranes, *Coffee and Peasants: The Origins of the Modern Plantation Economy in Guatemala, 1853–1897,* English version revised by Carla Clason-Hook (Stockholm: Institute of Latin American Studies, University of Stockholm, 1985), 128–35.

10. The best analysis of the liberal anti-ecclesiastical project in Guatemala is H. J. Miller, *La iglesia y el Estado.*

11. Clegern, *Origins of Liberal Dictatorship,* 127.

12. See "Decreto Num. 16" and "Decreto, Numero 18," in *Recopilación de las leyes,* 1:13, 14–15.

13. The relevant antichurch decrees initiated by Barrios in the 1871–73 period can be found in several places, including the document section in García Laguardia, *La reforma liberal,* 181–90.

14. Kauck, "Agricultural Commercialization," 147. Kauck draws on Shelton H. Davis, "Land of Our Ancestors: A Study of Land Tenure and Inheritance in the Highlands of Guatemala" (Ph.D. diss., Harvard University, 1970).

15. Kauck, "Agricultural Commercialization," 147. See also the more detailed discussion in García Laguardia, *La reforma liberal,* 137–38.

16. See Thomas R. Herrick, *Desarrollo económico y político de Guatemala durante el período de Justo Rufino Barrios (1871–1885)* (Guatemala: EDUCA, 1974), 174–75.

17. Clegern, *Origins of Liberal Dictatorship,* 142. Only 10,000 people actually voted in these elections.

18. On the González years in El Salvador, see José F. Figeac, *Recordatorio histórico de la República de El Salvador* (San Salvador: Talleres Gráficos Cisneros, 1952), 250–62; Kauck, "Agricultural Commercialization," 169; and Derek N. Kerr, "La edad de oro del café," *Mesoamérica* 3 (June 1982): 12–13.

19. Justo Rufino Barrios, *Mensaje que el Jeneral Presidente de la República de Guatemala dirije a la Asamblea Nacional Lejislativa* (Guatemala: Tipográfico de "El Progreso," March 1876).

20. White, *El Salvador,* 86.

21. For details, see Paul Burgess, *Justo Rufino Barrios: A Biography* (Philadelphia: Dorrance & Company, 1926), chap. 15; Gregorio Bustamante, *Historia militar de El Salvador: Desde la independencia de Centro América, hasta nuestros días (1821–1935)* (San Salvador: Talleres Gráficos Cisneros, 1935), 75–79; and Figeac, *Recordatorio histórico,* 262–67.

22. General background on Zaldívar can be found in the biographical section of Rodolfo Ramos Choto and Maria Leistenschneider, eds., *Primera parte de la biografía y administración del Dr. Rafael Zaldívar,* vol. 1 (San Salvador: Archivo General de la Nación, October 1972).

23. Aldo A. Lauria-Santiago, *An Agrarian Republic: Commercial Agriculture and the Politics of Peasant Communities in El Salvador, 1823–1914* (Pittsburgh: University of Pittsburgh Press, 1999), 123.

24. See Figeac, *Recordatorio histórico*, 270.

25. The phrase is the title of chapter 5 of Cambranes, *Coffee and Peasants*. See also Cambranes's comment on p. 177. Other scholars who share this understanding of the Barrios administration include Augusto Cazali Àvila, "El desarrollo del cultivo del café y su influencia en el régimen del trabajo agrícola: Época de la reforma liberal (1871–1885)," *Anuario de Estudios Centroamericanos* 2 (May 1976): 62; Alain Y. Dessaint, "Effects of the Hacienda and Plantation Systems on Guatemala's Indians," *América Indígena* 22 (October 1962): 330–31; Paul J. Dosal, *Power in Transition: The Rise of Guatemala's Industrial Oligarchy, 1871–1994* (Westport, Conn.: Praeger, 1995), 20–21; Valentín Solórzano F., *Evolución económica de Guatemala*, 2d ed. (Guatemala: Centro Editorial "José de Pineda Ibarra," 1963), chap. 12; and Torres-Rivas, *Interpretación del desarrollo*, 35.

26. Excellent accounts of the working of the Barrios dictatorship can be found in Burgess, *Justo Rufino Barrios*; Herrick, *Desarrollo económico*, 202–24; and David McCreery, *Development and the State in Reforma Guatemala, 1871–1885* (Athens: Ohio University, Center for International Studies, Latin America Program, 1983). Enrique Guzmán, a contemporary observer, wrote the following in his personal diary: "The Guatemalan press repeats until satiety the words *progress, reform, liberty, pueblo,* and *democracy;* but it is necessary not to forget that the author of *progress* is General Barrios; the initiator and propagator of *reform,* General Barrios; the supporter of *liberty,* General Barrios; the child of the *pueblo,* the father of the *pueblo,* the grandfather of the *pueblo,* General Barrios; and finally, the man of democracy, the same General Barrios." Quoted in Herrick, *Desarrollo económico*, 194 (emphasis in original).

27. David McCreery, *Rural Guatemala, 1760–1940* (Stanford: Stanford University Press, 1994), 173.

28. Herrick, *Desarrollo económico*, 219.

29. Kauck, "Agricultural Commercialization," 148–49 (emphasis added).

30. Cazali Àvila, "El desarrollo," 45.

31. Herrick, *Desarrollo económico*, 228–31; McCreery, *Rural Guatemala*, 183.

32. An example is the development of the National Bank of Guatemala in 1873, which used funds from the sale of Church properties. Although the bank was ostensibly created to provide loans for farmers, its resources were used primarily by the state, quite likely in the form of political patronage to allies of Barrios. See "Decreto, Num. 104," in *Recopilación de las leyes*, 1:194–96; V. Solórzano, *Evolución económica de Guatemala*, 356–58; Burgess, *Justo Rufino Barrios*, 124; and McCreery, *Development and the State*, 29.

33. Michael McClintock, *The American Connection*, vol. 2, *State Terror and Popular Resistance in Guatemala* (London: Zed Books, 1985), 10. See also

José Luis Cruz Salazar, "El ejército como una fuerza política," *Estudios Sociales* 6 (Guatemala: Universidad Rafael Landívar, 1972): 75.

34. "Decreto, Num. 85," in *Recopilación de las leyes,* 1:141–54.

35. McCreery, *Rural Guatemala,* 180. On the military reforms initiated in the 1871–73 period, see "Organización del batallón permanente," "Decreto, Num. 66," "Decreto, Num. 81," "Decreto, Num. 83," "Decreto, Num. 85," and "Decreto, Num. 98," in *Recopilación de las leyes,* 1:79–80, 103–5, 132–34, 135–37, 140–41, 183–84.

36. This is the primary interpretation of McClintock, *The American Connection,* 2:10–11.

37. McCreery, *Rural Guatemala,* 220.

38. "Decreto, Num 156," in *Recopilación de las leyes,* 2:206–7; Herrick, *Desarrollo económico,* 145–47; McCreery, *Development and the State,* 32–33.

39. "Decreto No. 109, 15 de diciembre de 1873," in *Recopilación de las leyes,* 1:238–39. See also "Decreto No. 112," 1:248–52; and the discussions in Cazali Àvila, "El desarrollo," 45, and R. G. Williams, *States and Social Evolution,* 59. Overviews of the infrastructure projects initiated by Barrios can be found in David J. McCreery, "Coffee and Class: The Structure of Development in Liberal Guatemala," *Hispanic American Historical Review* 56 (August 1976): 438–60; and Chester Lloyd Jones, *Guatemala: Past and Present* (Minneapolis: University of Minnesota Press, 1940), 246–47.

40. Cazali Àvila, "El desarrollo," 49–51.

41. McCreery, *Rural Guatemala,* 179.

42. This paragraph draws on especially Roland H. Ebel, "Political Modernization in Three Guatemalan Indian Communities," in A. L. Harrison and Robert Wauchope, eds., *Community Culture and National Change* (New Orleans: Middle American Research Institute, Tulane University, 1972); Herrick, *Desarrollo económico,* 219–24; and Kauck, "Agricultural Commercialization," 161.

43. McCreery, *Development and the State,* 18.

44. Herrick, *Desarrollo económico,* 220–21.

45. Ebel, "Political Modernization," 153.

46. "Acuerdo sobre enajenación de terrenos baldíos de la Costa Cuca y El Palmar," in Julio César Méndez Montenegro, ed., *444 años de legislación agraria, 1513–1957* (Guatemala: Revista de la Facultad de Ciencias Jurídicas y Sociales de Guatemala, 1960), 123–24. See also Cazali Àvila, "El desarrollo," 45–46; Herrick, *Desarrollo económico,* 236–38; Kauck, "Agricultural Commercialization," 151–53; McCreery, *Rural Guatemala,* 203–5; V. Solórzano, *Evolución económica de Guatemala,* 345–48; and R. G. Williams, *States and Social Evolution,* 61–63.

47. Méndez, *444 años,* 131–33, 153–54, 162–72.

48. Herrick, *Desarrollo económico,* 237.

49. R. G. Williams, *States and Social Evolution,* 63.

50. McCreery, *Rural Guatemala,* 203.

51. "Decreto Numero 170," in Méndez, *444 años,* 133–44. These pages also include subsequent reforms of this decree. Discussions of this legislation can be found in McCreery, *Rural Guatemala,* 185–86; Herrick, *Desarrollo económico,* 231–36; Kauck, "Agricultural Commercialization," 153; and R. G. Williams, *States and Social Evolution,* 60.

52. Herrick, *Desarrollo económico,* 231.

53. Kauck, "Agricultural Commercialization," 166.

54. Ibid., 150.

55. R. G. Williams, *States and Social Evolution,* 63. See also Greg Grandin, *The Blood of Guatemala: A History of Race and Nation* (Durham, N.C.: Duke University Press, 2000), 113.

56. McCreery, *Rural Guatemala,* 238.

57. David McCreery, "State Power, Indigenous Communities, and Land in Nineteenth-Century Guatemala, 1820–1920," in Carol A. Smith, ed., with the assistance of Marilyn M. Moors, *Guatemalan Indians and the State, 1540–1988* (Austin: University of Texas Press, 1990), 108–12.

58. Ibid., 107.

59. Kauck, "Agricultural Commercialization," 154–57.

60. McCreery, *Rural Guatemala,* 200–201.

61. This appears to have been more the case for communities located in the Alta Verapaz department, in the western highlands, and in areas adjacent to the western piedmont coffee region, as opposed to communities within the western piedmont itself. In this latter area, the privatization of land directly converted communities into plantation labor forces. See McCreery, *Rural Guatemala,* 241–46.

62. Carol Smith makes this point in "Beyond Dependency Theory: National and Regional Patterns of Underdevelopment in Guatemala," *American Ethnologist 5* (March 1978): 574–617.

63. David McCreery offers by far the best analysis of the coercive labor systems in liberal Guatemala. In addition to his book *Rural Guatemala,* see his articles "Debt Servitude in Rural Guatemala, 1876–1936," *Hispanic American Historical Review* 63 (November 1983): 735–59; and "'An Odious Feudalism': *Mandamiento* Labor and Commercial Agriculture in Guatemala, 1858–1920," *Latin American Perspectives* 13 (winter 1986): 99–117. This paragraph and the next two rely heavily on these sources.

64. McCreery, "'An Odious Feudalism,'" 105. See also Cazali Àvila, "El desarrollo," 68.

65. McCreery, "Debt Servitude," 746–47.

66. See Dana G. Munro, *The Five Republics of Central America: Their Political and Economic Development and Their Relations with the United States* (New York: Oxford University Press, 1918), 61–63; and McCreery, "Debt Servitude," 748.

67. This paragraph draws on R. G. Williams, *States and Social Evolution,* 121; and McCreery, "Debt Servitude," 748, 751–52.

68. For example, David Browning, *El Salvador: Landscape and Society* (Oxford: Clarendon Press, 1971), 172–73; Mario Flores Macal, *Origen, desarrollo y crisis de las formas de dominación en El Salvador* (San José: SECASA, 1983), 59, 63; Rafael Guidos Véjar, *El ascenso del militarismo en El Salvador,* 4th ed. (San Salvador: UCA Editores, 1988), 48; Arturo Taracena Arriola, "Liberalismo y poder político en Centroamérica (1870–1929)," in *Historia general de Centroamérica,* vol. 4, *Las repúblicas agroexportadoras (1870–1945),* ed. Víctor Hugo Acuña Ortega (Madrid: FLASCO, 1993), 187; and White, *El Salvador,* 80.

69. See Julio Alberto Domínguez Sosa, *Génesis y significado de la Constitución de 1886* (San Salvador: Departamento Editorial Ministerio de Cultura, 1958), 9; Figeac, *Recordatorio histórico,* 267–333; and Italo López Vallecillos, *El periodismo en El Salvador: Bosquejo histórico-documental, precedido de apuntes sobre la prensa colonial hispanoamericana* (San Salvador: Editorial Universitaria, 1964), 116–17.

70. Knut Walter, "Trade and Development in an Export Economy: The Case of El Salvador, 1870–1914" (M.A. thesis, University of North Carolina, Chapel Hill, 1977), 78–79.

71. Ibid., 71.

72. Ibid., table 17, p. 80.

73. Patricia Alvarenga, "Reshaping the Ethics of Power: A History of Violence in Western Rural El Salvador, 1880–1932" (Ph.D. diss., University of Wisconsin, Madison, 1994), 35–36; Héctor Lindo-Fuentes, *Weak Foundations: The Economy of El Salvador in the Nineteenth Century, 1821–1898* (Berkeley: University of California Press, 1990), 64.

74. "Cuadro de organización de la fuerza permanente," in Maria Leistenschneider, ed., *La Administración del Dr. Rafael Zaldívar,* vol. 1, pt. 2, Colección Maria Leistenschneider (San Salvador: Archivo General de la Nación, October 1972), 38–53.

75. "Presupuesto 1877," in Leistenschneider, *La Administración,* vol. 1, pt. 2:109–30. This figure probably only partially measures military expenditures because it is likely that some of the funds dedicated to the Department of Government (Gobernación) were used for security-related matters.

76. "Decreto sobre milicias," ibid., vol. 2 (May 1973), 138–40. In addition, there is evidence that Zaldívar oversaw the creation of powerful civilian auxiliary forces. See Patricia Alvarenga, "Auxiliary Forces in the Shaping of the Repressive System: El Salvador, 1880–1930," in Aviva Chomsky and Aldo Lauria-Santiago, eds., *Identity and Struggle at the Margins of the Nation-State: The Laboring People of Central America and the Hispanic Caribbean* (Durham, N.C.: Duke University Press, 1998), 122–50.

77. Alvarenga, "Reshaping the Ethics of Power," 35. See also Aldo Lauria, "An Agrarian Republic: Production Politics and the Peasantry in El Salvador, 1740–1920" (Ph.D. diss., University of Chicago, 1992), 532.

78. Alvarenga, "Reshaping the Ethics of Power," 35.

79. Ibid., 38.

80. Lindo-Fuentes, *Weak Foundations*, 136.

81. Héctor Lindo-Fuentes, "The Economy of Central America: From Bourbon Reforms to Liberal Reforms," in Lowell Gudmundson and Héctor Lindo-Fuentes, *Central America, 1821–1871: Liberalism before Liberal Reform* (Tuscaloosa: University of Alabama Press, 1995), 46–47; Rodolfo Cardenal, *El poder eclesiástico en El Salvador, 1871–1931* (San Salvador: UCA Editores, 1980), chap. 3.

82. This estimate is from Lauria-Santiago. Menjívar and Macal estimate that 40 percent of all land was targeted; Browning and Lindo-Fuentes, about 25 percent. See Lauria-Santiago, *An Agrarian Republic*, 193; Rafael Menjívar L., *Acumulación originaria y desarrollo del capitalismo en El Salvador* (San José: EDUCA, 1980), 99; Flores Macal, *Origen, desarrollo y crisis*, 60; Browning, *El Salvador*, 191–92; and Lindo-Fuentes, *Weak Foundations*, 130.

83. This paragraph draws on Browning, *El Salvador*, 181–203.

84. "Decreto Sobre Tierras en Comunidad," in Leistenschneider, *La Administración*, vol. 3, pt. 2 (1978): 328.

85. "Decreto—Extinguición en El Salvador de la Institución de Ejidos," ibid., 364–68.

86. For a particularly strong statement of this position, see Menjívar, *Acumulación originaria*, chap. 2.

87. For statistical support for many of Lauria-Santiago's conclusions, see the excellent comparative study by Mario Samper K., "El significado social de la caficultura costarricense y salvadoreña: Análisis histórico comparado a partir de los censos cafetaleros," in Héctor Pérez Brignoli and Mario Samper, eds., *Tierra, café y sociedad* (San José: FLASCO, 1994).

88. Lauria-Santiago, *An Agrarian Republic*, 165, 230–31.

89. Ibid., 168–69, 231.

90. Ibid., 231.

91. Ibid., 171, 178.

92. Ibid., 174, 181.

93. Ibid., 185, 191.

94. Lindo-Fuentes, *Weak Foundations*, 134; Samper, "El significado social," 195–96.

95. Lauria-Santiago, *An Agrarian Republic*, 231.

96. As Alvarenga suggests, "the ability to create a national-level army is what permitted Zaldívar to carry out a project of profound social transformations." Alvarenga, "Reshaping the Ethics of Power," 155.

97. Lauria-Santiago, *An Agrarian Republic*, 174–75.

98. Ibid., 174.

99. Kerr, "La edad de oro," 13.

100. Lauria-Santiago, *An Agrarian Republic*, 152–57.

101. R. G. Williams, *States and Social Evolution*, 124. See also Browning,

El Salvador, 169–71; Menjívar, *Acumulación originaria*, 91–92; and Samper, "El significado social," 197–98.

102. On the 1885 war between Guatemala and El Salvador, see Burgess, *Justo Rufino Barrios*, chaps. 17–22; Bustamante, *Historia militar*, 81–88; Cardenal, *El poder eclesiástico*, 125–28; and Figeac, *Recordatorio histórico*, 311–30.

103. R. G. Williams, *States and Social Evolution*, 64–67, 121–23.

104. McCreery, "'An Odious Feudalism'"; Jeffery M. Paige, *Coffee and Power: Revolution and the Rise of Democracy in Central America* (Cambridge: Harvard University Press, 1997), chap. 2.

105. McCreery, *Rural Guatemala*, 178; McClintock, *The American Connection*, 2:12.

106. James Wesley Bingham, "Guatemalan Agriculture during the Administration of President Manuel Estrada Cabrera, 1898–1920" (master's thesis, Tulane University, 1974), 26–27, 62, 105; quotation from p. 27.

107. Ibid., 105.

108. Munro, *The Five Republics of Central America*, 53.

109. This paragraph draws broadly from Bingham, "Guatemalan Agriculture."

110. This paragraph draws on Paul J. Dosal, *Doing Business with the Dictators: A Political History of United Fruit in Guatemala, 1899–1944* (Wilmington, Del.: Scholarly Resources, 1993); and Jim Handy, *Gift of the Devil: A History of Guatemala* (Boston: South End Press, 1984), chap. 4.

111. David Alejandro Luna, *Manual de historia económica de El Salvador* (San Salvador: Editorial Universitaria, 1971), 202–3.

112. The major work on this subject is Lauria-Santiago, *An Agrarian Republic.*

113. See the relevant decrees in Luna, *Manual de historia económica*, 188–92.

114. Lauria-Santiago, *An Agrarian Republic*, 233.

115. Ibid.

116. This paragraph draws on R. G. Williams, *States and Social Evolution*, 77–78.

117. Ibid., 77.

118. See Paige, *Coffee and Power*, table 1, p. 60.

119. Land area data are from Ralph Lee Woodward Jr., *Central America: A Nation Divided*, 2d ed. (New York: Oxford University Press, 1985), 363. Population data are from Victor Bulmer-Thomas, *The Political Economy of Central America since 1920* (Cambridge: Cambridge University Press, 1987), 310.

120. On labor in the Salvadoran coffee economy, see Cardoso, "Historia económica del café," 29–30; R. G. Williams, *States and Social Evolution*, 124–26; and Lauria-Santiago, *An Agrarian Republic.*

121. The general debate over which type of peasantry is most prone to rebellion and revolution is, of course, by no means settled. As the case of Costa Rica will more fully show, the evidence from Central America tends to contra-

dict the theories of scholars such as James C. Scott and Eric Wolf, who suggest
that smallholding peasants who derive their income from control over land are
most likely to rebel. The evidence is more consistent with Jeffery M. Paige's hypothesis that plantation wage laborers faced with an elite that derives income
principally from land are likely to lead revolutionary movements. Yet in order
to explain differences between El Salvador and Guatemala—specifically, why
peasant revolution occurred much earlier in El Salvador (in 1932)—Paige's theory must be reworked along the lines suggested by Theda Skocpol. Skocpol's theory, which highlights the role of direct landlord control over peasants as a key
factor in the occurrence of large-scale revolt, offers much insight into the overall similarities and specific differences between Guatemala and El Salvador. See
James C. Scott, *The Moral Economy of the Peasant: Rebellion and Subsistence
in Southeast Asia* (New Haven: Yale University Press, 1976); Eric Wolf, *Peasant
Wars of the Twentieth Century* (New York: Harper & Row, 1969); Jeffery M.
Paige, *Agrarian Revolution: Social Movements and Export Agriculture in the
Underdeveloped World* (New York: Free Press, 1975); and Theda Skocpol, *States
and Social Revolutions: A Comparative Analysis of France, Russia, and China*
(Cambridge: Cambridge University Press, 1979).

122. The size of the Salvadoran army in each department in 1892 is reflected in the following table.

	Top Officers and Generals	Officers	Troops
San Salvador	46	144	1,937
La Libertad	4	12	154
Cuscatlán	5	11	224
San Vicente	4	8	90
Chalatenango	2	8	125
La Paz	4	9	70
Cabañas	3	11	140
San Miguel	9	22	280
Usulután	2	6	65
Morazán	2	5	50
La Unión	4	21	221
Santa Ana	7	37	652
Sonsonate	4	12	156
Ahuachapán	3	15	316
Puerto La Libertad	2	2	36
Id. de Acajutla	1	4	31
Total	102	327	4,544

Source: "Ejército de la República," Sección Guerra y Marina, January 24, 1892,
Archivo General de la Nación, San Salvador.

123. Alvarenga, "Reshaping the Ethics of Power," 156.

124. Ibid., 163. See also Alvarenga, "Auxiliary Forces," 124.

125. Browning, Burns, and Cardoso all suggest that the mounted police force was a major presence in the daily lives of peasants in the western coffee zones. However, the revisionist research of Lauria-Santiago, Ching, and Alvarenga—which is based on new archival materials—suggests that this force was largely ineffective. See Cardoso, "Historia económica del café," 30; E. Bradford Burns, "The Modernization of Underdevelopment: El Salvador, 1858–1931," *Journal of Developing Areas* 18 (April 1984): 302; Browning, *El Salvador,* 218; Lauria-Santiago, *An Agrarian Republic,* 155–57; Erik Ching, "Patronage, Politics, and Power in El Salvador, 1840–1940" (book manuscript, 1998); and Alvarenga, "Reshaping the Ethics of Power," 169.

126. This paragraph draws on Alvarenga, "Reshaping the Ethics of Power," 173–78; Ching, "Patronage, Politics, and Power"; and Robert Varney Elam, "Appeal to Arms: The Army and Politics in El Salvador, 1931–1964" (Ph.D. diss., University of New Mexico, 1968), 11–15.

127. Ching, "Patronage, Politics, and Power," 188–89.

128. This paragraph and the next one are based on my interpretation of the evidence presented in the general secondary literature and official government bulletins for late-nineteenth and early-twentieth-century Central American history.

129. Paige, *Coffee and Power,* 54.

130. Ibid., chap. 2. On the strength of the commercial faction of the Salvadoran coffee elite during the late nineteenth and early twentieth centuries, see also Lauria-Santiago, *An Agrarian Republic,* 160–62.

131. Bingham, "Guatemalan Agriculture," 27–28.

132. Ibid., 43. See also p. 20.

133. See Everett Alan Wilson, "The Crisis of National Integration in El Salvador, 1919–1935" (Ph.D. diss., Stanford University, 1970), chap. 3; Ching, "Patronage, Politics, and Power," chap. 5.

134. McCreery, *Rural Guatemala,* 221; Cambranes, *Coffee and Peasants,* 289, 302–4; Segundo Montes, *El agro salvadoreño (1973–1980)* (San Salvador: UCA Editores, 1986), 40.

135. Kauck, "Agricultural Commercialization," 149; Bingham, "Guatemalan Agriculture," 62; Williams, *States and Social Evolution,* 75.

CHAPTER SIX: REFORMIST LIBERALISM

1. Ralph Lee Woodward Jr., "The Aftermath of Independence, 1821–c. 1870," in Leslie Bethell, ed., *Central America since Independence* (Cambridge: Cambridge University Press, 1991), 8.

2. Carolyn Hall, *El café y el desarrollo histórico-geográfico de Costa Rica* (San José: Editorial Costa Rica, 1991), 35; Rodrigo Facio, *Estudio sobre*

economía costarricense, reprinted in *Obras de Rodrigo Facio,* vol. 1 (San José: Editorial Costa Rica, 1972), 39; Ciro F. S. Cardoso, "The Formation of the Coffee Estate in Nineteenth-Century Costa Rica," in Kenneth Duncan and Ian Rutledge, eds., with the collaboration of Collin Harding, *Land and Labour in Latin America* (Cambridge: Cambridge University Press, 1977), 170.

3. José Luis Vega Carballo, *Orden y progreso: La formación del Estado nacional en Costa Rica* (San José: Instituto Centroamericano de Administración Pública, 1981), 50. Sáenz notes that "throughout the history of the coffee industry the state has been the main driving force behind its expansion." Carlos Joaquín Sáenz, "Population Growth, Economic Progress, and Opportunities on the Land: The Case of Costa Rica," Research Paper No. 47, University of Wisconsin, Madison, June 1972, 13.

4. Facio, *Estudio sobre economía costarricense,* 39; Robert G. Williams, *States and Social Evolution: Coffee and the Rise of National Governments in Central America* (Chapel Hill: University of North Carolina Press, 1994), 46; Cardoso, "Formation of the Coffee Estate," 170.

5. Cardoso, "Formation of the Coffee Estate," 172.

6. Hall, *El café y el desarrollo,* 39.

7. Iván Molina J., "Habilitadores y habilitados en el Valle Central de Costa Rica: El financiamiento de la producción cafetalera en los inicios de su expansión (1838–1850)," *Revista de Historia* 16 (July–December 1987): 88.

8. Hall, *El café y el desarrollo,* 73–74.

9. R. G. Williams, *States and Social Evolution,* 44.

10. Silvia Castro Sánchez, "Estado, privatización de la tierra y conflictos agrarios," *Revista de Historia* 21–22 (January–December 1990): 208–10; R. G. Williams, *States and Social Evolution,* 45.

11. Hall, *El café y el desarrollo,* 85.

12. Iván Molina Jiménez, *Costa Rica (1800–1850): El legado colonial y la génesis del capitalismo* (San José: EDUCA, 1991), 245. See also the similar data presented in Molina J., "Habilitadores y habilitados," 103–8.

13. Cardoso, "Formation of the Coffee Estate," 173–75.

14. Ibid., 175.

15. Lowell Gudmundson, *Costa Rica before Coffee: Society and Economy on the Eve of the Export Boom* (Baton Rouge: Louisiana State University Press, 1986), 82.

16. Ibid., 52–53; R. G. Williams, *States and Social Evolution,* 46.

17. José Antonio Salas Víquez, "La privatización de los baldíos nacionales en Costa Rica durante el siglo XIX: Legislación y procedimientos utilizados para su adjudicación," *Revista de Historia* 15 (January–June 1987): 63–118.

18. R. G. Williams, *States and Social Evolution,* 46; Castro Sánchez, "Estado," 210.

19. R. G. Williams, *States and Social Evolution,* 51.

20. Cardoso, "Formation of the Coffee Estate," 173.

21. Ibid., 176. It is important to recognize that this finding about the predominance of small coffee farms is based on comparative data from Central America. Within Costa Rica itself, not all coffee holdings were small; larger estates accounted for a significant part of total coffee production; and smaller holdings were often divided up over time such that by the mid-twentieth century, land concentration was a problem. In fact, drawing on a 1955 coffee census, Paige argues that "the most important small-holding class is *not* the family farmers but rather the sub-family farmers [i.e., farmers with less than 5 *manzanas* of land]. . . . The family farm is actually relatively insignificant in numbers, area, and production. Furthermore, a small number of large estates (184 of 22,000) controlled 30.6% of total coffee area and 37.5% of production." Jeffery M. Paige, *Coffee and Power: Revolution and the Rise of Democracy in Central America* (Cambridge: Harvard University Press, 1997), 65.

22. Gudmundson, *Costa Rica before Coffee*, 68.

23. Paige, *Coffee and Power*, 81. However, as we shall see, the landed elite in Honduras was actually the weakest in the region.

24. Gudmundson, *Costa Rica before Coffee*, 78, 80, 85. Samuel Z. Stone has shown conclusively the profound continuity of certain families within the Costa Rican elite from colonial times through the liberal reform up until the present period. See Samuel Stone, *La dinastía de los conquistadores: La crisis del poder en la Costa Rica contemporánea*, 3d ed. (San José: EDUCA, 1982); and Stone, "Los cafetaleros: Un estudio de los caficultores de Costa Rica," *Revista Conservadora del Pensamiento Centroamericano* 26 (March 1971): 11–31. More generally on Central America as a whole, see Samuel Z. Stone, *The Heritage of the Conquistadors: Ruling Classes in Central America from the Conquest to the Sandinistas* (Lincoln: University of Nebraska Press, 1990).

25. In the other key townships of the Meseta Central, large merchants were less likely to invest in coffee but still took advantage of land privatization. For example, wealthy individuals in Heredia often used early land reforms to establish estates dedicated to grain production. See Patricia Alvarenga Venutolo, "Las explotaciones agropecuarias en los albores de la expansión cafetalera," *Revista de Historia* 14 (July–December 1986): 115–31; and Hall, *El café y el desarrollo*, 73–74.

26. Gudmundson, *Costa Rica before Coffee*, 81, 85. See also Molina J., "Habilitadores y habilitados," 103.

27. Carrillo had served as president earlier, from 1835 to 1837. For discussions of the politics surrounding his first presidency and the coup of 1838, see Clotilde Obregón, *Carrillo: Una época y un hombre, 1835–1842* (San José: Editorial Costa Rica, 1990), chap. 1; Rodolfo Cerdas Cruz, *Formación del Estado en Costa Rica*, 2d ed. (San José: EDUCA, 1978), 145–65; Cleto González Víquez, *El sufragio en Costa Rica ante la historia y la legislación* (San José: Editorial Costa Rica, 1972), chap. 3; and Vega Carballo, *Orden y progreso*, 69–72. No general work on the ideology of Carrillo is available, but see the relevant

documents and letters in Carlos Meléndez, ed., *Documentos fundamentos del siglo XIX* (San José: Editorial Costa Rica, 1978), esp. 169–224. José Luis Vega Carballo has pointed out, "The governments that would come after the period that ended with the fall of Carrillo from power basically followed the path he had outlined. . . . From this point of view, [there followed] a long period of 'Carrillismo without Carrillo,' in which the basic institutional foundations that were needed for the agroexport society had already been constituted." Vega Carballo, *Orden y progreso*, 97.

28. Manuel Calderón Hernández, "Proceso y estructura del liberalismo en Costa Rica, 1821–1940," in Jaime Murillo, ed., *Desarrollo institucional de Costa Rica (de las sociedades indígenas a la crisis del 30)* (San José: EDUCA, 1991), 303; Obregón, *Carrillo*, 20.

29. "Ley de Bases y Garantías," in *Colección de leyes y decretos*, vol. 7 (San José: ANCR, March 28, 1841), 15. For good discussions of the historical significance of this legislation, see Obregón, *Carrillo*, 71–77; William Guido Madriz, "Don Braulio Carrillo y la Ley de Bases y Garantías" (tesis de grado, Universidad de Costa Rica, San José, 1971); and Alberto Sáenz Maroto, *Braulio Carrillo: Reformador agrícola de Costa Rica* (San José: EDUCA, 1987), chap. 10.

30. See Marina Volio de Kobe, "Estado y derecho en la Costa Rica del siglo XIX," in Murillo, *Desarrollo institucional de Costa Rica*, 240–42.

31. "Decreto 33," "Decreto 43," and "Orden 11," in *Colección de leyes y decretos*, vol. 5 (San José: ANCR, 1837–38), 102, 122, 273; Obregón, *Carrillo*, 87–93.

32. "Reglamento de Policía," in *Colección de leyes y decretos*, vol. 7 (San José: ANCR, December 1841), 153–61. On Carrillo's military reforms, see also Edwin Solís Salazar and Carlos E. González Pacheco, *El ejército en Costa Rica: Poder político, poder militar, 1821–1890* (San José: Editorial Alma Mater, 1991), 39–40, 45–50; Mercedes Muñoz Guillén, *El Estado y la abolición del ejército, 1914–1949* (San José: Editorial Porvenir, 1990), 15–16; and Muñoz Guillén, "El ejército costarricense y la conquista de los atributos de la estaticidad," in Murillo, *Desarrollo institucional de Costa Rica*, 259–60.

33. Fewer than 500 men is my estimate, based in part on a reading of the Codigo Militar of May 11, 1871, which refers to the military in the pre-1870 period.

34. Solís Salazar and González, *El ejército en Costa Rica*, 40.

35. This fact has led to a tension in much of the literature on Carrillo. Scholars often suggest that Carrillo's coup in 1838 corresponded with the rise to power of an incipient San José coffee elite, but they are then forced to acknowledge major conflicts between Carrillo and the San José elite. See, for example, Cerdas Cruz, *Formación del Estado*, 162–63, 172; Obregón, *Carrillo*, 61; and Vega Carballo, *Orden y progreso*, 71, 96, 106–8.

36. A discussion of the opposition movements against Carrillo can be found

in Rafael Obregón Loría, *De nuestra historia patria: Hechos militares y políticos* (Alajuela, Costa Rica: Museo Histórico Cultural Juan Santamaría, 1981), 48–55.

37. On Carrillo's agrarian reforms, see Castro Sánchez, "Estado," 210; Cardoso, "Formation of the Coffee Estate," 172–73; Facio, *Estudio sobre economía costarricense*, 40; Hall, *El café y el desarrollo*, 35; Dana G. Munro, *The Five Republics of Central America: Their Political and Economic Development and Their Relations with the United States* (New York: Oxford University Press, 1918), 141; Obregón, *Carrillo*, 82–83; Sáenz Maroto, *Braulio Carrillo;* and Volio de Kobe, "Estado y derecho," 235. On the labor market at this time, see Ciro Flamarion Santana Cardoso, "Historia económica del café en Centroamérica (siglo XIX): Estudio comparativo," *Estudios Sociales Centroamericanos* 4 (January–April 1975): 26; and José Luis Vega Carballo, "El nacimiento de un regimen de burguesía dependiente: El caso de Costa Rica," part 2, *Estudios Sociales Centroamericanos* 6 (September–December 1973): 93.

38. Deborah J. Yashar, *Demanding Democracy: Reform and Reaction in Costa Rica and Guatemala, 1870s–1950s* (Stanford: Stanford University Press, 1997), 60; R. G. Williams, *States and Social Evolution*, 127–28; Gudmundson, *Costa Rica before Coffee*, 74–77. The most detailed discussion of the labor market in the early coffee economy is Molina J., "Habilitadores y habilitados."

39. David M. Kauck, "Agricultural Commercialization and State Development in Central America: The Political Economy of the Coffee Industry from 1838 to 1940" (Ph.D. diss., University of Washington, 1988), 190.

40. The one exception was the military president Francisco Morazán (1842). Donna Lillian Cotton, "Costa Rica and the Era of Tomás Guardia, 1870–1882" (Ph.D. diss., George Washington University, 1972), 24.

41. With some minor variations, the suffrage was restricted to literate, wealthy, male property holders, and the electoral process was so fraudulent that the winning candidate was often known in advance. See Carlos Araya Pochet, "Esbozo histórico de la institución del sufragio en Costa Rica," in Paulino González Villalobos, ed., *Desarrollo institucional de Costa Rica (1523–1914)* (San José: SECASA, 1983), 119–24, esp. table 1, p. 122; Theodore S. Creedman, "The Political Development of Costa Rica, 1936–1944: Politics of an Emerging Welfare State in a Patriarchal Society" (Ph.D. diss., University of Maryland, 1971), 32–36; and González Víquez, *El sufragio en Costa Rica*. More generally on mid-nineteenth-century politics, see Eugenio Sancho-Riba, "Merchant-Planters and Modernization: An Early Liberal Experiment in Costa Rica, 1849–1870" (Ph.D. diss., University of California, San Diego), 1982.

42. Kauck, "Agricultural Commercialization," 190. See also Fernando Volio Jiménez, *El militarismo en Costa Rica y otros ensayos* (San José: Asociación Libro Libre, 1985), 15.

43. For example, Orlando Salazar Mora, *El apogeo de la república liberal en Costa Rica, 1870–1914* (San José: EDUCA, 1993), 23.

44. Cotton, "Costa Rica," 25–26.

45. Cardoso, "Formation of the Coffee Estate," 182.

46. Carlos Araya Pochet, "La minería y sus relaciones con la acumulación de capital y la clase dirigente de Costa Rica, 1821–1841," *Estudios Sociales Centroamericanos* 5 (May–August 1973): 36, 46.

47. José Luis Vega Carballo, *Hacia una interpretación del desarrollo costarricense: Ensayo sociológico*, 5th ed. (San José: Editorial Porvenir, 1986), chap. 2, esp. 65–66.

48. Vega's position is supported by Cardoso, "Formation of the Coffee Estate," 182. Molina Jiménez draws from both perspectives in *Costa Rica (1800–1850)*, 184–95.

49. Araya, "La minería," 39–40.

50. Vega Carballo, *Hacia una interpretación*, 64–70.

51. Robert Arthur Naylor, "British Commercial Relations with Central America, 1821–1851" (Ph.D. diss., Tulane University, 1958), 266, 267.

52. Tulio Halperín Donghi, *The Contemporary History of Latin America*, ed. and trans. John Charles Chasteen (Durham, N.C.: Duke University Press, 1993), 80.

53. Some scholars in fact date the beginning of the liberal reform period with the Guardia administration. Yet Guardia was building on several decades of earlier liberal reforms, including ones that had weakened the Church. In addition, Guardia did not initiate any significant agrarian legislation. On the ecclesiastical legislation promulgated between 1821 and 1870, see Claudio Antonio Vargas Arias, *El liberalismo, la iglesia y el Estado en Costa Rica* (San José: Ediciones Guayacán, 1991), 39–65.

54. See Eugenio Rodríguez, *Don Tomás Guardia y el Estado liberal*, 2d ed. (San José: EUNED, 1989), 37; Eduardo Rosés Alvarado, "La dictadura de Tomás Guardia: Un período de transición del Estado costarricense," in González Villalobos, *Desarrollo institucional de Costa Rica*, 107–9; Araya, "Esbozo histórico," 124–25; and O. Salazar, *El apogeo*, 21, 28, 31.

55. General historical information for this paragraph is from Obregón Loría, *De nuestra historia patria*, 159–67; González Víquez, *El sufragio en Costa Rica*, chaps. 17–18; and O. Salazar, *El apogeo*, 22–26.

56. Rosés Alvarado, "La dictadura de Tomás Guardia," 108; Volio Jiménez, *El militarismo*, 16.

57. O. Salazar, *El apogeo*, 24.

58. See Robert Howard Claxton, "Lorenzo Montúfar: Central American Liberal" (Ph.D. diss., Tulane University, 1970), 72–74.

59. O. Salazar, *El apogeo*, 29; Solís Salazar and González, *El ejército en Costa Rica*, 86–87, 138; Vega Carballo, *Orden y progreso*, 251.

60. Solís Salazar and González, *El ejército en Costa Rica*, 52, 99; Vega Carballo, *Orden y progreso*, 269.

61. The major military innovations completed by Guardia are the subject

of Solís Salazar and González, *El ejército en Costa Rica,* esp. 70–121. See also Edward Dennis Hernández, "Modernization and Dependency in Costa Rica during the Decade of the 1880s" (Ph.D. diss., University of California, Los Angeles, 1975), 75–84.

62. As Vega puts it: "The political authoritarianism of Guardia had served to eliminate the constant political-economic struggles among factions of the dominant class, and in spite of having enlarged the military apparatus of the state, it put officials outside of political activity and secured the control and absolute subjugation of the barracks to the presidency of the Republic." Vega Carballo, *Orden y progreso,* 270.

63. Ibid., 273.

64. Ibid. The size of the state bureaucracy should be seen in light of the overall population of Costa Rica, which was only about 140,000 at the time.

65. Cotton, "Costa Rica," chap. 2.

66. O. Salazar, *El apogeo,* 34.

67. Astrid Fischel, *Consenso y represión: Una interpretación socio-política de la educación costarricense* (San José: Editorial Costa Rica, 1990).

68. Héctor Lindo-Fuentes, *Weak Foundations: The Economy of El Salvador in the Nineteenth Century, 1821–1898* (Berkeley: University of California Press, 1990), 70.

69. Ralph Lee Woodward Jr., *Central America: A Nation Divided,* 2d ed. (New York: Oxford University Press, 1985), 173.

70. The best analysis of nation-building in Costa Rica is Steven Paul Palmer, "A Liberal Discipline: Inventing Nations in Guatemala and Costa Rica, 1870–1900" (Ph.D. diss., Columbia University, 1990). Palmer argues that the appearance of Costa Rican nationalism can be dated to the period between 1885 and 1895 (156).

71. For somewhat opposing interpretations of this reform process, see the discussions in Philip J. Williams, *The Catholic Church and Politics in Nicaragua and Costa Rica* (Pittsburgh: University of Pittsburgh Press, 1989); and Vargas Arias, *El liberalismo,* chap. 4.

72. O. Salazar, *El apogeo,* 178–81.

73. Orlando Salazar Mora, "Sobre la democracia liberal en Costa Rica (1889–1919)," in Paulino González Villalobos, *Desarrollo institucional de Costa Rica,* 148.

74. Araya, "Esbozo histórico," 128; O. Salazar, *El apogeo,* 45.

75. Creedman, "Political Development of Costa Rica," chap. 3; Fabrice Edouard Lehoucq, "The Origins of Democracy in Costa Rica in Comparative Perspective" (Ph.D. diss., Duke University, 1992), chap. 3; Munro, *The Five Republics of Central America,* 150–54; O. Salazar, "Sobre la democracia liberal"; Yashar, *Demanding Democracy.* Mario Samper argues that scholars who see electoral fraud as an aberration or imperfection of an essentially democratic system are grossly mistaken, for electoral fraud "was in reality not an 'anomaly' but a

basic feature of the system." Mario Samper K., "Fuerzas sociopolíticas y procesos electorales en Costa Rica," *Revista de Historia,* número especial (1988), 173.

76. For a discussion of early democratization in Europe and Latin America,
see Ruth Berins Collier, *Paths toward Democracy: The Working Class and Elites
in Western Europe and South America* (New York: Cambridge University Press,
1999).

77. See, for example, Halperín, *Contemporary History of Latin America,*
chap. 5.

78. The origins of the banana industry are discussed in Jeffrey Casey Gas-
par, *Limón, 1880–1940: Un estudio de la industria bananera en Costa Rica* (San
José: Editorial Costa Rica, 1979), chap. 1; Aviva Chomsky, *West Indian Work-
ers and the United Fruit Company in Costa Rica, 1870–1940* (Baton Rouge:
Louisiana State University Press, 1996), chap. 1; and Clarence F. Jones and
Paul C. Morrison, "Evolution of the Banana Industry of Costa Rica," *Economic
Geography* 28 (January 1952): 1–3. In addition to these sources, this section
draws on the general discussions of the Costa Rican banana industry in Charles
David Kepner Jr. and Jay Henry Soothill, *The Banana Empire: A Case Study of
Economic Imperialism* (New York: Russell & Russell, 1935), chap. 2; and
Woodward, *Central America: A Nation Divided,* chap. 7.

79. Kepner and Soothill, *The Banana Empire,* 44–45.

80. Jones and Morrison, "Evolution of the Banana Industry," 3.

81. See Kepner and Soothill, *The Banana Empire,* chap. 2.

82. Chomsky, *West Indian Workers,* 60. This paragraph draws on Chomsky's fine work, esp. pp. 30–31, 60–68.

83. Gaspar, *Limón,* 189.

84. Ibid.

CHAPTER SEVEN: ABORTED LIBERALISM

1. The notion of a "frustrated" liberal reform is from Edelberto Torres-
Rivas, *Interpretación del desarrollo social centroamericano: Procesos y estructuras de una sociedad dependiente,* 2d ed. (San José: EDUCA, 1971), 35.

2. Héctor Pérez Brignoli, *La reforma liberal en Honduras* (Tegucigalpa: Editorial Nuevo Continente, 1973), 12.

3. Charles Abbey Brand, "The Background to Capitalistic Underdevelopment: Honduras to 1913" (Ph.D. diss., University of Pittsburgh, 1972), 58.
Brand's study—arguably the best work available in English on the liberal reform
period in Honduras—also stresses the small size and weakness of the Honduran
elite, and especially its unwillingness to participate in and invest in liberal reform
projects.

4. This factor is highlighted by José Francisco Guevara-Escudero in "Nineteenth-Century Honduras: A Regional Approach to the Economic History of
Honduras" (Ph.D. diss., New York University, 1983).

5. This was true even though Soto and Rosa had served as ministers for Justo Rufino Barrios in the mid-1870s and developed their liberal political credentials in Guatemala. On the liberal ideological program embraced by Soto and Rosa, see especially José Reina Valenzuela and Mario Argueta, *Marco Aurelio Soto: Reforma liberal de 1876* (Tegucigalpa: Banco Central de Honduras, 1978); Rafael Heliodoro Valle, *Oro de Honduras: Antología de Ramón Rosa* (Tegucigalpa: Tipografía Nacional, 1948); and Marcos Carías, ed., *Ramón Rosa: Obra escogida* (Tegucigalpa: Editorial Guaymuras, 1980).

6. Aníbal Delgado Fiallos goes so far as to write that "the Conservative Party never existed in Honduras." A. Delgado, *Rosa: El político* (Tegucigalpa: Editorial Cultura, 1994), 43.

7. Juan Arancibia C., *Honduras: ¿Un Estado nacional?* 2d ed. (Tegucigalpa: Editorial Guaymuras, 1991), 29.

8. See Valenzuela and Argueta, *Marco Aurelio Soto,* chap. 10.

9. Arancibia, *Honduras,* 29–30.

10. Ibid., 30. See also Matías Funes h., *Los deliberantes. El poder militar en Honduras* (Tegucigalpa: Editorial Guaymuras, 1995), 44.

11. "Decreto en que se mandan recojer las armas nacionales que existen en poder de particulares," *Gaceta Oficial del Gobierno de Honduras,* ser. 1, no. 8 (December 30, 1876): 5–7; "Crónica interior," *Gaceta de Honduras,* ser. 2, no. 14 (March 25, 1877): 1.

12. In 1881, for example, over half of the national budget was allocated to the Department of War (502,016 pesos out of a total of 988,012 pesos). "Presupuesto de la renta," *Gaceta de Honduras,* ser. 5, no. 47 (May 26, 1879): 2–3. See also Funes, *Los deliberantes,* 52–53.

13. Marco Aurelio Soto, "Mensaje dirijio al Congreso de la República," *Gaceta de Honduras,* ser. 5, no. 48 (June 5, 1879): 2.

14. Guillermo Molina Chocano, *Estado liberal y desarrollo capitalista en Honduras* (Tegucigalpa: Banco Central de Honduras, 1976), 12–13.

15. Funes suggests that Soto believed a permanent army was simply too expensive for Honduras. See Funes, *Los deliberantes,* 59.

16. "Memoria de Fomento, agricultura i comercio," *La Gaceta,* ser. 5, no. 56 (November 20, 1879): 1–3; Luis Mariñas Otero, *Honduras* (Tegucigalpa: Editorial Universitaria, 1983), 356–57.

17. "Decreto en que se establece los que deben pagar los estractores i destazadores de ganado," *La Gaceta de Honduras,* ser. 2, no. 13 (February 28, 1877): 1–2; "Memoria de Hacienda, Crédito Público i Guerra," *La Gaceta,* ser. 5, no. 57 (November 27, 1879); Valenzuela and Argueta, *Marco Aurelio Soto,* 92.

18. Soto, "Mensaje dirijio al Congreso," 1.

19. On the defeat of the Medina and Vásquez uprisings, see "Manifesto del Señor Presidente de la República," *Gaceta de Honduras,* ser. 3, no. 29 (March 8, 1878): 1–2; and "Decreto Numero 44," *Gaceta de Honduras,* ser. 5, no. 46 (May 13, 1879): 3.

20. G. Molina, *Estado liberal*, 14. For a somewhat opposing view of the impact of Soto's state reforms, see Pérez Brignoli, *La reforma liberal*, 11. Pérez Brignoli uses a comparison with Guatemala as the basis for his assessment of Honduras. See also Darío A. Euraque, "Merchants and Industrialists in Northern Honduras: The Making of a National Bourgeoisie in Peripheral Capitalism" (Ph.D. diss., University of Wisconsin, Madison, 1990), 58.

21. Soto mentioned the success of "the dictatorship of Carrillo" in a February 1880 decree. See "Documento no. 8—situación de la agricultura del país," *Cuaderno de Ciencias Sociales*, no. 2 (1973): 53.

22. Quoted in Valenzuela and Argueta, *Marco Aurelio Soto*, 111. Soto wrote this passage in a letter in 1906, but it reflects the spirit of his reform efforts while he was in power.

23. Marco Aurelio Soto and Ramón Rosa, "Decreto en que se fomenta la agricultura," *Gaceta de Honduras*, ser. 2, no. 17 (May 1, 1877). Information for this paragraph and the next one is from this legislation.

24. Robert G. Williams, *States and Social Evolution: Coffee and the Rise of National Governments in Central America* (Chapel Hill: University of North Carolina Press, 1994), 93.

25. G. Molina, *Estado liberal*, 27.

26. Ibid., 28.

27. Beyond this, the government ordered that "idle" individuals who were capable of serving as day or permanent laborers be registered by local authorities and "apportioned" as needed to export-producing units. But this measure served primarily to encourage individuals to become small agricultural farmers, rather than provide Honduras's minuscule plantation-owner class with a ready-made workforce. R. G. Williams (*States and Social Evolution*, 140–41) also highlights the noncoercive aspects of Honduran labor policy. For a somewhat opposing view, see Brand, "Background to Capitalistic Underdevelopment," 109, 128.

28. G. Molina, *Estado liberal*, 44.

29. See, for example, Pérez Brignoli, *La reforma liberal*.

30. Brand, "Background to Capitalistic Underdevelopment," 110–13.

31. Charles David Kepner Jr. and Jay Henry Soothill, *The Banana Empire: A Case Study of Economic Imperialism* (New York: Russell & Russell, 1935), 95–96.

32. Brand, "Background to Capitalistic Underdevelopment," 114.

33. A traditional view, represented by the work of Charles Brand, suggests that the dominant class was largely uninterested and uninvolved in banana production, remaining content with traditional sources of wealth and property speculation. Ibid.

34. Darío A. Euraque, "La 'reforma liberal' en Honduras y la hipótesis de la 'oligarquía ausente': 1870–1930," *Revista de Historia* 23 (January–June 1991): 18.

35. Ibid. See also the discussion in Darío A. Euraque, *Reinterpreting the Banana Republic: Region and State in Honduras, 1870–1972* (Chapel Hill: University of North Carolina Press, 1996), 9–13.

36. G. Molina, *Estado liberal,* 44.

37. This paragraph and the subsequent ones in this section are based significantly on Kenneth V. Finney's doctoral dissertation, "Precious Metal Mining and the Modernization of Honduras: In Quest of El Dorado (1880–1900)" (Tulane University, 1973). Other especially valuable sources I consulted are Guillermo Molina Chocano, "La formación del Estado y el origen minero-mercantil de la burguesía hondureña," *Estudios Sociales Centroamericanos* 25 (January–April 1980): 55–89; Kenneth V. Finney, "Rosario and the Election of 1887: The Political Economy of Mining in Honduras," *Hispanic American Historical Review* 59 (February 1979): 81–107; and Brand, "Background to Capitalistic Underdevelopment," 88–107.

38. Finney, "Precious Metal Mining," 18; Brand, "Background to Capitalistic Underdevelopment," 89–90. Soto and his close advisor Enrique Gutiérrez had substantial personal investments in this mine.

39. The resignation of Soto in May 1883 occurred under pressure from Justo Rufino Barrios, who felt betrayed when Soto discussed the possibility of a Central American union without consulting him. See Mario Rodríguez, *Central America* (Englewood Cliffs, N.J.: Prentice-Hall, 1965), 97.

40. Finney, "Precious Metal Mining," table 1, p. 45.

41. G. Molina, *Estado liberal,* 44.

42. Ibid., 74–75.

43. Background for this paragraph is from Finney, "Rosario and the Election of 1887."

44. Finney, "Precious Metal Mining," 327–30, 423.

45. Euraque, "Merchants and Industrialists," 74. See also Víctor Meza and Héctor López, "Las inversiones extranjeras en Honduras antes del Mercado Común Centroamericano," *Economía Política* 6 (September–December 1973): 56.

46. Brand, "Background to Capitalistic Underdevelopment," 105.

47. G. Molina, "La formación del Estado," 63.

48. Euraque, "Merchants and Industrialists," 84.

49. Marvin A. Barahona, *La hegemonía de los Estados Unidos en Honduras (1907–1932)* (Tegucigalpa: Centro de Documentación de Honduras, 1989), 114.

50. As Charles Brand notes, by 1918 "the incorporation of the state's most viable surplus-producing export sectors into the international capitalistic economy [was completed], a process which began with foreign development and control of mining in the 1880s." Brand, "Background to Capitalistic Underdevelopment," 123.

51. See Arancibia, *Honduras,* 40.

52. Brand notes that 80 percent of all banana plantations in 1910 were

owned by North Americans. Given that these plantations were on average much larger than Honduran-owned ones, the U.S. plantations would certainly have accounted for much more than 80 percent of total exports by the conclusion of the reform period in 1919. See Brand, "Background to Capitalistic Underdevelopment," 159.

53. Arancibia, *Honduras,* 40.

54. For example, see Brand, "Background to Capitalistic Underdevelopment," table 6, p. 111.

55. Euraque, "Merchants and Industrialists," 90.

56. As Marvin Barahona suggests, "North American hegemony evolved, with time, toward a type of domination, but this domination was permitted, accepted, even used by Honduran political elites." Barahona, *La hegemonía,* xiii.

57. Vilma Laínez and Víctor Meza, "El enclave bananero en la historia de Honduras," *Estudios Sociales Centroamericanos* 5 (May–August 1973): 154.

58. On the Vacarros, see especially Laínez and Meza, "El enclave bananero," 120–24; Thomas L. Karnes, *Tropical Enterprise: The Standard Fruit and Steamship Company in Latin America* (Baton Rouge: Louisiana State University Press, 1978), chaps. 1–4; and Kepner and Soothill, *The Banana Empire,* 102.

59. Laínez and Meza, "El enclave bananero," 122.

60. A good account of Zemurray's career is Stephen J. Whitfield, "Strange Fruit: The Career of Samuel Zemurray," *American Jewish History* 82 (March 1984): 307–23. See also Thomas P. McCann, *An American Company: The Tragedy of United Fruit,* ed. Henry Scammell (New York: Crown Publishers, 1976), chap. 3.

61. Antonio Murga Frassinetti, *Enclave y sociedad en Honduras* (Tegucigalpa: Editorial Universitaria, 1978), 82.

62. For background for this paragraph and the next two, I relied on especially Mario R. Argueta, *Bananos y política: Samuel Zemurray y la Cuyamel Fruit Company en Honduras* (Tegucigalpa: Editorial Universitaria, 1989), 9–37; Brand, "Background to Capitalistic Underdevelopment," 168–81; and Kepner and Soothill, *The Banana Empire,* 105–10.

63. On the one hand, this move won Dávila some support from the U.S. State Department, which was then pursuing a policy of "dollar diplomacy" (and which in fact intervened to support the Valentine and Morgan venture). On the other hand, the move was highly unpopular in Honduras.

64. Brand, "Background to Capitalistic Development," 179.

65. Karnes, *Tropical Enterprise,* 45.

66. On the concept of embeddedness, see Peter Evans, *Embedded Autonomy: States and Industrial Transformation* (Princeton: Princeton University Press, 1995).

67. See William S. Stokes, *Honduras: An Area Study in Government* (Madison: University of Wisconsin Press, 1950), chap. 8; and Mario Posas and Rafael

del Cid, *La construcción del sector público y del Estado nacional en Honduras, 1876–1979,* 2d ed. (San José: EDUCA, 1983), 88–92.

68. Steve C. Ropp, "The Honduran Army in the Sociopolitical Evolution of the Honduran State," *The Americas* 30 (April 1974): 506 (emphasis in original).

69. Numerous authors have observed that Honduras never developed a powerful landed elite. For a review of this literature, see Euraque, "La 'reforma liberal,'" 9–11.

70. Torres-Rivas, *Interpretación del desarrollo.* The quotation is on p. 42; the comparison with Guatemala and El Salvador is on p. 40. Torres-Rivas further clarified his argument in "Poder nacional y sociedad dependiente: Las clases y el Estado en Centroamérica," in Rafael Menjívar, ed., *La inversión extranjera en Centroamérica* (San José: EDUCA, 1974). Other good discussions of how foreign capital stunted the development of a landed elite in Honduras can be found in Héctor Pérez Brignoli, "Economía y sociedad en Honduras durante el siglo XIX: Las estructuras demográficas," *Estudios Sociales Centroamericanos* 6 (September–December 1973): 51–52; Laínez and Meza, "El enclave bananero," 152–53; Murga, *Enclave y sociedad,* 68; and Euraque, "La 'reforma liberal.'"

71. This was due in part to the technical aspects of banana production, which favored control over transportation and commercial distribution by a single enterprise. See Torres-Rivas, *Interpretación del desarrollo,* 57.

72. See G. Molina, "La formación del Estado," 56.

73. Murga, *Enclave y sociedad,* chap. 3; Euraque, "La 'reforma liberal,'" 39.

74. See Jeffery M. Paige, *Agrarian Revolution: Social Movements and Export Agriculture in the Underdeveloped World* (New York: Free Press, 1975), 9–40, 48–58.

75. Representative examples include Oscar René Vargas, *La revolución que inició el progreso (Nicaragua, 1893–1909)* (Managua: Ecotextura, 1990); Ilva Fernández, "Nicaragua: Estructura económico-social y política del régimen de Zelaya" (licenciado thesis, Universidad Centroamericana, Managua, 1978); José Luis Velázquez Pereira, *Formación del Estado en Nicaragua* (Managua: Fondo Editorial, Banco Central de Nicaragua, 1992); Jaime Wheelock Román, *Imperialismo y dictadura: Crisis de una formación social* (Mexico City: Siglo Veintiuno Editores, 1975); Juan Manuel Ulloa Mayorga et al., *Apuntes de historia de Nicaragua* (León, Nicaragua: Editorial Universitaria, 1988), 25–26; and Juan Luis Vázquez, "Luchas políticas y Estado oligárquico," in Alberto Lanuza et al., eds., *Economía y sociedad en la construcción del Estado de Nicaragua* (San José: Instituto Centroamericano de Administración Pública, 1983).

76. See especially Charles L. Stansifer, "José Santos Zelaya: A New Look at Nicaragua's 'Liberal' Dictator," *Revista/Review Interamericana* 7 (fall 1977): 468–85; see also the various pieces that follow José Santos Quant's article "No-

tas sobre la Revolución Liberal en la historia económica de Nicaragua," *Boletín Nicaragüense de Bibliografía y Documentación* 6 (July–August 1975): 54–69.

77. On the opposition to Zelaya, see Ramón Ignacio Matus, "Revoluciones contra Zelaya," *Revista Conservadora del Pensamiento Centroamericano* 4 (April 1962): 4–12; and Enrique Aquino, *La personalidad del General José Santos Zelaya* (Managua: Talleres Gráficos Pérez, 1944), 83–91.

78. "Prefectura del Departamento," *Gaceta Oficial* (Managua), July 28, 1893, 2; "Acuerdo por el cual . . . ," ibid., August 9, 1893, 3; "Decreto relativo al mantenimiento del orden público," ibid., October 21, 1893, 1. It is not clear how effective the government was at actually collecting arms. In late 1897 the same basic decree was issued again: "Decreto relativo . . . ," ibid., December 1, 1897.

79. "Ley marcial," *Gaceta Oficial*, October 9, 1894, 1–2.

80. "Organización del ejército nacional," *Gaceta Oficial*, December 31, 1895, 2–3.

81. I derive these figures from readings of the *Gaceta Oficial* and the discussions in Emilio Àlvarez Montalván, *Las fuerzas armadas en Nicaragua: Sinopsis histórica, 1821–1994* (Managua: Edición Jorge Eduardo Arellano, 1994), chap. 5; Richard Millet, *Guardians of the Dynasty: A History of the U.S. Created Guardia Nacional de Nicaragua and the Somoza Family* (Maryknoll, N.Y.: Orbis Books, 1977); and Benjamin I. Teplitz, "The Political and Economic Foundations of Modernization in Nicaragua: The Administration of José Santos Zelaya, 1893–1909" (Ph.D. diss., Howard University, 1973), chap. 4. The government no doubt exaggerated in 1896 when it reported the size of the army to exceed six thousand men. See "El ejército nacional," *Gaceta Oficial*, March 4, 1896, 3. In his presidential message of 1901, Zelaya boasted that thirty-four thousand soldiers were available. See "Mensaje del Presidente de la República a la Asamble Nacional Legislativa," *Diaro Oficial* (Managua), August 7, 1901, 1.

82. In Nicaragua, the Church had been weakened considerably during the Thirty Years period. See chapter 4 of this study and Jorge Eduardo Arellano, *Breve historia de la iglesia en Nicaragua (1523–1979)* (Managua: CEHILA, 1980), chap. 2. Hence, we need not go into great depth here on Zelaya's anti-ecclesiastical politics. However, when the archbishop of Nicaragua came into conflict with the liberal government in 1899, Zelaya was quick to expel him and other León clergymen from the country. For a brief account, see Alejandro Cole Chamorro, *145 Años de historia política de Nicaragua* (Managua: Editora Nicaragüense, 1967), 69–71.

83. Teplitz, "Political and Economic Foundations," 108–9.

84. Velázquez, *Formación del Estado en Nicaragua*, 92.

85. For exact figures, see Vargas, *La revolución*, 112–20.

86. Ibid., 120. Furthermore, all agricultural laborers were required to work one week per year on the construction of public works. See Velázquez, *Formación del Estado en Nicaragua*, 58–59.

87. Amaru Barahona, *Estudio sobre la historia de Nicaragua: Del auge cafetalero al triunfo de la revolución* (Managua: INIES, 1989), 16.

88. This paragraph draws on Teplitz, "Political and Economic Foundations," chap. 8.

89. Ibid., 312–13.

90. Ibid., 320–21.

91. Charlip offers an excellent analysis of the coffee economy around the Carazo Plateau. See Julie A. Charlip, "Cultivating Coffee: Farmers, Land, and Money in Nicaragua, 1877–1930" (Ph.D. diss., University of California, Los Angeles, 1995).

92. See, for example, "Mensaje del Presidente del Estado a la Asamblea Nacional Legislativa," *Diario Oficial,* January 5, 1898, 3.

93. Teplitz, "Political and Economic Foundations," 214.

94. For the text of much of this legislation and a discussion, see Fernández, "Nicaragua," 58–75.

95. Teplitz, "Political and Economic Foundations," 216.

96. Ibid., 228, 231.

97. R. G. Williams, *States and Social Evolution,* 86.

98. Jeffrey L. Gould, "El trabajo forzoso y las comunidades indígenas nicaragüenses," in Héctor Pérez Brignoli and Mario Samper, eds., *El café en la historia de Centroamérica* (San José: FLASCO, 1993), 24–27, 39.

99. For good discussions, see J. Gould, "El trabajo forzoso"; and R. G. Williams, *States and Social Evolution,* 84–86, 177.

100. R. G. Williams, *States and Social Evolution,* 86. In contrast to Williams, Charlip argues that landholding patterns in Nicaragua more closely resembled those of Costa Rica than those found in either El Salvador or Guatemala. Based on a study of Carazo, she argues that the coffee economy was "dominated by small and medium landholders, who produced most of the coffee. Contrary to popular wisdom, access to land posed no significant problem; land was available and prices were relatively low." Charlip, "Cultivating Coffee," 1–2. Since both Williams and Charlip rely heavily on the same 1909 coffee census, however, the debate ultimately boils down to how one defines categories such as "small estate" and "large estate." Given Charlip's concern with overturning a "proletarianization" interpretation of the spread of coffee production in Nicaragua, she quite appropriately defines land categories in a manner such that the data suggest large capitalistic *fincas* were rare compared to medium and small-sized estates. By contrast, given Williams's concern with systematically comparing landholding structures across the Central American countries to uncover the agrarian roots of modern politics, he quite appropriately defines the categories such that capitalist estates include those that employed only relatively modest amounts of labor. Here I follow Williams's understanding of large estate.

101. Ibid., 86–91.

102. Teplitz, "Political and Economic Foundations," 225; see also Jeffrey L. Gould, "'¡Vana Ilusión!': The Highlands Indians and the Myth of Nicaragua Mestiza, 1880–1925," in Aviva Chomsky and Aldo Lauria-Santiago, eds., *Identity and Struggle at the Margins of the Nation-State: The Laboring People of Central America and the Hispanic Caribbean* (Durham, N.C.: Duke University Press, 1998), 62–65.

103. Ibid., 226–31.

104. Ibid., 226.

105. "Ley sobre agricultura y trabajadores," *Gaceta Oficial*, October 2, 1894, 1–3.

106. This paragraph draws on Teplitz, "Political and Economic Foundations," 195–212.

107. Ibid., 198.

108. "Se reglamenta la libreta de obrero," *Gaceta Oficial*, October 19, 1901.

109. Teplitz, "Political and Economic Foundations," 204.

110. See John Ellis Findling, "The United States and Zelaya: A Study in the Diplomacy of Expediency" (Ph.D. diss., University of Texas, Austin, 1971), chap. 3; Charles Edward Frazier, "The Dawn of Nationalism and Its Consequences in Nicaragua" (Ph.D. diss., University of Texas, Austin, 1958), 12–13; and Teplitz, "Political and Economic Foundations," 244. Nonetheless, there was some hostility to Zelaya among U.S. businesses based on the fact that he did not hesitate to cancel concessions when the terms were not fulfilled.

111. Walter LaFeber, *Inevitable Revolutions: The United States in Central America* (New York: Norton, 1984), 40.

112. For general historical background in this section, I have relied on Harold Norman Denny, *Dollars for Bullets: The Story of American Rule in Nicaragua* (New York: Dial Press, 1929), chap. 4; Frazier, "The Dawn of Nationalism"; LaFeber, *Inevitable Revolutions*, 46–49; Ivan Musicant, *The Banana Wars: A History of United States Military Intervention in Latin America from the Spanish-American War to the Invasion of Panama* (New York: Macmillan, 1990), chap. 4; Anna I. Powell, "Relations between the United States and Nicaragua, 1898–1916," *Hispanic American Historical Review* 8 (February 1928): 43–64; Teplitz, "Political and Economic Foundations," chap. 10; and "The United States and Central American Stability," *Foreign Policy Reports* 8 (July 8, 1931), esp. 169–76.

113. See, for example, Dana G. Munro, *Intervention and Dollar Diplomacy in the Caribbean, 1900–1921* (Princeton: Princeton University Press, 1964).

114. Roscoe R. Hill, *Fiscal Intervention in Nicaragua* (New York: Paul Maisel, 1933), 3. Hence, any claim that the uprising represented traditional landed elites who were opposed to the new coffee order cannot be easily sustained. Rather, conservative opposition at this point appears to have centered

more squarely on old partisan rivalries and the massive liberal state-building efforts that had taken place, especially the fact that Zelaya had built a national state structure that penetrated the country in the name of the Liberal Party. For a somewhat opposing interpretation, see Wheelock, *Imperialismo y dictadura,* 111–12.

115. Denny, *Dollars for Bullets,* 71.

116. Ibid., 81, 82.

117. Although these developments take us chronologically out of the liberal reform period (which concluded with the fall of Zelaya), it is important to consider them here to understand the configuration of state and class structures present in the years immediately following the reform period.

118. See John A. Booth, *The End and the Beginning: The Nicaraguan Revolution,* 2d ed. (Boulder, Colo.: Westview Press, 1985), chap. 3.

119. Denny, *Dollars for Bullets,* 121–22.

120. This paragraph draws from Knut Walter, *The Regime of Anastasio Somoza, 1936–1956* (Chapel Hill: University of North Carolina Press, 1993), 11–13; Hill, *Fiscal Intervention,* chaps. 2–3; and Carlos Quijano, *Nicaragua: Ensayo sobre el imperialismo de los Estados Unidos (1909–1927)* (Managua: Vanguardia, 1987), pts. 1 and 2.

121. Jeffery M. Paige, *Coffee and Power: Revolution and the Rise of Democracy in Central America* (Cambridge: Harvard University Press, 1997), 166–67.

122. See R. G. Williams, *States and Social Evolution,* 268–69.

123. Booth, *The End and the Beginning,* 33.

124. Walter, *The Regime of Anastasio Somoza,* 13.

125. Paige, *Coffee and Power,* chap. 2.

126. Ibid., 79–80.

CHAPTER EIGHT: AFTERMATH

1. Chacón was selected first designate for the presidency during the administration of José María Orellana and took office after Orellana died of a heart attack in 1926. Romero was the handpicked candidate of the powerful Meléndez-Quiñónez family and took office through a fraudulent election.

2. On Guatemala, see Héctor Pérez-Brignoli, *A Brief History of Central America,* trans. Ricardo B. Sawrey A. and Susana Stettri de Sawrey (Berkeley: University of California Press, 1989), 108; and Arturo Taracena Arriola, "Liberalismo y poder político en Centroamérica (1870–1929)," in *Historia general de Centroamérica,* vol. 4, *Las repúblicas agroexportadoras (1870–1945),* ed. Víctor Hugo Acuña Ortega (Madrid: FLASCO, 1993), 177. On El Salvador, see Everett Alan Wilson, "The Crisis of National Integration in El Salvador, 1919–1935" (Ph.D. diss., Stanford University, 1970), chap. 5; Patricia Alvarenga, "Reshaping the Ethics of Power: A History of Violence in Western Rural El Salvador,

1880–1932" (Ph.D. diss., University of Wisconsin, Madison, 1994), chap. 5; and Erik Ching, "Patronage, Politics, and Power in El Salvador, 1840–1940" (book manuscript, 1998), 253–56.

3. On the fall of Estrada Cabrera, see Joseph Apolonio Pitti, "Jorge Ubico and Guatemalan Politics in the 1920s" (Ph.D. diss., University of New Mexico, 1975), 20–30. Pitti's study is the best analysis of Guatemalan politics in the 1920s.

4. Ibid., 30.

5. On the Orellana government, see Pitti, "Jorge Ubico," chaps. 2–3.

6. Chacón and the other presidents of the 1920s are virtually unknown, even by Guatemala specialists. Unfortunately, the most detailed analysis of the Chacón administration focuses too much attention on his weak leadership and the criticisms of his administration presented by a variety of opposition actors. See Pitti, "Jorge Ubico," chaps. 4–8. Further historical research is needed on Chacón and indeed the entire 1920s period.

7. Pérez-Brignoli, *Brief History,* 108; Arturo Taracena Arriola, "El primer Partido Comunista de Guatemala (1922–1932): Diez años de una historia olvidada," *Anuario de Estudios Centroamericanos* 15 (1989): 79–80.

8. On the initial incorporation of the labor movement, see Ruth Berins Collier and David Collier, *Shaping the Political Arena: Critical Junctures, the Labor Movement, and Regime Dynamics in Latin America* (Princeton: Princeton University Press, 1991).

9. Pitti, "Jorge Ubico," 271.

10. The definitive work on Romero is yet to be published. But see the discussions in Ching, "Patronage, Politics, and Power," chap. 5; E. A. Wilson, "Crisis of National Integration," chap. 5; Mariano Castro Morán, *Función política del ejército salvadoreño en el presente siglo* (San Salvador: UCA Editores, 1984), chap. 2; and Alastair White, *El Salvador* (New York: Praeger, 1973), 95–99.

11. Robert Varney Elam, "Appeal to Arms: The Army and Politics in El Salvador, 1931–1964" (Ph.D. diss., University of New Mexico, 1968), chap. 2.

12. On the election, see Ching, "Patronage, Politics, and Power," chap. 5; Rafael Guidos Véjar, *El ascenso del militarismo en El Salvador,* 4th ed. (San Salvador: UCA Editores, 1988), 112–18; and E. A. Wilson, "Crisis of National Integration," 199–209.

13. Araujo's progressive platform also attracted some working-class votes from the capital. See E. A. Wilson, "Crisis of National Integration," 206–8.

14. See Ching, "Patronage, Politics, and Power," 306–7; and Kenneth J. Grieb, "The United States and the Rise of General Maximiliano Hernández Martínez," *Journal of Latin American Studies* 3 (November 1971): 153.

15. This paragraph draws on Kenneth J. Grieb, *Guatemalan Caudillo: The Regime of Jorge Ubico* (Athens: Ohio University Press, 1979), chap. 1; and Pitti, "Jorge Ubico," chap. 8.

16. For a discussion of the U.S. role, see Kenneth J. Grieb, "American Involvement in the Rise of Jorge Ubico," *Caribbean Studies* 10 (April 1970): 5–21.

17. James Dunkerley, *The Long War: Dictatorship and Revolution in El Salvador* (London: Verso, 1982), 23; Thomas Anderson, *Matanza*, 2d ed. (Willimantic, Conn.: Curbstone Press, 1992; originally published in 1971), 77–78.

18. Elam, "Appeal to Arms," 20–22; Grieb, "The United States," 154.

19. T. Anderson, *Matanza*, 73–78; Dunkerley, *The Long War*, 23.

20. On this coup, see Elam, "Appeal to Arms," chap. 3.

21. Grieb, "The United States," 155.

22. See Grieb, "American Involvement," and Grieb, "The United States."

23. The standard interpretation remains T. Anderson, *Matanza*. Valuable accounts are also found in Erik Ching, "In Search of the Party: The Communist Party, the Comintern, and the Peasant Rebellion of 1932 in El Salvador," *The Americas* 55 (October 1998): 204–39; Roque Dalton, *Miguel Mármol* (San José: EDUCA, 1972), 229–367; Dunkerley, *The Long War*, chap. 2; Guidos, *El ascenso del militarismo*, chap. 3; Douglas Kincaid, "Peasants into Rebels: Community and Class in Rural El Salvador," *Comparative Studies in Society and History* 29 (July 1989): 466–94; and E. A. Wilson, "Crisis of National Integration."

24. Ching, "Patronage, Politics, and Power," 260–61.

25. See Jeffery M. Paige, *Coffee and Power: Revolution and the Rise of Democracy in Central America* (Cambridge: Harvard University Press, 1997), 122.

26. Charles W. Anderson, "El Salvador: The Army as Reformer," in Martin C. Needler, ed., *Political Systems of Latin America* (Princeton: D. Van Nostrand Company, 1964), 58.

27. Grieb, "The United States," 163.

28. On the paramilitary forces, see Philip J. Williams and Knut Walter, *Militarization and Demilitarization in El Salvador's Transition to Democracy* (Pittsburgh: University of Pittsburgh Press, 1997), 23–25.

29. The best source on the Ubico government is probably Grieb, *Guatemalan Caudillo*.

30. Deborah J. Yashar, *Demanding Democracy: Reform and Reaction in Costa Rica and Guatemala, 1870s–1950s* (Stanford: Stanford University Press, 1997), 44–45.

31. Elam, "Appeal to Arms," 55. See also Patricia Parkman, *Nonviolent Insurrection in El Salvador: The Fall of Maximiliano Hernández Martínez* (Tucson: University of Arizona Press, 1988), 25–27; Williams and Walter, *Militarization and Demilitarization*, 26–29; and E. A. Wilson, "Crisis of National Integration," 257–58.

32. Grieb, *Guatemalan Caudillo*, 22–23 (emphasis in original).

33. Ibid., 34.

34. During the 1930s, rice cultivation increased by 700 percent; corn cultivation by 500 percent. Jim Handy, *Gift of the Devil: A History of Guatemala* (Boston: South End Press, 1984), 94.

35. For a discussion, see David McCreery, *Rural Guatemala, 1760–1940* (Stanford: Stanford University Press, 1994), 316–22.

36. Handy argues that coffee planters had come to believe that the debt peonage system was outdated and that they favored a more efficient system. By contrast, Grieb views the abolition of debt peonage as a measure that benefited peasants at the expense of the coffee elite. See Handy, *Gift of the Devil*, 98; and Grieb, *Guatemalan Caudillo*, 38.

37. See the discussion in Yashar, *Demanding Democracy*, 48.

38. Kenneth J. Grieb, "The Guatemalan Military and the Revolution of 1944," *The Americas* 32 (July–April 1975–76): 526. See also Piero Gleijeses, *Shattered Hope: The Guatemalan Revolution and the United States, 1944–1954* (Princeton: Princeton University Press, 1991), 14–16; and Grieb, *Guatemalan Caudillo*, 47.

39. See Grieb, "The Guatemalan Military," 526–27; Grieb, *Guatemalan Caudillo*; and José Luis Cruz Salazar, "El ejército como una fuerza política," *Estudios Sociales* 6 (Guatemala: Universidad Rafael Landívar, 1972): 77.

40. Grieb, *Guatemalan Caudillo*, 45.

41. Grieb, "The Guatemalan Military," 527.

42. Ibid.

43. Parkman, *Nonviolent Insurrection*, 25. Parkman offers an excellent discussion of the position of the dominant class in the Martínez government on pp. 20–25.

44. David Luna, "Análisis de una dictadura fascista Latinoamericana: Maximiliano Hernández Martínez, 1931–1944," *La Universidad*, no. 5 (September–October 1969): 99, 101.

45. For example, Williams and Walter, *Militarization and Demilitarization*, chap. 2. Miguel Marmol presents the view endorsed here, arguing that "Martínez was a one-man dictatorship, not an army dictatorship. [He] never governed with the monolithic support of the army." Quoted in Tommie Sue Montgomery, *Revolution in El Salvador: From Civil Strife to Civil Peace*, 2d ed. (Boulder, Colo.: Westview Press, 1995), 39. See also Elam, "Appeal to Arms," 108.

46. Luna, "Análisis de una dictadura," 94, 98; Elam, "Appeal to Arms," 46–47; Parkman, *Nonviolent Insurrection*, 20–21.

47. See Michael McClintock, *The American Connection*, vol. 1, *State Terror and Popular Resistance in El Salvador* (London: Zed Books, 1985), 127–28; and Elam, "Appeal to Arms," 59–60.

48. This was especially true among junior officers, who were aggrieved by Martínez's politicized promotional system. By contrast, senior officers were more likely to remain loyal. See Parkman, *Nonviolent Insurrection*, 57–58.

49. McClintock, *The American Connection*, 1:127 (emphasis in original).

50. Williams and Walter, *Militarization and Demilitarization*, 25–26.

51. Ching, "Patronage, Politics, and Power," chap. 7.

52. This paragraph and the next two draw heavily on Parkman's excellent

study, *Nonviolent Insurrection,* esp. chaps. 3–6. I also consulted Luna, "Análisis de una dictadura"; Castro Morán, *Función política,* chap. 5; and Williams and Walter, *Militarization and Demilitarization,* 32–33.

53. Elam, "Appeal to Arms," 61–64. See also Alberto Pena Kampy, *"El General Martínez": Un patriarcal presidente dictador* (San Salvador: Editorial Tipográfica Ramírez, 1972), chap. 3.

54. Parkman, *Nonviolent Insurrection.*

55. Ibid., 80.

56. Williams and Walter, *Militarization and Demilitarization,* 33–35.

57. See the brief comment in White, *El Salvador,* 104. Despite these major parallels, no serious comparative study yet exists of the 1940s in Guatemala and El Salvador.

58. Elam, "Appeal to Arms," 87–90.

59. Williams and Walter, *Militarization and Demilitarization,* 33.

60. Elam, "Appeal to Arms," 100–104.

61. McClintock, *The American Connection,* 1:131. For an alternative view of this reform, see the discussion in Elam, "Appeal to Arms," 123–24.

62. Elam, "Appeal to Arms," 115–20. See also Williams and Walter, *Militarization and Demilitarization,* 37–39.

63. See John Holger Peterson, "The Political Role of University Students in Guatemala, 1944–1968" (Ph.D. diss., University of Pittsburgh, 1970), esp. 60–75; Baltasar Morales, *Derrocamiento de una tiranía: La caída de Jorge Ubico* (Guatemala: La Tipografía Nacional de Guatemala, 1958), esp. 41–45; and Manuel Galich, *Del pánico al ataque* (Guatemala: Editorial Universitaria, 1977).

64. On the decision of Ubico to resign, see Grieb, *Guatemalan Caudillo.*

65. Ibid., 275, 276.

66. Grieb, "The Guatemalan Military," 538.

67. Grieb, "The Guatemalan Military." See also Galich, *Del pánico al ataque,* 374–75.

68. For works that emphasize the influence of communists, see Daniel James, *Red Design for the Americas: Guatemalan Prelude* (New York: Day, 1954); and Norman La Charité et al., *Case Studies in Insurgency and Revolutionary Warfare: Guatemala, 1944–1954* (Washington, D.C.: American University, 1964). For critiques of this position, see Susanne Jonas Bodenheimer, *Guatemala: Plan piloto para el continente* (San José: EDUCA, 1981); and Cole Blasier, *The Hovering Giant: U.S. Responses to Revolutionary Change in Latin America, 1910–1985,* rev. ed. (Pittsburgh: University of Pittsburgh Press, 1985), 203.

69. See, for example, Jonas, *Guatemala;* and Stephen Schlesinger and Stephen Kinzer, *Bitter Fruit: The Untold Story of the American Coup in Guatemala* (Garden City, N.Y.: Anchor Books, 1982).

70. See, for example, John F. McCamant, "Intervention in Guatemala: Implications for the Study of Third World Politics," *Comparative Political Studies* 17 (October 1984): 373–407; Gordon L. Bowen, "U.S. Foreign Policy toward

Radical Change: Covert Operations in Guatemala, 1950–1954," *Latin American Perspectives* 36 (winter 1983): 88–102; and Richard H. Immerman, *The CIA in Guatemala: The Foreign Policy of Intervention* (Austin: University of Texas Press, 1982).

71. This position is now supported by most analysts. For several quite different examples that all share this position, see Yashar, *Demanding Democracy;* Susanne Jonas, *The Battle for Guatemala: Rebels, Death Squads, and U.S. Power* (Boulder, Colo.: Westview Press, 1991), 36; Manuel Galich, "Causas internas de una derrota," in Eduardo Antonio Velásquez Carrera, ed., *La revolución de Octubre: Diez años de lucha por la democracia en Guatemala, 1944–1954,* vol. 2 (Guatemala: CEUR, Universidad de San Carlos, 1994); and Jim Handy, *Revolution in the Countryside: Rural Conflict and Agrarian Reform in Guatemala, 1944–1954* (Chapel Hill: University of North Carolina Press, 1994), 179, 203.

72. On the Arévalo administration, see Gleijeses, *Shattered Hope,* chap. 2; Handy, *Gift of the Devil,* chap. 5; Handy, *Revolution in the Countryside,* chap. 2; and the relevant articles in Velásquez Carrera, *La revolución de Octubre.*

73. Bowen, "U.S. Foreign Policy," 88.

74. Illiterate women—usually indigenous women—were excluded from voting. Voting was mandatory for all literate men and was optional for illiterate men and literate women. For a discussion, see Yashar, *Demanding Democracy,* 122.

75. Handy, *Revolution in the Countryside,* 4.

76. The best analysis of the agrarian reform is Handy, *Revolution in the Countryside.* Also useful are Gleijeses, *Shattered Hope,* chap. 8; Piero Gleijeses, "The Agrarian Reform of Jacobo Arbenz," *Journal of Latin American Studies* 21 (October 1989): 451–80; and Robert Wasserstrom, "Revolution in Guatemala: Peasants and Politics under the Arbenz Government," *Comparative Studies in Society and History* 17 (October 1975): 443–78. The general interpretation offered here follows Handy quite closely.

77. A 1950 census found that 72 percent of all agricultural land was controlled by roughly 2 percent of farming units, whereas only 14 percent of the land was controlled by 88 percent of farming units. For further details, see Handy, *Revolution in the Countryside,* 82–83.

78. Ibid., 93–95; quotation from 94–95.

79. Ibid., 169.

80. Ibid., 180.

81. Ibid., 179–90, 239 n. 36.

82. Ibid., 184.

83. Ibid., 187.

84. Gleijeses, "Agrarian Reform," 473.

85. Orlando Salazar Mora, *Política y reforma en Costa Rica, 1914–1958* (San José: Editorial Porvenir, 1981), 62. See also Orlando Salazar Mora, *Crisis liberal y Estado reformista: Análisis político-electoral, 1914–1949* (San José: EDUCA, 1995); Eugenio Rodríguez Vega, *Los días de Don Ricardo* (San José:

Editorial Costa Rica, 1971); and Carlos Monge Alfaro, *Historia de Costa Rica,* 14th ed. (San José: Librería Trejos, 1976), 257–68.

86. In 1932, there was a failed coup—the so-called *bellavistazo*—that developed in response to a division "between factions of the dominant class and liberal parties." See O. Salazar, *Crisis liberal,* 154. The most detailed analysis of the Tinoco dictatorship is Hugo Murillo Jiménez, *Tinoco y los Estados Unidos: Génesis y caída de un régimen* (San José: Editorial Universidad Estatal a Distancia, 1981).

87. O. Salazar, *Política y reforma;* O. Salazar, *Crisis liberal,* chap. 2; Monge, *Historia de Costa Rica,* 266–68; Theodore S. Creedman, "The Political Development of Costa Rica, 1936–1944: Politics of an Emerging Welfare State in a Patriarchal Society" (Ph.D. diss., University of Maryland, 1971), 48.

88. See fig. 6.1.

89. Mario Samper distinguishes between the far less competitive elections before 1914 and the more competitive—though still not democratic—elections after this time. See his article "Fuerzas sociopolíticas y procesos electorales en Costa Rica," *Revista de Historia,* número especial (1988), 164–66. More generally on the electoral system, see O. Salazar, *Crisis liberal,* chaps. 3–4.

90. Fabrice Edouard Lehoucq, "The Origins of Democracy in Costa Rica in Comparative Perspective" (Ph.D. diss., Duke University, 1992), 70–71. See also Creedman, "Political Development of Costa Rica," 46–53.

91. Because these reforms gave opposition groups a greater stake in the system, they may have contributed to a decline in armed violence. See Lehoucq, "Origins of Democracy," chap. 3.

92. Víctor Hugo Acuña Ortega and Iván Molina Jiménez, *Historia económica y social de Costa Rica, 1750–1950* (San José: Editorial Porvenir, 1991), chap. 5.

93. For basic historical background on the Calderón administration, I referred to John Patrick Bell, *Crisis in Costa Rica: The 1948 Revolution* (Austin: Institute of Latin American Studies, University of Texas Press, 1971), chap. 2; Manuel Rojas Bolaños, *Lucha social y guerra civil en Costa Rica* (San José: Editorial Porvenir, 1979); John W. Gardner, "The Costa Rican Junta, 1948–1949" (Ph.D. diss., St. John's University, 1971); Lehoucq, "Origins of Democracy"; Mark Rosenberg, "Social Reform in Costa Rica: Social Security and the Presidency of Rafael Angel Calderón Guardia," *Hispanic American Historical Review* 61 (May 1981): 278–96; O. Salazar, *Crisis liberal;* O. Salazar, *Política y reforma;* and Yashar, *Demanding Democracy.*

94. Rosenberg, "Social Reform in Costa Rica," 284.

95. Ibid., 289.

96. Ibid.; O. Salazar, *Política y reforma,* 91.

97. Creedman, "Political Development of Costa Rica," 119, 141–44; Lehoucq, "Origins of Democracy," chap. 5; O. Salazar, *Política y reforma,* 79–82; and Yashar, *Demanding Democracy,* 74–76.

98. Rosenberg, "Social Reform in Costa Rica," 292. The fact that the Center was primarily a middle-class organization clearly shows that class interests did not fully predict political orientation in Costa Rica.

99. The Church's backing of Calderón reflected the progressive, paternalistic reform program advocated by Archbishop Víctor Sanabria, whose social ideology was probably quite close to Calderón's. In addition, the Church hierarchy included many progressive Catholic reformers who had served in earlier reform movements such as that led by Jorge Volio. Details on the politics of the Church's alliance with Calderón can be found in James Backer, *La iglesia y el sindicalismo en Costa Rica* (San José: Editorial Costa Rica, 1978); and Philip J. Williams, *The Catholic Church and Politics in Nicaragua and Costa Rica* (Pittsburgh: Pittsburgh University Press, 1989).

100. In reaction to the gains that Communists were making in urban areas, President Ricardo Jiménez (1932–36) had banned the Communist Party from overseeing voting polls. Moreover, he made voting obligatory in an attempt "to counter the vote of city workers with votes from the countryside." Bell, *Crisis in Costa Rica*, 13. This move highlights the conservative voting orientation of the Costa Rican peasantry.

101. For a brief account of the development of the Communists before 1949, see Eugene D. Miller, "Labour and the War-Time Alliance in Costa Rica, 1943–1948," *Journal of Latin American Studies* 25 (October 1993): 515–41. On the working class more generally, see Marielos Aguilar H., *Clase trabajadora y organización sindical en Costa Rica, 1943–1971* (San José: Editorial Porvenir, 1989).

102. O. Salazar, *Política y reforma*, 91. See also Yashar, *Demanding Democracy*, 72.

103. Rojas, *Lucha social*, 88.

104. Rosenberg, "Social Reform in Costa Rica," 279.

105. Creedman, "Political Development of Costa Rica," 224; Lehoucq, "Origins of Democracy," 180–84, 187–93.

106. Yashar, *Demanding Democracy*, 172.

107. Oscar Aguilar Bulgarelli, *La constitución de 1949: Antecedentes y proyecciones* (San José: Editorial Costa Rica, 1986), 185. The magnitude of fraud in these elections was probably not great enough to have affected the general outcome. See Lehoucq, "Origins of Democracy," 252–55.

108. The on-again, off-again process through which the opposition united is discussed in Lehoucq, "Origins of Democracy," 215–24.

109. A good discussion is found in Yashar, *Demanding Democracy*, 170–79.

110. Ibid., 179.

111. See the discussion in Lehoucq, "Origins of Democracy," 318–20.

112. O. Salazar, *Política y reforma*, 133.

113. The reasons why the Costa Rican military did not participate have not

been adequately explored in the literature. Schifter and Salazar have independently suggested that the Picado government seemed remarkably unprepared for the war, and the absence of military preparation was a major reason why the government lost the war. Jacobo Schifter, *Las alianzas conflictivas: Las relaciones de Costa Rica y Estados Unidos de la Segunda Guerra Mundial a los inicios de la Guerra Civil* (San José: Libro Libre, 1986), 277; O. Salazar, *Política y reforma,* 133.

114. Yashar, *Demanding Democracy,* 183; Lehoucq, "Origins of Democracy," 3.

115. Too often this division has been reduced to a class-based split among actors of the oligarchy. For example, Orlando Salazar makes this error (*Política y reforma,* 142–43).

116. On the basic points of this agreement, see Gardner, "The Costa Rican Junta," 65–66.

117. Yashar, *Demanding Democracy,* 184.

118. Gardner, "The Costa Rican Junta," 107–8; Jacobo Schifter S., "La democracia en Costa Rica como producto de la neutralización de clases," in Chester Zelaya et al., *¿Democracia en Costa Rica? Cinco opiniones polémicas* (San José: Editorama, 1993), 207; O. Salazar, *Política y reforma,* 154–58.

119. Yashar, *Demanding Democracy,* 187.

120. Cynthia H. Chalker, "Elections and Democracy in Costa Rica," in Mitchell A. Seligson and John A. Booth, eds., *Elections and Democracy in Central America Revisited* (Chapel Hill: University of North Carolina Press, 1995), 106.

121. Yashar, *Demanding Democracy,* 189.

122. Darío A. Euraque, *Reinterpreting the Banana Republic: Region and State in Honduras, 1870–1972* (Chapel Hill: University of North Carolina Press, 1996), 46. See also Theodore P. Wright Jr., "Honduras: A Case Study of United States Support for Free Elections in Central America," *Hispanic American Historical Review* 40 (May 1960): 216–17.

123. Euraque, *Reinterpreting the Banana Republic,* 48.

124. Edward Boatan, quoted in Mario Posas and Rafael del Cid, *La construcción del sector público y del Estado nacional en Honduras, 1876–1979,* 2d ed. (San José: EDUCA, 1983), 71.

125. Charles David Kepner Jr. and Jay Henry Soothill, *The Banana Empire: A Case Study of Economic Imperialism* (New York: Russell & Russell, 1935), 115.

126. This paragraph and the next one draw on Euraque, *Reinterpreting the Banana Republic,* 27–52.

127. Ibid., 37.

128. Marvin A. Barahona, *La hegemonía de los Estados Unidos en Honduras (1907–1932)* (Tegucigalpa: Centro de Documentación de Honduras, 1989), 209–10.

129. Juan Arancibia C., *Honduras: ¿Un Estado nacional?* 2d ed. (Tegucigalpa: Editorial Guaymuras, 1991), 48.

130. Euraque, *Reinterpreting the Banana Republic,* 50.

131. Mario Argueta, *Tiburcio Carías: Anatomía de una época, 1923–1948* (Tegucigalpa: Editorial Guaymuras, 1989), chaps. 2–3; Euraque, *Reinterpreting the Banana Republic,* 55–56.

132. Argueta, *Tiburcio Carías,* 59.

133. Euraque, *Reinterpreting the Banana Republic,* 57–59; Argueta, *Tiburcio Carías,* chap. 6.

134. The class underpinnings of Liberal and Conservative parties in the early twentieth century still need to be clarified. During Zelaya's rule, coffee planters from Managua had become central within the Liberal Party. But histories of the U.S. protectorate years generally assert that Liberals were based primarily in their historic stronghold of León, not Managua. As for the Conservatives, we can be more certain that they continued to maintain a significant support base among wealthy merchants in Granada and among elite coffee families identified with the conservative cause during the Thirty Years period. However, after 1923, they were increasingly split, with one major faction (the Republican Conservatives) drawing at least some support from coffee growers of the northern department of Jinotega.

135. For more detailed historical accounts, see Karl Bermann, *Under the Big Stick: Nicaragua and the United States since 1848* (Boston: South End Press, 1986), chaps. 9–10; John A. Booth, *The End and the Beginning: The Nicaraguan Revolution,* 2d ed. (Boulder, Colo.: Westview Press, 1985), chap. 3; William Kamman, *A Search for Stability: United States Diplomacy toward Nicaragua, 1925–1933* (Notre Dame: University of Notre Dame Press, 1968); Dana G. Munro, *The United States and the Caribbean Republics, 1921–1933* (Princeton: Princeton University Press, 1974), chaps. 5–6; Carlos Quijano, *Nicaragua: Ensayo sobre el imperialismo de los Estados Unidos (1909–1927)* (Managua: Vanguardia, 1987); and Knut Walter, *The Regime of Anastasio Somoza, 1936–1956* (Chapel Hill: University of North Carolina Press, 1993), chaps. 1–2.

136. This paragraph and the next two draw on Bermann, *Under the Big Stick,* 176–84.

137. Two standard works on the Sandino rebellion are Neill Macaulay, *The Sandino Affair* (Chicago: Quadrangle Books, 1971); and Gregorio Selser, *Sandino* (New York: Monthly Review Press, 1981). A good work on the ideology of Sandino is Donald C. Hodges, *Intellectual Foundations of the Nicaraguan Revolution* (Austin: University of Texas Press, 1986), chaps. 1–4.

138. Booth, *The End and the Beginning,* 49.

139. The standard work on the National Guard is Richard Millet, *Guardians of the Dynasty: A History of the U.S. Created Guardia Nacional de Nicaragua and the Somoza Family* (Maryknoll, N.Y.: Orbis Books, 1977). This paragraph draws on esp. pp. 108–20.

140. Ibid., 130.

141. Ibid., 135.

142. This paragraph draws on Millet, *Guardians of the Dynasty,* chaps. 7–8; and Walter, *The Regime of Anastasio Somoza,* chap. 2.

143. Walter, *The Regime of Anastasio Somoza,* 53–58.

CHAPTER NINE: REGIME HERITAGE

1. On land concentration in Costa Rica, see Mitchell A. Seligson, "Agrarian Reform in Costa Rica: The Impact of the Title Security Program," *Inter-American Economic Affairs* 35 (1982): 31–56; and Mario Samper K., "El significado social de la caficultura costarricense y salvadoreña: Análisis histórico comparado a partir de los censos cafetaleros," in Héctor Pérez Brignoli and Mario Samper, eds., *Tierra, café y sociedad* (San José: FLASCO, 1994).

2. Commission for Historical Clarification, "Guatemala: Memory of Silence." This report can be found in English and Spanish on the Internet at <http://hrdata.aaas.org/ceh/report>.

3. This section draws on the following sources for basic data: George Black, with Milton Jamail and Norma Stoltz Chinchilla, *Garrison Guatemala* (New York: Monthly Review Press, 1984); Robert M. Cammack, ed., *Harvest of Violence: The Mayan Indians and the Guatemalan Crisis* (Norman: University of Oklahoma Press, 1988); José Luis Chea, *Guatemala: La cruz fragmentada* (San José: FLASCO, 1988); Shelton H. Davis, "State Violence and Agrarian Crisis in Guatemala," in Martin Diskin, ed., *Trouble in Our Backyard: Central America and the United States in the Eighties* (New York: Pantheon Books, 1983); James Dunkerley, *Power in the Isthmus: A Political History of Modern Central America* (London: Verso, 1988), chap. 9; Jim Handy, *Gift of the Devil: A History of Guatemala* (Boston: South End Press, 1984); Susanne Jonas, *The Battle for Guatemala: Rebels, Death Squads, and U.S. Power* (Boulder, Colo.: Westview Press, 1991); Michael McClintock, *The American Connection,* vol. 2, *State Terror and Popular Resistance in Guatemala* (London: Zed Books, 1985); and Mario Solórzano Martínez, *Guatemala: Autoritarismo y democracia* (San José: EDUCA, 1987).

4. Dunkerley, *Power in the Isthmus,* 430.

5. Commission for Historical Clarification, "Guatemala."

6. Jonas, *The Battle for Guatemala,* 42. See also Miguel Angel Albizures, "Struggles and Experiences of the Guatemalan Trade Union Movement," *Latin American Perspectives* 7 (spring and summer 1980): 145–59.

7. Deborah Levenson-Estrada, *Trade Unionists against Terror: Guatemala City, 1954–1985* (Chapel Hill: University of North Carolina Press, 1994), 8.

8. Edelberto Torres-Rivas, "Guatemala: Crisis and Political Violence," *NACLA* 6 (November–December 1985): 24.

9. Dunkerley, *Power in the Isthmus,* 445. See also Jerry L. Weaver, "Politi-

cal Style of the Guatemalan Military Elite," *Studies in Comparative International Development* 5 (1969–70): 64.

10. Deborah J. Yashar, *Demanding Democracy: Reform and Reaction in Costa Rica and Guatemala, 1870s–1950s* (Stanford: Stanford University Press, 1997), 223; Weaver, "Political Style," 69.

11. On bureaucratic authoritarianism, see Guillermo O'Donnell, *Modernization and Bureaucratic-Authoritarianism: Studies in South American Politics,* Politics of Modernization No. 9 (Berkeley: Institute of International Studies, University of California, Berkeley, 1973); David Collier, ed., *The New Authoritarianism in Latin America* (Princeton: Princeton University Press, 1979); and Gerardo L. Munck, *Authoritarianism and Democratization: Soldiers and Workers in Argentina, 1976–1983* (University Park: Pennsylvania State University Press, 1998).

12. See Hector E. Schamis, "Reconceptualizing Latin American Authoritarianism in the 1970s: From Bureaucratic-Authoritarianism to Neoconservativism," *Comparative Politics* 23 (January 1991): 201–20.

13. See especially McClintock, *The American Connection,* vol. 2.

14. For an excellent multivariate analysis of guerrilla-movement formation in Guatemala and Latin America, see Timothy Wickham-Crowley, *Guerrillas and Revolution in Latin America: A Comparative Study of Insurgents and Regimes since 1956* (Princeton: Princeton University Press, 1992).

15. Robert G. Williams, *Export Agriculture and the Crisis in Central America* (Chapel Hill: University of North Carolina Press, 1986), 189.

16. This section draws on the following studies: Enrique A. Baloyra, *El Salvador in Transition* (Chapel Hill: University of North Carolina Press, 1982), chaps. 1–4; James Dunkerley, *The Long War: Dictatorship and Revolution in El Salvador* (London: Verso, 1982); Robert Varney Elam, "Appeal to Arms: The Army and Politics in El Salvador, 1931–1964" (Ph.D. diss., University of New Mexico, 1968), chap. 9; Michael McClintock, *The American Connection,* vol. 1, *State Terror and Popular Resistance in El Salvador* (London: Zed Books, 1985); Tommie Sue Montgomery, *Revolution in El Salvador: From Civil Strife to Civil Peace,* 2d ed. (Boulder, Colo.: Westview Press, 1995), 43–49; William Stanley, *The Protection Racket State: Elite Politics, Military Extortion, and Civil War in El Salvador* (Philadelphia: Temple University Press, 1996); Roberto Turcios, *Autoritarismo y modernización: El Salvador, 1950–1960* (San Salvador: D. R. Ediciones Tendencias, 1993); and Philip J. Williams and Knut Walter, *Militarization and Demilitarization in El Salvador's Transition to Democracy* (Pittsburgh: University of Pittsburgh Press, 1997).

17. Dunkerley, *Power in the Isthmus,* 351–52.

18. On developmentalism in Latin America, see Kathryn Sikkink, *Ideas and Institutions: Developmentalism in Brazil and Argentina* (Ithaca: Cornell University Press, 1991), chap. 1.

19. Williams and Walter, *Militarization and Demilitarization,* 115.

20. Baloyra, *El Salvador in Transition.*

21. Edward S. Herman and Frank Brodhead, *Demonstration Elections: U.S.-Staged Elections in the Dominican Republic, Vietnam, and El Salvador* (Boston: South End Press, 1984).

22. See especially Williams and Walter, *Militarization and Demilitarization*, 111–13.

23. Wickham-Crowley, *Guerrillas and Revolution*.

24. John A. Booth, "Costa Rican Democracy," in Larry Diamond, ed., *Political Culture and Democracy in Developing Countries* (Boulder, Colo.: Lynne Rienner, 1993). Since 1959, voting has been mandatory, though penalties are not imposed for nonparticipation. Cynthia H. Chalker, "Elections and Democracy in Costa Rica," in Mitchell A. Seligson and John A. Booth, eds., *Elections and Democracy in Central America Revisited* (Chapel Hill: University of North Carolina Press, 1995), 107.

25. Jorge Rovira Mas, *Estado y política económica en Costa Rica, 1948–1970* (San José: Editorial Porvenir, 1988).

26. Chalker, "Elections and Democracy," 108–9.

27. Bruce M. Wilson, *Costa Rica: Politics, Economics, and Democracy* (Boulder, Colo.: Lynne Rienner, 1998), 65; John A. Booth, *Costa Rica: Quest for Democracy* (Boulder, Colo.: Westview Press, 1998), 68; Chalker, "Elections and Democracy," 110–13. The anti-PLN orientation of much of the working class grows out of their identification with Calderón (rather than the PLN forces) during the civil war. Since that time, the PLN's electoral strength has been based on historical party loyalty, rather than socioeconomic factors. See Mitchell A. Seligson, "Costa Rica and Jamaica," in Myron Weiner and Ergun Ozbudun, eds., *Competitive Elections in Developing Countries* (Durham, N.C.: Duke University Press, 1987), 172–73.

28. Anthony Winson, "One Road to Democracy with Development: José Figueres and the Social Democratic Project after 1948," in John M. Kirk and George W. Schuler, eds., *Central America: Democracy, Development, and Change* (New York: Praeger, 1988), 89–100; Yashar, *Demanding Democracy*, 220.

29. Chalker, "Elections and Democracy," 112.

30. Wilson, *Costa Rica*, 96.

31. All statistics are from Luis Garita, "The Bureaucratization of the Costa Rican State," in Marc Edelman and Joanne Kenen, eds., *The Costa Rica Reader* (New York: Grove Weidenfeld, 1989), 139–40; and Dunkerley, *Power in the Isthmus*, 605–6. On state employment, see also Ana Sojo, *Estado empresario y lucha política en Costa Rica* (San José: EDUCA, 1984), 56; and Winson, "One Road to Democracy," 97–98.

32. See Wilson, *Costa Rica*, 54–57.

33. John A. Booth, "Costa Rica: The Roots of Democratic Stability," in Larry Diamond, Juan J. Linz, and Seymour Martin Lipset, eds., *Politics in Developing Countries: Comparing Experiences with Democracy* (Boulder, Colo.: Lynne Rienner, 1990), 404.

34. Chalker, "Elections and Democracy," 114.

35. Ibid., 115, 118.

36. Booth, "Costa Rica," 405.

37. Wilson, Costa Rica, chaps. 5–6.

38. Evelyne Huber, "Options for Social Policy in Latin America: Neoliberal versus Social Democratic Models," in Gosta Esping-Anderson, ed., Welfare States in Transition: National Adaptations in Global Economics (London: Sage Publications, 1996).

39. See figures in Booth, Costa Rica, 167.

40. Mitchell A. Seligson and Miguel Gómez B., "Ordinary Elections in Extraordinary Times: The Political Economy of Voting in Costa Rica," in John A. Booth and Mitchell A. Seligson, eds., Elections and Democracy in Central America (Chapel Hill: University of North Carolina Press, 1989).

41. Unfortunately, very little systematic comparative work has been done on the Ubico, Martínez, Carías, and Somoza dictatorships.

42. The best work on the Carías administration is Mario Argueta, Tiburcio Carías: Anatomía de una época, 1923–1948 (Tegucigalpa: Editorial Guaymuras, 1989). On the historiography of this government, see Darío A. Euraque, "Social, Economic, and Political Aspects of the Carías Dictatorship in Honduras: The Historiography," Latin American Research Review 29, no. 1 (1994): 238–48. The best work on the government of Anastasio Somoza is Knut Walter, The Regime of Anastasio Somoza, 1936–1956 (Chapel Hill: University of North Carolina Press, 1993).

43. The Pro-Patria Party in El Salvador during the Martínez dictatorship may have played a similar role.

44. See Mario Posas, Luchas del movimiento obrero hondureño (San José: EDUCA, 1981); and Darío A. Euraque, Reinterpreting the Banana Republic: Region and State in Honduras, 1870–1972 (Chapel Hill: University of North Carolina Press, 1996), 36–38.

45. Walter, The Regime of Anastasio Somoza, 55–57.

46. Richard Millet, Guardians of the Dynasty: A History of the U.S. Created Guardia Nacional de Nicaragua and the Somoza Family (Maryknoll, N.Y.: Orbis Books, 1977), 198.

47. Euraque, "Social, Economic, and Political Aspects," 245.

48. See Leticia Salomón, Militarismo y reformismo en Honduras (Tegucigalpa: Editorial Guaymuras, 1982); Matías Funes h., Los deliberantes: El poder militar en Honduras (Tegucigalpa: Editorial Guaymuras, 1995), 134–45; and Argueta, Tiburcio Carías, chap. 8.

49. An especially good analysis of Somoza's state-building activities is found in Walter, The Regime of Anastasio Somoza.

50. Euraque, Reinterpreting the Banana Republic, 69.

51. This paragraph draws on Walter, The Regime of Anastasio Somoza, chap. 4.

52. Euraque, *Reinterpreting the Banana Republic,* 69.

53. Ibid.

54. Mark B. Rosenberg, "Can Democracy Survive the Democrats? From Transition to Consolidation in Honduras," in Booth and Seligson, *Elections and Democracy in Central America,* 41–42.

55. In making this argument, I draw on the descriptions of the Honduran political system offered in James A. Morris, *Honduras: Caudillo Politics and Military Rulers* (Boulder, Colo.: Westview Press, 1984); and Donald E. Schulz and Deborah Sundloff Schulz, *The United States, Honduras, and the Crisis in Central America* (Boulder, Colo.: Westview Press, 1994).

56. Schulz and Schulz, *The United States,* 316. See also the excellent studies of J. Mark Ruhl, "Agrarian Structure and Political Stability in Honduras," *Journal of Latin American Studies and World Affairs* 26 (February 1984): 33–68; and Rachel Sieder, "Honduras: The Politics of Exception and Military Reformism (1972–1978)," *Journal of Latin American Studies* 27, pt. 1 (February 1995): 99–127.

57. Schulz and Schulz, *The United States,* 41.

58. Ibid., 319.

59. On the family dynasty, see especially John A. Booth, *The End and the Beginning: The Nicaraguan Revolution,* 2d ed. (Boulder, Colo.: Westview Press, 1985), chap. 5.

60. I derive this interpretation from Thomas Walker, *Nicaragua: The Land of Sandino* (Boulder, Colo.: Westview Press, 1986), 29.

61. Shirley Christian, *Nicaragua: Revolution in the Family* (New York: Random House, 1985), 24.

62. Millet, *Guardians of the Dynasty,* 229.

63. Booth, *The End and the Beginning,* 54–57, 91–93; Millet, *Guardians of the Dynasty,* chap. 9.

64. Richard Snyder, "Explaining Transitions from Neopatrimonial Dictatorships," *Comparative Politics* 24 (1992): 379–99; Wickham-Crowley, *Guerrillas and Revolution,* esp. chaps. 11–12.

65. A huge literature—much of it journalistic—offers assessments of the Central American crisis of the 1980s. A voluminous literature has also developed around the role of the United States during the crisis period. For books in English on these subjects, see Cynthia J. Arnson, *Crossroads: Congress, the President, and Central America, 1976–1993,* 2d ed. (University Park: Pennsylvania State University Press, 1993); Edward Best, *U.S. Policy and Regional Security in Central America* (New York: St. Martin's Press, 1987); Morris J. Blachman, William M. LeoGrande, and Kenneth Sharpe, eds., *Confronting Revolution: Security through Diplomacy in Central America* (New York: Pantheon, 1986); Roger Burbach and Patricia Flynn, *The Politics of Intervention: The United States in Central America* (New York: Monthly Review Press, 1984); Thomas Carothers, *In the Name of Democracy: U.S. Policy toward Latin America in the*

Reagan Years (Berkeley: University of California Press, 1991); Kenneth Coleman and George Herring, eds., *Understanding the Central American Crisis* (Wilmington, Del.: Scholarly Resource Books, 1991); Giuseppe Di Palma and Laurence Whitehead, eds., *The Central American Impasse* (New York: St. Martin's Press, 1986); Martin Diskin, ed., *Trouble in Our Backyard: Central America and the United States in the Eighties* (New York: Pantheon Books, 1983); Marlene Dixon and Susanne Jonas, *Revolution and Intervention in Central America* (San Francisco: Synthesis Publications, 1983); Richard Fagen, *Forging Peace: The Challenge of Central America* (New York: Basil Blackwell, 1987); Mark Falcoff and Robert Royal, ed., *The Continuing Crisis: U.S. Policy in Central America and the Caribbean* (Washington, D.C.: Ethics and Public Policy Center, 1986); Richard Feinberg, *Central America: International Dimensions of the Crisis* (New York: Holmes & Meier, 1982); Marvin E. Gettleman et al., eds., *El Salvador: Central America in the New Cold War* (New York: Grove Weidenfeld, 1986); Roy Gutman, *Banana Diplomacy: The Making of American Foreign Policy in Nicaragua, 1981–1987* (New York: Simon & Schuster, 1988); Nora Hamilton et al., eds., *Crisis in Central America: Regional Dynamics and U.S. Policy in the 1980s* (Boulder, Colo.: Westview Press, 1984); Richard Harris and Carlos M. Vilas, *Nicaragua: A Revolution under Siege* (London: Zed Books, 1985); George Irvin and Xavier Gorostiaga, eds., *Towards an Alternative for Central America and the Caribbean* (London: George Allen & Unwin, 1985); Robert S. Leiken, ed., *Central America: Anatomy of a Conflict* (New York: Pergamon Press, 1984); Robert S. Leiken and Barry Rubin, eds., *The Central American Crisis Reader* (New York: Summit Books, 1987); Thomas M. Leonard, *Central America and the United States: The Search for Stability* (Athens: University of Georgia Press, 1991); Abraham F. Lowenthal, ed., *Exporting Democracy: The United States and Latin America* (Baltimore: Johns Hopkins University Press, 1991); Darío Moreno, *U.S. Policy in Central America: The Endless Debate* (Miami: Florida International University Press, 1990); Jack Nelson-Pallmeyer, *War against the Poor: Low-Intensity Conflict and Christian Faith* (Maryknoll, N.Y.: Orbis Books, 1989); Steve C. Ropp and James A. Morris, eds., *Central America: Crisis and Adaptation* (Albuquerque: University of New Mexico Press, 1984); Stanford Central America Action Network, *Revolution in Central America* (Boulder, Colo.: Westview Press, 1983); Washington Institute Task Force on Central America, *Central America in Crisis* (Washington, D.C.: Washington Institute for Values in Public Policy, 1984); Howard J. Wiarda, ed., *Rift and Revolution: The Central American Imbroglio* (Washington, D.C.: American Enterprise Institute, 1984); and Ralph Lee Woodward Jr., ed., *Central America: Historical Perspectives on the Contemporary Crisis* (New York: Greenwood Press, 1988). A gigantic literature is also specifically focused on the Nicaraguan Revolution of 1979. For an entry into the scores of works on the subject, see Ralph Lee Woodward Jr., comp., *Nicaragua* (Oxford: Clio, 1994).

66. R. G. Williams, *Export Agriculture,* 189.

67. In addition to R. G. Williams, *Export Agriculture*—which is probably the single best work on the Central American crisis—see also John A. Booth and Thomas W. Walker, *Understanding Central America* (Boulder, Colo.: Westview Press, 1989); Jan L. Flora and Edelberto Torres-Rivas, "Sociology of Developing Societies: Historical Bases of Insurgency in Central America," in Flora and Torres-Rivas, eds., *Sociology of "Developing Societies": Central America* (New York: Monthly Review Press, 1989); Peter H. Smith, "The Origins of the Crisis," in Blachman, LeoGrande, and Sharpe, *Confronting Revolution;* and Carlos M. Vilas, *Between Earthquakes and Volcanoes: Market, State, and the Revolutions in Central America* (New York: Monthly Review Press, 1995), chap. 3.

68. This paragraph draws on insights from the literature on Third World revolutions. See John Foran, ed., *Theorizing Revolutions* (London: Routledge Press, 1997); Jeff Goodwin, *No Other Way Out: State and Revolution, 1945–1991* (Cambridge: Cambridge University Press, 2001); and Wickham-Crowley, *Guerrillas and Revolution.*

69. Manus I. Midlarsky and Kenneth Roberts, "Class, State, and Revolution in Central America: Nicaragua and El Salvador Compared," *Journal of Conflict Resolution* 29 (June 1985): 163–93; Ruhl, "Agrarian Structure."

70. For a similar argument, see Sieder, "Honduras," 113.

71. The transition to democracy in Central America is beginning to receive systematic comparative attention. See, for example, Einar Berntzen, "Democratic Consolidation in Central America: A Qualitative Comparative Approach," *Third World Quarterly* 14 (1993): 589–604; Booth and Seligson, *Elections and Democracy in Central America;* Jorge I. Domínguez and Marc Lindenberg, eds., *Democratic Transitions in Central America and Panama* (Boston: World Peace Foundation, 1993); Jorge I. Domínguez and Abraham F. Lowenthal, eds., *Constructing Democratic Governance: Mexico, Central America, and the Caribbean in the 1990s* (Baltimore: Johns Hopkins University Press, 1996); Seligson and Booth, *Elections and Democracy in Central America, Revisited;* Edelberto Torres-Rivas, "Authoritarian Transition to Democracy in Central America," in Jan L. Flora and Edelberto Torres-Rivas, eds., *Sociology of "Developing Societies": Central America* (New York: Monthly Review Press, 1989); and Carlos M. Vilas, "Prospects for Democratisation in a Post-revolutionary Setting: Central America," *Journal of Latin American Studies* 28 (May 1996): 461–503.

72. On this perspective, see Richard Snyder and James Mahoney, "The Missing Variable: Institutions and the Study of Regime Change," *Comparative Politics* 32 (October 1999): 103–22.

73. Samuel Huntington, *The Third Wave: Democratization in the Late Twentieth Century* (Norman: University of Oklahoma Press, 1991), 98.

74. Jeffery M. Paige, *Coffee and Power: Revolution and the Rise of Democracy in Central America* (Cambridge: Harvard University Press, 1997), 316.

75. Vilas, "Prospects for Democratisation," 476, 479. This theme is developed in many of the works cited in n. 65 above.

76. Vilas, "Prospects for Democratisation," 463, offers a refreshing commentary from a Marxist political-economy perspective on this point.

77. An especially good account of the Sandinista regime is Dennis Gilbert, *Sandinistas: The Party and the Revolution* (Cambridge: Basil Blackwell, 1988). On the 1990 transition and subsequent events, see Thomas W. Walker, ed., *Nicaragua without Illusions: Regime Transition and Structural Adjustment in the 1990s* (Wilmington, Del.: Scholarly Resources, 1997).

78. On the Honduran transition, see J. Mark Ruhl, "Honduras: Militarism and Democratization in Troubled Waters," in Thomas Walker and Ariel C. Armony, eds., *Repression, Resistance, and Democratic Transition in Central America* (Wilmington, Del.: Scholarly Resources, 2000); Mark B. Rosenberg, "Honduran Scorecard: Military and Democrats in Central America," *Caribbean Review* 12 (winter 1983): 3–19; Mark B. Rosenberg, "Honduras: An Introduction," in Mark B. Rosenberg and Philip H. Shepherd, eds., *Honduras Confronts Its Future* (Boulder, Colo.: Lynne Rienner, 1986); and Schulz and Schulz, *The United States.*

79. The expression "hovering giant" is from Cole Blasier's classic study, *The Hovering Giant: U.S. Responses to Revolutionary Change in Latin America, 1910–1985,* rev. ed. (Pittsburgh: University of Pittsburgh Press, 1985).

80. Paige, *Coffee and Power,* 336.

CHAPTER TEN: CONCLUSION

1. Barrington Moore Jr., *Social Origins of Dictatorship and Democracy: Lord and Peasant in the Making of the Modern World* (Boston: Beacon Press, 1966); Gregory M. Luebbert, *Liberalism, Fascism, or Social Democracy: Social Classes and the Political Origins of Regimes in Interwar Europe* (New York: Oxford University Press, 1991); Ruth Berins Collier and David Collier, *Shaping the Political Arena: Critical Junctures, the Labor Movement, and Regime Dynamics in Latin America* (Princeton: Princeton University Press, 1991).

2. Moore, *Social Origins,* xi.

3. Ibid., 430–31.

4. Ibid., 433–38.

5. Ibid., chap. 9.

6. Jeffery M. Paige, *Coffee and Power: Revolution and the Rise of Democracy in Central America* (Cambridge: Harvard University Press, 1997); Lowell Gudmundson, "Lord and Peasant in the Making of Modern Central America," in Evelyne Huber and Frank Safford, eds., *Agrarian Structure and Political Power* (Pittsburgh: University of Pittsburgh Press, 1995); Dietrich Rueschemeyer, Evelyne Huber Stephens, and John D. Stephens, *Capitalist Development and Democracy* (Chicago: University of Chicago Press, 1992).

7. Paige, *Coffee and Power.*

8. Rueschemeyer, Stephens, and Stephens, *Capitalist Development and Democracy.*

9. On democratization in Britain, see Ruth Berins Collier, *Paths toward Democracy: The Working Class and Elites in Western Europe and South America* (New York: Cambridge University Press, 1999), 61–66. On democratization in Chile, see J. Samuel Valenzuela, "Class Relations and Democratization: A Reassessment of Barrington Moore's Model," in Miguel Angel Centeno and Fernando López-Alves, eds., *The Other Mirror: Grand Theory through the Lens of Latin America* (Princeton: Princeton University Press, 2000).

10. See especially Paige, *Coffee and Power,* 326–29.

11. For a balanced assessment of the Sandinista Revolution, see Dennis Gilbert, *Sandinistas: The Party and the Revolution* (Cambridge: Basil Blackwell, 1988).

12. See Moore, *Social Origins,* xvi, chap. 6, and the concluding remarks on India in chaps. 7–9.

13. Ibid., 316, 353–70.

14. Luebbert summarizes his argument in chapter 1 of *Liberalism, Fascism, or Social Democracy.* See also the summary in Thomas Ertman, "Democracy and Dictatorship in Interwar Western Europe Revisited," *World Politics* 50 (April 1998): 493–97.

15. Luebbert, *Liberalism, Fascism, or Social Democracy,* 308–9.

16. Andrew C. Gould, *The Origins of Liberal Dominance: State, Church, and Party in Nineteenth-Century Europe* (Ann Arbor: University of Michigan Press, 1999).

17. Collier and Collier, *Shaping the Political Arena,* chap. 4.

18. Ibid., 750.

19. Ibid., 769.

20. Evelyne Huber Stephens, "Capitalist Development and Democracy in South America," *Politics and Society* 17, no. 3 (1989): 281–352.

21. Seymour Martin Lipset and Stein Rokkan, "Cleavage Structures, Party Systems, and Voter Alignments: An Introduction," in Seymour Martin Lipset and Stein Rokkan, eds., *Party Systems and Voter Alignments: Cross-National Perspectives* (New York: Free Press, 1967), 47–50; Timothy R. Scully, *Rethinking the Center: Party Politics in Nineteenth and Twentieth Century Chile* (Stanford: Stanford University Press, 1992).

22. On the neoliberal project in Central America, see Victor Bulmer-Thomas, "The Balance of Payments Crisis and Adjustment Programmes in Central America," in Rosemary Thorp and Laurence Whitehead, eds., *Latin American Debt and the Adjustment Crisis* (Pittsburgh: University of Pittsburgh Press, 1987); Victor Bulmer-Thomas, *The Political Economy of Central America since 1920* (Cambridge: Cambridge University Press, 1987); James Dunkerley, *The Pacification of Central America* (London: Verso, 1994); Jolyne

Melmed-Sanjak, Carlos E. Santiago, and Alvin Magid, eds., *Recovery or Relapse in the Global Economy: Comparative Perspectives on Restructuring in Central America* (Westport, Conn.: Praeger, 1993); and Wim Pelupessy and John Weeks, *Economic Maladjustment in Central America* (New York: St. Martin's Press, 1993).

SELECT BIBLIOGRAPHY OF WORKS ON CENTRAL AMERICAN POLITICS AND HISTORY

The following bibliography lists the major studies of Central American history and politics that I consulted in developing the argument of this book. The various works on theory and method cited in the notes to Part I and the Conclusion are not included here; nor have I listed the primary source documents and general works on Latin American history found in the notes for Part III.

Acuña Ortega, Víctor Hugo. "La ideología de los pequeños y medianos productores cafetaleros costarricenses (1900–1961)." *Avances de Investigación* 23 (1987): 1–19.

———. "Clases subalternas y movimientos sociales en Centroamérica (1870–1930)." In *Historia general de Centroamérica,* vol. 4, *Las repúblicas agroexportadoras,* edited by Víctor Hugo Acuña Ortega. Madrid: FLASCO, 1993.

———, ed. *Historia general de Centroamérica.* Vol. 4, *Las repúblicas agroexportadoras.* Madrid: FLASCO, 1993.

Acuña Ortega, Víctor Hugo, and Iván Molina Jiménez. *Historia económica y social de Costa Rica, 1750–1950.* San José: Editorial Porvenir, 1991.

Aguilar Bulgarelli, Oscar. *Costa Rica y sus hechos políticos de 1948: Problemática de una decada.* San José: Progreso Editorial, 1983.

———. *La constitución de 1949: Antecedentes y proyecciones.* San José: Editorial Costa Rica, 1986.

Aguilar H., Marielos. *Clase trabajadora y organización sindical en Costa Rica, 1943–1971.* San José: Editorial Porvenir, 1989.

Aguilera, Gabriel. "The Development of Military Autonomy and Corporateness in Central America." In *Democracy under Siege: New Military Power in Latin America,* edited by Augusto Varas. New York: Greenwood Press, 1989.

Albizures, Miguel Angel. "Struggles and Experiences of the Guatemalan Trade Union Movement." *Latin American Perspectives* 7 (spring and summer 1980): 145–59.

Alvarenga, Patricia. "Reshaping the Ethics of Power: A History of Violence in Western Rural El Salvador, 1880–1932." Ph.D. diss., University of Wisconsin, Madison, 1994.

———. *Cultura y ética de la violencia: El Salvador, 1880–1932.* San José: EDUCA, 1996.

———. "Auxiliary Forces in the Shaping of the Repressive System: El Salvador, 1880–1930." In *Identity and Struggle at the Margins of the Nation-State: The Laboring People of Central America and the Hispanic Caribbean,* edited by Aviva Chomsky and Aldo Lauria-Santiago. Durham, N.C.: Duke University Press, 1998.

Alvarenga Venutolo, Patricia. "Las explotaciones agropecuarias en los albores de la expansión cafetalera." *Revista de Historia* 14 (July–December 1986): 115–31.

Àlvarez Montalván, Emilio. *Las fuerzas armadas en Nicaragua: Sinopsis histórica, 1821–1994.* Managua: Edición Jorge Eduardo Arellano, 1994.

Amador, Armando. *Un siglo de lucha de los trabajadores en Nicaragua.* Managua: Centro de Investigación de la Realidad de America Latina, 1990.

Amurrio, Jesús Julián. *El positivismo en Guatemala.* Guatemala: Universidad de San Carlos, 1970.

Anderson, Charles W. "El Salvador: The Army as Reformer." In *Political Systems of Latin America,* edited by Martin C. Needler. Princeton: D. Van Nostrand Company, 1964.

Anderson, Ken, and Jean-Marie Simon. "Permanent Insurgency in Guatemala." *Telos* 73 (fall 1987): 9–46.

Anderson, Thomas P. *Matanza.* 2d ed. Willimantic, Conn.: Curbstone Press, 1992. Originally published in 1971.

———. *Politics in Central America: Guatemala, El Salvador, Honduras, and Nicaragua.* Rev. ed. New York: Praeger, 1988.

Andino Martínez, Carlos. "El estamento militar en El Salvador." *Estudios Centroamericanos* 34 (1970): 615–30.

Aquino, Enrique. *La personalidad del General José Santos Zelaya.* Managua: Talleres Gráficos Pérez, 1944.

Arancibia C., Juan. *Honduras: ¿Un Estado nacional?* 2d ed. Tegucigalpa: Editorial Guaymuras, 1991.

Araya Pochet, Carlos. "La minería y sus relaciones con la acumulación de capital y la clase dirigente de Costa Rica, 1821–1841." *Estudios Sociales Centroamericanos* 5 (May–August 1973): 31–64.

———. *Historia económica de Costa Rica: 1821–1971.* San José: Editorial Fernández-Arce, 1982.

———. "Esbozo histórico de la institución del sufragio en Costa Rica." In *Desarrollo institucional de Costa Rica (1523–1914),* edited by Paulino González Villalobos. San José: SECASA, 1983.

Arellano, Jorge Eduardo. *Breve historia de la iglesia en Nicaragua (1523–1979).* Managua: CEHILA, 1980.

Argueta, Mario. *Historia laboral de Honduras: De la conquista al siglo XIX.* Tegucigalpa: Imprenta Offset/Cultura y Turismo de la República de Honduras, 1985.

———. *Bananos y política: Samuel Zemurray y la Cuyamel Fruit Company en Honduras.* Tegucigalpa: Editorial Universitaria, 1989.

———. *Tiburcio Carías: Anatomía de una época, 1923–1948.* Tegucigalpa: Editorial Guaymuras, 1989.

———. *Diccionario histórico-biográfico hondureño.* Tegucigalpa: Editorial Universitaria, 1990.

Arnson, Cynthia J. *Crossroads: Congress, the President, and Central America, 1976–1993.* 2d ed. University Park: Pennsylvania State University Press, 1993.

Backer, James. *La iglesia y el sindicalismo en Costa Rica.* San José: Editorial Costa Rica, 1978.

Baires, Sonia, and Mario Lungo. "San Salvador (1880–1930): La lenta consolidación de la capital salvadoreña." *Anuario de Estudios Centroamericanos* 7 (1981): 71–83.

Baloyra, Enrique A. *El Salvador in Transition.* Chapel Hill: University of North Carolina Press, 1982.

Baloyra-Herp, Enrique A. "Reactionary Despotism in Central America." *Journal of Latin American Studies* 15, pt. 2 (1983): 295–319.

Bancroft, Hubert Howe. *History of Central America.* Vol. 3. San Francisco: The History Company, 1887.

Baquero, Sara L. *Gobernantes de Nicaragua.* Managua: Tipografía Gordillo, 1937.

Barahona, Amaru. *Estudio sobre la historia de Nicaragua: Del auge cafetalero al triunfo de la revolución.* Managua: INIES, 1989.

Barahona, Marvin A. *La hegemonía de los Estados Unidos en Honduras (1907–1932).* Tegucigalpa: Centro de Documentación de Honduras, 1989.

———. *La evolución histórica de la identidad nacional.* Tegucigalpa: Editorial Guaymuras, 1991.

Bardales Bueso, Rafael. *Imagen de un líder: Manuel Bonilla.* Tegucigalpa: Editorial Universitaria, 1985.

Barón Castro, Rodolfo. *La población de El Salvador: Estudio acerca de su desenvolvimiento desde la época prehispánica hasta nuestros días.* Madrid: Consejo Superior de Investigaciones Científicas, 1942.

Barry, Tom. *Roots of Rebellion: Land and Hunger in Central America.* Boston: South End Press, 1987.

Barry, Tom, Beth Wood, and Deb Preusch. *Dollars and Dictators: A Guide to Central America.* New York: Grove Press, 1983.

Bell, John Patrick. *Crisis in Costa Rica: The 1948 Revolution.* Austin: Institute of Latin American Studies, University of Texas Press, 1971.

Belli, Humberto. "Un ensayo de interpretación sobre las luchas políticas nicaragüenses (de la independencia hasta la Revolución Cubana)." *Revista del Pensamiento Centroamericano* 32 (October–December 1977): 50–59.

Bermann, Karl. *Under the Big Stick: Nicaragua and the United States since 1848.* Boston: South End Press, 1986.

Berntzen, Einar. "Democratic Consolidation in Central America: A Qualitative Comparative Approach." *Third World Quarterly* 14 (1993): 589–604.

Best, Edward. *U.S. Policy and Regional Security in Central America.* New York: St. Martin's Press, 1987.

Bethell, Leslie, ed. *Central America since Independence.* Cambridge: Cambridge University Press, 1991.

Biderman, Jaime. "Class Structure, the State, and Capitalist Development in Nicaraguan Agriculture." Ph.D. diss., University of California, Berkeley, 1982.

————. "The Development of Capitalism in Nicaragua: A Political Economic History." *Latin American Perspectives* 10 (1983): 7–32.

Bingham, James Wesley. "Guatemalan Agriculture during the Administration of President Manuel Estrada Cabrera, 1898–1920." Master's thesis, Tulane University, 1974.

Blachman, Morris J., William M. LeoGrande, and Kenneth Sharpe, eds. *Confronting Revolution: Security through Diplomacy in Central America.* New York: Pantheon, 1986.

Black, George. *Triumph of the People: The Sandinista Revolution in Nicaragua.* London: Zed Books, 1981.

————. "Central America: Crisis in the Backyard." *New Left Review* 135 (September–October 1982): 5–34.

Black, George, with Milton Jamail and Norma Stoltz Chinchilla. *Garrison Guatemala.* New York: Monthly Review Press, 1984.

Blanco Segura, Ricardo. *Historia eclesiástica de Costa Rica, 1502–1850.* San José: Editorial Universidad Estatal a Distancia, 1983.

Blasier, Cole. *The Hovering Giant: U.S. Responses to Revolutionary Change in Latin America, 1910–1985.* Rev. ed. Pittsburgh: University of Pittsburgh Press, 1985.

Booth, John A. *The End and the Beginning: The Nicaraguan Revolution.* 2d ed. Boulder, Colo.: Westview Press, 1985.

————. "Costa Rica: The Roots of Democratic Stability." In *Politics in Developing Countries: Comparing Experiences with Democracy,* edited by Larry Diamond, Juan J. Linz, and Seymour Martin Lipset. Boulder, Colo.: Lynne Rienner, 1990.

————. "Socioeconomic and Political Roots of National Revolts in Central America." *Latin American Research Review* 26 (1991): 33–73.

————. "Costa Rican Democracy." In *Political Culture and Democracy in Developing Countries,* edited by Larry Diamond. Boulder, Colo.: Lynne Rienner, 1993.

————. *Costa Rica: Quest for Democracy.* Boulder, Colo.: Westview Press, 1998.

Booth, John A., and Mitchell A. Seligson, eds. *Elections and Democracy in Central America.* Chapel Hill: University of North Carolina Press, 1989.

Booth, John A., and Thomas W. Walker. *Understanding Central America.* Boulder, Colo.: Westview Press, 1989.

Bourgois, Philippe I. *Ethnicity at Work: Divided Labor on a Central American Banana Plantation.* Baltimore: Johns Hopkins University Press, 1989.

Bowen, Gordon L. "U.S. Foreign Policy toward Radical Change: Covert Operations in Guatemala, 1950–1954." *Latin American Perspectives* 36 (winter 1983): 88–102.

Brand, Charles Abbey. "The Background to Capitalistic Underdevelopment: Honduras to 1913." Ph.D. diss., University of Pittsburgh, 1972.

Brockett, Charles D. "The Commercialization of Agriculture and Rural Economic Insecurity: The Case of Honduras." *Studies in Comparative International Development* 32 (spring 1987): 82–102.

———. 1988. *Land, Power, and Poverty: Agrarian Transformation and Political Conflict in Central America.* Boston: Unwin Hyman.

Browning, David. *El Salvador: Landscape and Society.* Oxford: Clarendon Press, 1971.

Bulmer-Thomas, Victor. "Economic Development over the Long Run—Central America since 1920." *Journal of Latin American Studies* 15 (1983): 269–94.

———. "The Balance of Payments Crisis and Adjustment Programmes in Central America." In *Latin American Debt and the Adjustment Crisis,* edited by Rosemary Thorp and Laurence Whitehead. Pittsburgh: University of Pittsburgh Press, 1987.

———. *The Political Economy of Central America since 1920.* Cambridge: Cambridge University Press, 1987.

———. "La crisis de la economía de agroexportación: 1930–1945." In *Historia general de Centroamérica,* vol. 4, *Las repúblicas agroexportadoras,* edited by Víctor Hugo Acuña Ortega. Madrid: FLASCO, 1993.

Burbach, Roger, and Patricia Flynn. *The Politics of Intervention: The United States in Central America.* New York: Monthly Review Press, 1984.

Burgess, Paul. *Justo Rufino Barrios: A Biography.* Philadelphia: Dorrance & Company, 1926.

Burns, E. Bradford. *The Poverty of Progress: Latin America in the Nineteenth Century.* Berkeley: University of California Press, 1980.

———. "The Modernization of Underdevelopment: El Salvador, 1858–1931." *Journal of Developing Areas* 18 (April 1984): 293–316.

———. "The Intellectual Infrastructure of Modernization in El Salvador, 1870–1900." *The Americas* 41 (January 1985): 57–82.

———. *Patriarch and Folk: The Emergence of Nicaragua, 1798–1858.* Cambridge: Harvard University Press, 1991.

Busey, James L. "The Presidents of Costa Rica." *The Americas* 18 (July 1961): 55–70.

Bushnell, David, and Neill Macaulay. *The Emergence of Latin America in the Nineteenth Century.* 2d ed. New York: Oxford University Press, 1994.

Bustamante, Gregorio. *Historia militar de El Salvador: Desde la independencia de Centro América, hasta nuestros días (1821–1935).* San Salvador: Talleres Gráficos Cisneros, 1935.

Cáceres Lara, Victor. *Gobernantes de Honduras en el siglo 19.* Tegucigalpa: Banco Central de Honduras, 1978.

Calderón Hernández, Manuel. "Proceso y estructura del liberalismo en Costa Rica, 1821–1940." In *Desarrollo institucional de Costa Rica (de las sociedades indígenas a la crisis del 30),* edited by Jaime Murillo. San José: EDUCA, 1991.

Cambranes, Julio Castellanos. "Origins of the Crisis of the Established Order in Guatemala." In *Central America: Crisis and Adaptation,* edited by Steve C. Ropp and James A. Morris. Albuquerque: University of New Mexico Press, 1984.

———. *Coffee and Peasants: The Origins of the Modern Plantation Economy in Guatemala, 1853–1897.* English version revised by Carla Clason-Hook. Stockholm: Institute of Latin American Studies, University of Stockholm, 1985.

Cammack, Robert M., ed. *Harvest of Violence: The Mayan Indians and the Guatemalan Crisis.* Norman: University of Oklahoma Press, 1988.

Cardenal, Rodolfo. *El poder eclesiástico en El Salvador, 1871–1931.* San Salvador: UCA Editores, 1980.

———. *Manual de historia de Centroamérica.* San Salvador: Universidad Centroamericana, n.d.

Cardoso, Ciro Flamarion Santana. "Historia económica del café en Centroamérica (siglo XIX): Estudio comparativo." *Estudios Sociales Centroamericanos* 4 (January–April 1975): 9–55.

———. "Características básicas de la economía latinoamericana (siglo XIX): Algunos problemas de la transición neo-colonial." *Revista de Historia* 4 (January–June 1977): 47–76.

———. "The Formation of the Coffee Estate in Nineteenth-Century Costa Rica." In *Land and Labour in Latin America,* edited by Kenneth Duncan and Ian Rutledge, with the collaboration of Collin Harding. Cambridge: Cambridge University Press, 1977.

———. "The Liberal Era, c. 1870–1930." In *Central America since Independence,* edited by Leslie Bethell. Cambridge: Cambridge University Press, 1991.

Cardoso, Ciro F. S., and Héctor Pérez Brignoli. *Centroamérica y la economía occidental, 1520–1930.* San José: EDUCA, 1977.

Cardoza y Aragón, Luis. "Guatemala y el imperio bananero." *Cuadernos Americanos* 74 (1954): 19–45.

Carías, Marcos, ed. *Ramón Rosa: Obra escogida.* Tegucigalpa: Editorial Guaymuras, 1980.

Carmack, Robert M. "Spanish-Indian Relations in Highland Guatemala, 1800–1944." In *Spaniards and Indians in Southeastern Mesoamerica: Essays on the History of Ethnic Relations,* edited by Murdo J. MacLeod and Robert Wasserstrom. Lincoln: University of Nebraska Press, 1983.

Carothers, Thomas. *In the Name of Democracy: U.S. Policy toward Latin America in the Reagan Years.* Berkeley: University of California Press, 1991.

Castrillo Gámez, Manuel. *Reseña histórica de Nicaragua: Comprende desde el año 1887 hasta fines de 1895.* Managua: Talleres Nacionales, 1963.

Castro López, Guillermo de Jesús. "Historia económica de Nicaragua (período 1887–1899)." Licenciado en Economía, Universidad Nacional Autónoma de Nicaragua, Managua, 1971.

Castro Morán, Mariano. *Función política del ejército salvadoreño en el presente siglo.* San Salvador: UCA Editores, 1984.

Castro Sánchez, Silvia. "Estado, privatización de la tierra y conflictos agrarios." *Revista de Historia* 21–22 (January–December 1990): 207–30.

Cazali Ávila, Augusto. "El desarrollo del cultivo del café y su influencia en el régimen del trabajo agrícola: Época de la reforma liberal (1871–1885)." *Anuario de Estudios Centroamericanos* 2 (May 1976): 35–93.

Cerdas Albertazzi, Ana Luisa. "El surgimiento del enclave bananero en el Pacífico sur." *Revista de Historia* 28 (1993): 117–59.

Cerdas Albertazzi, Ana Luisa, and Gerardo A. Vargas Cambronero. *La abolición del ejército en Costa Rica: Hito de un camino de democracia y paz.* San José: Comisión Nacional de Conmemoraciones Históricos, 1988.

Cerdas Cruz, Rodolfo. *Formación del Estado en Costa Rica.* 2d ed. San José: EDUCA, 1978.

———. "Costa Rica since 1930." In *Central America since Independence,* edited by Leslie Bethell. Cambridge: Cambridge University Press, 1991.

Chalker, Cynthia H. "Elections and Democracy in Costa Rica." In *Elections and Democracy in Central America Revisited,* edited by Mitchell A. Seligson and John A. Booth. Chapel Hill: University of North Carolina Press, 1995.

Chamorro, Diego Manuel. "El conservatismo de los años '30.'" *Revista Conservadora del Pensamiento Centroamericano* 51 (1964): 35–36.

Chamorro, Pedro Joaquín. *Historia de la Federación de la América Central, 1823–1840.* Madrid: Ediciones Cultura Hispánica, 1951.

Charlip, Julie A. "Cultivating Coffee: Farmers, Land, and Money in Nicaragua, 1877–1930." Ph.D. diss., University of California, Los Angeles, 1995.

———. "At Their Own Risk: Coffee Farmers and Debt in Nicaragua, 1870–1930." In *Identity and Struggle at the Margins of the Nation-State: The Laboring People of Central America and the Hispanic Caribbean,* edited by Aviva Chomsky and Aldo Lauria-Santiago. Durham, N.C.: Duke University Press, 1998.

Chasteen, John C. "Manuel Enrique Araujo and the Failure of Reform in El Salvador, 1911–13." *Southeastern Latin Americanist* 28 (September 1984): 1–16.

Chea, José Luis. *Guatemala: La cruz fragmentada*. San José: FLASCO, 1988.

Ching, Erik. "Patronage, Politics, and Power in El Salvador, 1840–1940." Ph.D. diss., University of California, Santa Barbara, 1997.

———. "In Search of the Party: The Communist Party, the Comintern, and the Peasant Rebellion of 1932 in El Salvador." *The Americas* 55 (October 1998): 204–39.

———. "Patronage, Politics, and Power in El Salvador, 1840–1940." Book manuscript, 1998.

Chomsky, Aviva. *West Indian Workers and the United Fruit Company in Costa Rica, 1870–1940*. Baton Rouge: Louisiana State University Press, 1996.

Chomsky, Aviva, and Aldo Lauria-Santiago, eds. *Identity and Struggle at the Margins of the Nation-State: The Laboring People of Central America and the Hispanic Caribbean*. Durham, N.C.: Duke University Press, 1998.

Christian, Shirley. *Nicaragua: Revolution in the Family*. New York: Random House, 1985.

Claxton, Robert Howard. "Lorenzo Montúfar: Central American Liberal." Ph.D. diss., Tulane University, 1970.

Clegern, Wayne M. "Transition from Conservativism to Liberalism in Guatemala, 1865–1871." In *Hispanic-American Essays in Honor of Max Leon Moorhead*, edited by William S. Coker. Pensacola: Perdido Bay Press, 1979.

———. *Origins of Liberal Dictatorship in Central America: Guatemala, 1865–1873*. Niwot, Colo.: University Press of Colorado, 1994.

Close, David. *Nicaragua: Politics, Economics, and Society*. London: Pinter, 1988.

Cole Chamorro, Alejandro. *145 Años de historia política de Nicaragua*. Managua: Editora Nicaragüense, 1967.

Coleman, Kenneth, and George Herring, eds. *Understanding the Central American Crisis*. Wilmington, Del.: Scholarly Resource Books, 1991.

Colindres, Eduardo. "La tenencia de la tierra en El Salvador." *Estudios Centroamericanos* 31 (September–October 1976): 463–72.

———. *Fundamentos económicos de la burguesía salvadoreña*. San Salvador: UCA/Editores, 1977.

Cotton, Donna Lillian. "Costa Rica and the Era of Tomás Guardia, 1870–1882." Ph.D. diss., George Washington University, 1972.

Creedman, Theodore S. "The Political Development of Costa Rica, 1936–1944: Politics of an Emerging Welfare State in a Patriarchal Society." Ph.D. diss., University of Maryland, 1971.

Cruz, Consuelo. "Identity and Persuasion: How Nations Remember Their Pasts and Make Their Futures." *World Politics* 52 (April 2000): 275–312.

Cruz Salazar, José Luis. "El ejército como una fuerza política." *Estudios Sociales* 6. Guatemala: Universidad Rafael Landívar, 1972.

Cuadra Pasos, Carlos. *Historia de medio siglo*. 2d ed. Managua: Editorial Unión, 1964.

Cullather, Nick. *Secret History: The CIA's Classified Account of Its Operations in Guatemala, 1952–1954.* Stanford: Stanford University Press, 1999.

Dalton, Roque. *Miguel Mármol.* San José: EDUCA, 1972.

Davis, Shelton H. "State Violence and Agrarian Crisis in Guatemala." In *Trouble in Our Backyard: Central America and the United States in the Eighties,* edited by Martin Diskin. New York: Pantheon Books, 1983.

del Cid, Rafael. *Honduras: Crisis económica y proceso de democratización política.* Tegucigalpa: Lithopress Industrial, 1990.

Delgado, Santiago. "El café en la economía nacional." *Revista Conservadora del Pensamiento Centroamericano* 3 (October 1961): 38–41.

Delgado Fiallos, Aníbal. *Rosa: El político.* Tegucigalpa: Editorial Cultura, 1994.

Denny, Harold Norman. *Dollars for Bullets: The Story of American Rule in Nicaragua.* New York: Dial Press, 1929.

Dessaint, Alain Y. "Effects of the Hacienda and Plantation Systems on Guatemala's Indians." *América Indígena* 22 (October 1962): 323–54.

Di Palma, Giuseppe, and Laurence Whitehead, eds. *The Central American Impasse.* New York: St. Martin's Press, 1986.

Diskin, Martin, ed. *Trouble in Our Backyard: Central America and the United States in the Eighties.* New York: Pantheon Books, 1983.

Dixon, Marlene, and Susanne Jonas. *Revolution and Intervention in Central America.* San Francisco: Synthesis Publications, 1983.

Domínguez, Jorge I., and Marc Lindenberg, eds. *Democratic Transitions in Central America and Panama.* Boston: World Peace Foundation, 1993.

Domínguez, Jorge I., and Abraham F. Lowenthal, eds. *Constructing Democratic Governance: Mexico, Central America, and the Caribbean in the 1990s.* Baltimore: Johns Hopkins University Press, 1996.

Domínguez Sosa, Julio Alberto. *Génesis y significado de la Constitución de 1886.* San Salvador: Departamento Editorial Ministerio de Cultura, 1958.

Domínguez T., Mauricio. "The Development of the Technological and Scientific Coffee Industry in Guatemala, 1830–1930." Ph.D. diss., Tulane University, 1970.

Dore, Elizabeth. "Land Privatization and the Differentiation of the Peasantry: Nicaragua's Coffee Revolution, 1850–1920." *Journal of Historical Sociology* 8 (September 1995): 303–26.

———. "Patriarchy and Private Property in Nicaragua, 1860–1920." In *Patriarchy and Economic Development: Women's Positions at the End of the Twentieth Century,* edited by Valentine M. Moghadam. Oxford: Clarendon Press, 1996.

———. "Property, Households, and Public Regulation of Domestic Life: Diriomo, Nicaragua, 1840–1900." *Journal of Latin American Studies* 29 (1997): 591–611.

Dosal, Paul J. *Doing Business with the Dictators: A Political History of United*

Fruit in Guatemala, 1899–1944. Wilmington, Del.: Scholarly Resources, 1993.

———. *Power in Transition: The Rise of Guatemala's Industrial Oligarchy, 1871–1994.* Westport, Conn.: Praeger, 1995.

———. "Recent Developments in Central American Studies: A Review of Trends and Prospects." *Latin American Research Review* 34, no. 3 (1999): 225–40.

Doubleday, C. W. *Reminiscences of the "Filibuster" War in Nicaragua.* New York: G. P. Putnam's Sons, 1886.

Dunkerley, James. *The Long War: Dictatorship and Revolution in El Salvador.* London: Verso, 1982.

———. *Power in the Isthmus: A Political History of Modern Central America.* London: Verso, 1988.

———. *The Pacification of Central America.* London: Verso, 1994.

Dunlop, Robert. *Travels in Central America.* London: Longman, Brown, Green, & Longmans, 1847.

Durham, William H. *Scarcity and Survival in Central America: Ecological Origins of the Soccer War.* Stanford: Stanford University Press, 1979.

Durón, Rómulo E. *Bosquejo histórico de Honduras.* 2d ed., no. 1. Tegucigalpa: Ministerio de Educación Pública, 1956.

Ebel, Roland H. "Political Modernization in Three Guatemalan Indian Communities." In *Community Culture and National Change,* edited by A. L. Harrison and Robert Wauchope. New Orleans: Middle American Research Institute, Tulane University, 1972.

Edelman, Marc. *The Logic of the Latifundio: The Large Estates of Northwestern Costa Rica since the Late Nineteenth Century.* Stanford: Stanford University Press, 1992.

Edelman, Marc, and Joanne Kenen, eds. *The Costa Rica Reader.* New York: Grove Weidenfeld, 1989.

Elam, Robert Varney. "Appeal to Arms: The Army and Politics in El Salvador, 1931–1964." Ph.D. diss., University of New Mexico, 1968.

Enríquez, Laura J. *Harvesting Change: Labor and Agrarian Reform in Nicaragua, 1979–1990.* Chapel Hill: University of North Carolina Press, 1991.

Euraque, Darío A. "Merchants and Industrialists in Northern Honduras: The Making of a National Bourgeoisie in Peripheral Capitalism." Ph.D. diss., University of Wisconsin, Madison, 1990.

———. "La 'reforma liberal' en Honduras y la hipótesis de la 'oligarquía ausente': 1870–1930." *Revista de Historia* 23 (January–June 1991): 7–56.

———. "Social, Economic, and Political Aspects of the Carías Dictatorship in Honduras: The Historiography." *Latin American Research Review* 29, no. 1 (1994): 238–48.

———. *Reinterpreting the Banana Republic: Region and State in Honduras, 1870–1972.* Chapel Hill: University of North Carolina Press, 1996.

————. "The Banana Enclave, Nationalism, and Mestizaje in Honduras, 1910s–1930s." In *Identity and Struggle at the Margins of the Nation-State: The Laboring People of Central America and the Hispanic Caribbean,* edited by Aviva Chomsky and Aldo Lauria-Santiago. Durham, N.C.: Duke University Press, 1998.

Everingham, Mark. *Revolution and the Multiclass Coalition in Nicaragua.* Pittsburgh: University of Pittsburgh Press, 1996.

Facio, Rodrigo. *Estudio sobre economía costarricense,* reprinted in *Obras de Rodrigo Facio.* Vol. 1. San José: Editorial Costa Rica, 1972.

Facio B., Rodrigo. *La Federación de Centroamérica: Sus antecedentes, su vida y su disolución.* San José: Escuela Superior de Administración Pública, 1960.

Fagen, Richard. *Forging Peace: The Challenge of Central America.* New York: Basil Blackwell, 1987.

Falcoff, Mark, and Robert Royal, eds. *The Continuing Crisis: U.S. Policy in Central America and the Caribbean.* Washington, D.C.: Ethics and Public Policy Center, 1986.

Fallas Monge, Carlos Luis. *El movimiento obrero en Costa Rica, 1830–1902.* San José: Editorial Universidad Estatal a Distancia, 1983.

Feinberg, Richard. *Central America: International Dimensions of the Crisis.* New York: Holmes & Meier, 1982.

Fernández, Ilva. "Nicaragua: Estructura económico-social y política del régimen de Zelaya." Licenciado thesis, Universidad Centroamericana, Managua, 1978.

Fernández Guardia, Ricardo. *Historia de Costa Rica: La independencia.* 2d ed. San José: Librería Lehmann, 1941.

————. *Cartilla histórica de Costa Rica.* San José: Lehmann Editores, 1984.

Figeac, José F. *Recordatorio histórico de la República de El Salvador.* San Salvador: Talleres Gráficos Cisneros, 1952.

Findling, John Ellis. "The United States and Zelaya: A Study in the Diplomacy of Expediency." Ph.D. diss., University of Texas, Austin, 1971.

Finney, Kenneth V. "Precious Metal Mining and the Modernization of Honduras: In Quest of El Dorado (1880–1900)." Ph.D. diss., Tulane University, 1973.

————. "Rosario and the Election of 1887: The Political Economy of Mining in Honduras." *Hispanic American Historical Review* 59 (February 1979): 81–107.

Fischel, Astrid. *Consenso y represión: Una interpretación socio-política de la educación costarricense.* San José: Editorial Costa Rica, 1990.

Flemion, Philip F. *Historical Dictionary of El Salvador.* Metuchen, N.J.: Scarecrow Press, 1972.

————. "States Rights and Partisan Politics: Manuel José Arce and the Struggle for Central American Union." *Hispanic American Historical Review* 53 (November 1973): 600–618.

Flora, Jan L., and Edelberto Torres-Rivas. "Sociology of Developing Societies: Historical Bases of Insurgency in Central America." In *Sociology of "Developing Societies": Central America,* edited by Jan L. Flora and Edelberto Torres-Rivas. New York: Monthly Review Press, 1989.

———, eds. *Sociology of "Developing Societies": Central America.* New York: Monthly Review Press, 1989.

Flores Macal, Mario. *Origen, desarrollo y crisis de las formas de dominación en El Salvador.* San José: SECASA, 1983.

Flores Valeriano, Enrique. *La explotación bananera en Honduras.* Tegucigalpa: Editorial Universitaria, 1987.

Floyd, Troy S. "The Guatemalan Merchants, the Government, and the *Provincianos,* 1750–1800." *Hispanic American Historical Review* 41 (February 1961): 90–110.

Fonseca, Elizabeth. *Costa Rica colonial: La tierra y el hombre.* San José: EDUCA, 1983.

Fowler, William R., Jr. "Cacao, Indigo, and Coffee: Cash Crops in the History of El Salvador." *Research in Economic Anthropology* 8 (1987): 139–67.

Frazier, Charles Edward. "The Dawn of Nationalism and Its Consequences in Nicaragua." Ph.D. diss., University of Texas, Austin, 1958.

Funes h., Matías. *Los deliberantes: El poder militar en Honduras.* Tegucigalpa: Editorial Guaymuras, 1995.

Galich, Manuel. *Del pánico al ataque.* Guatemala: Editorial Universitaria, 1977.

———. "Causas Internas de una derrota." In *La revolución de Octubre: Diez años de lucha por la democracia en Guatemala, 1944–1954,* vol. 2, edited by Eduardo Antonio Velásquez Carrera. Guatemala: CEUR, Universidad de San Carlos, 1994.

García Laguardia, Jorge Mario. *El pensamiento liberal de Guatemala (antología).* San José: EDUCA, 1977.

———. *La reforma liberal en Guatemala.* 3d ed. Guatemala: Editorial Universitaria, USAC, 1985.

Gardner, John W. "The Costa Rican Junta, 1948–1949." Ph.D. diss., St. John's University, 1971.

Garita, Luis. "The Bureaucratization of the Costa Rican State." In *The Costa Rica Reader,* edited by Marc Edelman and Joanne Kenen. New York: Grove Weidenfeld, 1989.

Gaspar, Jeffrey Casey. *Limón, 1880–1940: Un estudio de la industria bananera en Costa Rica.* San José: Editorial Costa Rica, 1979.

Gettleman, Marvin E., et al., eds. *El Salvador: Central America in the New Cold War.* New York: Grove Weidenfeld, 1986.

Gilbert, Dennis. *Sandinistas: The Party and the Revolution.* Cambridge: Basil Blackwell, 1988.

Gleijeses, Piero. "The Agrarian Reform of Jacobo Arbenz." *Journal of Latin American Studies* 21 (October 1989): 451–80.

————. *Shattered Hope: The Guatemalan Revolution and the United States, 1944–1954.* Princeton: Princeton University Press, 1991.

Gonzáles-Vegas, Claudio, and Víctor Hugo Céspedes. "Costa Rica." In *The Political Economy of Poverty, Equity, and Growth: Costa Rica and Uruguay,* edited by Simon Rottenberg. Oxford: Oxford University Press, 1993.

González Cabezas, Fabio. *Hechos históricos de 1848 a 1885: Biografía del Mariscal Don Santiago González.* San Salvador: Talleres Gráficos Cisneros, 1930.

González García, Yamileth. "Desintegración de bienes de cofradías y de fondos píos en Costa Rica, 1805–1845." *Mesoamérica* 8 (1984): 22–34.

González Villalobos, Paulino, ed. *Desarrollo institucional de Costa Rica (1523–1914).* San José: SECASA, 1983.

González Víquez, Cleto. *El sufragio en Costa Rica ante la historia y la legislación.* San José: Editorial Costa Rica, 1972.

Goodman, Louis W., William M. LeoGrande, and Johanna Mendelson Forman, eds. *Political Parties and Democracy in Central America.* Boulder, Colo.: Westview Press, 1992.

Gould, Jeffrey L. *To Lead as Equals: Rural Protest and Political Consciousness in Chinandega, Nicaragua, 1912–1979.* Chapel Hill: University of North Carolina Press, 1990.

————. "El trabajo forzoso y las comunidades indígenas nicaragüenses." In *El café en la historia de Centroamérica,* edited by Héctor Pérez Brignoli and Mario Samper. San José: FLASCO, 1993.

————. *To Die in This Way: Nicaraguan Indians and the Myth of Mestizaje, 1880–1965.* Durham, N.C.: Duke University Press, 1998.

————. "'¡Vana Ilusión!': The Highlands Indians and the Myth of Nicaragua Mestiza, 1880–1925." In *Identity and Struggle at the Margins of the Nation-State: The Laboring People of Central America and the Hispanic Caribbean,* edited by Aviva Chomsky and Aldo Lauria-Santiago. Durham, N.C.: Duke University Press, 1998.

Gould, Jeffery L., and Lowell Gudmundson. "Central American Historiography after the Violence." *Latin American Research Review* 32, no. 2 (1997): 244–56.

Grandin, Greg. *The Blood of Guatemala: A History of Race and Nation.* Durham, N.C.: Duke University Press, 2000.

Grieb, Kenneth J. "American Involvement in the Rise of Jorge Ubico." *Caribbean Studies* 10 (April 1970): 151–72.

————. "The United States and the Rise of General Maximiliano Hernández Martínez." *Journal of Latin American Studies* 3 (November 1971): 5–21.

————. "The Guatemalan Military and the Revolution of 1944." *The Americas* 32 (July–April 1975–76): 524–43.

————. "The Myth of a Central American Dictators' League." *Journal of Latin American Studies* 10 (1978): 329–45.

——. *Guatemalan Caudillo: The Regime of Jorge Ubico.* Athens: Ohio University Press, 1979.

Griffith, William J. "Attitudes toward Foreign Colonization: The Evolution of Nineteenth-Century Guatemalan Immigration Policy." In *Applied Enlightenment: 19th Century Liberalism,* edited by Mario Rodríguez et al. New Orleans: Middle American Research Institute, Tulane University, 1972.

Gudmundson, Lowell. "Nueva luz sobre la estratificación socio-económica costarricense al iniciarse la expansión cafetalera." *Revista de Historia* 4 (January–June 1977): 149–89.

——. "El campesino y el capitalismo agrario de Costa Rica: Una crítica de la ideología como historia." *Revista de Historia* 8 (January–June 1979): 59–81.

——. "Costa Rica before Coffee: Occupational Distribution, Wealth Inequality, and Élite Society in the Village Economy of the 1840s." *Journal of Latin American Studies* 15 (November 1983): 427–52.

——. *Hacendados, precaristas y políticos: La ganadería y el latifundismo guanacasteco, 1800–1950.* San José: Editorial Costa Rica, 1983.

——. "Peasant Movements and the Transition to Agrarian Capitalism: Freeholding versus Hacienda Peasantries and Agrarian Reform in Guanacaste, Costa Rica, 1880–1935." *Peasant Studies* 10 (1983): 145–62.

——. *Costa Rica before Coffee: Society and Economy on the Eve of the Export Boom.* Baton Rouge: Louisiana State University Press, 1986.

——. "Lord and Peasant in the Making of Modern Central America." In *Agrarian Structure and Political Power,* edited by Evelyne Huber and Frank Safford. Pittsburgh: University of Pittsburgh Press, 1995.

Gudmundson, Lowell, and Héctor Lindo-Fuentes. *Central America, 1821–1871: Liberalism before Liberal Reform.* Tuscaloosa: University of Alabama Press, 1995.

Guerra Borges, Alfredo. "Apuntes para una interpretación de la revolución guatemalteca y de su derrota en 1954." *Anuario de Estudios Centroamericanos* 14 (1988): 109–20.

Guevara-Escudero, José Francisco. "Nineteenth-Century Honduras: A Regional Approach to the Economic History of Honduras." Ph.D. diss., New York University, 1983.

Guido Madriz, William. "Don Braulio Carrillo y la Ley de Bases y Garantías." Tesis de grado, Universidad de Costa Rica, San José, 1971.

Guidos Véjar, Rafael. *El ascenso del militarismo en El Salvador.* 4th ed. San Salvador: UCA Editores, 1988.

Gutiérrez Espeleta, Nelson. "Notas sobre la evolución del Estado costarricense, 1821–1978." *Estudios Centroamericanos* 28 (January–April 1981): 69–86.

Gutman, Roy. *Banana Diplomacy: The Making of American Foreign Policy in Nicaragua, 1981–1987.* New York: Simon & Schuster, 1988.

Habib, Fawzi. "The Course and Problems of an Export Economy: The Case of El Salvador." Ph.D. diss., Duke University, 1958.

Hale, Charles A. *The Transformation of Liberalism in Late Nineteenth-Century Mexico.* Princeton: Princeton University Press, 1989.

Hale, Charles R. *Resistance and Contradiction: Miskitu Indians and the Nicaraguan State, 1894–1987.* Stanford: Stanford University Press, 1994.

Hall, Carolyn. *El café y el desarrollo histórico-geográfico de Costa Rica.* San José: Editorial Costa Rica, 1991.

Hamilton, Nora, et al., eds. *Crisis in Central America: Regional Dynamics and U.S. Policy in the 1980s.* Boulder, Colo.: Westview Press, 1984.

Handy, Jim. *Gift of the Devil: A History of Guatemala.* Boston: South End Press, 1984.

———. "The Most Precious Fruit of the Revolution: The Guatemala Agrarian Reform, 1952–1954." *Hispanic American Historical Review* 68 (November 1988): 675–705.

———. "National Policy, Agrarian Reform, and the Corporate Community during the Guatemalan Revolution." *Comparative Studies in Society and History* 30 (October 1988): 698–724.

———. *Revolution in the Countryside: Rural Conflict and Agrarian Reform in Guatemala, 1944–1954.* Chapel Hill: University of North Carolina Press, 1994.

Harris, Richard, and Carlos M. Vilas. *Nicaragua: A Revolution under Siege.* London: Zed Books, 1985.

Herman, Edward S., and Frank Brodhead. *Demonstration Elections: U.S.-Staged Elections in the Dominican Republic, Vietnam, and El Salvador.* Boston: South End Press, 1984.

Hernández, Edward Dennis. "Modernization and Dependency in Costa Rica during the Decade of the 1880s." Ph.D. diss., University of California, Los Angeles, 1975.

Herrate, Alberto. *La unión de Centroamérica: Tragedia y esperanza.* Guatemala: Editorial del Ministerio de Educación Pública, 1955.

Herrera Balharry, Eugenio. *Los alemanes y el Estado cafetalero.* San José: Editorial Universidad Estatal a Distancia, 1988.

Herrera Calix, Tomas. "Guatemala: Del gobierno de 'mano fuerte' de Ubico al gobierno del 'socialismo espiritual' de Arévalo." *Estudios Sociales Centroamericanos* 16 (January–April 1977): 168–94.

Herrick, Thomas R. *Desarrollo económico y político de Guatemala durante el período de Justo Rufino Barrios (1871–1885).* Guatemala: EDUCA, 1974.

Hill, Roscoe R. *Fiscal Intervention in Nicaragua.* New York: Paul Maisel, 1933.

Hodges, Donald C. *Intellectual Foundations of the Nicaraguan Revolution.* Austin: University of Texas Press, 1986.

Holden, Robert H. "The Real Diplomacy of Violence: United States Military

Power in Central America, 1950–1990." *International History Review* 20 (1993): 283–322.

————. "Constructing the Limits of State Violence in Central America: Towards a New Research Agenda." *Journal of Latin American Studies* 28 (May 1996): 435–59.

Holleran, Mary P. *Church and State in Guatemala.* New York: Columbia University Press, 1949.

Iglesias, Francisco María. *Braulio Carrillo: Tributo patrio.* San José: Editorial Costa Rica, 1971.

Immerman, Richard H. *The CIA in Guatemala: The Foreign Policy of Intervention.* Austin: University of Texas Press, 1982.

Ingersoll, Hazel Marylyn Bennett. "The War of the Mountain: A Study of Reactionary Peasant Insurgency in Guatemala, 1837–1873." Ph.D. diss., George Washington University, 1972.

Irvin, George, and Xavier Gorostiaga, eds. *Towards an Alternative for Central America and the Caribbean.* London: George Allen & Unwin, 1985.

Irving, T. B. "On the Enlightenment in Central America." In *The Ibero-American Enlightenment,* edited by A. Owen Aldridge. Urbana: University of Illinois Press, 1971.

James, Daniel. *Red Design for the Americas: Guatemalan Prelude.* New York: Day, 1954.

Jiménez Castro, Wilburg. *Génesis del Gobierno de Costa Rica.* San José: Editorial Alma Mater, 1986.

Jonas, Susanne. *The Battle for Guatemala: Rebels, Death Squads, and U.S. Power.* Boulder, Colo.: Westview Press, 1991.

Jonas Bodenheimer, Susanne. *Guatemala: Plan piloto para el continente.* San José: EDUCA, 1981.

Jones, Chester Lloyd. *Guatemala: Past and Present.* Minneapolis: University of Minnesota Press, 1940.

Jones, Clarence F., and Paul C. Morrison. "Evolution of the Banana Industry of Costa Rica." *Economic Geography* 28 (January 1952): 1–19.

Jones, Oakah L., Jr. *Guatemala in the Spanish Colonial Period.* Norman: University of Oklahoma Press, 1994.

Jung, Harald. "Class Struggles in El Salvador." *New Left Review* 122 (July 1980): 3–25.

Kaimowitz, David. "New Perspectives on Central American History, 1838–1945." *Latin American Research Review* 31, no. 1 (1996): 201–10.

Kamman, William. *A Search for Stability: United States Diplomacy toward Nicaragua, 1925–1933.* Notre Dame: University of Notre Dame Press, 1968.

Kantor, Harry. *The Costa Rican Election of 1953: A Case Study.* Gainesville: University of Florida Press, 1958.

Karl, Terry. "Imposing Consent? Electoralism vs. Democratization in El Salvador." In *Elections and Democratization in Latin America, 1980–85,* edited by Paul W. Drake and Eduardo Silva. San Diego: Center for Iberian and Latin American Studies, University of California, San Diego, 1986.

Karnes, Thomas L. *The Failure of Union: Central America, 1824–1960.* Chapel Hill: University of North Carolina Press, 1961.

——. *Tropical Enterprise: The Standard Fruit and Steamship Company in Latin America.* Baton Rouge: Louisiana State University Press, 1978.

Karush, G. E. "Plantations, Population, and Poverty: The Roots of Demographic Crisis in El Salvador." *Studies in Comparative International Development* 8 (1978): 59–75.

Kauck, David M. "Agricultural Commercialization and State Development in Central America: The Political Economy of the Coffee Industry from 1838 to 1940." Ph.D. diss., University of Washington, 1988.

Kenyon, Gordon. "Mexican Influence in Central America, 1821–1823." *Hispanic American Historical Review* 41 (May 1961):175–205.

Kepner, Charles David Jr., and Jay Henry Soothill. *The Banana Empire: A Case Study of Economic Imperialism.* New York: Russell & Russell, 1935.

Kerr, Derek N. "La edad de oro del café." *Mesoamérica* 3 (June 1982): 1–25.

Kincaid, Douglas. "Peasants into Rebels: Community and Class in Rural El Salvador." *Comparative Studies in Society and History* 29 (July 1989): 466–94.

Krehm, William, and Salomon de la Selva. *Nicaragua en la primera mitad del siglo XX.* Managua: Ediciones Populares, 1976.

Kuznesof, Elizabeth. "Comentarios sobre 'La Costa Rica cafetalera: Economía, sociedad y estructuras de poder.'" *Revista de Historia* 14 (1986): 31–39.

La Charité, Norman, et al. *Case Studies in Insurgency and Revolutionary Warfare: Guatemala, 1944–1954.* Washington, D.C.: American University, 1964.

LaFeber, Walter. *Inevitable Revolutions: The United States in Central America.* New York: Norton, 1984.

Laínez, Vilma and Víctor Meza. "El enclave bananero en la historia de Honduras." *Estudios Sociales Centroamericanos* 5 (May–August 1973): 115–55.

Lanuza, Alberto. "La formación del Estado nacional en Nicaragua: Las bases económicas, comerciales y financieras entre 1821 y 1873." In *Economía y sociedad en la construcción del Estado de Nicaragua,* edited by Alberto Lanuza et al. San José: Instituto Centroamericano de Administración Pública, 1983.

Lanuza, Alberto, Juan Luis Vázquez, Amaru Barahona, and Amalia Chamorro, eds. *Economía y sociedad en la construcción del Estado de Nicaragua.* San José: Instituto Centroamericano de Administración Pública, 1983.

Lanuza Matamoras, Alberto. "Estructuras socioeconómicas, poder y Estado en Nicaragua, de 1821 a 1875." Tesis de Grado, Universidad de Costa Rica, n.d.

Lapper, Richard, and James Painter. *Honduras: State for Sale.* London: Latin American Bureau, 1985.

Larde y Larín, Jorge. *El Salvador: Historia de sus pueblos, villas y ciudades.* San Salvador: Ministerio de Cultura, 1957.

Larín, Arístides Augusto. "Historia del movimiento sindical de El Salvador." *La Universidad,* no. 4 (July–August 1971): 135–80.

Lauria, Aldo. "An Agrarian Republic: Production Politics and the Peasantry in El Salvador, 1740–1920." Ph.D. diss., University of Chicago, 1992.

Lauria-Santiago, Aldo. "Introduction: Identity and Struggle in the History of the Hispanic Caribbean and Central America, 1850–1950." In *Identity and Struggle at the Margins of the Nation-State: The Laboring People of Central America and the Hispanic Caribbean,* edited by Aviva Chomsky and Aldo Lauria-Santiago. Durham, N.C.: Duke University Press, 1998.

———. *An Agrarian Republic: Commercial Agriculture and the Politics of Peasant Communities in El Salvador, 1823–1914.* Pittsburgh: University of Pittsburgh Press, 1999.

Lehoucq, Fabrice Edouard. "Class Conflict, Political Crisis, and the Breakdown of Democratic Practices in Costa Rica: Reassessing the Origins of the 1948 Civil War." *Journal of Latin American Studies* 23 (February 1991): 37–60.

———. "The Origins of Democracy in Costa Rica in Comparative Perspective." Ph.D. diss., Duke University, 1992.

———. "The Institutional Foundations of Democratic Cooperation in Costa Rica." *Journal of Latin American Studies* 28 (May 1996): 329–55.

Lehoucq, Fabrice Edouard, and Iván Molina. "Stuffing the Ballot Box: Fraud, Electoral Reform, and Democratization in Costa Rica." Book manuscript, 2000.

Leiken, Robert S., ed. *Central America: Anatomy of a Conflict.* New York: Pergamon Press, 1984.

Leiken, Robert S., and Barry Rubin, eds. *The Central American Crisis Reader.* New York: Summit Books, 1987.

LeoGrande, William M., and Carla Anne Robbins. "Oligarchs and Officers: The Crisis in El Salvador." *Foreign Affairs* 58 (1980): 1084–1103.

Leonard, Thomas M. *Central America and the United States: The Search for Stability.* Athens: University of Georgia Press, 1991.

Levenson-Estrada, Deborah. *Trade Unionists against Terror: Guatemala City, 1954–1985.* Chapel Hill: University of North Carolina Press, 1994.

Levy, Pablo. "Notas geográficas y económicas sobre la República de Nicaragua." *Revista Conservadora del Pensamiento Centroamericana* 12–13 (August–December 1965): 7–293.

Lindenberg, Marc. "World Economic Cycles and Central American Political Instability." *World Politics* 42 (April 1990): 397–421.

Lindo-Fuentes, Héctor. *Weak Foundations: The Economy of El Salvador in the*

Nineteenth Century, 1821–1898. Berkeley: University of California Press, 1990.

Longley, Kyle. *The Sparrow and the Hawk: Costa Rica and the United States during the Rise of José Figueres.* Tuscaloosa: University of Alabama Press, 1997.

López Vallecillos, Italo. *El periodismo en El Salvador: Bosquejo histórico-documental, precedido de apuntes sobre la prensa colonial hispanoamericana.* San Salvador: Editorial Universitaria, 1964.

———, ed. *Gerardo Barrios y su tiempo.* 2 vols. San Salvador: Ministerio de Educación, 1967.

Love, Joseph L. "Structural Change and Conceptual Response in Latin America and Romania, 1860–1950." In *Guiding the Invisible Hand: Economic Liberalism and the State in Latin American History,* edited by Joseph L. Love and Nils Jacobsen. New York: Praeger, 1988.

Luna, David. "Análisis de una dictadura fascista Latinoamericana: Maximiliano Hernández Martínez, 1931–1944." *La Universidad,* no. 5 (September–October 1969): 39–130.

———. *Manual de historia económica de El Salvador.* San Salvador: Editorial Universitaria, 1971.

Macaulay, Neill. *The Sandino Affair.* Chicago: Quadrangle Books, 1971.

MacCameron, Robert. *Bananas, Labor, and Politics in Honduras: 1954–1963.* Syracuse, N.Y.: Maxwell School of Citizenship and Public Affairs, Syracuse University, 1983.

MacLeod, Murdo J. "Ethnic Relations and Indian Society in the Province of Guatemala, ca. 1620–ca. 1800." In *Spaniards and Indians in Southeastern Mesoamerica: Essays on the History of Ethnic Relations,* edited by Murdo J. MacLeod and Robert Wasserstrom. Lincoln: University of Nebraska Press, 1983.

Mariñas Otero, Luis. *Honduras.* Tegucigalpa: Editorial Universitaria, 1983.

Marroquín, Alejandro D. "Estudio sobre la crisis de los años treinta en El Salvador." *Anuario de Estudios Centroamericanos* 3 (1977): 115–60.

Marure, Alejandro. *Bosquejo histórico de las revoluciones de Centro-América: Desde 1811 hasta 1834.* Vols. 1–2. Guatemala: Tipografía de "El Progreso," 1877.

———. *Efemérides de los hechos notables acaecidos en la república de Centro América.* Guatemala: Tipografía Nacional, 1895.

Mas Rovira, Jorge. *Estado y política económica en Costa Rica, 1948–1970.* San José: Editorial Porvenir, 1988.

Matus, Ramón Ignacio. "Revoluciones contra Zelaya." *Revista Conservadora del Pensamiento Centroamericano* 4 (April 1962): 1–44.

McCamant, John F. "Intervention in Guatemala: Implications for the Study of Third World Politics." *Comparative Political Studies* 17 (October 1984): 373–407.

McCann, Thomas P. *An American Company: The Tragedy of United Fruit,* edited by Henry Scammell. New York: Crown Publishers, 1976.

McClintock, Michael. *The American Connection.* Vol. 1, *State Terror and Popular Resistance in El Salvador.* London: Zed Books, 1985.

———. *The American Connection.* Vol. 2, *State Terror and Popular Resistance in Guatemala.* London: Zed Books, 1985.

McCreery, David J. "Coffee and Class: The Structure of Development in Liberal Guatemala." *Hispanic American Historical Review* 56 (August 1976): 438–60.

———. "Debt Servitude in Rural Guatemala, 1876–1936." *Hispanic American Historical Review* 63 (November 1983): 735–59.

———. *Development and the State in Reforma Guatemala, 1871–1885.* Athens: Ohio University, Center for International Studies, Latin America Program, 1983.

———. "'An Odious Feudalism': *Mandamiento* Labor and Commercial Agriculture in Guatemala, 1858–1920." *Latin American Perspectives* 13 (winter 1986): 99–117.

———. "State Power, Indigenous Communities, and Land in Nineteenth-Century Guatemala, 1820–1920." In *Guatemalan Indians and the State, 1540–1988,* edited by Carol A. Smith with the assistance of Marilyn M. Moors. Austin: University of Texas Press, 1990.

———. *Rural Guatemala, 1760–1940.* Stanford: Stanford University Press, 1994.

Mejía, Medardo. *Historia de Honduras.* Vols. 4, 5. Tegucigalpa: Editorial Universitaria, 1988–89.

Meléndez, Carlos. *Historia de Costa Rica.* San José: Editorial Universidad Estatal a Distancia, 1979.

———, ed. *Documentos fundamentos del siglo XIX.* San José: Editorial Costa Rica, 1978.

Melmed-Sanjak, Jolyne, Carlos E. Santiago, and Alvin Magid, eds. *Recovery or Relapse in the Global Economy: Comparative Perspectives on Restructuring in Central America.* Westport, Conn.: Praeger, 1993.

Mena Solórzano, Luis. "Los arquitectos de la victoria liberal." *Revista Conservadora del Pensamiento Centroamericano* 26 (1971): 1–53.

Méndez Montenegro, Julio César. *444 años de legislación agraria, 1513–1957.* Guatemala: Revista de la Facultad de Ciencias Jurídicas y Sociales de Guatemala, 1960.

Menjívar, Rafael. *Formación y lucha del proletariado industrial salvadoreño.* San José: Editorial Universitaria Centroamericana, 1982.

Menjívar L., Rafael. *Acumulación originaria y desarrollo del capitalismo en El Salvador.* San José: EDUCA, 1980.

Merrill, Tim L. *Honduras: A Country Study.* Washington, D.C.: Library of Congress, 1995.

Meza, Víctor. *Historia del movimiento obrero hondureño.* Tegucigalpa: CEDOH, 1991.

Meza, Víctor, and Héctor López. "Las inversiones extranjeras en Honduras antes del Mercado Común Centroamericano." *Economía Política* 6 (September–December 1973): 47–79.

Miceli, Keith L. "Rafael Carrera: Defender and Promoter of Peasant Interests in Guatemala, 1837–1848." *The Americas* 31 (July 1974): 72–95.

Midlarsky, Manus I., and Kenneth Roberts. "Class, State, and Revolution in Central America: Nicaragua and El Salvador Compared." *Journal of Conflict Resolution* 29 (June 1985): 163–93.

Miller, Eugene D. "Labour and the War-Time Alliance in Costa Rica, 1943–1948." *Journal of Latin American Studies* 25 (October 1993): 515–41.

Miller, Hubert J. *La iglesia y el Estado en tiempo de Justo Rufino Barrios.* Guatemala: Universidad de San Carlos, 1976.

———. "Liberal Modernization and Religious Corporate Property in Nineteenth-Century Guatemala." In *Liberals, the Church, and Indian Peasants: Corporate Lands and the Challenge of Reform in Nineteenth-Century Spanish America,* edited by Robert H. Jackson. Albuquerque: University of New Mexico Press, 1997.

Millet, Richard. *Guardians of the Dynasty: A History of the U.S. Created Guardia Nacional de Nicaragua and the Somoza Family.* Maryknoll, N.Y.: Orbis Books, 1977.

———. "Praetorians or Patriots? The Central American Military." In *Central America: Anatomy of a Conflict,* edited by Robert S. Leiken. New York: Pergamon Press, 1984.

Molina Chocano, Guillermo. *Estado liberal y desarrollo capitalista en Honduras.* Tegucigalpa: Banco Central de Honduras, 1976.

———. "La formación del Estado y el origen minero-mercantil de la burguesía hondureña." *Estudios Sociales Centroamericanos* 25 (January–April 1980): 55–89.

———. "Población, estructura productiva y migraciones internas en Honduras (1950–1960)." *Estudios Sociales Centroamericanos* 12 (September–December 1975): 9–39.

Molina Jiménez, Iván. "El Valle Central de Costa Rica en la independencia." *Revista de Historia* 14 (July–December 1986): 85–114.

———. "Habilitadores y habilitados en el Valle Central de Costa Rica: El financiamiento de la producción cafetalera en los inicios de su expansión (1838–1850)." *Revista de Historia* 16 (July–December 1987): 85–128.

———. *Costa Rica (1800–1850): El legado colonial y la génesis del capitalismo.* San José: EDUCA, 1991.

Molina J., Iván, and Steven Palmer. *Costa Rica, 1930–1996: Historia de una sociedad.* San José: Editorial Porvenir, 1997.

Monge Alfaro, Carlos. *Historia de Costa Rica.* 14th ed. San José: Librería Trejos, 1976.

Monterrey, Francisco J. *Historia de El Salvador: Anotaciones cronológicas, 1843–1871.* Vol. 2. 2d ed. San Salvador: Editorial Universitaria, 1978.

Montes, Segundo. *El agro salvadoreño (1973–1980)*. San Salvador: UCA Editores, 1986.

Montgomery, Tommie Sue. *Revolution in El Salvador: From Civil Strife to Civil Peace*. 2d ed. Boulder, Colo.: Westview Press, 1995.

Montúfar, Lorenzo. *Reseña histórica de Centroamérica*. Vol. 1. Guatemala: Tipografía de "El Progreso," 1878.

Morales, Baltasar. *Derrocamiento de una tiranía: La caída de Jorge Ubico*. Guatemala: La Tipografía Nacional de Guatemala, 1958.

Morales, Jorge. "El ferrocarril nacional de Honduras: Su historia e incidencia sobre el desarrollo económico." *Estudios Sociales Centroamericanos* 2 (May–August 1972): 7–20.

Moreno, Darío. *U.S. Policy in Central America: The Endless Debate*. Miami: Florida International University Press, 1990.

Morris, James A. *Honduras: Caudillo Politics and Military Rulers*. Boulder, Colo.: Westview Press, 1984.

Morris, James A., and Steve C. Ropp. "Corporatism and Dependent Development: A Honduran Case Study." *Latin American Research Review* 12, no. 2 (1977): 27–68.

Mosk, Sanford A. "The Coffee Economy of Guatemala, 1850–1918: Development and Signs of Instability." *Inter-American Economic Affairs* (winter 1955): 6–20.

Muñoz Guillén, Mercedes. *El Estado y la abolición del ejército, 1914–1949*. San José: Editorial Porvenir, 1990.

———. "El ejército costarricense y la conquista de los atributos de la estaticidad." In *Desarrollo institucional de Costa Rica (de las sociedades indígenas a la crisis del 30)*, edited by Jaime Murillo. San José: EDUCA, 1991.

Munro, Dana G. *The Five Republics of Central America: Their Political and Economic Development and Their Relations with the United States*. New York: Oxford University Press, 1918.

———. *Intervention and Dollar Diplomacy in the Caribbean, 1900–1921*. Princeton: Princeton University Press, 1964.

———. *The United States and the Caribbean Republics, 1921–1933*. Princeton: Princeton University Press, 1974.

Murga Frassinetti, Antonio. *Enclave y sociedad en Honduras*. Tegucigalpa: Editorial Universitaria, 1978.

Murillo, Jaime, ed. *Desarrollo institucional de Costa Rica (de las sociedades indígenas a la crisis del 30)*. San José: EDUCA, 1991.

Murillo Jiménez, Hugo. *Tinoco y los Estados Unidos: Génesis y caída de un régimen*. San José: Editorial Universidad Estatal a Distancia, 1981.

Musicant, Ivan. *The Banana Wars: A History of United States Military Intervention in Latin America from the Spanish-American War to the Invasion of Panama*. New York: Macmillan, 1990.

Naylor, Robert Arthur. "British Commercial Relations with Central America, 1821–1851." Ph.D. diss., Tulane University, 1958.

Nelson, Harold D., ed. *Costa Rica: A Country Study.* Washington, D.C.: American University, 1984.

Nelson-Pallmeyer, Jack. *War against the Poor: Low-Intensity Conflict and Christian Faith.* Maryknoll, N.Y.: Orbis Books, 1989.

North, Liisa. *Bitter Grounds: Roots of Revolt in El Salvador.* Toronto: Between the Lines, 1981.

Obregón, Clotilde. *Carrillo: Una época y un hombre, 1835–1842.* San José: Editorial Costa Rica, 1990.

Obregón Loría, Rafael. *Costa Rica en la independencia y en la federación.* 2d ed. San José: Editorial Costa Rica, 1979.

———. *De nuestra historia patria: Hechos militares y políticos.* Alajuela, Costa Rica: Museo Histórico Cultural Juan Santamaría, 1981.

Oqueli, Ramón. *1862.* Tegucigalpa: Editorial Universitaria, 1990.

Ortega Arancibia, Francisco. *Cuarenta años de historia de Nicaragua (1838–1878).* 4th ed. Managua: Fondo de Promoción Cultural—BANIC, 1993.

Oseguera de Ochoa, Margarita. *Honduras hoy: Sociedad y crisis política.* 2d ed. Tegucigalpa: CEDOH, 1990.

Paige, Jeffery M. "Coffee and Politics in Central America." In *Crisis in the Caribbean,* edited by Richard Tardanico. Newbury Park: Sage, 1987.

———. "The Social Origins of Dictatorship, Democracy, and Socialist Revolution in Central America." *Journal of Developing Societies* 6 (1990): 37–42.

———. *Coffee and Power: Revolution and the Rise of Democracy in Central America.* Cambridge: Harvard University Press, 1997.

Palacios, Julio E. *La huelga de 1944.* Guatemala City: Editorial del Ministerio de Educación Pública, 1950.

Palmer, Frederick. *Central America and Its Problems: An Account of a Journey from the Rio Grande to Panama.* New York: Moffat, Yard & Company, 1910.

Palmer, Steven Paul. "A Liberal Discipline: Inventing Nations in Guatemala and Costa Rica, 1870–1900." Ph.D. diss., Columbia University, 1990.

Parada, Alfredo. *Etapas políticas.* San Salvador, 1950.

Parkman, Patricia. *Nonviolent Insurrection in El Salvador: The Fall of Maximiliano Hernández Martínez.* Tucson: University of Arizona Press, 1988.

Pearce, Jenny. *Under the Eagle: U.S. Intervention in Central American and the Caribbean.* London: Latin American Bureau, 1981.

Pearson, Heale J. "Peasant Pressure Groups and Agrarian Reform in Honduras, 1962–1977." In *Rural Change and Public Policy,* edited by William Avery, Richard E. Lonsdale, and Ivan Volgyes. New York: Pergamon Press, 1980.

Peccorini Letona, Francisco. *La voluntad del pueblo en la emancipación de El Salvador.* San Salvador: Ministerio de Educación, Dirección de Publicaciones, 1972.

Peckenham, Nancy, and Annie Street, eds. *Honduras: Portrait of a Captive Nation.* New York: Praeger, 1985.

Peeler, John A. *Latin American Democracies: Colombia, Costa Rica, and Venezuela.* Chapel Hill: University of North Carolina Press, 1985.

Pelupessy, Wim, and John Weeks. *Economic Maladjustment in Central America.* New York: St. Martin's Press, 1993.

Pena Kampy, Alberto. *"El General Martínez": Un patriarcal presidente dictador.* San Salvador: Editorial Tipográfica Ramírez, 1972.

Pérez Estrada, Francisco. "Breve historia de la tenencia de la tierra en Nicaragua." *Revista Conservadora del Pensamiento Centroamericano* 51 (December 1964): 15–33.

Pérez Brignoli, Héctor. "Economía y sociedad en Honduras durante el siglo XIX: Las estructuras demográficas." *Estudios Sociales Centroamericanos* 6 (September–December 1973): 51–81.

———. *La reforma liberal en Honduras.* Tegucigalpa: Editorial Nuevo Continente, 1973.

———. *A Brief History of Central America,* translated by Ricardo B. Sawrey A. and Susana Stettri de Sawrey. Berkeley: University of California Press, 1989.

———. "Crecimiento agroexportador y regímenes políticos en Centroamérica: Un ensayo de historia comparada." In *Tierra, café y sociedad,* edited by Héctor Pérez Brignoli and Mario Samper. San José: FLASCO, 1994.

———. "Indians, Communists, and Peasants: The 1932 Rebellion in El Salvador." In *Coffee, Society, and Power in Latin America,* edited by William Roseberry, Lowell Gudmundson, and Mario Samper Kutschbach. Baltimore: Johns Hopkins University Press, 1995.

Pérez Brignoli, Héctor, and Mario Samper, eds. *El café en la historia de Centroamérica.* San José: FLASCO, 1993.

Peterson, John Holger. "The Political Role of University Students in Guatemala, 1944–1968." Ph.D. diss., University of Pittsburgh, 1970.

Pinto Soria, Julio César. *Raíces históricas del Estado en Centroamérica.* Guatemala: Editorial Universitaria de Guatemala, 1983.

Pitti, Joseph Apolonio. "Jorge Ubico and Guatemalan Politics in the 1920s." Ph.D. diss., University of New Mexico, 1975.

Posas, Mario. *Notas sobre las sociedades artesanales y los orígenes del movimiento obrero hondureño.* Tegucigalpa: ESP Editorial, 1977.

———. *Luchas del movimiento obrero hondureño.* San José: EDUCA, 1981.

———. "La plantación bananera en Centroamérica: 1870–1929." In *Historia general de Centroamérica,* vol. 4, *Las repúblicas agroexportadoras,* edited by Víctor Hugo Acuña Ortega. Madrid: FLASCO, 1993.

Posas, Mario, and Rafael del Cid. *La construcción del sector público y del Estado nacional en Honduras, 1876–1979.* 2d ed. San José: EDUCA, 1983.

Powell, Anna I. "Relations between the United States and Nicaragua, 1898–1916." *Hispanic American Historical Review* 8 (February 1928): 43–64.

Quant, José Santos. "Notas sobre la Revolución Liberal en la historia económica de Nicaragua." *Boletín Nicaragüense de Bibliografía y Documentación* 6 (July–August 1975): 54–69.

Quijano, Carlos. *Nicaragua: Ensayo sobre el imperialismo de los Estados Unidos (1909–1927)*. Managua: Vanguardia, 1987.

Radell, David R. "Historical Geography of Western Nicaragua: The Spheres of Influence of León, Granada, and Managua, 1519–1965." Ph.D. diss., University of California, Berkeley, 1969.

Ramírez, Sergio. "The Kid from Niquinohomo." *Latin American Perspectives* 16 (1989): 48–82.

———. "Entre dos revoluciones." *El Semanario,* no. 3, Suplemento Especial Coleccionable (1993), 1–2.

Ramírez B., Mario A. "La polémica de la concentración de la tierra en Costa Rica: Mitos e ideologías." *Revista de Ciencias Sociales* 21–22 (March–October 1981): 35–54.

Rippy, Fred J. "Justo Rufino Barrios and the Nicaraguan Canal." *Hispanic American Historical Review* 20 (May 1940): 190–97.

———. "Relations of the United States and Guatemala during the Epoch of Justo Rufino Barrios." *Hispanic American Historical Review* 22 (November 1942): 595–605.

Rodríguez, Eugenio. *Don Tomás Guardia y el Estado liberal.* 2d ed. San José: EUNED, 1989.

Rodríguez, Mario. *Central America.* Englewood Cliffs, N.J.: Prentice-Hall, 1965.

———. *The Cádiz Experiment in Central America, 1808 to 1826.* Berkeley: University of California Press, 1978.

Rodríguez, Olvin E., ed. *100 Años de historia.* Tegucigalpa: Graficentro Editores, 1991.

Rodríguez S., Eugenia. "Las interpretaciones sobre la expansión del café en Costa Rica y el papel jugado por el crédito." *Revista de Historia* 18 (1988): 163–86.

Rodríguez Vega, Eugenio. *Los días de Don Ricardo.* San José: Editorial Costa Rica, 1971.

Rojas Bolaños, Manuel. *Lucha social y guerra civil en Costa Rica.* San José: Editorial Porvenir, 1979.

———. "El proceso democrático en Costa Rica." In *Costa Rica: La democracia inconclusa,* edited by Manuel Rojas Bolaños. San José: Editorial Departamento Ecumémico de Investigaciones, 1989.

Ropp, Steve C. "The Honduran Army in the Sociopolitical Evolution of the Honduran State." *The Americas* 30 (April 1974): 504–28.

Ropp, Steve C., and James A. Morris, eds. *Central America: Crisis and Adaptation.* Albuquerque: University of New Mexico Press, 1984.

Roseberry, William, Lowell Gudmundson, and Mario Samper Kutschbach, eds. *Coffee, Society, and Power in Latin America.* Baltimore: Johns Hopkins University Press, 1995.

Rosenberg, Mark B. "Honduras: An Introduction." In *Honduras Confronts Its*

Future, edited by Mark B. Rosenberg and Philip H. Shepherd. Boulder, Colo.: Lynne Rienner, 1986.

———. "Social Reform in Costa Rica: Social Security and the Presidency of Rafael Angel Calderón Guardia." *Hispanic American Historical Review* 61 (May 1981): 278–96.

———. "Honduran Scorecard: Military and Democrats in Central America." *Caribbean Review* 12 (winter 1983): 3–19.

———. "Can Democracy Survive the Democrats?: From Transition to Consolidation in Honduras." In *Elections and Democracy in Central America,* edited by John A. Booth and Mitchell A. Seligson. Chapel Hill: University of North Carolina Press, 1989.

Rosés Alvarado, Eduardo. "La dictadura de Tomás Guardia: Un período de transición del Estado costarricense." In *Desarrollo institucional de Costa Rica (1523–1914),* edited by Paulino González Villalobos. San José: SECASA, 1983.

Rosset, Peter, and John Vandermeer, ed. *The Nicaraguan Reader: Documents of a Revolution under Fire.* New York: Grove Press, 1983.

Rovira Mas, Jorge. *Estado y política económica en Costa Rica: 1948–1970.* San José: Editorial Porvenir, 1988.

Rubio Sánchez, Manuel. *Historia del añil o xiquilite en Centroamérica.* 2 vols. San Salvador: Ministerio de Educación, 1976.

Ruhl, J. Mark. "Agrarian Structure and Political Stability in Honduras." *Journal of Latin American Studies and World Affairs* 26 (February 1984): 33–68.

———. "Honduras: Militarism and Democratization in Troubled Waters." In *Repression, Resistance, and Democratic Transition in Central America,* edited by Thomas Walker and Ariel C. Armony. Wilmington, DE: Scholarly Resources, 2000.

Ruiz Granadino, Santiago. "Modernización agrícola en El Salvador." *Estudios Sociales Centroamericanos* 22 (January–April 1979): 71–100.

Sáenz, Carlos Joaquín. "Population Growth, Economic Progress, and Opportunities on the Land: The Case of Costa Rica." Research Paper No. 47, University of Wisconsin, Madison, June 1972.

Sáenz Maroto, Alberto. *Braulio Carrillo: Reformador agrícola de Costa Rica.* San José: EDUCA, 1987.

Safford, Frank. "Bases for Political Alignment in Early Independent Spanish America." In *New Perspectives in Latin American History,* edited by Richard Graham. Austin: University of Texas Press, 1978.

Salas Víquez, José Antonio. "El liberalismo positivista en Costa Rica: La lucha entre ladinos e indígenas en Orosi, 1881–1884." *Revista de Historia* 5 (July–December 1977): 187–217.

———. "La privatización de los baldíos nacionales en Costa Rica durante el siglo XIX: Legislación y procedimientos utilizados para su adjudicación." *Revista de Historia* 15 (January–June 1987): 63–118.

Salazar, Ramón A. *Historia de veintiún años: La independencia de Guatemala.* 2d ed., tomo 2, vol. 5. Guatemala: Editorial del Ministerio de Educación Pública, 1956.

Salazar Mora, Jorge Mario. *Calderón Guardia.* San José: Editorial Universidad Estatal a Distancia, 1980.

———. "Estado liberal y luchas sociales en Costa Rica (1870–1920)." *Revista de Ciencias Sociales* 36 (1987): 91–102.

Salazar Mora, Orlando. *Política y reforma en Costa Rica, 1914–1958.* San José: Editorial Porvenir, 1981.

———. "Sobre la democracia liberal en Costa Rica (1889–1919)." In *Desarrollo institucional de Costa Rica (1523–1914),* edited by Paulino González Villalobos. San José: SECASA, 1983.

———. *El apogeo de la república liberal en Costa Rica, 1870–1914.* San José: EDUCA, 1993.

———. *Crisis liberal y Estado reformista: Análisis político-electoral, 1914–1949.* San José: EDUCA, 1995.

Salisbury, Richard V. *Costa Rica y el istmo, 1900–1934.* San José: Editorial Costa Rica, 1984.

Salomón, Leticia. *Militarismo y reformismo en Honduras.* Tegucigalpa: Editorial Guaymuras, 1982.

———. *Política y militares en Honduras.* Tegucigalpa: Centro de Documentación de Honduras, 1992.

Samper Kutschbach, Mario. "Los productores directos en el siglo del café." *Revista de Historia* 7 (July–December 1978): 123–217.

———. "Uso de la tierra y unidades productivas al finalizar el siglo XIX: Noreste del Valle Central, Costa Rica." *Revista de Historia* 14 (1986): 133–77.

———. "Fuerzas sociopolíticas y procesos electorales en Costa Rica." *Revista de Historia,* número especial (1988), 157–222.

———. *Generations of Settlers: Rural Households and Markets on the Costa Rican Frontier, 1850–1935.* Boulder, Colo.: Westview Press, 1990.

———. "Café, trabajo y sociedad en Centroamérica (1870–1930): Una historia común y divergente." In *Historia general de Centroamérica,* vol. 4, *Las repúblicas agroexportadoras,* edited by Víctor Hugo Acuña Ortega. Madrid: FLASCO, 1993.

———. "El significado social de la caficultura costarricense y salvadoreña: Análisis histórico comparado a partir de los censos cafetaleros." In *Tierra, café y sociedad,* edited by Héctor Pérez Brignoli and Mario Samper. San José: FLASCO, 1994.

Sancho-Riba, Eugenio. "Merchant-Planters and Modernization: An Early Liberal Experiment in Costa Rica, 1849–1870." Ph.D. diss., University of California, San Diego, 1982.

Schifter, Jacobo. *La fase oculta de la Guerra Civil en Costa Rica.* San José: EDUCA, 1986.

————. *Las alianzas conflictivas: Las relaciones de Costa Rica y Estados Unidos de la Segunda Guerra Mundial a los inicios de la Guerra Civil.* San José: Libro Libre, 1986.

Schifter S., Jacobo. "La democracia en Costa Rica como producto de la neutralización de clases." In *¿Democracia en Costa Rica? Cinco opiniones polémicas,* edited by Chester Zelaya et al. San José: Editorama, 1993.

Schlesinger, Stephen, and Stephen Kinzer. *Bitter Fruit: The Untold Story of the American Coup in Guatemala.* Garden City, N.Y.: Anchor Books, 1982.

Schmolt-Haberlein, Michaela. "Continuity and Change in a Guatemalan Indian Community: San Cristóbal-Verapaz, 1870–1940." *Hispanic American Historical Review* 76 (1996): 227–48.

Schoonover, Thomas. "Imperialism in Middle America: United States, Britain, Germany, and France Compete for Transit Rights and Trade, 1820s–1920s." In *Eagle against Empire: American Occupation to European Imperialism, 1914–1982,* edited by Rhodri Jeffreys-Jones. Cedex: Université de Provence, 1983.

————. "Metropole Rivalry in Central America, 1820s–1929: An Overview." In *Central America: Historical Perspectives on the Contemporary Crisis,* edited by Ralph Lee Woodward Jr. New York: Greenwood Press, 1988.

————. *The United States in Central America: Episodes of Social Imperialism and Imperial Rivalry in the World System.* Durham, N.C.: Duke University Press, 1991.

Schulz, Donald E., and Deborah Sundloff Schulz, *The United States, Honduras, and the Crisis in Central America.* Boulder, Colo.: Westview Press, 1994.

Scroggs, William O. *Filibusters and Financiers: The Story of William Walker and His Associates.* New York: Macmillan, 1916.

Seligson, Mitchell A. *Peasants of Costa Rica and the Development of Agrarian Capitalism.* Madison: University of Wisconsin Press, 1980.

————. "Agrarian Reform in Costa Rica: The Impact of the Title Security Program." *Inter-American Economic Affairs* 35 (1982): 31–56.

————. "Costa Rica and Jamaica." In *Competitive Elections in Developing Countries,* edited by Myron Weiner and Ergun Ozbudun. Durham, N.C.: Duke University Press, 1987.

————. "Development, Democratization, and Decay: Central America at the Crossroads." In *Authoritarians and Democrats: Regime Transition in Latin America,* edited by James M. Malloy and Mitchell A. Seligson. Pittsburgh: University of Pittsburgh Press, 1987.

Seligson, Mitchell A., and John A. Booth, eds. *Elections and Democracy in Central America Revisited.* Chapel Hill: University of North Carolina Press, 1995.

Seligson, Mitchell A., and Miguel Gómez B. "Ordinary Elections in Extraordinary Times: The Political Economy of Voting in Costa Rica." In *Elections and Democracy in Central America,* edited by John A. Booth and Mitchell A. Seligson. Chapel Hill: University of North Carolina Press, 1989.

Selser, Gregorio. *Sandino*. New York: Monthly Review Press, 1981.

Selva, Carlos. "Un poco de historia de cuando se luchaba contra Zelaya." *Revista Conservadora del Pensamiento Centroamericano* 16 (May 1967): 1–46.

Sieder, Rachel. "Honduras: The Politics of Exception and Military Reformism (1972–1978)." *Journal of Latin American Studies* 27, pt. 1 (February 1995): 99–127.

Slutzky, Daniel, and Ester Alonso. *Empresas transnacionales y agricultura: El caso del enclave bananero en Honduras*. Tegucigalpa: Editorial Universitaria, 1980.

Slutzky, Daniel, and Ester Slutzky. "El Salvador: Estructura de la explotación cafetalera." *Estudios Sociales Centroamericanos* 30 (May–August 1972): 101–25.

Smith, Carol. "Beyond Dependency Theory: National and Regional Patterns of Underdevelopment in Guatemala." *American Ethnologist* 5 (March 1978): 574–617.

———. "Local History in Global Context: Social and Economic Transitions in Western Guatemala." *Comparative Studies in Society and History* 26 (1984): 193–228.

———. "Origins of the National Question in Guatemala: A Hypothesis." In *Guatemalan Indians and the State, 1540–1988*, edited by Carol Smith, with the assistance of Marilyn M. Moors. Austin: University of Texas Press, 1990.

Smith, Carol A., ed., with the assistance of Marilyn M. Moors. *Guatemalan Indians and the State, 1540–1988*. Austin: University of Texas Press, 1990.

Smith, Hazel. *Nicaragua: Self-Determination and Survival*. London: Pluto Press, 1993.

Smith, Peter H. "The Origins of the Crisis." In *Confronting Revolution: Security through Diplomacy in Central America*, edited by Morris J. Blachman, William M. LeoGrande, and Kenneth Sharpe. New York: Pantheon, 1986.

Smith, Robert S. "Origins of the Consulado of Guatemala." *Hispanic American Historical Review* 26 (May 1946): 150–61.

———. "Forced Labor in the Guatemalan Indigo Works." *Hispanic American Historical Review* 36 (August 1956): 319–28.

———. "Indigo Production and Trade in Colonial Guatemala." *Hispanic American Historical Review* 39 (May 1959): 181–211.

———. "Financing the Central American Federation, 1821–1838." *Hispanic American Historical Review* 43 (November 1963): 483–510.

Sojo, Ana. *Estado empresario y lucha política en Costa Rica*. San José: EDUCA, 1984.

Solís Salazar, Edwin, and Carlos E. González Pacheco. *El ejército en Costa Rica: Poder político, poder militar, 1821–1890*. San José: Editorial Alma Mater, 1991.

Solórzano F., Juan Carlos. "Rafael Carrera, ¿Reacción conservadora o revolución campesina? Guatemala 1837–1873." *Anuario de Estudios Centroamericanos* 13 (1987): 5–35.

Solórzano F., Valentín. *Evolución económica de Guatemala.* 2d ed. Guatemala: Centro Editorial "José de Pineda Ibarra," 1963.

Solórzano Martínez, Mario. *Guatemala: Autoritarismo y democracia.* San José: EDUCA, 1987.

Squire, Ephraim George. *The States of Central America.* New York, 1858.

———. *Nicaragua: Its People, Scenery, Monuments, Resources, Condition, and Proposed Canal.* New York: Harper & Brothers, 1860.

———. *Notes on Central America, Particularly the States of Honduras and San Salvador: Their Geography, Topography, Climate, Population, Resources, Productions, Etc., Etc. and the Proposed Honduras Inter-Oceanic Railway.* New York: Praeger, 1969.

Stanford Central America Action Network, *Revolution in Central America.* Boulder, Colo.: Westview Press, 1983.

Stanley, William. *The Protection Racket State: Elite Politics, Military Extortion, and Civil War in El Salvador.* Philadelphia: Temple University Press, 1996.

Stansifer, Charles L. "José Santos Zelaya: A New Look at Nicaragua's 'Liberal' Dictator." *Revista/Review Interamericana* 7 (fall 1977): 468–85.

Stephens, John L. *Incidents of Travel in Central America, Chiapas and Yucatan.* 2 vols. New Brunswick: Rutgers University Press, 1949.

Stokes, William S. "The Land Laws of Honduras." *Agricultural History* 21 (1947): 148–54.

———. *Honduras: An Area Study in Government.* Madison: University of Wisconsin Press, 1950.

Stone, Samuel Z. "Los cafetaleros: Un estudio de los caficultores de Costa Rica." *Revista Conservadora del Pensamiento Centroamericano* 26 (March 1971): 11–31.

———. *La dinastía de los conquistadores: La crisis del poder en la Costa Rica contemporánea.* 3d ed. San José: EDUCA, 1982.

———. *The Heritage of the Conquistadors: Ruling Classes in Central America from the Conquest to the Sandinistas.* Lincoln: University of Nebraska Press, 1990.

Strobeck, Susan Emily. "The Political Activities of Some Members of the Aristocratic Families of Guatemala, 1821–1839." M.A. thesis, Tulane University, 1958.

Sullivan-González, Douglas. "'A Chosen People': Religious Discourse and the Making of the Republic of Guatemala, 1821–1871." *The Americas* 54 (July 1997): 17–38.

Taracena Arriola, Arturo. "El primer Partido Comunista de Guatemala (1922–1932): Diez años de una historia olvidada." *Anuario de Estudios Centroamericanos* 15 (1989): 71–91.

———. "Liberalismo y poder político en Centroamérica (1870–1929)." In *Historia general de Centroamérica,* vol. 4, *Las repúblicas agroexportadoras (1870–1945),* edited by Víctor Hugo Acuña Ortega. Madrid: FLASCO, 1993.

Teplitz, Benjamin I. "The Political and Economic Foundations of Modernization in Nicaragua: The Administration of José Santos Zelaya, 1893–1909." Ph.D. diss., Howard University, 1973.

Torres-Rivas, Edelberto. *Interpretación del desarrollo social centroamericano: Procesos y estructuras de una sociedad dependiente.* 2d ed. San José: EDUCA, 1971.

———. "Poder nacional y sociedad dependiente: Las clases y el Estado en Centroamérica." In *La inversión extranjera en Centroamérica,* edited by Rafael Menjívar. San José: EDUCA, 1974.

———. *Crisis del poder en Centroamérica.* San José: Editorial Universitaria Centroamericana, 1981.

———. "The Beginning of Industrialization in Central America." Latin American Program, no. 141. Washington, D.C.: The Woodrow Wilson International Center for Scholars, 1984.

———. "Guatemala: Crisis and Political Violence." *NACLA* 6 (November–December 1985): 3–34.

———. "Escenarios, sujetos, desenlaces (reflexiones sobre la crisis centroamericana)." Working Paper No. 68, Kellogg Institute, University of Notre Dame, March 1986.

———. "Authoritarian Transition to Democracy in Central America." In *Sociology of "Developing Societies": Central America,* edited Jan L. Flora and Edelberto Torres-Rivas. New York: Monthly Review Press, 1989.

Trudeau, Robert H. *Guatemalan Politics: The Popular Struggle for Democracy.* Boulder, Colo.: Lynne Rienner, 1993.

Tulchin, Joseph S., ed. *Is There a Transition to Democracy in El Salvador?* Boulder, Colo.: Lynne Rienner, 1992.

Turcios, Roberto. *Autoritarismo y modernización: El Salvador, 1950–1960.* San Salvador: D. R. Ediciones Tendencias, 1993.

Ulloa Mayorga, Juan Manuel, et al. *Apuntes de historia de Nicaragua.* León, Nicaragua: Editorial Universitaria, 1988.

Ungo, Guillermo Manuel. "El Salvador: 'Democratization' to Halt the Insurgency." In *Central America: Democracy, Development, and Change,* edited by John M. Kirk and George W. Schuler. New York: Praeger, 1988.

Valenzuela, José Reina and Mario Argueta. *Marco Aurelio Soto: Reforma liberal de 1876.* Tegucigalpa: Banco Central de Honduras, 1978.

Valle, Rafael Heliodoro. *Oro de Honduras: Antología de Ramón Rosa.* Tegucigalpa: Tipografía Nacional, 1948.

Vargas, Oscar René. *La revolución que inició el progreso (Nicaragua, 1893–1909).* Managua: Ecotextura, 1990.

Vargas Arias, Claudio Antonio. *El liberalismo, la iglesia y el Estado en Costa Rica.* San José: Ediciones Guayacán, 1991.

Vázquez, Juan Luis. "Luchas políticas y Estado oligárquico." In *Economía y sociedad en la construcción del Estado de Nicaragua,* edited by Alberto Lanuza, et al. San José: Instituto Centroamericano de Administración Pública, 1983.

Vega Carballo, José Luis. "Etapas y procesos de la evolución sociopolítica de Costa Rica." *Estudios Sociales Centroamericanos* 1 (January–April 1972): 45–72.

———. "El nacimiento de un regimen de burguesía dependiente: El caso de Costa Rica." Parts 1 and 2. *Estudios Sociales Centroamericanos* 5 (January–April 1973): 157–85; 6 (September–December 1973): 83–118.

———. *Orden y progreso: La formación del Estado nacional en Costa Rica.* San José: Instituto Centroamericano de Administración Pública, 1981.

———. *Hacia una interpretación del desarrollo costarricense: Ensayo sociológico.* 5th ed. San José: Editorial Porvenir, 1986.

Velásquez Carrera, Eduardo Antonio, ed. *La revolución de Octubre: Diez años de lucha por la democracia en Guatemala, 1944–1954.* Tomo 1. Guatemala: CEUR, Universidad de San Carlos, 1994.

Velázquez, José Luis. "La incidencia de la formación de la economía agroexportadora en el intento de formación del Estado nacional en Nicaragua (1860–1930)." *Revista Conservadora del Pensamiento Centroamericano* 32 (October–December 1977): 11–31.

Velázquez Pereira, José Luis. *Formación del Estado en Nicaragua.* Managua: Fondo Editorial, Banco Central de Nicaragua, 1992.

Vilas, Carlos M. "Family Affairs: Class, Lineage and Politics in Contemporary Nicaragua." *Journal of Latin American Studies* 24 (1992): 309–41.

———. *Between Earthquakes and Volcanoes: Market, State, and the Revolutions in Central America.* New York: Monthly Review Press, 1995.

———. "Prospects for Democratisation in a Post-revolutionary Setting: Central America." *Journal of Latin American Studies* 28 (May 1996): 461–503.

Villalobos, Bernardo. *La mesocracia de Costa Rica, 1821–1926.* San José: Editorial Costa Rica, 1986.

Volio Jiménez, Fernando. *El militarismo en Costa Rica y otros ensayos.* San José: Asociación Libro Libre, 1985.

Volio de Kobe, Marina. "Estado y derecho en la Costa Rica del siglo XIX." In *Desarrollo institucional de Costa Rica (de las sociedades indígenas a la crisis del 30),* edited by Jaime Murillo. San José: EDUCA, 1991.

Volk, Steven. "Honduras: On the Border of War." *NACLA Report on the Americas* 15 (1981): 2–37.

Walker, Thomas. *Nicaragua: The Land of Sandino.* Boulder, Colo.: Westview Press, 1986.

Walker, Thomas W., ed. *Nicaragua without Illusions: Regime Transition and*

Structural Adjustment in the 1990s. Wilmington, Del.: Scholarly Resources, 1997.

Walker, William. *The War in Nicaragua.* Tucson: University of Arizona Press, 1985.

Walter, Knut. "Trade and Development in an Export Economy: The Case of El Salvador, 1870–1914." M.A. Thesis, University of North Carolina, Chapel Hill, 1977.

———. *The Regime of Anastasio Somoza, 1936–1956.* Chapel Hill: University of North Carolina Press, 1993.

Wasserstrom, Robert. "Revolution in Guatemala: Peasants and Politics under the Arbenz Government." *Comparative Studies in Society and History* 17 (October 1975): 443–78.

Weaver, Frederick Stirton. *Inside the Volcano: The History and Political Economy of Central America.* Boulder, Colo.: Westview Press, 1994.

Weaver, Jerry L. "Political Style of the Guatemalan Military Elite." *Studies in Comparative International Development* 5 (1969–1970): 68–84.

Weeks, John. *The Economies of Central America.* New York: Holmes & Meier, 1985.

———. "An Interpretation of the Central American Crisis." *Latin American Research Review* 21, no. 3 (1986): 31–54.

Wheelock Román, Jaime. *Imperialismo y dictadura: Crisis de una formación social.* Mexico City: Siglo Veintiuno Editores, 1975.

———. *Raíces indígenas de la lucha anticolonialista en Nicaragua.* 2d ed. Managua: Editorial Nueva Nicaragua, 1985.

White, Alastair. *El Salvador.* New York: Praeger, 1973.

Whitfield, Stephen J. "Strange Fruit: The Career of Samuel Zemurray." *American Jewish History* 82 (March 1984): 307–23.

Wiarda, Howard J., ed. *Rift and Revolution: The Central American Imbroglio.* Washington, D.C.: American Enterprise Institute, 1984.

Williams, Philip J. *The Catholic Church and Politics in Nicaragua and Costa Rica.* Pittsburgh: University of Pittsburgh Press, 1989.

Williams Philip J., and Knut Walter. *Militarization and Demilitarization in El Salvador's Transition to Democracy.* Pittsburgh: University of Pittsburgh Press, 1997.

Williams, Robert G. *Export Agriculture and the Crisis in Central America.* Chapel Hill: University of North Carolina Press, 1986.

———. *States and Social Evolution: Coffee and the Rise of National Governments in Central America.* Chapel Hill: University of North Carolina Press, 1994.

Williamson, Edwin. *The Penguin History of Latin America.* London: Penguin, 1992.

Wilson, Bruce M. *Costa Rica: Politics, Economics, and Democracy.* Boulder, Colo.: Lynne Rienner, 1998.

Wilson, Everett Alan. "The Crisis of National Integration in El Salvador, 1919–1935." Ph.D. diss., Stanford University, 1970.

Winson, Anthony. "One Road to Democracy with Development: José Figueres and the Social Democratic Project after 1948." In *Central America: Democracy, Development, and Change,* edited by John M. Kirk and George W. Schuler. New York: Praeger, 1988.

———. *Coffee and Democracy in Modern Costa Rica.* New York: St. Martin's Press, 1989.

Woodward, Ralph Lee Jr. "Guatemalan Cotton and the American Civil War." *Inter-American Economic Affairs* (winter 1964): 87–94.

———. "Economic and Social Origins of the Guatemalan Political Parties (1773–1823)." *Hispanic American Historical Review* 45 (November 1965): 544–66.

———. "The Guatemalan Merchants and National Defense: 1810." *Hispanic American Historical Review* 45 (August 1965): 452–62.

———. *Class Privilege and Economic Development: The Consulado de Comercio of Guatemala, 1793–1871.* Chapel Hill: University of North Carolina Press, 1966.

———. "Social Revolution in Guatemala: The Carrera Revolt." In *Applied Enlightenment: Nineteenth Century Liberalism,* edited by Mario Rodríguez et al. New Orleans: Middle American Research Institute, Tulane University, 1972.

———. ""Liberalism, Conservatism, and the Response of the Peasants of La Montaña to the Government of Guatemala, 1821–1850." *Plantation Society* 1 (February 1979): 109–29.

———. "The Rise and Decline of Liberalism in Central America: Historical Perspectives on the Contemporary Crisis." *Journal of Interamerican Studies and World Affairs* 26 (August 1984): 291–312.

———. *Central America: A Nation Divided.* 2d ed. New York: Oxford University Press, 1985.

———. "Changes in the Nineteenth-Century Guatemalan State and Its Indian Policies." In *Guatemalan Indians and the State, 1540–1988,* edited by Carol A. Smith with the assistance of Marilyn M. Moors. Austin: University of Texas Press, 1990.

———. "The Aftermath of Independence, 1821–c.1870." In *Central America since Independence,* edited by Leslie Bethell. Cambridge: Cambridge University Press, 1991.

———. *Rafael Carrera and the Emergence of the Republic of Guatemala, 1821–1871.* Athens: University of Georgia Press, 1993.

———, ed. *Positivism in Latin America, 1850–1900: Are Order and Progress Reconcilable?* Lexington, Mass.: D. C. Heath & Company, 1971.

———, ed. *Central America: Historical Perspectives on the Contemporary Crisis.* New York: Greenwood Press, 1988.

Wortman, Miles. "Government Revenue and Economic Trends in Central America, 1787–1819." *Hispanic American Historical Review* 55 (May 1975): 251–86.

———. *Government and Society in Central America, 1680–1840.* New York: Columbia University Press, 1982.

Wright, Theodore P. Jr. "Honduras: A Case Study of United States Support for Free Elections in Central America." *Hispanic American Historical Review* 40 (May 1960): 212–23.

Yashar, Deborah J. "Civil War and Social Welfare: The Origins of Costa Rica's Competitive Party System." In *Building Democratic Institutions: Parties and Party Systems in Latin America,* edited by Scott Mainwaring and Timothy R. Scully. Stanford: Stanford University Press, 1995.

———. *Demanding Democracy: Reform and Reaction in Costa Rica and Guatemala, 1870s–1950s.* Stanford: Stanford University Press, 1997.

———. "The Quetzal is Red: Military States, Popular Movements, and Political Violence in Guatemala." In *The New Politics of Inequality in Latin America: Rethinking Participation and Representation,* edited by Douglas A. Chalmers et al. Oxford: Oxford University Press, 1997.

Zamosc, Leon. "Class Conflict in an Export Economy: The Social Roots of the Salvadoran Insurrection of 1932." In *Sociology of "Developing Societies": Central America,* edited by Jan L. Flora and Edelberto Torres-Rivas. New York: Monthly Review Press, 1989.

Zúñiga Huete, José Angel. *Presidentes de Honduras.* Vol. 2. Mexico City: IPGH, 1988.

INDEX

Library of Congress Cataloging-in-Publication Data
Mahoney, James, 1968–
   The legacies of liberalism : path dependence and political regimes in
Central America / James Mahoney.
      p.   cm.
Includes bibliographical references (p.   ) and index.
   ISBN 0-8018-6552-2 (alk. paper)
1. Central America—Politics and government—20th century.
2. Liberalism—Central America.   3. Democratization—Central America.
4. Comparative government.   I. Title.
JL1410.M34 2001
320.9728—dc21

                                             00-011212

DATE		

HIGHSMITH #4